Catherine Larkin

QUEEN MARY
AND OTHERS

Osbert Sitwell

QUEEN MARY AND OTHERS

THE JOHN DAY COMPANY

NEW YORK

Library of Congress Cataloging in Publication Data

Sitwell, Sir Osbert, bart., 1892–1969.
  Queen Mary and others.

    1. Sitwell, Sir Osbert, bart., 1892–1969—Biography.
I. Title.
PR6037.I83Q4   1974   828'.9'1209 [B]   74-9361
ISBN 0–381–98279–3
1 2 3 4 5 6 7 8 9 10

First United States Publication 1975

Printed in the United States of America

Contents

———◇———

Illustrations

The publishers would like to give grateful thanks to the following for their help with the illustrations: Reresby Sitwell (1, 6, 7); Raleigh Trevelyan (2, 3, 4, 5).

Foreword

---◇---

THOSE who have not had the rare pleasure of knowing Sir
Osbert Sitwell personally will derive some idea of his conversation from these essays, many of which he was too infirm
to polish. They contain much of his gallant spirit and keen
perceptiveness, and they will therefore be valued by admirers
of his *œuvre*. Uncommon common sense and humour they
contain in abundance though they cannot compare with the
densely woven tapestry of his longer-winded prose. The
essays are in his minor rather than his major manner—how
grand it is all the same! His will to continue writing was
strong, but he was handicapped by the crippling progress of
disease.

Everything Sir Osbert wrote is saturated in his personality.
His autobiography will remain his best monument. So
accurately has he portrayed himself in its glowing pages that
others can only add the palest of postscripts. To have known
him since I was young, to have basked in the warmth of his
presence, has been one of my life-enhancing experiences. Even
when he was stricken with palsy he set a brave example to
those of us who complain of lesser ailments. He had the
liberal breadth of outlook which one associates with the finest
eighteenth-century philosophers. *Winters of Content* and
Escape with Me! seem like twentieth-century sequels to
William Beckford's travel books, suavely discursive, im-
aginatively poetical, but richer than rich Beckford in red
corpuscles and humanity.

In his prime Sir Osbert resembled the early portraits of King George III. Tall, fair and clean-shaven, his features were cast in a Hanoverian mould: the prominent nose might be described as Roman with a Northern complexion, the eyes were blue and penetrating, ever watchful. Frank Dobson's head in gleaming brass conveys his youthful appearance, and Mr John Lehmann's *A Nest of Tigers* is the most skilful and informative account of his association with his elder sister and younger brother, united in the vanguard to defend poetry and every form of art, mocking the shibboleths of pedants and bureaucrats and trampling on the ubiquitous Philistine. All three owed more to their erudite father than is generally realised. I was very young when I first met Sir George, a dignified figure with the formal courtesy correctly labelled 'old world'. A suitable model for Van Dyck, but he was linked with a more distant past by his passion for the Middle Ages, he looked and walked and talked like the lord of an English manor at large, and it was easy to fancy him in the role of domestic tyrant. When he spoke of 'the boys' it was with an odd mixture of pride and faint disapproval, as if they were not sufficiently serious. I do not remember any reference to his daughter. Evidently her parents failed to appreciate Edith's genius.

Sir George shared my father's predilection for formal gardens and art collecting, and together they used to browse in the local antique shops. To me he was noteworthy as parent of the poets I admired in *Wheels*, but I found him evasive when I questioned him about their work. He presented my mother with a handsome edition of his *Tales of My Native Village*. 'The scene of these stories,' he wrote in the preface, 'is laid at the place I know best, my old house in Derbyshire, where for more than seventy years I have been lord of the manor.' Besides a glorification of Chaucer's England, in which he tilts at 'the young men of the present day ... always writing to the newspapers about the genius of youth', he dwells nostalgically on the time when 'Merry England was something more than an empty phrase,' and 'there was a joy in life which the modern world has thrown away'. Many of his sentences—for instance, 'Walter de Biblesworth speaks of ladies dancing the carole, their heads encircled by garlands of the blaverole or blue-bottle flower'—suggest that his children inherited his love of rare locutions as well as a deep consciousness of their ancestry.

As a result of her generous review of *The Eton Candle* I happened to meet Dame Edith before her brothers. I was immediately captivated by her extraordinary grace and refinement combined with a tart sense of humour, but being ignorant of the literary feuds that obsessed her, I could not feel quite at ease. When I mentioned Wyndham Lewis, who had painted her portrait and contributed to a journal edited by Osbert, she said sharply: 'Let's change the subject,' and an awkward silence followed. D. H. Lawrence was also anathema. With Osbert and Sacheverell, however, there were no awkward silences: on the contrary, there was plenty of laughter. All three enjoyed battling with their enemies, including the tweed-and-pipe songsters of the Georgian School and their impresarios Sir J. C. Squire and Sir Edward Marsh, but delicate Edith seemed to lead in the battle.

Osbert and Sacheverell were nearer my age and I scarcely felt the difference, though the former had survived the horrors of existence in the trenches. I met them not in Florence but in London—a London galvanised for me by their literary activities. Everything of aesthetic significance appeared to be happening within their orbit. More than other English writers they had affinities with Italy.

Accustomed to the unimpeded rational flow of Italian talk, I was rather surprised at first by the casual quality of their discourse, which zigzagged abruptly in various directions, seldom settling on a single topic or argument, as if that might incur boredom or ponderous earnestness. The modulation of Osbert's voice was amber-mellow and his remarks often had an underlying chuckle. While in London I usually encountered him at luncheons and dinners, by far the pleasantest of which were in his house at 2, Carlyle Square. Its interior, described in this book, expressed his personality. Like an exotic conservatory it appealed to several senses at once, tempting exploration if not kleptomania. The heterogeneous pictures looked happy on the walls. One expected the carved dolphins of the furniture to come to life and gambol in the sea-grotto dining-room. Rococo mirrors reflected the shell-shaped chairs, the frigates in bottles, the Victorian figures and fruit under glass domes. This patchwork quilt of objects was the antithesis of modish decoration in the twenties, which was chromium-plated and clinically austere, with beige prevailing until pure white came into vogue with Syrie Maugham.

Osbert had the gift of conjuring fantasy; he also tended to attract it from outside. Stranger things happened to him and to Edith than to most of us, as when a taxi-driver, wearing a large sombrero and a loose loud necktie, told him: 'I often drive my taxi at night on the astral plane and I sometimes see you there.' The stout female intruder who demanded that he should take down in embroidery the colours that she would sing to him was another typical example. He was a magnet for curious characters and situations and he enjoyed mingling them in impromptu comedies. His old friend Mrs Leverson, who had been christened The Sphinx by Oscar Wilde, often contributed to the fun, as he has related in *Noble Essences*.

At the Magnasco Society, which he and his brother helped to found in 1924, he waved an invisible wand over his fellow members, inspiring them with his magnificent enthusiasm. Sir Sacheverell's *Southern Baroque Art* had recently kindled a fresh interest in those seventeenth- and eighteenth-century painters, mostly Italian, who had fallen under a shadow since Ruskin's totalitarian reign, while many splendid examples of their work were hanging in English country houses. How few bothered about Conca and Solimena in the twenties, or visited Naples for the sake of its baroque monuments! The very word baroque, described in the Oxford Dictionary as 'grotesque, whimsical', had assumed pejorative connotations. After Wölfflin, Geoffrey Scott's *Architecture of Humanism* had paved the way for the few, but Sacheverell's *Southern Baroque Art* and Osbert's *Discursions* had reached the many, especially at our universities. Magnasco's name was chosen for the society because he had been the most neglected artist of the period: he also seemed to summarise its *Zeitgeist*. Nature is reduced to a nervous wreck in his landscapes: there is thunder and lightning in the sultry air, more *scuro* than *chiaro*, in the manner of Salvator Rosa, for whom he was often mistaken at the time of Lady Morgan's romantic biography. But it is more in his groups of gesticulating gypsies, monks and brigands, in his crumbling refectories and synagogues, that he achieves a restless individuality that endeared him to Gian Gastone, the last of the Medici Grand Dukes.

Each of the Magnasco Society's exhibitions was celebrated by a banquet in a private room of the Savoy Hotel, as Sir Osbert has related here. Though Lord Gerald Wellesley (later Duke of Wellington) presided, Osbert was the true master of ceremonies, supported by the genial Finnish art critic Dr Tancred Borenius and a galaxy of connoisseurs, some of whom lent their pictures to embellish the dining-room. As the youngest member I was dazzled when the venerable Walter Sickert delivered a panegyric on the paintings, which wound up with imitations of the *lions comiques* he had depicted in the nineties. The fruits of this aesthetic revival were apparent in the National Gallery's subsequent acquisitions.

In London, however, I had few opportunities of seeing Osbert alone. He was a public figure representing the avant garde, and incessant demands were made on him by lion-hunting hostesses whose foibles he satirized in his *Mrs Kinfoot* series:

'The joy of catching tame elephants
And finding them to be white ones,
Still gleams from the jungle eyes

Of Mrs Kinfoot,
But her mind is no jungle
Of Ethiopia,
But a sound British meadow.'

As he could find little freedom for composition at Montegufoni I seldom saw him there. He preferred to spend winter at Amalfi without parental interruption. It was not until he came to Peking, where he rented a typical Chinese house on Kan Yü Hutung that I saw him frequently and concluded that more than other writers I had known, he was all of a piece with his writings: his natural command of style and very English sense of humour were combined with aristocratic reserve: he would never unbutton himself. 'This age of frankness', as he prophesied, 'will wither before another age of discretion. "Sex-appeal" will lose its sway over the hearts of the young and will take on a hundred variations of name. It will become the fashion to disguise the sentiments just as, perhaps, once more to disguise the male countenance with whiskers.' He flinched visibly from Rabelaisian jest. I suspect I used to shock him with my absence of disguise: his expression at such moments delighted me, for the twinkling eyes and twitching mouth struggled with his resolve to remain impassive. For all his urbanity he was fundamentally shy like Edith, and it must have cost both of them agonies to overcome this shyness before large audiences. In conversation he hardly ever mentioned his work, but he analysed the characters of mutual friends and speculated on the pretensions and absurdities of Peking's cosmopolitan colony with a Dickensian gusto. I introduced him to several of my Chinese colleagues and students of Peking National University, and he was quick to appreciate their subtle qualities, for to modify the Chinese saw, all *courteous* men are brothers.

Through our friend Laurence Sickman he became acquainted with the distinguished artist Prince P'u Ju, a cousin of the ex-Emperor P'u Yi, and his evocation of the Prince's

Foreword

garden party in honour of his blossoming crab-apple trees
(in *Old Worlds for New*) is another fine sample of his talent
for seeing the past behind the present and bringing it into
focus. Looking back, it is curious to recall that he was engaged
on a book about Brighton in Peking, where the pale sand from
the Gobi desert silted through paper windows and powdered
the furniture.

After working all morning he would set forth on excursions
in the afternoon, to the Forbidden City, to Buddhist and
Taoist and Confucian temples, antique shops and local fairs,
and to paraphrase his own comment, everything he saw was,
in a sense, work; as much as writing itself. Nothing was too
far for his keen eyes to follow; he missed nothing of beauty
and significance, and his *Escape with Me!* conveys the sensuous
fascination of Peking when 'the effervescence of spring was
everywhere to be felt' during that lull before the Japanese
invasion. Collecting articles of virtu was contagious, and with
the adornment of his sister in mind he gradually formed a
collection of old Chinese belt-buckles inlaid with semi-
precious stones, all of which he would arrange on tables,
delighting in their kaleidoscopic design. Among the foreign
community he was most entertained by that adventurous 'old
China hand' L. C. Arlington, a sinologist who could spin
picaresque yarns about his forty-odd years in the Chinese
Maritime Customs, many of which are incorporated in his
book *Through the Dragon's Eyes*.

Apart from a visit to Renishaw in 1940—but it is needless
here to expatiate on the place he loved best—I did not see
Osbert again till the war was over. More than other friends he
could sympathise with my plight as an Englishman whose
home had always been in Italy, a fact that was held against
me by hidebound jingoes. His scorn of politicians, 'the real
authors of the prevailing disaster', had been voiced in his
eloquent *Letter to My Son*. In the meantime *Left Hand, Right
Hand!* was acclaimed as a masterpiece by authoritative critics
on both sides of the Atlantic.

15

Osbert had visited America in 1927, as recorded in this book. His return there with Edith for a joint lecture tour in 1948 was a resounding personal triumph, often repeated. Neither had to seek publicity: publicity sought them. To encounter them in a New York street or in the caravanserai de luxe where they were staying was always a surprise. Both stood out a mile, as it were, from their environment, heraldic figures from a different sphere and century. The American lady who remarked to Osbert: 'You Englishmen all wear armour,' was not utterly at fault, for Osbert did seem to wear a coat of mail, while Edith seemed to have strayed from a Gothic arras.

In contrast with the restrictions and austerities of life in London during the post-war period New York entertainments were lavish, but there was none of the alcoholic hullabaloo of the Prohibition era described in Osbert's article on *New York in the Twenties*, when he was impelled to take refuge under a large supper table with Muriel Draper for a quiet chat. In retrospect it is depressing to compare the sociable Montmartre-Harlem of the 'twenties with the hostile fastness it has become. Much as I enjoyed *The Blackbirds* and Josephine Baker at the Casino de Paris, the spontaneous Terpsichoreans of the Harlem Savoy were far more thrilling, the frenzy of the jazz-players more inspired. Madam Walker, known as the 'Antikink Queen' since she had made a fortune out of a product that flattened Negro curls, was innocent of racial prejudice. Now the curls are defiantly exaggerated in fuzzy-wuzzy mops which are sometimes dyed red.

An experience which I also shared was a visit to the art collection of Mr Goldman, who in spite of his blindness accompanied his guests from picture to picture, particularising the virtues of each in turn as if he could still see it. 'A lesson of courage,' wrote Osbert, who showed the same kind of courage when he was stricken with what he apologetically dismissed as 'the shakes'. He would rush or stagger through a room to greet one at the constant risk of falling. Even when thus afflicted he could not resist another invitation to give readings in New York. During a rough Atlantic passage he was injured, but he invariably made light of such accidents. I was often present at the same parties, especially at Mrs Murray Crane's, one of the last intellectual hostesses in the French tradition who encouraged literary discussion and organised lectures in her Fifth Avenue salon, and I noticed that his composure and ready repartee seemed to dominate his ailment. James Fosburgh painted his portrait at this time and it is a touching likeness: the heavy frame had shrunk, but the eyes were still watchful, the lips about to break into a smile.

Eventually he retired from his beloved Renishaw to the castle of Montegufoni. There I was able to visit him frequently until he died. Embarrassed by his condition and afraid of causing embarrassment, he was increasingly reluctant to meet strangers. Though he recovered from a dangerous new operation on the brain its success was only partial. His inability to control his movements was humiliating for him and harrowing to witness but he was quite without bitterness or self-pity, and his patience under strain was exemplary. One grew accustomed to his muffled articulation. The tremors attacked him in startling fits, especially during meals, when I made a point of talking steadily above the clatter of knife and fork until it had subsided.

In the long airy drawing-room facing the terrace parterre of clipped box hedges and lemon trees in pots with its serene panorama of the olive and vine-clad Val di Pesa Osbert sat hunched and rigid beside piles of books and art magazines from London. The handicap that chiefly distressed him was his inability to write, for he confessed that he did not feel his age: he still felt young and longed for creative activity.

Friends from England came for brief spells: Christabel, Lady Aberconway, Sir Malcolm Bullock, L. P. Hartley, John Lehmann, Fr. Caraman and others, who read aloud to him and cheered him with nuggets of news from the world he had left behind. Conversation with such old friends involved no strain. It flowed as naturally as possible in spite of his jerky diction—how unlike the rolling sentences and musical cadences of his best writing.

The day of the hermit might be over, but Montegufoni had become his hermitage. He saw even fewer friends after the death of Dame Edith, who had told me that one of the reasons for her conversion to Catholicism was to promote Osbert's recovery. His clever and enterprising majordomo— the vintner of Montegufoni's superlative Chianti—had succumbed to spinal cancer; his old companion David Horner had been partly paralysed; and his sister's death had been a final blow. Now he exercised his power of minute observation on a few stray cats and kittens which had been cherished by Dame Edith. While the caprices of these felines diverted him they were no protection against the rats that infested the place. In his enforced immobility the rodents were an added threat to his peace of mind. Supposing they attacked him in swarms during the night? A professional rat-killer was engaged to exterminate them.

I lunched with him often, and he made the supreme effort of coming to lunch with me. The difficulty of moving in and out of a motor car and up and down steps, of being wheeled into the drawing- and dining-room across pavements of different levels, made these excursions hazardous, even with the assistance of his devoted attendant secretary Frank Magro. But it was obvious that he enjoyed these occasional outings: his good appetite was flattering, his vocation for happiness undimmed. Aware of his objection to 'the kind people, the well-meaning, who feel sorry for you *because* you are alone', I tried to conduct myself as if nothing were amiss, hoping that my cheerful act was not overdone like the bedside manner of fashionable physicians.

His essay *On the Horror of Solitude* shows that he had given thought to the question and come to terms with the relative solitude forced upon him. His anecdote of Pachmann who, when asked by a hostess: 'Dear Master, I do hope you don't mind being alone?' replied: 'Madam, I am never alone. I am with Pachmann,' must have occurred to him amid the spacious silence of Montegufoni. His fabulous memory kept him company. If I forgot or bungled a name, he could always correct me, and I felt sure that like his deaf friend Ada Leverson he had sessions of silent laughter, 'at incidents which had occurred, and at incidents which had not occurred, at things people had said or that, in fact they had not said', but which had been suggested to him by his witty imagination. As an emperor of anecdotes historical and social he has not been surpassed.

Harold Acton

Queen Mary

———◇———

IT would have been impossible to know Queen Mary at all, or even only to have seen her, and not to entertain for her a very genuine admiration. At the beginning of the pages that follow, I attempt to sketch her character and the impression she made, and then go on to depict Her Majesty as she was in the war years, under circumstances quite new to her. But chiefly I apply my hand to the portrait of her in a phase of life that was so far from typical, because I enjoyed exceptional opportunities for observing it. Further, Queen Mary's life at Badminton, and the existence of those round her during that period, had about them something very unusual yet characteristic, perhaps a little resembling those of a court in exile. For example, for five whole years no mention was allowed to be made in the press of Her Majesty's retreat, in case the attention of the enemy should be drawn to it, and in consequence comparatively few people knew where she was living. Her small, formal world still revolved round her as before, but she was no longer at the hub of things; news took some time to reach her. Never before had she been allowed to spend more than a month or two at most in the same place, and now she found herself obliged to remain at Badminton without moving at all for five whole years, after a long career in which every moment—not every spare moment, because for her no moments were spare—had been allotted for months beforehand, whether to a state function or a private visit to a friend. Moreover the style in which Her Majesty then lived in this temporary seclusion may be of interest, for though to her it must have seemed comparatively simple, it is scarcely likely to be revived, and may soon be as far removed from the current ways of life as is to us the court of Queen Charlotte or even that of Queen Anne. This I realised at the time, and therefore during each of my visits to Badminton I made careful notes from which much of this material is drawn, and I have included many small details and minute comedies, in order to build up the picture.

First, a few facts must be stated in order to establish the identity of the subject. Queen Mary was born on May 26th, 1867, at Kensington Palace. She was the daughter of the Duke of Teck and the Duchess, formerly Princess Mary of Cambridge, in her time the most popular of English princesses, and a granddaughter of King George III. It was to be expected, therefore, that Queen Mary should manifest in her presence, as undoubtedly she did, much of the same imposing physique and dignified royal air as marked the members of the English royal family in the late eighteenth and early nineteenth centuries. Throughout her career she refused to yield to the epoch, just as, in the latter decades of it, she refused to give in to old age (saying once, I remember, when she was over eighty-three, 'I am beginning to lose my memory —but I mean to get it back!'). It used to be said that Queen Mary was the only person in the twentieth century who, on any given occasion, entertained no doubts concerning how to act or what judgment to pass, and I think this remark very accurately summed up both her strength and her weakness. Doubt never entered in. She saw the world's moral and social problems in terms of black and white, with no gradations. In addition, she possessed enormous energy, and had been well educated. She spoke foreign languages with ease and care for their idiom (what most struck her in listening to a broadcast by Hitler was the abominable German he spoke); she had amassed an infinite store of dynastic history, and in her life-time had accumulated whole histories of pictures, furniture and jewels in which she had been interested.

Queen Mary's character must have developed steadily from the beginning, and always along its own lines. Augustus Hare, writing some fifty-nine years before I set myself to make this portrait, publishes in his *Story of My Life* the following extract from his diaries, dated September 30th, 1899:

> I have been at Swaylands to meet the Duchess of York, and as there were scarcely any other guests, saw a great deal of her, and was increasingly filled with admiration for the dignified simplicity, and single-mindedness, and the high sense of duty by which her naturally merry, genial nature is pervaded, and which will be the very salvation of England some day. Before her, scandal sits dumb: she has a quiet but inflexible power of silencing everything which seems likely to approach ill-natured gossip, yet immediately after gives such a genial kindly look and word to the silenced one as prevents any feeling of mortification. All the morning the Duchess was occupied with her lady in real hard work, chiefly letters, I believe; in the afternoons we went for long drives and sight-seeings—of Penshurst, Knole, Groombridge, Hever, Igtham, and she was full of interest in the history and associations of these old-world places.

Only those who were privileged to go round some old house with Her Majesty could be aware how thoroughly she would have seen the places to which the writer alludes, and how much knowledge and enthusiasm she would have brought to the expeditions. Throughout her life she retained a liking for, and habit of, hard work. Though she was tolerant, I think laziness, untidiness, and waste of any description—including waste of time—were the faults she found most difficult to condone or overlook. Certainly she disliked untidiness in every form, even in plants that grew in a dishevelled manner and harboured dirt or dust: for this reason, among others, she was an inveterate and implacable foe to ivy, advising always that it should be cut down, and pulling it off walls herself and making others do so.

When I first met Her Majesty at Windsor Castle in April 1937, the same qualities which Hare had observed were visible, as will be noticed in a moment, though others too were evident; for example, the Queen had in the interval become a very ardent collector of many different kinds of things, and hardly had I been shown my room at Windsor Castle—it was the first time I had stayed there—when Queen Mary's page, in scarlet livery, arrived in my sitting-room carrying a huge leather book, which he thrust toward me, saying 'Queen Mary would like to have your autograph.' At dinner one night, I found myself placed between Queen Elizabeth and Queen Mary, and during the course of the meal I ventured to ask Queen Mary the history of what looked, from where I was sitting, to be a magnificent piece of silver standing on a sideboard. She saw that I really wanted to know, but she could not recollect it, and for a moment or two was plainly worried, in the way one is when some familiar fact becomes temporarily elusive. However, she talked of other things, and I returned to London the next day without finding out. But a few mornings later there arrived for me from Marlborough House an envelope bearing Queen Mary's cypher. It contained a letter from the lady-in-waiting, and ran, 'I am commanded by Queen Mary to send you the enclosed commentary on a subject between you and the Queen, as Her Majesty thought you might like to have the answer to your conundrum.' Attached was a page and a half written in Her Majesty's own bold and well-formed hand: 'Twenty-four hours after you asked me the history of the silver equestrian statue of William III, the name of the horse who won it came back to me—"Bacaldine". The statue was given by the last King of the Netherlands as a prize for a race at Ascot in 1882—I believe. The statue was I think bought by King Edward VII or given to him. I suppose the owner sold it.' How few old ladies would have taken the matter up in this way; how few possess the requisite energy! Moreover in the realm of the decorative arts, Her Majesty's knowledge was that of a specialist and in the park at Windsor she had furnished Frogmore House, over which she showed me, with so many objects of interest and historical association that it was in effect a museum. More particularly, she understood palace-objects—by which I mean to denote works of high luxury and intricate workmanship, which, to look their best, need to be displayed against the background of palace rooms—more than anyone living: for today, taste has altered, and a cottage is preferred, both for comfort and style, to a palace.

To take, for example, the changed manner in which the leaders of the modern world treat objects formerly much prized, and which Queen Mary greatly loved, it is only necessary to recall a story Joey Legh* told me when I was a guest at Windsor Castle in the spring of 1937. Mr Bevin, the Foreign Secretary, and Mrs Bevin had been spending a few days there just before I arrived. Queen Elizabeth called their attention one afternoon to the cases filled with pearl-pink and rose-pink Sèvres china bought in Paris after the French Revolution by King George IV, which stands in the Long Corridor. Made for Louis Quinze, this china, the height of aristocratic art, its shapes lacerated and painted in the most extravagant way, exhibits an absolute technical perfection and is such work as a French collector would travel over the world to see. Mr Bevin, on the contrary, was rather nonplussed by it, but after regarding it for a moment with a reflective eye, remarked to the Queen, 'I'm sure I'm very glad to see it—the wife an' me 'ave always 'ad a taste for pottery.'

Queen Elizabeth delighted in this typical comment: I doubt whether Queen Mary would have been similarly

---

* Sir Piers Legh, Master of the Household.

amused. Yet, all the same, she might have liked it: for it was her own mingling of stateliness and innocence, of a sense of enjoyment and a sense of duty, that made Queen Mary's character such a feature and support of contemporary English life.

After this first meeting with Queen Mary at Windsor, I was asked by Princess Alice to stay at Brantridge to meet Her Majesty again. This visit proved to be rather a strain, for I have a horror of English breakfasts, and like to remain in my room in the morning till I decide to come down; but this was the only house in England at which Queen Mary appeared at breakfast, and I had to be waiting at the bottom of the staircase ready to make my bow every morning at 8.55 a.m. Unpunctuality was not allowed, and conversation I found difficult at that hour. Queen Mary never failed to be impressive, even at breakfast: her personality was very strong. In those days I had a motor-car and a chauffeur—a lively intelligent scamp, called Walter Cooper, whose name occurs once or twice in my autobiography. He thought every matter out for himself, was most unconventional, questioned automatically all authority, and was frightened of nothing and nobody in heaven or hell, or on earth—except Queen Mary, who had obtained this effect by meeting him unexpectedly in a passage, and by looking at him and saying, 'Good-morning'. The house was rather small, but henceforth in his anxiety not to cross Her Majesty's path he used to dart and scuttle about it like a crab in the rocks. It was a real tribute to her individual quality in temperament, appearance and clothes. ... It was while I was staying at Brantridge that Queen Mary told me with great enjoyment how, during her tour in Canada, when she was Princess of Wales, she had been mistaken for her maid. The incident had taken place in Quebec; she had gone straight up to her room, and was sitting in a chair, when a porter arrived with some of her luggage, and said to her, 'What are you doing, sitting there, Miss? Can't you give us an 'and?'

During my stay at Brantridge, we worked very hard at sightseeing, inspecting, among other monuments, the Royal Pavilion at Brighton. I recall that various aldermen connected with the management of the building were there to receive Queen Mary, and one of them, over-excited at the prospect of the royal visit, had got rather drunk. He kept on pointing in the direction of the ball-room, and saying to Queen Mary 'Imagine the shene! The room all lit up, and all the ladies in their low lashivious dresshes.' Queen Mary did not care for such reflections on the company kept by her great-uncle, King George IV. . . . It was at Brantridge, too, that another episode occurred. Queen Mary was just getting into her motor-car to take us to see her niece, Lady Cambridge, at Bognor, when her page came out of the house and handed Her Majesty a telegram. It was to inform her of the death of a cousin in Germany, I think the Grand Duke of Hesse. In the motor Queen Mary expounded, for the benefit of her royal relations, the smallest genealogical details, with a great grasp of their intricacy. Then for a time she lapsed into silence, but after a while, with a reversion to the more direct and simple side of her nature, remarked 'I do hope they give us shrimps or one of those nice sea things for tea!' I can place on record that Lady Cambridge provided shrimps, but an inadequate supply.

Towards the end of September 1938, I went to stay at Badminton with my cousins the Duke* and Duchess of Beaufort to meet Queen Mary, who, as it later turned out, was in reality staying there at the suggestion of the Government, so as to inspect the great house and see whether it would suit her as a retreat if war were to come. The house-party included Lady Beatrice Pole-Carew, Lord Mildmay of Flete, Mr and Mrs Simon Rodney and the Duchess of Beaufort's younger brother, Lord Frederick Cambridge. My stay there, though overshadowed during the whole of the week by news of the Munich crisis, was of a different kind from the later visits, since the old traditional England and its social

* Henry, 10th Duke of Beaufort. Known to his friends as *Master*.

life, which ended one year later, in September 1939, then still continued.... Again we devoted hard hours to sightseeing which sometimes occupied the entire day from 9.45 a.m. to 7 p.m. I remember particularly, because of a small incident that occurred, a day spent in and near Bath, where Queen Mary had many engagements to fill. As we left the city to return home, we passed a large building in a wooded park. Queen Mary, no doubt rather tired after so many arduous hours, was very quiet, but as we passed this mansion—obviously an institution of some kind—her energy returned, and she said 'How interesting! That must be the School for the Orphan Daughters of Officers that my Mother used to take such an interest in!' At that moment the children began to converge on the road; they were carrying hockey-sticks, and stared in a desultory, adenoidal kind of way at the large royal motor and its august occupant, who on this occasion as usual, sat just behind the driver in a small upright seat, so that she was very visible. As Queen Mary passed the girls, she waved her hand and smiled at them, but they merely stood still, mooning at Her Majesty vacantly, and then I heard Queen Mary observe to herself, '*Cheer*, little idiots, can't you?'

Among the places we saw at this time was Tottenham, a Palladian country-house magnificently situated in Savernake Forest, and the home of Lord and Lady Ailesbury. That afternoon was coloured for me by the fact that, when we had nearly arrived there, Queen Mary, who had been very silent hitherto, suddenly exclaimed to the four or five of us who were in the motor with her, 'Of course, I remember Lady Ailesbury now! Nearly forty years ago! She was a Miss Madden, and flirted outrageously with my cousin the Grand Duke of Mecklenburg-Strelitz—the Grand Duchess was quite jealous!' This remark gave us a new idea both of Lady Ailesbury and of Queen Mary, who appeared to take a more tolerant, lighter view of the matter than one would have expected. By this time the car had drawn up at Tottenham. Lady Ailesbury was on the steps to meet Queen Mary, who, as we entered the house, observed to her seriously, but with, to those who knew her, an air of undisguised mischief, 'I believe you were a great friend of my cousin, the Grand Duke of Mecklenburg-Strelitz?'

'Yes,' replied Lady Ailesbury, in a tone of agony, and added, in the manner of one grasping at a life-belt in a rough sea, '*and of the Grand Duchess!*'

Whatever Lady Ailesbury may have looked like as a pretty and dashing young girl, she resembled now an enormous pyramid of red granite decked out in black velvet and strung with pearls. But what was really extraordinary was that she had managed to assemble in the same house three other women, who, though they were not related to her, approximated to her in appearance. One, I remember, was a Duchess of Grafton. Lady Ailesbury herself was a woman of character, but she possessed a one-track mind. Today it was devoted exclusively to Queen Mary, so that when, continually, our hostess pointed out things to Her Majesty with the black ebony cane she carried, she swept the eyes of many guests with it in the process, though she never noticed their cries of fright or pain. Plainly she bullied her husband, and Mary Beaufort told me later that, when she had motored to Tottenham a few days earlier to make arrangements for Queen Mary to come over, and had been discussing the details with Lord Ailesbury, Lady Ailesbury had walked up to them, and looking at her husband, with great severity, had said to him, 'Be quiet, Chandos, pray, while *I* talk to the Duchess!'

As one result of the afternoon in question, Queen Mary recollected that, if the King were to visit Savernake Forest, it was the duty of his Hereditary Ranger, Lord Ailesbury, to greet His Majesty by blowing on a horn. Queen Mary reminded the King of this fact, and in consequence, during the war, he snatched an hour one day from inspecting the troops at Aldershot, and motored to Tottenham, where Lord Ailesbury greeted His Majesty under the Palladian portico by tooting his horn at him, while Lady Ailesbury watched proudly, though not without a detached air that implied possible musical criticism at some subsequent quiet moment.

One day during this visit, Queen Mary had an important engagement in Bath. It was accordingly arranged that the whole party should motor over in the morning and go to see Prior Park and other places of interest in the city. Then, for luncheon, the party broke in two, since there were so many of us. Queen Mary, the Beauforts and a few others, including myself, were entertained by Horace Annesley Vachell, even then in 1938 an old gentleman—he is still alive at the time of my writing this in 1952—an author of novels and plays, and what romantic journalists like to call a *raconteur*, which means an indefatigable monopolist in conversation, and a prop of the Wine and Food Society, that contemporary collection of aspiring gourmets. (Thus Mr Vachell prided himself on being able to spot a Château Yquem 1921 or a Crofts 1892 at a hundred yards, as it were.) He lived just outside the city, at Widcombe Manor, the most beautiful of small country houses in the neighbourhood, planned like a miniature palace. Inside, the furniture was in keeping, though the ancestral portraits on the wall gave occasion for doubt. Mr Vachell had living in the house with him his only daughter, a young woman with a pronounced squint, and her husband,* who was a nephew of our host and her first cousin. Husband and wife looked very alike, and their child, a girl of eight or nine, who was also present at luncheon, exactly resembled both of them. Mr Vachell had recently suffered from a severe attack of laryngitis, during which he had lost his voice, but he was so determined to recover it in time for his luncheon for Queen Mary, to which he had long eagerly looked forward, that in order to save energy and his vocal chords, he had, so his son-in-law confided in me, spent the last ten days in bed, during which period he had refused to speak a word, even to answer an important question. When

---

* Some years later, he met a strange death, by sawing off a branch on which he was standing.

the great day came, he certainly made up for his previous term of self-imposed silence.

From the very beginning of the meal, everything went wrong. Our host had taken great trouble over the food, but it was all burnt, and too discouragingly large in size—there was placed before Queen Mary a whole, enormous partridge, roasted to a cinder. The wines, which changed colour with the courses, were all corked; the servants in the dining-room lost their heads completely, and above all, Mr Vachell never stopped talking for an instant and was far too familiar in what he said. Queen Mary disliked being too near her neighbours, but was that day pitilessly clamped against her host. Almost he dug Her Majesty in the ribs, as he drank glass after glass of wine, without, in his excitement, noticing anything wrong with it, and made to her such remarks as, 'We had another great friend in common', or, 'I know another old friend of yours in Florence.' He continued to press food and drink upon Queen Mary, who, though she liked food to be good, was very abstemious. She froze under this treatment; but still he laughed and talked without ceasing, and urged her to eat and drink more, ending up by trying to insist that Her Majesty should consume the old brandy from a balloon glass, a third full. Of the Vachell family only the son-in-law was aware of the atmosphere, and said to me, when we were alone for a moment after luncheon, 'Is Her Majesty *always* as stiff as that?' But Mr Vachell was quite happy still, and secured a photograph of the whole group, including Queen Mary, standing on some steps in the garden. In after years, I sometimes alluded to Mr Vachell and his luncheon party in front of Queen Mary, who invariably smiled and said, 'Disgusting, drunken old man.'

One or two other incidents occurred during this visit. I recall that Queen Mary went to see Ramsbury, a fine house, said to be by Inigo Jones, which belonged to an ancient Mrs Pleydell Bouverie, who lived in it with two daughters. The poor old lady was so frightened at the prospect of receiving

Queen Mary that she telephoned to the Dowager Duchess of Beaufort to implore her help, and as a result she and I were sent over first, to help stiffen the garrison, as it were.

On another occasion during this same week at Badminton Queen Mary was taking the Duke of Beaufort and me in her motor car, again to see over a house, when, just as we were arriving, Her Majesty was suddenly assailed by one of those recurrent conundrums that worry royal heads. (Besides, Queen Mary liked to know the minutiae of things, and she recognised that there were many details of many kinds of life that she did not comprehend fully.) So, turning to Beaufort after a lengthy silence, she enquired, 'Master, I've always meant to ask you; I'm sure you'll know—do hens have fleas?'

'Yes, Ma'am.'

'But do they bite human beings?', she pursued.

At this moment, however, the motor drew up at the door, and his answer to this important question in natural history had to be reserved. I do not know if Queen Mary ever reverted to this particular step in her quest for knowledge, but this small incident was typical of the innocence, in some matters, of the royal mind, in others so sophisticated.

*　　*　　*

Queen Mary left London at the wish of the Government, who did not want her to stay there and by so doing to add to their responsibilities, at a moment, too, when they were engaged in an effort to evacuate as many persons as possible from the overcrowded city. There can be no doubt, I think, that, had the decision been left to her, she would have chosen to remain in London, her home and birthplace. Nevertheless, she liked Badminton—though I do not doubt that she grew tired of it during the long years she was obliged to spend there —and once said to me, 'I've adopted the house and the family as my own!' And at Windsor, when Queen Mary first talked to me, after telling me how as a child she used to play with my mother in the gardens of Berkeley Square, she added that, until she had been ten or eleven, she had not known which were the members of her own family and which the Somersets, so intimate were they. It was indeed a very old connection or alliance; Lady Augusta Somerset in the forties of the last century had wanted to marry Queen Mary's uncle, the then young Duke of Cambridge, and, because of her obvious love for him, had been requested by Queen Victoria to leave Windsor Castle, where she was staying. (Lady Augusta was soon afterwards safely married off to Baron Neumann, the Austrian Minister in London and an illegitimate son of Metternich.) Later her half-sister, Lady Geraldine, formed a hopeless, life-long attachment for him. In short, the family of the Duke of Cambridge and that of the Duke of Beaufort had long been on intimate terms, and finally, in my generation, the Duke of Beaufort of the day had married Lady Mary Cambridge, the daughter of the Duke of Teck, Queen Mary's eldest brother, and a great-niece of the old Duke of Cambridge.

The rather singular basic arrangement that had been made for what turned out to be Queen Mary's long sojourn at Badminton—where she arrived in October 1939, with some seventy pieces of personal luggage—was that Her Majesty should take the house for the whole of the war years, except for the bedrooms and sitting-room used by the Beauforts. They were to stay there with their own servants, though they had their meals at her table, in fact, to become guests in their own home. Though Master and Mary were fond of Queen Mary and revered her, this system of dyarchy was not altogether a success: for one thing, the Dowager Duchess, Louisa, a very pretty and exquisite old lady, who lived at the edge of the park in a cottage filled with pastels by Liotard, and immensely enjoyed the decorative position of being the chief old lady in the region, now to her dismay found herself outshone by a much bigger setting sun. Then, too, the cohort of royal servants proved difficult; they missed their domestic life in London, or in cottages at Sandringham and

elsewhere. On October 19th, 1939, I received a letter from
Mary Beaufort from London, in which she wrote,

> I hope to return on Sunday or Monday. Queen Mary has
> gone to Badminton for the duration. Oh, how I longed for
> you to be there when she and about fifty-five servants
> arrived. Pandemonium was the least it could be called!
> The servants revolted, and scorned our humble home. They
> refused to use the excellent rooms assigned to them. Fear-
> ful rows and battle royals [were] fought over my body—but
> I won in the end and reduced them to tears and to pulp.
> ... I can laugh now, but I have never been so angry! ...
> The Queen, quite unconscious of the stir, has settled in
> well, and is busy cutting down trees and tearing down ivy.
> Tremendous activity.

Thus the servants complained from the outset, and continued
to repine throughout.

Queen Mary first sent for me to Badminton in January
1941, when she had been there some fifteen months. I arrived
there on a Saturday, and was curious to see how matters were
progressing. One sad change was immediately evident between this visit and that of 1938—the gap left by the death on
active service of Lord Frederick Cambridge, a charming and
lively personality, with a little the air of an eighteenth-
century prince, who had made his home at Badminton with
his sister and brother-in-law. Everyone, including his aunt,
Queen Mary, greatly missed him. ... The party was small,
consisting of Queen Mary, her lady-in-waiting, Miss Margaret
Wyndham, and Mary Beaufort and Master, who, on the
outbreak of war, had rejoined his regiment, the Blues, but
was at home on leave for one night. ... The days were
bright and opaline with frost. Worcester Lodge, the fantastic
masterpiece of William Kent, was clearly visible from the
upper windows at the other end of the Long Avenue every
morning, nor had I ever seen the interior of the house look

finer, perhaps because after a period of some years when certain rooms were not much used, now again it appeared as if the whole extent of it were lived in. It had always, moreover, preserved a peculiar air of the past, because things had been left alone, and objects left where they were. Thus in the hall, the white light radiating from the thin and scintillant layer of frost outside played on the dry, white Italian plasterwork, on dark frescoes by Richard Wootton depicting the sports of the first Duke, and sparkled on the silver tops of the maces, which, carried by footmen in the time of Queen Anne, still stood in a corner near the fireplace. Though an air of extra prosperity and polish now prevailed, the rooms in general were untouched: nothing had been moved: the only visible change consisted in the presence of a guard outside the house, which added to the atmosphere a suggestion that its occupants might be prisoners, and thereby induced a distant sense of gloom or doom.

In Queen Mary herself I saw no alteration, though Mary Beaufort told me that the air-raids in the immediate district had greatly shaken Her Majesty, but that with her great power of self-control she would not allow any outward sign of this to appear. Further, and more altruistically, Queen Mary had been much affected by the raids on her beloved London, and by the wrecking of the City churches and especially by the loss of the Guildhall—to which she constantly alluded—and of the many beautiful buildings and works of art throughout the country; so much of her time had been given to tracing, classifying and collecting together objects of interest—to finding, for example, a piece of tapestry mentioned in inventories of Queen Elizabeth I, or matching a silver vase made for King George IV, or buying a chair that had escaped from some famous set, and then to presenting these to the place from which they had originally come—let us say to the Guildhall or the Royal Pavilion at Brighton or to the Queen's House at Greenwich—that this continuous and insensate destruction, which both raised old and pleasant memories of the monuments and objects now wrecked in this fashion, and at the same time affronted her strong sense of historic tradition, had hit her particularly hard.

It was evident, too, that Queen Mary must have found her life greatly changed from its former normal course. Her Majesty always showed herself very strict in observing all the war regulations concerning food, dress, coal and motoring. Thus with the current petrol shortage, she was deprived of what was her chief recreation in ordinary times, and could not—or rather would not, for of course the Government would have granted her a special allowance of petrol had she chosen to ask for it—any longer drive over to see places of historic or artistic interest in the neighbourhood. So, with time at last on her hands, but determined not to waste a moment of it, Queen Mary had taken to sorting out papers and letters, and had put a new floor, and installed electric light and heating, in the Muniment Room, which occupied one of the two pavilions added by William Kent to the ends of the house. Queen Mary's energy, derived no doubt in part from the wonderful Guelph physique, had been driven in on itself. Directly after breakfast the lady-in-waiting had first to read aloud to Her Majesty for an hour, and then to start pasting together books that had become untidy; there followed a walk, and work in the woods—a phrase which in this case denotes that Queen Mary was now able to spend a larger part of the day in her enjoyable but unprofitable crusade against nature.

I have already mentioned that she had for many years carried on a regular feud against ivy: now she was able to add the fallen branches and twigs of trees to the small list of her enemies. Every day she spent two or three hours in the Verge—the wooded strip, some ten miles in length, that runs round the edge of the park at Badminton—tidying and arranging. Alas! As soon as a portion of it had become neat, a storm would ensue, and once more down came leaves, twigs and branches, while, in addition, bits of paper and odd fragments of cigarettes had been known to blow over the boundary wall from the road. In the manner of all royal persons, Queen Mary had never before been allowed to stay long enough in one place to realise that the Ministry-of-Works brand of tidiness appertaining to royal residences is an expensive and unnatural condition: but now she had remained at Badminton for over a year, and had seen—and it had been a great disillusionment—the ivy she had already once destroyed, grow again, and had comprehended that because it does grow, it is a particularly difficult foe to vanquish. So, instead of the ivy being merely picked off the walls, its trunks were now cut, and the roots, where possible, torn up. Even then this sly, treacherous foe would be liable to creep back. And here is perhaps the place to interpolate an episode from two years before.

Queen Mary had arranged to motor over from Harewood to Renishaw, to see the house and gardens, in September 1939, an expedition which the outbreak of war on the third of that month prevented. I had been uneasy beforehand, wondering how to fill Her Majesty's afternoon, and aware that every minute must be occupied. Moreover, I realised that if time was on our hands, Queen Mary, who was most observant in such matters, would notice, even more than she would otherwise, the age and shabbiness of many curtains and carpets at Renishaw, and the other faults of an old house which had not been much refurbished. I remembered how Mrs Greville had, on hearing of a proposed afternoon visit from Queen Mary, rushed up to London and returned to Polesden Lacey with twenty-four small deerskin rugs, and when I asked why, had replied, 'I bought them to cover up the holes in the carpets, or Queen Mary will discover them with the end of her umbrella, which acts like a divining-rod for such things.' I could not afford a similar disguise for the defects of Renishaw, but an idea came to me that would have left Queen Mary with small leisure for such discoveries, and in writing to the Queen—Queen Elizabeth, the Queen Mother

—I mentioned it. I explained my quandary: that the carpets were in holes; the ceilings were in one or two places discoloured; the furniture was not sufficiently polished for Queen Mary's taste, and that, in order to leave as little time as possible in which for her to note these defects, I had told Maynard Hollingworth, my agent, to cut all the ivy he could find on the estate, and hang it over the stables, so that the party could pick it off the walls without stubbing our nails. A day or two before England declared war on Germany, I dined alone with the King and Queen at Buckingham Palace. After dinner, the King said to me, 'What's all this, about ivy? Very good idea. . . . You know Queen Mary once gave me and Lillybett* ivy-poisoning by making us pick it off walls at Sandringham!'

To return, however, to life at Badminton. On Sunday afternoon Queen Mary took me for a walk in the park, occasionally pausing to flick a stick or twig from the path with one of her two canes. She talked mostly about *Two Generations*, which book—the diaries respectively of a great-aunt and an aunt of mine, edited by myself—had then lately been published. Queen Mary liked best, as I did, the second part of the book, crammed with religious details of the 1870s, and with period interest, and she greatly appreciated its curious absurdity. Some parts of it she made her lady-in-waiting read over to her twice running, and she told me that the kind of existence described in it greatly resembled her own early life.

Dinner was at 8.30 every night. Queen Mary appeared in a sequined dress, with an ostrich-feather cape and several rows of pearls, but no other jewels. The food was good, though confined to the regulation three courses, and by no means over-plentiful. A note of austerity had been introduced, and I remarked that instead of having fresh tablecloths, we had, in order to save washing, one of oilcloth disguised to look like linen, which could just be sponged down afterwards. I have

* The Queen.

never paid attention to the shibboleths of the fashionable world—though I have found the cataloguing of them instructive—but I remember being brought up to regard napkin-rings as very vulgar (on a par with saying 'serviette' when you meant napkin), and it was therefore with pleasure that I observed at dinner the first night that every member of the party had been provided with this useful adjunct, for I could deduce that, if only temporarily, it would become *de rigueur*, and that all the people who had formerly been so horrified at the idea of a napkin-ring would now have to adopt it with enthusiasm. Those living in the house plainly possessed their own—Queen Mary, for example, had a heavy silver ring, with the crown and her monogram engraved on it; the rest had rings of coloured celluloid or plastic. Queen Mary herself perfectly appraised the position, for during my final visit to Badminton while it was in the occupation of Queen Mary, at Christmas 1944, one afternoon when tea was over, she first very deliberately furled her napkin and tucked it through the ring, and then pointed with it at her deaf old courtier, Sir Richard Molyneux, at the same time saying to me, 'I believe Dick over there disapproves of my doing this, but I've had to do it now for nearly five years!' At the end of the meal I always disgraced myself by showing my incapacity for rolling a napkin; I would first make several bungling and amateurish attempts, until, finding Queen Mary's eye watching me as I struggled with it, I had eventually to continue the battle under the table, where it could not be seen until in the end I had been able to impose some sort of order upon chaos.

Dinner, a quick meal, was always over by nine o'clock, when we listened to the news on the radio, with its interminable lists of destruction at home and abroad. The moment the radio was turned on, Queen Mary and her lady whipped out their knitting, for during a war, even more than during peace, no moment must be idle. (In the week or two before Beaufort had re-joined his regiment, he had been compelled to knit a scarf on a wooden framework of pegs during these post-prandial moments.) Queen Mary would listen attentively to the good news and bad—mostly, in 1941, bad—but never by the flicker of an eyelash would she show that she was disturbed, or make any comment. Only once did I see Her Majesty's expression change during the news. On Sunday night, Hungary or Romania was under discussion, and the word 'Transylvania' occurred. At this, Queen Mary smiled rather archly, and caught the eye of her niece, nodded to her, and repeated softly, in her rather deep voice 'Transylvania, Transylvania!' and then, seeing that I had observed this, explained, 'The joke is that some of us came from there.' I was amused, because there had been a similar reference at Brantridge a year before, by Queen Mary and her brother Lord Athlone. Queen Mary's grandmother—the mother of the Duke of Teck—hailed from Transylvania, but evidently the Guelph strain is so strong that none of her family can believe in their possession of such outlandish blood. Nevertheless, Queen Mary's beautiful Magyar or Romanian grandmother accounts for many traits in her—her eyebrows, and her eyes, set at an angle; the manner in which she smoked cigarettes; her love of jewels, and the way she wore them; and the particular sort of film-star glamour that in advanced age overtook her appearance, and made her, with the stylisation of her clothes, such an attractive as well as imposing figure. The quality in Her Majesty which I most admired was her— it is difficult to express—'all-throughness'. Her personality and temperament permeated everything she did, said, or wore. Her clothes, elaborate to a degree, for she liked detail in everything, had in the early days of King George V's reign been much criticised—who else, it must be asked, could have worn them with success?—and she displayed the same taste throughout, in her choice of jewels, decoration, furniture and pictures. This intense individuality, maturing through the length of her career, caused her to be loved and admired increasingly. And Her Majesty's awareness of how people felt about her afforded her that continually increasing self-confidence which caused her to blossom into the magnificent person she became: in early life and by nature she was shy, and perhaps she did not really come into her own until the Jubilee of 1935.

As soon as the news finished, Queen Mary rose and left, and we all followed her immediately—for she did not permit the men to sit on in the dining-room after dinner, as is the usual habit in England—into the drawing-room. There, I noticed, on the first night of my visit, for I knew the room well, that a chair had been introduced into it which had not been there before—not an arm-chair, but a high chair with a rounded back of red leather, made in the reign of King William IV. It did not particularly suit the room, which was of the period of Charles II, but it did exactly suit Queen Mary. It might have been designed specially for her, and when I asked its history, Mary Beaufort told me that Her Majesty had spotted it in a lumber-room upstairs, and had immediately ordered it to be brought down for her own use. After dinner, then, she would sit in this chair, placed in the middle of the room, away from the fire, and look at illustrated books. For example, the first evening she showed me a collection of coloured plates of soldiers in British and foreign uniforms, belonging to her nephew, Lord Cambridge, and on Sunday night we examined the papers which concerned the purchase in Rome by the third Duke of Beaufort of an entire gallery of works of art from Cardinal Alberoni who had formed it. These documents were extraordinarily interesting, since, in addition to unfolding a fascinating story of ingenious fraud on the part of the Duke's chief agent in the matter, they made clear the method by which such an enormous collection, including many famous pictures, pieces of sculpture and antique vases, was moved; the manner in which it was conveyed to England; and how it was embarked at Ostia, together with letters from the captains of the ships and from the agents, Italian and English, involved in the transactions, and they included minute descriptions of the journey from Rome to the sea, and the actual bills of lading.* From the lists, Queen Mary had been able to identify several objects, the history of which had long since been forgotten. Later she showed me a box of letters docketed by my great-aunt Lady Geraldine Somerset, and talked a little of her, of her intense character, of her violent temper and great kindness in combination, and of how cultivated she and her sisters had been—much more cultivated than later generations—able to speak French, Italian and German correctly and fluently, and to write a fine hand. Geraldine I remembered as a genial but intimidating old lady, armed with an enormous ear-trumpet edged with a black silk fringe, who lived in a small house in Upper Brook Street, each room of which resembled a tent made of faded photographs. And I called to mind the poignant death-bed scene of which I had been told, when Queen Alexandra had come to say good-bye to her old friend. Geraldine sat up, and said loudly, 'Go away, Ma'am, I am too old and too ugly for you to come to see me.' Queen Alexandra, who was also deaf, misunderstood, and said, 'That is *too* much! She says I am too old and too ugly!' And on this note, the friendship of a lifetime ended.

On Monday morning Queen Mary sent for me to her sitting-room upstairs to take my leave of her. She showed me various pieces of furniture which had belonged to her grandmother, the Duchess of Cambridge, as well as various objects she had lately acquired—a chinoiserie clock, for example, a Chinese butterfly-cage, and a little jade figure, Moghul, which Queen Mary, who collected Moghul objects, pronounced *Mōrgul*, so that it was some time before I understood what she was saying.

I paid a second visit to Queen Mary on May 5th, 1941. Her Majesty was not very well, and there prevailed in the house, like a fog, that curious air of mystery that always

---

* This material I subsequently edited at Her Majesty's suggestion, and published in a book of essays, called *Sing High, Sing Low*, under the title of *The Red Folder*.

surrounds any illness, however slight, in a member of the royal family. This arises, I suppose, because kings and queens must not appear to be in any sense fallible. Though, unlike Roman Emperors, they now make no pretensions to downright divinity, yet a faint odour of ex-officio immortality still surrounds them, and the possibility of an illness attacking them always brings a sense of shock, reminds them—and still more those in waiting upon them—of the transitoriness of their human splendour. A year or so after writing this passage I read Lord Hervey's *Memoirs** and found that he had observed exactly the same conditions prevalent, but in a very exaggerated form, during the illness of any member of the royal family in the court of King George II and Queen Caroline. The relevant passage is appended.** By the next morning, however, Queen Mary had recovered her usual energy. Some of the huge old trees in the Long Avenue were being cut—though professionally and not by the royal party— and the ground cleared for agriculture, and Queen Mary enthusiastically supported, and aided as far as she could, this work. At 10.15 on a very cold May morning Her Majesty

* Edited by Romney Sedgwick.
** The day before the King's birthday the Court removed from Kensington to London, and the Queen, who had long been out of order with a cough and a little lurking fever, notwithstanding she had been twice blooded, grew every hour worse and worse. However, the King lugged her the night she came from Kensington, the first of Farinelli's performances, to the opera, and made her the next day go through all the tiresome ceremonies of drawing-rooms and balls, the fatigues of heats and crowds, and every other disagreeable appurtenance to the celebration of a birthday. There was a strange affection of an incapacity of being sick that ran through the whole Royal Family which they carried so far that no one of them was more willing to own any other of the family ill than to acknowledge themselves to be so. I have known the King get out of his bed, choking with a sore throat, and in a high fever, only to dress and have a levee, and in five minutes undress and return to his bed till the same ridiculous farce of health was to be presented the next day at the same hour. With all his fondness for the Queen, he used to make her in the like circumstances commit the like extravagances, but never with more danger and uneasiness than at this time. In the morning drawing-room she found herself so near swooning that she was forced to send Lord Grantham to the King to beg he would retire, for that she was unable to stand any longer. Notwithstanding which, at night he brought her into still a greater crowd at the ball, and there kept her till eleven o'clock.

accordingly conducted the Princess Royal, who was also staying in the house, the lady-in-waiting and myself to a distant portion of the park, where we were made to set to and clear great clumps of young trees, shrubs and brambles, for the battle Queen Mary now waged against Nature's untidiness knew no respite. Indeed, she had extended her war against the foe still further. Mary Beaufort told me how interesting it had been lately to watch the battle of two strong wills. Queen Mary was determined to cut down the large cedar outside the drawing-room windows, giving as her reason that its branches excluded the light: this was true, but it happened also to be the tree in which Lord Fitzroy Somerset, afterwards Lord Raglan, the famous soldier who had commanded troops during the Crimean War, had played as a boy, and Beaufort, so tolerant in all else, was equally resolved to support family tradition and to prevent the tree being sacrificed. The tussle continued for several years, but at the time of writing, 1951, the tree is still standing.

Added to these extensions of her private war, Queen Mary had lately taken up enthusiastically the campaign to collect scrap. Her sense of domestic economy, as much as of order and tidiness, made her enjoy the amassing of it, and if she found a piece of bone deposited by a fox, or a fragment of old iron, she would at once pick it up and hand it, usually to a somewhat reluctant lady-in-waiting, to take home; though on one occasion I had to carry a really filthily dirty old glass bottle for several miles. Queen Mary's fanatical collection of scrap continued until the end of the war, and was reported to have culminated in an episode which I here record, though without being able to vouch for its truth. It was said that one fine spring noon Her Majesty returned to the house in triumph after a walk, dragging behind her a large piece of rusty old iron to add to the royal dump. A few minutes later, however, one of her pages brought an urgent message from a neighbouring farmer. 'Please, Your Majesty, a Mr Hodge has arrived, and he says Your Majesty has taken his plough, and will Your Majesty graciously give it back to him, please, at once, as he can't get on without it!'

On the occasion of which I am writing, when we went wooding, Queen Mary, attended by a despatch-rider on a motor-bicycle, in person conducted our operations, poking at recalcitrant branches with her walking-stick. The work certainly seemed to be quite dangerous. The despatch-rider of that morning was a new recruit to the post, temporarily replacing a more permanent predecessor who had already been injured: two chauffeurs had been knocked out, and another man, now helping, still wore a black patch over one eye which, I was told, a splinter had entered. We were made to begin attacking an enormous centuries-old thicket of hawthorn, bramble and wild rose, with a few quite tall but scrubby oaks: by the time we left, the ground was clear, albeit I only just succeeded in rescuing the Princess Royal from a falling tree-top. The journey back to the house, too, was somewhat alarming, for Humphries, Queen Mary's chauffeur, whether because he felt it to be in keeping with the rustic, fête-champêtre atmosphere that prevailed that day, or whether because he knew the surface of the road to be bad (we were returning by another way), now chose to desert the drive, and begin to lumber and bump across-country over the grass. The large, old-fashioned Daimler rocked and swayed in a most frightening fashion, to the consternation of all its occupants except Queen Mary, who did not seem to mind much, though she muttered to herself once or twice, 'Oh dear! I wish he wouldn't do it!' Albeit Humphries was, as the saying goes, 'long past it'. Queen Mary maintained a kind belief in his driving, because he had been for so many years in her service that, though perfectly aware of his shortcomings, she would not discharge him.

I had already at Brantridge had some experience of Humphries's capacity, for, returning from an expedition, he lost Queen Mary and her party, including myself, for a whole hour and a half in Ashdown Forest. He was, indeed, as much celebrated for his bad driving as for the arguments into which he entered downstairs: the Daimler under his care was always breaking down, and on one occasion an amusing incident, of which Lady Desborough told me, had ensued. It occurred during the latter part of the reign of King George V, when Queen Mary was Queen of England. She left Windsor Castle one morning by motor, with Lady Desborough, her Lady of the Bedchamber, to go to Oxford where Her Majesty was to have luncheon with the Chancellor, and subsequently to open some new building. On the journey there, in the loneliest place on the road, the motor broke down, and of course Humphries could not repair it or get the engine to start again. The hour at which Queen Mary should have reached Oxford grew nearer and nearer, until at last the Queen told Lady Desborough to stop the next motor-car she saw, and ask the driver to give Her Majesty a lift into Oxford. The situation seemed somewhat irregular; however, Lady Desborough got out, and started to walk slowly up and down the road. She paced it for a long time: there seemed to be no traffic passing, until at last she saw in the distance a small car advancing from the wrong direction. She signalled to the driver to stop, and said to him, 'Would you mind giving the Queen a lift into Oxford? She has to be there by one o'clock, and the royal motor has broken down.'

'Surely Her Majesty would not consent to be driven by a commoner?' the driver countered.

Lady Desborough reassured Mr Titmuss—for such his name proved to be—on this point, and said that, on the contrary, the Queen *wished* it. Mrs Titmuss was sitting next to her husband in the front seat, and the back of the car was full of onions.

Lady Desborough now hurried back to the Queen and announced, 'I've succeeded in stopping a motor, Ma'am. And the owner of it, Mr Titmuss, would be delighted to turn round and take Your Majesty into Oxford. He says he can just do it in the time—the only thing is, the back of the motor is full of onions.'

'Do they smell?' enquired the Queen.

'Not more than usual, Ma'am,' Lady Desborough, who had begun to feel desperate, replied.

The onions were then piled on the floor of the car and the party started for Oxford, the Queen sitting beside Mr Titmuss, and Lady Desborough and Mrs Titmuss sitting at the back among the onions. They reached Oxford at the right time, and the Chancellor and other academic dignitaries received the Queen as had been arranged.

Now, too, though Humphries drove off the road and across the rough grass of the park at Badminton, we arrived safely at the house in spite of him, but most of us in a rather exhausted and hungry condition. At luncheon, I note, we found a new and rather horrible war-time dish had been prepared for us, called Lord Woolton Pie (Lord Woolton was Minister of Food at the time). Queen Mary's chef had died recently, and she had appointed in his place a former kitchen-maid, Mary Douglas. One day Queen Mary had remarked to the chief of the several stately and pompous major-domos in her service, 'Mary Douglas seems to be doing quite well, Jenkins.'

'I am glad', he replied, 'that she is giving Your Majesty satisfaction. She has had considerable experience. I understand that for thirteen years she was in the cold larder!'

In the afternoon, Queen Mary, the Princess Royal and I set out in the vast royal Daimler to visit some antique-shops in Bath and afterwards to have tea with Lady Noble in Lansdowne Crescent. Humphries was, as usual, driving, and next to him, in the front, sat a large detective. Queen Mary and the Princess Royal were in the back, with myself between them. On the way, Queen Mary, always anxious to do any kindness that she could, remarked that if we saw any man in the forces at the side of the road, waiting to be given a lift into Bath, we must stop and take him. Presently, about five miles from the city, Her Majesty observed an aircraftsman waiting, and tapped with her umbrella on the window in front, behind Humphries's head. The motor pulled up, and Queen Mary told the detective to get down and fetch the airman.

The detective at once kidnapped him and ushered him right into the motor-car. He was very young and totally unprepared for the company in which he found himself. He entered in a jaunty manner, and then saw the Princess Royal. A frantic look of fright came into his eyes, and, as if unwilling to accept the testimony they offered him, he cast them round widly—and beheld Queen Mary, about whose very individual appearance there could be no mistake! Every fair hair on his head stood up, and his eyes darted here and there in search of escape. But by now he was sitting down, and the motor had started. Queen Mary saw that he was nervous and shy, and talked to him so charmingly that she soon reassured him. It was now his turn, though he remained quite unconscious of it, to give Queen Mary a shock, for when she asked him what his profession had been before the war, he replied, 'I worked in a hospital—in the maternity ward.'

Silence followed, and he was released on the outskirts of Bath, though subsequently I have often wondered whether we did not carry him in the wrong direction. After he had got out, I sat in the place he had vacated, and could hear Queen Mary and the Princess Royal in the back of the motor murmuring together for some minutes, 'How very odd!' 'He said he was working in the *maternity ward*!' 'What can he have been doing?' 'It seems very strange!' 'We ought to have asked him.' 'In the *maternity ward*!' And subsequently for the rest of the day they would from time to time revert to the subject in a low voice.

In the evening I sat next to Queen Mary at dinner, and happened to remark how difficult I found it to save or be economical. This avowal surprised Queen Mary, who confessed that she was by nature very careful in small ways: she

Osbert Sitwell at Montegufoni

Renishaw

The view from Renishaw

Montegufoni

The view
from
the house

Lady Ida
Sitwell's
bedroom,
recently used
as a winter
dining room

Montegufoni
a distant view

added that she used every piece of soap until it could be used no more, and that what most particularly riled her was to have to discard a pair of long white kid gloves after wearing them only once, and to be obliged by custom to put on a new pair. Later Queen Mary told me that she was terrified of being kidnapped by the Nazis. It was her abiding fear, and she had made arrangements for an airplane to take her away from Badminton to a secret destination, should a German landing occur. The Duchess of Beaufort, to whom afterwards I mentioned this, said that Queen Mary always had three suitcases packed ready, in case of such trouble. Her Majesty kept one herself, and the other two were handed over to the two dressers separately, one for each of them to guard. If an alert were given of an air-raid, it was also their duty to pack a fourth suitcase, filling it with tiaras and other jewels. This, the lady-in-waiting had to hold.

One morning during this visit, Queen Mary set off to have luncheon with the King and Queen at Windsor Castle. It was the only time she had been there since the war. The party consisted of two motor-cars, preceded by two despatch-riders on motor-bicycles. The first motor contained Queen Mary, the second, two dressers and a page.

I paid several other visits to Badminton, but there was nothing particular to note (until the last—Christmas 1944— which I shall describe in a moment), except for one ridiculous incident before I arrived to stay there for a few days in 1942. I was going straight to Badminton from Renishaw without touching London, and, having been misled by the time-table, I had asked to be met at Mangotsfield, the nearest station on that line. To my consternation I discovered while in the train that, owing to the chaotic conditions prevailing on the railways in time of war, the schedule had been altered, and it no longer stopped there. Queen Mary with her hatred of waste would certainly be annoyed at petrol being consumed in this way for no purpose, and further the chauffeur would not know what to do, and might wait for hours outside the station. I was at a complete loss, and as I was in the restaurant-car having tea at the time I found out, I took the steward, an intelligent man I had deduced, into my confidence and explained the situation. After hearing my story, he said, 'There's only one thing to do, sir. Write a message of explanation to the chauffeur, telling him to meet you at Bristol, and I'll put it in a bottle and throw it out of the window as we pass through Mangotsfield Station.' This was a method of communication I had always imagined only to be practised by mariners wrecked in rough seas, but it worked. I addressed the message and wrote it; the steward then folded it, put it in an empty lemonade bottle attached to a piece of string, and threw it carefully out of the window on to an empty part of the platform, letting go of the string at the same time—and, sure enough, soon after I reached Bristol, the royal motor drew up to fetch me.

After leaving Badminton, I sent Queen Mary my essay *The Red Folder*, to which I have already referred. In her letter dated May 12th, 1942, thanking me, she commented on the bombing of Bath, 'Poor beautiful Bath, it is tragic, so much spoilt. I went there last week, Lansdowne Crescent, Royal Crescent, the Circus, Queen's Square terribly scarred and houses burnt out, as for the poorer parts, one out of every three houses gone—the noise was terrific. The country round here is looking so lovely just now, one hates to think of those barbarities.' Enclosed in the letter was the page of pencilled notes which follows:

Royal Cres.	(small portion damaged.)
Circus	(19, 20 & 21 still on fire
	large bomb dropped in centre of road.)
Assembly Room	Gutted with fire, nothing saved.
Gay St.	Very little damage.
Hotels	Lansdowne Grove, Francis Hotel
	Queen Sq. & Bennett St. badly
	damaged.

Churches	Abbey, broken windows, St. James gutted by fire, St. John's South Parade and St. Mary's Julian Rd. badly damaged with fire.
Prior Park College	small damage to building and grounds.
Pulteney St.	considerable damage to property.
Milsom St.	only broken windows in certain premises.
New Site for Royal Mineral Water Hospital	considerable damage to site and surrounding shops.

1 Inspector and 7 other ranks of Special Constabulary were killed on Saturday night. Five regular Police Officers were wounded.

One P.C. of Somerset County Constabulary has failed to return today and is believed to have been killed.

Military Hospital and R.V.H. not damaged.

In November 1944 I received a letter from Queen Mary asking me to spend from December 22nd to 28th at Badminton. I wrote to Her Majesty at once to accept, at the same time declaring immediately, so that there could be no mistake about it, that my doctor absolutely forbade me to clear or cut timber. . . . Claud Hamilton,* the Comptroller of Queen Mary's Household, and a former brother-officer of mine in the Grenadiers, telephoned to me a few days before I left Renishaw to tell me (for war always makes inroads on royal privilege) that, after five years of war, it was not possible to guarantee a reserved seat for me, but that if I reported to the station-master's office at one o'clock on Friday the 22nd—the train started at two—that important person had promised to do all he could to find me a place. Accordingly, as I was anxious not to have to stand in the corridor the

* Lord Claud Nigel Hamilton, seventh son of the 2nd Duke of Abercorn.

entire way—since though the whole journey should only occupy two hours, it was plain that, in their war-Christmas state of overcrowding, the trains would run very late—I arrived at the station at twelve-thirty, only to find a howling pack of distracted people rushing about in every direction. There were no porters, and I had been obliged to take a good deal of luggage with me. Eventually I discovered a dazed adolescent who seemed not unwilling to help, and, making him mount guard over my suitcases, I left him with strict instructions not to move, even for an instant, until I returned. Next, I fought my way to the station-master's office, and back again to the entrance with a porter. My luggage was still where I had left it, but without the boy in charge of it; he had absolutely disappeared. I then accompanied the luggage to the office, where I was given a chair, and sat in a corner, hearing the trampling of the mob outside.

The station-master's real office had been bombed, so the staff were using temporarily the royal waiting-room, a pretty octagonal room, crowned with a shallow dome and having on one wall a rather pretty plaster medallion of Queen Victoria as a young woman. There were three men and two girls working, and the sound of feet outside was accompanied within by the tapping and click of typewriters, and the continual ringing of a telephone bell. The station-master himself often rang up a mysterious higher authority, active elsewhere. This power he approached rather as a mortal might attempt to speak to those who dwell on Olympus.

'Is Mr Williams there? . . . I want to speak to Mr Williams Himself. It's the Station-Master. Yes, I said HIMSELF. . . . Is that you Mr Williams? The lawns are dangerously crowded, sir. I thought you might care to inspect them, and pass your opinion. You may think the gates should be shut.' (It was the first time I had heard platforms referred to as *lawns*, and this interested me. It must be, I think, a relic of days when platforms were open strips of grass.)

Five telephones were now in use at once, when suddenly

a sixth bell rang loudly, and the younger of the girl-clerks, abandoning her own instrument, rushed to it. She lifted the receiver, and I heard her say, ' "Are we the Ivy Restaurant?" . . . Certainly not!' All present seemed hurt by the suggestion, and the four other clerks laid down their receivers to discuss the matter until at last the other girl clerk relieved the situation by saying, 'The place is ever so posh—not ordinary at all. Mr Noel Coward goes there, and you have to order a table. No queues.'

At this moment, attention was diverted, for from his olympian retreat the great Mr Williams gave the order to shut the gates of the station, and this was done, so that now two crowds roared and raved, one inside, the other outside and besieging the yellow bulk of Paddington.... From the office, the noise they made sounded like a rough sea.... After an hour the station-master told me that his deputy would take me over to the platform: it was impossible, he said, to reserve a carriage, but he hoped to be able to put me in one with only three other people, if it could be done. He explained the identity of the others, who included the wife of the Medical Officer at Swindon. Her I shall always remember; a short, stocky, tweed-clad, determined-looking woman, who was already seated on her box on the platform, reading a book while waiting, with such resolution that she did not look up when we were introduced but shook hands in the void, as it were, over the cover. I recognised at once the book she was reading—a novel of mine. I was interested—because it is seldom that an author catches a reader red-handed—and so I said to her, 'That book is very familiar to me.'

She cannot have heard my name, for she said, somewhat morosely, 'You mean, you've read it?'

'No,' I answered, 'I mean I wrote it.'

A strong expression of disbelief and disapproval clamped down on her face. She thought, I apprehended, either that I was not telling the truth or that I was boastful. When we got into the train, she read the book without a single pause for the whole of the journey, which took four and a half hours instead of two; nor did she smile once. At the same time it was gratifying to me as an author to note that the general atmosphere of holiday (far from being only four in the carriage, we were eight in the seats, with several children crawling under and over us) in no whit caused her attention to wander. People and children bumped and screamed, but she read grimly on.

When I arrived at Badminton very late, I found Queen Mary seated at the tea-table in the drawing-room. Her Majesty must have been waiting a long time, and I am afraid must have found it trying—though she showed no sign of annoyance—for the next day when the Princess Royal's train coming from Leeds was three hours late, Queen Mary fretted, and said to me 'I'm afraid I'm dreadfully impatient: it is one of my faults.' At tea that afternoon, she told me of the following incident which had occurred in the summer, when King George VI was visiting the British armies in Italy.

The King had arrived on the coast in the late afternoon, and was spending the night with his staff in a nissen hut by the sea, at Amalfi, just below Ravello, where King Victor Emmanuel and the Queen of Italy were living at this time in a house belonging to the Duca di Sangro. King George did not call on them that day, for he thought it might embarrass Mr Churchill and the Government. A motor-boat was coming to fetch His Majesty at an early hour the following morning, to join Field-Marshal Alexander. When it arrived the next morning at 6 a.m., the captain noticed in the immediate vicinity on the shore, just where the King would embark, a tall, robust woman dressed in black, who stood by herself, fishing. He sent an officer to tell her to move. She paid no attention. He sent three officers. Still she paid no attention. Finally he went himself to remonstrate with her. She continued to fish, and kept her eye on the float, but this time dextrously flicked at him a visiting-card, on which was written 'S.M. La Regina d'Italia'.

Queen Mary was as energetic as when she had first come to live at Badminton, and looked no older. She usually never mentioned, and perhaps seldom thought of, her age—though indeed, on this visit I heard her refer to it. One afternoon when I was walking with Her Majesty we met a young woman with a child of three or four years of age: a charming little boy in whom Queen Mary took an interest. Queen Mary stooped down, grasped both the child's hands in her own, and whirled him round several times, in a rather stiff-jointed dance, saying 'Never forget, you've waltzed with an old lady of seventy-five!' This interested me, for she was seventy-seven at the time, and I wondered whether this minimisation, so unlike her character, was intentional or the fruit of feminine vanity.

The Christmas house-party consisted of Queen Mary, the Princess Royal and Lord Harewood, the Beauforts, Lady Constance Milnes-Gaskell, who was in waiting, Lord Claud Hamilton and Sir Richard Molyneux. Of these, apart from the Beauforts, I knew best Harry Harewood, with whom I had served in the 1914–18 war. In the trenches, I had grown to know him well, and I recall that, while in those miserable quarters, he told me of how—for he had been rather a rake and spendthrift—he had applied for a loan to a moneylender called Sanguinetti, who proved to be his great-uncle, the second Marquess of Clanricarde, the celebrated miser and collector of works of art. This old gentleman, who in later life never visited his great Irish estates, but lived in London, was often mistaken for a tramp, as he sat on a bench in Hyde Park, and ate unappetising scraps of food from a paper bag or parcel which he brought with him. It was known that he had amassed several millions, and various relations were so sure of inheriting that they had already built houses in which to reside when they received his fortune. Lascelles, on the other hand, entertained, after the Sanguinetti episode, no such hopes. But nevertheless when Lord Clanricarde died in 1916, it was found that he had left his entire enormous fortune to Lascelles. He was supposed to have said, 'It has to go to someone—it had better go to the one who will get through it quickest!' Other people believed that, hating Lascelles's father, he had left the money to the son to annoy him, and certainly, in favour of this view, is the fact that the elder Lord Harewood was made an executor and trustee.

I had always liked Harry, for he knew a great deal about pictures and works of art, and really cared for them, and he was broadminded and kind, as well as intelligent. He was also —a quality which he lost in later life—a dandy, and would emerge from the muddiest trench unsullied, and as if straight out of a bandbox: for this characteristic he was much admired by his company of Grenadiers. I could never make out why he was not equally popular elsewhere, but he was not generally liked. In 1944, the weather at Badminton, like our treatment of Christmas, was strictly traditional. Harry was ill with bronchitis and did not go out, but sat by the drawing-room fire. He amused me, for he told me he had just read a pamphlet I had recently published about the war and the position in it of the artist. When I asked him what he thought of it, he replied 'It's full of your own brand of mad common sense.' Both the Princess Royal and he were worried and unhappy, as their elder son, a prisoner of war, had been sent to a special German camp established for the sons of eminent men, and it was suspected that the Nazis intended to use them as hostages.

The chief change visible was that Queen Mary had given shelter to the fine statue of William III on horseback, which had been moved here for safety from Bristol after the first bombing of that city. It now faced the Long Avenue. The food was still good if exiguous, and the servants, though all old or in ill-health, and for these reasons not in the Services, tumbled over each other. There were seven men waiting in the small dining-room on Christmas night. During the daytime, they seemed always to be in the process of carrying in larger and larger tables, because Queen Mary insisted always on a two-foot space each side of her at meals. By this time the royal pages had been obliged to abandon their scarlet coats, and were wearing the blue battle dress, with the royal cypher on the breast, that had been designed for them recently by King George. Some of them much resented the change, and one of Queen Mary's pages had actually left when obliged to discard the scarlet livery which he had worn for thirty years. Queen Mary sent for him and told him that it was an act of direct rebellion against the King's commands.

Christmas grew nearer. Presents had been my great worry, for I had been warned that the traditional Sandringham ritual still continued. An enormous table was placed in the hall. It was divided up into sections by ribbons, themselves relics of thirty or forty years. Each section was labelled, beginning next to the window with Queen Mary's; then came that of the Princess Royal, and the series ended with mine, on the extreme right. To find gifts for so many people in shops that had been depleted by war, was no easy matter. Moreover, at a moment when taxes were unprecedentedly high, it could be most costly. I had written to grumble about this to Mary Beaufort, who wrote back to me, saying, yes, it was very ruinous, but I need not buy presents for her or Master; would I, instead, bring down something I already possessed or would have to buy soon, for them to give me, and she would choose two objects from a lumber-room, or perhaps take two books from the library, for me to give them. In this fashion we should get what we wanted, and not be put to extra expense. Accordingly, I brought to Badminton a hundred Turkish cigarettes, made by Sullivan Powell (which I always smoked) for Master's present to me, and a recent book on Sickert, which I needed for reference for an essay I was writing, for Mary to give me. In return Mary found a green-shagreen *étui*, circa 1780, for me to give her, and a book on hunting for me to give Master. On the afternoon of Christmas Eve, which fell on a Sunday, the tree which had been placed in the middle of the hall was lighted up, and the purple cloth which had covered the table was removed to show the presents. Queen Mary examined them all in detail, and evinced some curiosity concerning the *étui* I had given her niece; she asked where I had discovered it; you did not often find such things nowadays. I was obliged to improvise in reply as best I could: but I think Her Majesty had no inkling of the deceit we practised. To Queen Mary, I presented a copy of the book describing Lord Castlemain's special embassy to the Pope—the last sent to a pontiff by an English monarch, James II: it is a fine baroque book, profusely illustrated with large folding plates of the coaches and horses and liveries employed, and of the presents offered and bestowed, the banquets and the galas that took place. For the Princess Royal I had found a book on the theatrical performances organised at Windsor Castle for Queen Victoria. Each chapter carried a programme for its heading. Her Majesty gave me the Phaidon Press book of the Holbein drawings in the library of Windsor Castle, and four volumes she had bought in Bath one day, with delightful mid-nineteenth-century French engravings. In the evening I moved the presents I had been given up to my room, remembering Queen Mary's passion for tidiness, but I believe I thereby committed a solecism, for Harewood told me later that members of the Royal Family were very fond of coming down in any spare moment to gloat over the presents, other people's as much as their own.

On the afternoon in question, before the presents were unveiled, a few guests had come over for tea, including Lord and Lady Cambridge, and two American officers. Queen Mary liked American soldiers and was amused by their frankness, and by their turns of phrase—and I heard her say to one of them, 'Perhaps we should still be one country, if my great-grandfather hadn't been so obstinate,'—a remark which seemed to span the interval between the War of Independence and 1944 with remarkable ease and directness.

On Christmas Day, and on Christmas Eve, the whole

party attended morning service, walking through the series of drawing-rooms to the family pew, from which the aspect of the tombs of the first four Dukes by Rysbrack is superb. This pew hangs over the back of the church like a box at the theatre, but at the same time has the air of a living-room. On both days the morning was cold and foggy, and a log fire blazed and crackled in the fireplace at the back of the pew, and flickered its light over the eighteenth-century religious paintings and prints hanging on the walls. On the ledge of the box and on the shelves were many handsome old prayer-books and bibles, bound in green morocco leather and carrying on the cover a label 'Her Grace The Dutchess (sic) of Beau-fort'. Queen Mary sat in an arm-chair in the middle, at the front, with the Princess Royal next to her, and I noticed that she knelt during the prayers, though she was an old lady, and the knifeboards provided for the purpose were an agony.

On Christmas evening as I was going upstairs to change for dinner, I met old Dick Molyneux, who roared at me, 'You and I have had all the hard work to do in this party. Would you like a glass of champagne before dinner? I don't expect we'll get any at dinner. Claud's too mean! I think we deserve it, and I've brought a bottle down with me in my luggage.'

I said I should like nothing better. His room was near mine, and I arrived there at 8.15—dinner was due at 8.30. His servant was just leaving, having put out on the table, and having opened, a bottle of Perier Jouet 1928, and placed near it a plate of biscuits. The old gentleman himself was sitting by the table in a chair by the fire; he poured me out a glass, and said 'I think it's wiser to have half a biscuit.' Just then he tasted the champagne, and a look of complete tragedy came into his eye. 'It's corked,' he shouted 'and the only bottle!' So we went downstairs, to find that we were being given champagne. Dick Molyneux sat opposite me, and as he tasted it, I saw a look in his eye that I had seen before. 'It's corked,' it stated as plainly as possible. A second bottle was produced, but proved to be similarly afflicted. Dick Molyneux was by now in a courtier's rage, though outwardly calm; he took me into corners after dinner to complain, 'I don't mind about the champagne, but I'm *so thirsty,* ' he kept on saying. 'It's all Claud Hamilton's fault. Queen Mary never drinks champagne herself, and so doesn't know. It's left to Claud, and he's too mean to give us the best. I shall speak to him about it this time.' But when he remonstrated, he received an answer which made him still more angry. 'The champagne was getting old, and I wanted to see if it was still fit to be drunk—and we're all old friends, so it doesn't matter. And I knew you'd tell me.'

Several people from the neighbourhood dined with Queen Mary that night, including an officer with the imposing title of Captain of the Garrison, but I could not help feeling that she must be thinking of other Christmases in the past. Now, with her, she had only the Princess Royal. The Duke of Windsor had abdicated, and lived abroad; the King was fully occupied; the Duke of Gloucester was away; and her favourite son, the Duke of Kent, who so much resembled her in her tastes, and who could do anything with her he liked had been killed in an airplane accident.* Certainly she looked superb, wearing enormous sapphires, a pearl collar, and huge diamond and pearl brooches and pendants. With her clear skin, she could wear white and such colours as usually only girls can wear, and look well in them, even by daylight. Tonight she wore silver. As this magnificent figure, blazing and sparkling, led the way from the room, Dick Molyneux turned to me and said in his loud, deaf voice, like that of a man shouting from a cave into a strong wind, 'I wonder if you realise it, but after that old lady has gone, you'll never see anything like this, or like her, again!' And, indeed, the England Queen Mary knew is dead; the empire over which she travelled is in part dispersed; the rigid life she led belongs to the past, before democracy swept Britain bare like a tide. Nor

---

* Killed in an aircraft accident, on August 25th 1942.

are we likely to meet again that particular combination of high personal dignity, dynastic pride, sense of history, knowledge of court life and the intricacies of princely pedigrees, and appreciation of works of art, all combined in one highly individual person, and presented in her own stylised manner by Queen Mary.

*　　*　　*

Epilogue

In May of the following year, I wrote to Mary Beaufort. In my letter I said—for I had heard Queen Mary was leaving Badminton—that I expected she was in the throes of packing. In her reply, dated May 18th, 1945, she wrote 'The Queen is here until 11th of June. I expect it is Marlborough House that is in a state of eruption, revolt and tumult. Vans of boxes and hampers and trunks all marked with the royal cypher continually leave the house. Today I saw such a van leaving with royal crowns and M.R.s bursting from every side, but at the very back and perched on the top of these dignified boxes sat, very cheerily and cheekily a common enamel slop-pail—very plebeian, and showing no sign of its royal ownership.'

Fortune-Tellers

DURING both day and night Peking—I write of this great capital before the Communists engulfed it—is profoundly quiet; peace reigns, in spite of the more minute sounds; sounds such as you will discover, perhaps, in no other large city in the world. In the day-time there reach you, of course, the shouts and cries of coolies running, their bodies like shining copper in the noonday sun, and, in addition, the more diminutive and insect-like notes which compose the symphony of Peking life; a composition orchestrated on the grand scale. Indeed, a thousand castanetted sounds, clangings and drummings and cicada-like crepitations, vibrate through the golden air and every now and then there will be wafted to your ears the gentle beating of a gong—not such a gong as summons all true Britons to their most hideous meals, but a sound that holds in it something tragic and not of this world, a mournful tintinnabulation. This signifies, to those who have become acquainted with the streets of Peking and with this kind of sound-hieroglyphic, that a blind fortune-teller is making his way through one of the numberless lanes, pausing every instant to lean on his long stick, the while he disengages his other arm and sounds the gong which he carries in his right hand. For in Peking those who cannot read the signs of the day before them, who can hardly tell dark from light, can plainly discern, it is believed, the course through the years.

The Chinese, indeed, are intensely superstitious, though they would hardly admit this, since they prefer to regard their practices as scientific; and, moreover, their superstition has often genuinely benefited science, for the fact that they possessed the earliest astronomical instruments in the world is actually only a by-product of their ancient reliance on superstition. Marco Polo, most accurate of historical observers, tells us that in his time there were in the city of Kanbalu (or Peking, as it was subsequently called) 'amongst Christians, Saracens and Cathaians, about five thousand astrologers and soothsayers. . . .' (When I was there, there were almost as many—only instead of 'astrologers' we must read 'fortune-tellers'.) The Emperor, we are told, provided for them, so that they could spend their time in the constant exercise of their art.

Marco Polo also informs us that they had their astrolabes, upon which appeared the signs of the zodiac, the hours and their various aspects for the year. The different schools of astrologers examined their respective tables every year, in order to discover the course of the planets in relation to one another. From this they could forecast the weather and natural phenomena for each month of the ensuing year. 'For instance,' he says, 'they predict that there shall be thunder and storms in a certain month, and earthquakes; in another, strokes of lightning and violent rains; in another, diseases, mortality, wars, discords, conspiracies.' The predictions were recorded upon 'certain small squares' and sold to the public, and those astrologers with the largest number of correct forecasts to their credit were, very reasonably, ranked the highest in their art.

The early astronomical apparatuses used by the Chinese have many of them survived to this day. You can still see the shapes of some of these beautiful instruments outlined against the sky above the Eastern Wall. Two of them, originally designed for Kubla Khan, were taken to Berlin after the Boxer Rebellion in 1901. Referring to these, Bertrand Russell, in *The Problem of China*, says: 'I understand they have been restored [to China] in accordance with one of the provisions of the

Treaty of Versailles. If so, this was probably the most important benefit which that Treaty secured to the world.'

Though these bronze machines for reading the heavens are no longer used, no Chinese would have started on any project or undertaken any course of action without acting on auguries, and many different methods of fortune-telling are, of course, in existence; such, for instance, as the temples of the Three Hundred and Sixty-Five Worthies; each of these represents a day in the year, so that you can tell what your fortune will be from the appearance of the worthy under whom you were born. . . . I remember being much impressed by the fact that my Chinese chauffeur, on enquiring from the custodian the identity of his tutelary guardian, was shown a great golden face so identical with his own that, unless he had moved, it would have been difficult to tell one from the other.

At every fair, too, there are those who divine by pouring sand on to the ground before them, and others who tell fortunes by an arrangement of beans or nuts. The blind, again, tell from the feel of the hand. But the oldest of all these methods, so its exponents claim, is that of telling the fortune from the lines of the face. And this art is not one to be lightly undertaken, since ten years of intensive study are needed for it. Those who practise this style of prophecy are men of professional repute, called in for every wedding of wealthy people. The fees seem high. Though life in China is inexpensive, to have your fortune told by this method costs at least a pound, while if called in, following on a marriage, to foretell the birth of children, the charges of the soothsayer mount still higher. Women being still despised, if he forecasts the birth of a daughter the charges will be reduced; but a prophecy of this nature is so unpopular with any but the most freaky parents that he would scarcely venture to make it.

You can imagine the scene. It is a hot day, and so you are sitting in the courtyard. The painting of cornices and doors and windows—the cornices in bright blues and greens, the doors and windows in the shade of red lacquer—glow in the spring sun, the light of which attains a particular brilliancy in this country. The doors stand open on to the quiet street beyond, guarded by a devil-screen which protects you from visitors both earthly and aerial. The bushes, maple or lilac, send a flicker of shadow over the intent face of the diviner and record their shapes on the paper windows, which gleam with a slight translucence. The man regards you with a pitiless stare; no line in your face escapes him. He begins at the forehead and reads down. A Chinese servant helps him by translating his forecast, but this is not so easy, for a simple fact may be of considerable portent. When, for instance, I was informed that in ten years' time I should grow a moustache—and this, indeed, was to be one of the central events of my career—I did not at first realise the political importance which is attached to such an embellishment in China. Only a person of power would dare to indulge in those few drooping and sparse hairs. . . .

The idiom of the language, too, is often picturesque. The fortune-teller prophesied the birth of several male children of my impending marriage. Though they would eventually attain success in life, there were difficulties ahead; when, he prophesied, I told them to go to the east, they would go to the west.

What It Feels Like to Be an Author

———————◇———————

HUNTING the author, painter and musician is a traditional and popular sport. In this country poet-baiting at an early stage assumed the place of bull-baiting. The critics drove Keats to death, Shelley to Italy and Swinburne to Putney. . . . After visiting the old Protestant Cemetery in Rome, and seeing there Keats's tomb, bearing on it the inscription: 'Here lies one whose name was writ in water'—words written by the poet himself and placed there at his especial request by his friend Severn—after reading, in addition, his letters, it is, I apprehend, impossible to doubt that the critics *did* kill Keats; though the bare recording of this fact in any public journal still causes them to defend themselves, crying out that if he were so weak a creature as *that*, then there was no hope for him, and it does not matter. Thereby they shirk a statement of the real truth, which is that it was 'grand sport', because, for killers who love their work, to tear to pieces a poet like Keats, one of the most sensitive beings who can ever have lived, with genius, too, so clearly indicated in his appearance that they could be quite certain of the quality of their victim—for, says Severn, he had the 'hazel eyes of a young gypsy maid in colour, set in the face of a young god'—this, all this, must have constituted it an infinitely more enjoyable sensation than, for example, to hunt Tennyson and fail to kill him.

A poet dead has always been worth a dozen alive, both literally and metaphorically. . . . This should have been particularly brought home to the public by the death of Sir

William Watson some years ago. The facts of his career as presented in the obituary columns must have caused a pleasant glow to warm the heart of many a reader. ... Every poet becomes a 'Famous Poet!' on the posters announcing his demise: but here was one who, to a name familiar enough for easy lip-service, joined every attribute that such a being should possess; he had lived and written in the reign of good Queen Victoria (a great aid to any poet), had remained uncomfortably poor during most of his life (as poets ought), was yet a knight (it is not often, by some strange coincidence, that the knight of today is a poor man) and, further, had been gifted—so the obituarists united to declare—with that elusive quality 'the authentic note'; of which I hope to have more to say one day in an essay entirely devoted to it. Yet he wrote verse which the man-in-the-street—who, together with the Archbishop of Canterbury, is recognised today in this country to be sole arbiter of art, as of politics and economics—could easily understand, if only he would read it. ... And many, no doubt, wondered, as they perused the columns before them, what was really the life, the *private* life, of an author.

None: he has none: comes the answer. Whether poet, novelist or essayist, a writer possesses, when his profession is compared with other trades, one supreme advantage combined with disadvantage—he can never stop working. Everything he sees or does is, in a sense, work: as much as writing itself. Thus he can never be idle for a moment, never live for the sake of living, never take an absolute rest. When he says: 'Now I will stop work,' it is only in order to begin labouring in another medium. Moreover, being in this way both inside and outside his work, he is at the same time, or should be, abnormally sensitive and abnormally insensitive. In consequence he is able to watch himself in action at the dentist's or when annoyed by some noise at night, and to observe with amusement his own responses and ruses.

If, however, the author has *his* own way of looking at life, so have the members of the public *their* way of looking at him.

68

They well know that every writer—and more especially every poet—is sent down from above as much for the counselling of all aspiring amateurs as for the entertainment of the crowd: and they consider that his sense of duty should oblige him to read carefully every manuscript forwarded to him, accompanied by the usual egotist's screed, and then annotate it and comment at length upon its merits. . . . All this the author must do without payment: indeed it is only fair, since writing in general consists of pure inspiration, poetry in particular being crooned, as it were, directly across the ether by the Great Invisible Crooner. No hours of labour, therefore, are needed for composition.

Ever has it been thus with poetry since, instead of being sung, it first began to be written down. Doubtless Chaucer, Shakespeare, Ben Jonson, Dryden—although manuscripts in those days were less easy to land on authors by post—found themselves similarly victimised. Pope, we know, felt himself obliged to spend countless hours in inventing excuses for not reading the imitative echoes of his own verse with which unknown persons continually favoured him. In consequence, he incurred much blame for the lies he told so profusely in order to avoid having to hurt the feelings of innumerable young people. And unless the world has changed, moreover, not only *young* people—for we seem, really, to be a nation of would-be poets rather than of successful shopkeepers. Old ladies and young ladies, cabinet ministers and porters, housemaids and aldermen and gamekeepers, hunting men, fishwives and interior decorators; all of them appear, at one time or another, to have essayed The Easy Art. . . . And war, which stirs the emotions and numbs the brain, only increases the number of aspiring poets and addled poems.

Nevertheless, these treasures which every post brings to an author of any celebrity constitute by no means his most serious infliction. His standing being that of an unpaid public servant, he is expected to bestow his time and the benefit of his advice upon anyone, whatever his need may be, who sees fit to claim them. And how diverse is the range of the necessity! It varies from giving instruction in the proper control of a hot-water bottle in the winter bed to an opinion upon psychic dancing or the principles of Schopenhauer. Chaperonage, too, apparently forms part of his job: for only a little while before the war, a lady of whom I had never heard, but who wanted to write a book which obliged her to contemplate spending some hours every day in the Reading Room of the British Museum, telephoned to command me to escort her there every morning, and to fetch her back home every evening; because, as she phrased it, 'The museum's such a grimy old place, it makes me feel quite nervous going in and out of it by myself'. And, on another occasion, a stout woman rang the front-door bell, and when I answered it, put her foot between the jamb and the door so as to prevent my shutting it, and demanded that I should take down in embroidery—one of the few arts of which I am altogether ignorant—the colours that she would sing to me—and, at this point, she burst into loud, unbidden song.

In growing numbers, too, there are the hordes of charity harpies begging books, a most unpleasant and persistent species. I refer particularly to the organisers of bazaars for eleemosynary causes, who never think twice before demanding from an author, almost with menaces, a signed copy of one or more of his works: though at the same time he is expected to pay his taxes and contribute in the ordinary way to deserving objects. And how frank and unabashed in tone is this great army of cadgers. 'Our idea is', runs a paragraph in a letter, headed 'Famous Authors Books Fund', which has just reached me from a hospital situated in a distant part of the country to that in which I live, 'to collect autographed books from famous authors, and auction them to book-lovers and well-to-do people.' (I like particularly, do you not, gentle reader, the distinction so wisely drawn between 'book-lovers' and 'well-to-do people'?) 'All of the money', it continues reassuringly, 'thus raised will be put to the Fund. The Appeals Committee will be tremendously grateful', the writer goes on, 'if you will autograph and give us a copy of one of your books, preferably the book which you consider to be your best, as that will add to the interest of the sale. . . .' So even the gift of a volume, and its signature by a 'famous author', is not enough; no, he must deliver judgment upon himself as well! . . . Yet the writer of this letter is in private life a nice, kind person, I should hazard, who would never dream of writing to a fishmonger, saying 'Our idea is to collect your best fish, ask you to sign them and then auction them to fish-lovers and well-to-do people.' He only writes in this way because he, together with the general public, shares the crooning conception of the author's work which I have adumbrated earlier.

Both of them consider that printed books fall upon the author like manna from heaven. Never does it begin to dawn on the acquaintance who says to you, with the insinuating whine that authors know so well: 'You never sent me your last book!' that he is demanding the equivalent of a postal order for 25s. Yet he would seldom dare to ask you for that amount outright. On the contrary, as his accompanying wheedling smile indicates, he regards his request as in some mysterious way a compliment to yourself. For every fool, however double-dyed in his folly, considers that his wishing to read a book must flatter its author. Or perhaps he bases his request on economic grounds of a different sort, understanding the real truth, now so often denied, that the only kind of money worth having is inherited, unearned money, and thus feeling that, if you earn the money by writing, you cannot mind giving it away, for you will certainly not have time in which to spend it.

Sometimes, of course, the organisers of bazaars are more generous and provide the books themselves: but even this can end badly. I remember, in this connection, a friend who asked me to sign some of my books which she had purchased and was giving to be auctioned for charity. Being vague by nature, she sent me round the *Forsyte Saga* instead, with a note saying: 'Would you mind signing these as you so kindly promised. . . .'

I did not feel I could disappoint her, as apparently I had given my word, so I signed them and they were auctioned, but I never learned what prices the admirers of Mr Galsworthy gave for these unique items.

The most peculiar of all the special attitudes which members of the outside world manifest towards writers, though, is that reserved for them by servants. They take a kindly care of us, as if we were rather mad children, albeit they generally refuse to look upon authorship as a profession and regard themselves as entirely free to interrupt their masters whenever they feel inclined to do so. . . . I remember, for example, how when I asked a servant, now dead, whether my sister was busy, because I wanted to show her a letter I had just received, he replied at once: 'Oh no, she's only writing!' And there can be little doubt that some deep instinct guides them very surely to burst in at *the* critical moment of inspiration, and generally to pursue the author with radios, gramophones, bumping, singing, stamping, smashing, dusting and other ingenious tortures.

Yet, I suppose, authors have only themselves to blame for conduct of the kind I have described. They are for the most part a kindly, talkative lot, interested in everything and everybody—even if the interest is, perhaps, a little professional, like that of Granny Wolf in *Red Riding Hood*. And often, after the pattern of all artists, they are passionately conceited and self-centred, which tends to render them slightly ridiculous. 'Let's have a little fun with them. Let's stick a pin or two into them and the bubbles they blow'; that is the general reaction to them. But if the author hits back, then his opponent, the Little Man—that degraded and hideous personification of a contemporary ideal—yells to his brother: 'Look! He's hitting someone smaller than himself!', forgetting, though the Press daily and flatteringly reminds him of the fact, that, however small, it is the Little Man who composes the big battalions: the packs, flocks and droves. Collectively, indeed, his methods resemble those of the herds of dwarf pigs which sweep through the forests of Central America, harrying and killing any living creature they meet that is bigger than themselves. They chase their victim for miles, and when they catch up with him gore him to death. If a man climbs a tree to elude them, they saw through the trunk with their tusks, and so get him just the same. Yet individually these little black porkers would harm no one, and are said to make charming pets, and can often be seen in the cities of their native region going shopping with their mistresses.

But I wander. . . . The reasons for the Little Man's attacks upon anyone over the normal size are, of course, easily to be comprehended. He is playing for safety, as well as enjoying the fun, and, further, there is the common desire to hit something bigger than yourself, to spit at the creative forces, to burn books, to debunk the great, to picnic in the ruins of a temple or palace—and, above all, the hitting is due to fright, downright funk. The Little Man suspects an author—often wrongly—of being 'clever'. This, by itself, would terrify him, but there is, in addition, his permanent, haunting nightmare of 'being put in a book'. A kind of humiliating form of individual preservation, he feels it to be, as though he were a foetus or freak preserved in spirits of wine in a bottle, for future ages to wonder and wince at. . . . And the duller-minded and more boring he is, the more he dreads this fate, which he regards as inevitable if he should meet a novelist, for the Little Man is unaware that his own fear of 'being put in a book' is surpassed only by the author's terror of the little beast getting himself there; an exploit which may involve a libel suit and impose upon the writer the payment of several thousands of pounds in damages.

The Little Man, therefore, relies upon persecution to rid himself of his terror, and constantly seeks—and finds—new methods. Of these, noise is the chief. The arrival of an author in a hotel, for example, inspires the most extraordinary phenomena. All the parents staying there will, swayed by some peculiar herd instinct, at once bestow upon their children the most raucous and ear-splitting toys, whistles, croakers, toy trumpets, crackers, miniature whizz-bangs, hooters, watch-men's rattles, plates to smash, fog-horns and dogs that have been taught to bark in an especially prolonged and attractive manner, and are encouraged to exercise this art by their dear little masters' perpetual teasing. And then, without adventitious help, the children themselves can cry and shout and sing —and do we not all love children's voices? . . . Down below, perhaps, a child of about fifteen, with fingers like a fox-terrier's paws, or sometimes, you may think, like an elephant's feet, is being given lessons on a piano by a professional torturer, who does not mind what suffering he inflicts on innocent listeners so long as he obtains his fees. This is the kind of pest who should be prosecuted and imprisoned. . . . The man in the next bedroom is learning to typewrite by day, and practises his snoring by night. (When you make a complaint about a snorer, he will always protest that he has 'never been known to snore before': and I think this is probably true; his unconscious mind has been tempted by the proximity of an author.) During the daytime, in every direction sound Salvation Army bands, the bands of the mutilated and every kind of professional howling and bawling by beggars, while the perpetual dripping of taps, tattooing of hot-water pipes—now cold—and an occasional burst of wireless news or music, gives variety to the nights.

Many other methods of annoying an author are known, however, to the *cognoscenti*. Invitations, for example, are extended to him, not by friends, but by those who contrive to remember his existence only at certain periods. Thus, every time a book appears, he is sure to receive an invitation from Lady Flinteye, or from soulful persons who claim to have known him in some other existence which they have rendered tragic for him, and who are determined, equally, to prevent him from enjoying this one. . . . Worst of all, there are the clubs run for artistic ladies; institutions which exist to enable their three hundred members to boast 'I met Mr So-and-So at dinner', and, more especially, to provide a meeting-place for all those who wish to insult at their ease any painter, author or musician whom they have been able to decoy thither to eat their rather indifferent food. Moreover, it meets the difficulty that etiquette precludes them from being rude in their own or in other people's houses: but in a *club*, specially organised for the purpose! What *could* be better! For the Little Woman favours sex equality and intends to be every bit as rude as the Little Man. . . . And how expert she has become! . . . I remember my initial experience of one of these meals. I was placed next to a gentle-looking, white-haired old lady with a soft manner and a slight but genial palsy. She turned to me at once, and said with a sweet, old-fashioned smile: 'Do you know, Mr Sitwell, I believe I've read nearly all your books'—a pause (during which I clamped across my face a mask of expectancy and pleasure appropriate to the coming compliment), then she added, *con brio*: 'and I don't like a single one of them!' . . . The insults are, indeed, often ingenious and sometimes amusing, even to those who are the object of them. On another occasion, I remember, I was introduced to a woman who was sitting next to me. . . . She at once burst into tears. My voice, I am sure, showed the interest and concern that I genuinely felt, as I enquired what was the matter. Giving a loud, yelp-like sob, she replied: 'For a long time I have looked forward intensely to meeting you, and now that I *have* met you, it is *such* a disappointment! . . .' It was impossible not to sympathise with a display of so much virtuosity and feeling.

Men, nevertheless, are no whit behind women in this direction. Thus, I recall an incident after a large dinner-party in Madeira a few years ago, when an individual, who was obviously a prey to a peculiarly intense inferiority complex—for he was stressing his individuality in the most painful manner by means of an eye-glass strung on a wide ribbon, and by a red-lined evening cloak, and every other possible, and impossible, attempt at originality of outward aspect—came up to me, solely in order to be rude. . . . By this time, for I had already been writing for many years, I knew that look in the eye, so when, by way of prologue—having already been carefully introduced to me once—he said: 'Your name is Sitwell, isn't it?', I replied loudly and clearly: '*No! Shakespeare!*'

However, he proceeded: 'Well, I know you are an author, and I want to tell you how much I despise all people who write books.'

'You ought to try to read one of them,' I suggested.

I should, perhaps, merely have replied: 'Little Man, You've had a Busy Day!' Because some instinct seems to prompt such people to be insolent to—it is true—all authors, but more particularly to that precise type of author who can most neatly or most severely answer them back. . . . Is it kind, one might enquire, to be rude to Pope or Dr Johnson or Sheridan or Shaw—or Sitwell? Is it *kind*; but, above all, is it *wise*?

Portrait of a Very Young Man

⋄

IF someone chanced to ask me who was the most lively, quick, well-informed, and in general, most intelligent young man I had ever met, I should have no difficulty in finding at once the answer: Constant Lambert.

It must have been in the winter of 1920 or in 1921, for I had already left Swan Walk and was settled in Carlyle Square, that one day, when I was alone in the house, the front-door bell rang, and I answered it. On the doorstep stood a pleasant-looking young, very young, man, who said, handing me an envelope, 'I have a letter of introduction.' I looked at him again, and noticed that he had a courageous look—which he might well have, for I did not like letters of introduction. However, I said, 'Come in, won't you?' And soon we were talking like old friends. And, indeed, a letter of introduction— I forget from whom—was hardly necessary, for though until that moment I had never heard of Constant, I had met once or twice his father, a well-known portrait painter, who had originally come from Australia. His mother, to whom he was devoted, I had never seen, nor as yet his elder brother, Manuel Lambert, the sculptor.

Although Constant was so young—seventeen—his character at once established itself without difficulty or self-assertiveness. That which made this all the more remarkable was that he suffered from partial deafness, which no doubt accounted for the eager look on his face, an expression which said clearly, 'I don't want to miss anything', and for the manner in which his eyes followed the speaker. This deafness, which troubled him a lot, but nobody else, was the result of a serious illness which had attacked him at school towards the end of the War to end War: a disease which was then known—and perhaps still is—as septicaemia. This illness lasted for many months, but fortunately he had made a good recovery, though he was still lame and walked with a stick, but he never permitted this disability, any more than his deafness, to obtrude.

We all of us—that is to say my sister, my brother, William Walton and myself—became friends with him, and he often came in those early days to spend the month of August, or part of it, with us at Renishaw. During these visits, he made a special study of my father, who was a source of never-failing interest to him. Of Constant's first glimpse of my father, I have written elsewhere, but it seems to me that I must adumbrate it here again. Well then, Constant had arrived late in the evening when my father had already 'retired for the night'. The next morning Constant was down early for breakfast. He helped himself and sat down facing the garden. Looking out, he was much surprised to see in the foreground a dignified old gentleman, crawling on all fours, with a stick in his mouth. Except that the old gentleman was neatly turned out, and his beard well trimmed, the scene bore a strong resemblance to William Blake's picture of Nebuchadnezzar. It was my father, testing the soil for the new level of the lawn he was making. (Elsewhere in the garden that summer, there was a light wooden instrument used for battering down the walls of cities during the Crusades. He would clamber up the ladder to his airy platform and spend hours with his binoculars clamped to his eyes, to see where the best place would be for the cascade he was planning.) Constant followed my father's every movement with rapt attention, and my father, for his part, must have felt this interest and would confide in him, as when, for example, he gave him his views of my first novel, *Before the Bombardment*. 'It will be an odd sort of book; no love interest and no hero or heroine.'

78

Portrait of a very Young Man

At Renishaw, the only pianos were a Bechstein, an enormous obsolete instrument, so old and unused as to count as an antique, and a younger one hired from Sheffield. But William and Constant would devote their days to them, and the sound of their musical skirmishes would reach me in various distant parts of the house. I must say here that their music was full of the personalities of the composers, and Constant's music seems to me to have a special nostalgia of its own; his choral setting of my brother's poem 'Rio Grande', which I have heard several times, is magnificent and beguiling. His book *Music Ho!* rivals Berlioz's *Soirées dans l'Orchestre*. Berlioz was one of his gods, as was the Abbé Liszt. But in light mood he would praise Sousa: indeed, he had founded a club to demand more and superior performances of his work.

Constant always defined his attitude to life in the words of Nietzsche as 'yea-saying'. This attitude applied to anything, to everything his friends suggested: a drink, a drive in a motor, a cinema, an opera; his first instinct was to say 'yes', but it was not a passive acquiescence, but a muffled fury of eagerness and of expected enjoyment. Yet he never seemed disillusioned. In fact, he was a natural convivial, always the first guest at the buffet and the last to leave. For this reason, when he was older, during the dreary decades that followed, he looked back on the twenties with great longing, as he did to those parties so beautifully described by Mr Evelyn Waugh in *Vile Bodies*.

Even as a young man, Constant had a surprisingly large circle of friends, made up of people of every kind. He and William Walton, as I have said, had soon become great friends; with their common interest in music, this was not to be wondered at, any more than were his friendships with Bernard van Dieren and Philip Heseltine—alias Peter Warlock. But he was also a friend of Edmund Dulac—that brilliant caricaturist in three dimensions who played the nose-flute—and of Sir Edmund Davis—who, I remember, had just bought a village near Zanzibar for the sake of its

79

Moorish tiles—and of innumerable others. All were people of character and distinction—he was, for example, a great friend of the brilliant young English painter, Christopher Wood— but then Constant's humour and wit, two qualities so seldom united in the same person, made him a perfect companion.

I shall never forget his delight when he received a copy of the magazine of the school where he had been so ill, and found in it a photograph of the churchyard there; under it was the legend: 'Boys who die during the term-time are usually buried in the churchyard.' This, in its turn, raised all sorts of questions. How many boys as a rule died during the average term? Where were the boys not fortunate enough to be 'buried in the churchyard' interred? At the cross-roads, perhaps? Or were their graves on the cricket-field or the football-ground? But it would surely have to be soccer rather than rugby because a scrum over the bodies would surely be a failure of respect!

As I write at Montegufoni, I naturally recall him here, as he was at the time of the dinner for the delegates of the International Festival of Modern Music, held in Siena in 1929—a feast I have already described in *Tales my Father Taught Me*—which nobody enjoyed more than Constant. Moreover, every night when the rest of the house party had gone to bed, William and Constant would carouse with Henry Moat at his special invitation . . . The Podesta of Siena had decided to give a special *Palio* in honour of the delegates of the Music Festival. This was crowded and I recollect that, just as the Campo had been cleared to make the race-course and to allow the horses to enter, the spectators were lined up behind ropes, in addition to cramming themselves into every door and window, William and Constant arrived, after what had plainly been a good late luncheon. They entered the Campo with something of the air of two young bulls entering the arena, and so impressive were they that the Italian crowd, always quick to seize the chance for a demonstration, began to cheer.

A Bunch of Snowdrops

FOR those who are no longer children, Christmas, whether they enjoy it or not, must inevitably be a brief season of nostalgia—and this is all the more to be savoured in a foreign land whose habits at this season greatly resemble those one knew at home. (*Foreign* is a word inapt to describe how an Englishman feels in the States or, I hope, how an American feels in England.) In Italy, on the other hand, Christmas is very different from ours: there are the old, indigenous customs, many of them pagan in origin, others touchingly and tenderly Christian and medieval, as when the *Pifferi* come from the mountains to blow their bagpipes in front of the lighted images of the Virgin throughout the length of Italy. But the American Christmas so greatly resembles our own—or let me qualify that by saying the English Christmas of thirty years ago—that it is bound to bring back memories. In an age of catastrophe and dissolution, these memories, albeit they may in themselves be happy, are bound to give life to old regrets.

One Christmas, then, I passed at Boston—and, as might be expected, the occasion itself was happy. To one fresh from the splendours and exaggerative beauties of New York, which I so greatly love, Boston seems as English in its architecture, in the houses on Beacon Hill, and the shell-like spires of its churches, as does its climate at Christmas. The actual eve of Christmas I spent in the house of my two dearest friends in Boston, and in the atmsophere of pervading hospitality and affection which they evoked—and under the influence, I may

add, of the delectable society and excellent claret they provided—all feelings of sadness were quickly forgotten, and I
enjoyed every moment of the evening, the company of the
people in the room, the crowds outside, the lighted candles in
the windows, the carols. . . . Only in the darkness of the night,
when I woke up, a sudden scent of snowdrops assailed me—
are snowdrops also an American flower?—and it seemed to me
suddenly that I had come a long and tiring way from the
point at which I started. I was now, I believed—but how could
one ever be sure?—a celebrated writer, I was certainly delivering lectures in a great and distant land, at fifty-six years of age.
In a way it sounded comforting. By today's standard, fifty-six
is no great age: but the people I knew as a child were dead,
the world in which they lived was dead, and even though I
had not liked all of them or it, it was borne in on me how
quickly life could change its surface.

As I lay there in the darkness, the Christmas Days I had
spent in my childhood loomed up at me like beads on a chain,
or snowdrops gathered in a bunch. . . . The first I remember
was spent under the hospitable roof of Ganton, the country-
house of the Legards in Yorkshire, and a name known to all
lovers of memoirs because of its frequent occurrence in the
pages of the Comtesse de Boigne's reminiscences. Sir Charles
Legard, portly and affable in the manner of the Prince of
Wales (for we are still in Queen Victoria's reign), wearing a
bowler hat and a dark suit, and Lady Legard, my godmother,
tight-waisted, charitable, dressed in lilac and white, are drawn
for ever in my memory against a background of snow.

There was a famous frost that winter, and they were forced
to walk delicately when they went out, as if walking on ropes—
and I remember that the cold had obliged the rabbits to nibble
every morsel of stick or leaf left above snow level. The
memory is sweet, tender and bitter as the smell of the bunches
of early snowdrops from Renishaw, which reached us when
we returned to our house at Scarborough; and which remain
for me ever associated with the festival.

A Bunch of Snowdrops

The first snow must have gone at Renishaw, or the flowers would not have come out. It was early for them. As they lay there, before my nurse took them from their damp box, I well remember my rapture at seeing those delicate, green-veined, frosty flowers, gothic in shape and edged with green, and with a particularly evasive and enticing scent; indeed, invented for what reason except to please human beings, because assuredly no insects are present at that season to be attracted?

After that first festival to be recalled, when I was three or four, came a Christmas spent in London. At that stage of infancy, the fact of mortality was still beyond my understanding, and I remember wondering what my father meant as, looking at a letter received from his father-in-law, Lord Londesborough, he remarked to my mother: 'As they've been invited, the children had better spend Christmas in London, with your father and mother. They're growing old, and may not be here much longer.'

What, I wondered, did he mean, and where would old people like that go to, at their age? (About their destination, perhaps, a doubt still lingers in my mind.) However, I entered enthusiastically into the idea of spending Christmas in London. It meant, I knew, that we should be taken on the night of Boxing Day to the opening of the Christmas pantomime at Drury Lane—an occasion for which all children longed —and see the great Dan Leno as the Widow Twankey in *Aladdin*.

The atmosphere of London at Christmas proved over-whelming: the moment we reached the station, after a journey of five unheated hours, it came at us. The station was a cavern of iron, with a glass roof, crammed with the fog and smoke of eons: from its menacing, dark shelter, full of shouts and bustle, we stepped into a four-wheeler, bitterly cold and smelling of oats, beer and fog in equal proportions. Even the hoarse voice of the red-nosed cabman carried out, as it were, the same stupendous epitome of the season.

We drove to Grosvenor Square, where was the family

mansion, and in it an exotic air of warmth, excitement and Christmas delights and surprises; which prevailed, too, in the day-time in the near-by streets, in the bouquets of sweet-scented flowers in the windows, in the toy-shops, crowded with ingenious mechanical treasures, and the fruit-shops, now full of southern fruits, such as tangerines, Elvas plums, starred with coloured paper, dates and raisins.

The size of London, in its thick muffling canopy of white or yellow fog, was immense, imposing: a fog lit by flares and torches, and through its often impenetrable texture would sound perpetually the cheerful, faintly contaminated Cockney vowels, as the shoppers at stalls and small stores called, one to another, and spoke of the weather, and of Christmas.

Yet, in spite of that urban experience of it, Christmas remains for me essentially a rural feast. Only a few Christmases did we spend at Renishaw—and these were overshadowed by my father's disapproval of the whole occasion, and by his fear of 'getting the children into extravagant habits by giving them presents'. (He hated to give presents to people who expected them, or when they expected them, and I still recall, with tremors of discomfort, the Christmas I spent with him in Venice some decades after, and how, when the amiable Italian waiter remarked to him: 'Good morning, Sir George, and a happy Christmas!', he replied in a tone of disillusioned comprehension: 'I know!')

My mother certainly made up for our lack of amusements as much as she could: yet Christmas at home remained a rather barren festival. But when I was about eight, my grandfather died and we began to spend Christmas every year in the house of his son. And it was this series of ten or so Christmases, spent under the roof of my uncle and aunt Londesborough at Blankney, that have subsequently conditioned and defined my ideas of Christmas, its horrors and pleasures.

It was perhaps not a typical Christmas, being more inter-national and exotic, and scarcely Christian, except for brief desultory, purely formal appearances in church. No, pleasure, comfort, warmth, sport were the objectives, and these were obtained.

The large house was always full of relatives of every age, from second childhood down to first: some were in bathchairs, others in perambulators, some remembered King George IV and the great Duke of Wellington, some remembered nothing, from having left off remembering, others had not yet begun to remember. There would often be foreign connections present as well as English.

As for the children, we were tied to compulsory pleasure, as later, at school, to compulsory games. We took part certainly in the feasting of our elders. We watched them hunting, shooting and engaged in other diverse and repulsive sports, such as clubbing rabbits on the head, but we were, on the other hand, made to perform a French play, under the tuition of a whole platoon of governesses. This would be given before villagers who understood no word of French, and were there by a kind of corvée.

But, above all, Christmas was henceforth to be associated for me with my giant and genial uncle and his two passions, for music and mechanics. In the passages he had accumulated some twelve or fourteen mechanical organs; cases with glass fronts that revealed trumpets and drums that, when set in motion, could be seen indulging in an orgy of self-blowing and self-beating. This elementary, if expensive, form of juke-box greatly pleased the children, even if it acerbated the nerves of our elders, who did not like their favourite selections from Verdi—for such they usually were—played in this fashion.

But now the music is stilled, the machines are obsolete; the fashionable beauties and the plain, poor relations are equally unfashionable, for they are dead, even most of those who were young children fifty years ago—and the dead are always unfashionable.

As I look back, I see the vast tents of the rooms, lighted during the day's dark as well as the night's, shining out for miles over untrodden fields of snow that ended beyond our vision in the white-fringed sea; rooms that were filled with the contemporary symbols of luxury, palm trees of exceptional stature, poinsettias that seemed to bear as flowers stars cut out of red flannel; a fragrance of wood-smoke, and jonquils and freesias, hung in the air. . . . But, framing all these and bringing them back to me, is the more rustic smell of snow-drops, edged with a few prickly green leaves, their stalks tied roughly, inexpertly, with thin, damp string, lying in a damp cardboard box that has just been opened.

Dining-Room Piece

---◇---

I WANT now to paint for you a still-life of things that are eaten in far-away lands, with, in the background, the likeness of those who evolved the dishes and, beyond them, a glimpse of the strange and imposing landscape which brought them forth. This picture aims to be a piece of the kind that was once so popular, hanging in every large English dining-room, but has now been set aside; by Snyders, or—as in the superlative examples of this *genre*—by that artist and Jordaens in conjunction. Differences, however, will at once be manifest, for instead of the peacock or the death-divining swan forming, as it were, the feathery explosive nucleus of my canvas, and lording it over the corpses of turkey, lobster and domestic fowl, here it will be that bird of fabulous beauty, the quetzal, who queens it over iguana and armadillo, and the background will resemble ruins depicted by Pannini rather than some Flemish hall. . . . But you shall judge.

The quetzal, indeed, plays a part at the beginning, for it is the national emblem of Guatemala, and was formerly, before the Spanish Conquest, the sacred bird of the indigenous clans. Clothed in green plumage of incredible brilliance and loveliness, and in appearance akin to a bird of paradise, it is so shy, so rare, as to be almost legendary except in the inmost prides of zoological gardens the world over. Nevertheless, even the coinage is named after it, a franc is—or was—a quetzal; and the strain of imagination touching practical affairs, which this nomenclature exemplifies, runs through the whole natural life, and begins to form a national style inspired by the original people of the country, albeit in many directions it is also intensely Spanish. Everywhere this Indian influence, Maya or Aztec, is to be felt; everywhere, beneath the disguises it has assumed, this national flavour obtrudes—and not least in the food.

It pervades everything—the things to be bought and sold, the houses, the clothes and, above all, is to be detected in the dark interiors of the gigantic churches, cloudy with incense, glittering with threads of gold where the flickering light catches the gilding; because all the illumination comes from the floor. For an hour or more each worshipper kneels on the stone pavers, strewn with rose petals, within a circle of candles that form, as it were, the footlights, and gesticulates, threatens and implores the Christian Deity for help, in one of the innumerable Maya dialects—and then leaves the church and returns to some dark nook in the mountains, there to renew the same pleas to the monstrous stone images that his tribe still worships in secret. Everywhere, as I have said, you will find the old gods evoking the old culture within the Christian forms; and it is surely more sensible to cultivate this sentiment to the full than to reject it—and yet, where deliberately it has been set aside, that, too, goes so far to the other extreme as to introduce an original atmosphere, and so I will mention here that many of the larger villages and towns in Guatemala have in their dusty centres, or in no-man's-lands on the outskirts, set in a gesticulating swirl of cactuses, and with, behind them, the essentially non-European outlines of their numerous volcanoes, a Doric temple, erected in white plaster by dusky workmen. These were decreed by the edict of a former President, in love with Greek culture, and determined to forge a classical pedigree for his country: the plaster is already falling, and the temples look anaemic, mean, unhappy; poor white trash, in fact.

The provisions for every *ménage* in Guatemala have to be bargained for at the market. It is impossible to obtain supplies outside, because the peasants throughout the country so much enjoy the occasion, which develops, for the man into a kind of club for drinking, and for the woman into the equivalent—though certainly more democratic—of Ascot and Longchamp. If you meet these Indian peasants upon the road, and stop them—they are running—and offer to buy some of the chickens, ducks, pigs, vegetables, fruit and flowers, under which they are weighed down, for treble the price they could, at the best, hope to extort for them from tyros in the market-place, they will assuredly refuse, otherwise they will miss the talk, the fun of a function, discussion of scandal and the showing-off of clothes. And upon *clothes* we must lay emphasis. Living for the rest on fruit and a little dried armadillo, in semi-transparent establishments woven of wattle, with mud added to it for substance, both men and women lavish their whole fortunes—and they are not peons, are by no means so intensely poor as the natives in other regions of Central and South America—upon dress. These costumes vary entirely in cut and in colour with each village, but in every case their origin is to be sought for in the Spanish fashions of two or three centuries ago, though the decorative motives which they embody are of Indian inspiration. They add a wonderful splendour and strangeness to the landscape and a sense of fantasy to the towns.

It is for these reasons, then, that the broad tracks along the sides of the roads are perpetually crowded with Indians, always at the run, padding along on their silent naked feet at a particular quick running trot, for they never walk, and markets are frequent and universal. And thus it is that in the morning, when the forests and the plantations of coffee and sugar round the city of Antigua are still thick with dew, and when, as the sun rises, the world of insect life within these balmy wildernesses sets up with voice and castanetted wing so great a clamour, loud and brief as a shriek, a sound that can only be described as a rhapsody of triumph, these peasants in their dresses, diverse but always gay, can be seen converging from

all sides upon the city, the women trotting too, some with long
plaited pigtails of coarse black hair hanging down behind, and
some with a baby fastened to their backs by a shawl, its nose
level with the mother's shoulders.

I have chosen Antigua for the market, since though this is
no finer than another, I know it the best. And though the scene
lacks the Doric temple that graces so many of these towns, it
has its own beauties and advantages of Nature and architecture.
Formerly the capital of one whole quarter of the Indies, it was
partly destroyed by a great earthquake in the 1760s, and its
ground space is in consequence too vast for the present population, and therefore no wave of modern American construction
has ensued. It remains today a partly ruined city of enormous,
crumbling, seventeenth- and eighteenth-century churches,
made of golden stone, or of adobe of the same rich tone, the
intricate sculptural and arabesque decoration fitted in between
the twisting pillars and round the pompous coats of arms upon
the façades being the work of Indian craftsmen trained by the
Jesuits. Some of the façades are so covered with deeply incised
decoration that they look in the distance as though they were
scrawled all over with handwriting. A few of the palaces—
notably those with the three arcaded storeys in the chief *plaza*
—exist only as to their fronts. The sky now shows through the
windows of their theatrical *décor*; but the majority, in this
resembling the houses of Andalusia—from which province,
surely, the conquistadores who first settled here must have set
forth—are of one storey, enclosing *patios*, and therefore sus-
tained less injury than the lofty and aspiring churches. All these
old palaces have fine iron grilles over their windows, and doors
of smooth cypress wood with ornate bosses and designs of iron
nails and studs, almost Byzantine in appearance. And several
of them, of which the finest example is perhaps the former
university and present museum, were designed by an eclectic
architect from Seville, who lived here during the forties and
fifties of the eighteenth century, and whose declared aim it was
to invent a manner which would represent the style wherein

the descendants of the Moorish builders in Andalusia *would have* worked, had their ancestors never been turned out by the Spaniards! And this ingenious adaptation of Saracenic, embodying rococo themes, which he deliberately evolved, is singularly delightful and to be seen nowhere else, even in Guatemala. The resemblance between, let us say, certain courts of the Alhambra and that of the university here, with its gaily fretted arcade and its lion-fountain, is unmistakable; though, in addition, since all the workmen employed were peons, the Indian influence is again to be felt.

In this town, then, the great market—for every day there is a market of a kind—takes place twice a week. More even than on Sunday, and though—in spite of the comparative size of the city to its population—the life in it is always vivid, vital, it imparts a tremendous air of festival to the days on which it occurs. In the first light of the morning the peasants begin to arrive, and you detect the well-known silent padding on the pavement. Soon after, a military band is heard practising. It is time to set out now, for, as elsewhere, the market here must be visited at an early hour. The streets are deserted, since everyone has already started, but on the way you notice the bakers' shops, for bread is not to be bought in the market, and the bread of Guatemala will be the most delicious and varied that you have ever eaten. At breakfast three or four kinds of roll at least would appear, in either private house or hotel. Otherwise, the shops are rather empty; empty vaults with cigarettes, rank cigars and postage stamps exposed for sale. But you must hurry.

The market is held in the gigantic *plazas* formed by the chapels, refectories and cloisters of a roofless monastery. . . . In flawless sunlight, the rays of which, though you feel them on your body under your thin clothes, are never *too* hot, this fantastic setting acts as background for a spectacle that never allows the visitor for a moment to forget his surroundings; the violence of it reminds him that, though not so far from the Equator, yet Antigua stands at a height of some five or six thousand feet above sea-level, upon the central plateau of Guatemala, and so the tropics have not sapped the energy of the people. Moreover, wherever you move here, you will see the feather-tufted cones of the two enormous volcanoes, their bulk being the colour of the bloom upon purple grapes, except when snow covers their tops; mountains which dominate the scene.

You see them, these monstrous twins, rising far over the tops of the towering, broken walls of adobe and stone that frame the market, over the sagging cornices festooned with tropical weeds and foliage, over the immense and disintegrating arches, laced with grotesque decorative motives, through the gaping windows. The best view of them, perhaps, is to be obtained from the one large roof which still exists, a green meadow supported upon arches. Mounted thus, and squatting upon the ground with their wares spread round them, in brilliant sunshine or under the flickering mauve-blue shadow of jacaranda trees that have seeded themselves within the precincts, or of square sails pitched above them, for their shade, on rough wooden supports, sit in long lines these beautiful little golden men and women, clad in dresses which create an amazingly rich effect; coarse homespun linens encrusted with embroidery that, being of fine design, coalesces into splashes of purple and mauve and rose and crimson, of blue and green and yellow and gold. The noise that rises in the air is hardly credible, the general chatter—for these people seem very gay, always chattering, except when they giggle silently, for they seldom laugh aloud—mingles with shouting, with the hammering of blacksmiths, with singing, and with the squealing of pigs, bleating of lambs and lowing of calves. In one room alone is there comparative silence, because the women in it—and you notice few here, except the cooks—are eating, resting and regarding one another, examining minutely each stitch of embroidery within range.

You might think this difficult, for at first, when you enter from the sun-drenched courts, it takes you a little time to see at all. Formerly a refectory, this room still possesses a roof and its windows are blocked up: no light enters save through the door from the cloister beyond; but the glowing charcoal fires of the cooks, who crouch above their stoves, stirring unknown concoctions, outline their figures and those of their customers, and flicker redly over the groups of mothers and restless, clawing children sitting on the ground. Eyes and teeth gleam from these sepia shadows, but everything else is gilded only in silhouette, seems to be smouldering, so that the forms take on most curious effects of light and shade, rich blooming darkness and sullen glow. Indeed, this interior, in the contrast it affords between the magnificence of its ruined setting and the un-expectedness of its inhabitants—the last people one would look for in such surroundings—can be compared in strangeness to those scenes of gypsies, fantastically garbed and feathered, feasting in the Gothic kitchens and dilapidated refectories of deserted monastic houses, which the eighteenth-century Genoese painter, Alessandro Magnasco, loved to depict.

But you must stop looking at the people and go to see what they sell and buy. First you will come to a cloister filled with flowers, placed within its lightly vaulted shade so as not to wither; huge mixed bouquets, arranged with skill which this race shows always in its use of colour, gigantic bunches of Harrisi lilies, of orchids, stacks of tuberoses, the scent of which lies on the air and wanders far, and many flowers of which I never found out the name, orange and flame-coloured and scarlet. But you must notice especially one flower, that here is bought either for decoration or to be eaten. This is the yucca; large spikes, clustering spires of cup-like blossom, creamy and green, ivory and white. The petals, cool, crisp and aromatic, of these flowers, sprinkled with their golden centres shredded over them, dressed with oil and vinegar and rubbed with garlic, form one of the usual dishes of this country. Texture and flavour are both excellent. The stalk is then cooked and eaten as a vegetable, but to me—though I seldom recognised what it was until I enquired—it seemed always rather tasteless and pithy, with a suggestion of soft wood and badly cooked root vegetables. . . . I cannot say whether these yuccas, though they look precisely the same, only larger and more florescent, are identical with those grown in English gardens, and I have not dared to find out empirically.

Passing on, you reach a court devoted to the sale of Guatemalan blankets, and, beyond it, another that displays embroidered shirts for men and shawls and scarves for women. In its turn, this leads into a colossal, sunny *plaza* where the native pottery is to be bought, mounds of earthenware pots and jars, their shape, the perfection of their irreproachable line, seeming more Greek than Spanish—a remark even more applicable to the neighbouring collections of flat dishes, made of an earthenware that is almost rose-coloured, which are used for cooking *tortillas*. Indeed, these large, flat, round plates resemble the discs of the *Discobolus*, so suave and stream-lined are they. From the next immense court, over which hangs a mantle of dust, issues that mingled lowing, bleating and squealing which you have already remarked.

Here, among the young pink porkers on string leads, who so resolutely make an inevitably ineffectual dash for freedom upon their short, apparently unjointed legs, here among the tufted calves attempting to escape—and indeed perhaps the cause of the general frantic behaviour of the animal world—sits a woman with a large round linen-basket full of the strangest cattle, the greatest living delicacy of the land: iguanas. These giant lizards, three or four feet long, are tied, like whitings upon an English breakfast-table, or the symbol of eternity, mouth to tail. Otherwise they would thresh out with their tails, which are spiked and can inflict formidable injuries. Their jaws, too, are bound together to prevent their snapping at and biting their prospective devourers, already bargaining over their bodies. Incidentally, the customers cannot poke them in the ribs, in the same manner in which they prod the calves and small pigs, to see if they are fat, because, even if an iguana possesses ribs—and at this point my knowledge of reptilian anatomy breaks down—the knobs and spikes of its armour would defeat prying fingers. Weight, alone, is the criterion.

A clean feeder, the creature lives in the tree-tops of the steaming jungles on sea-level, and subsists on the green leaves round it. The iguana-catcher is trained to net his prey, a difficult profession that needs a long schooling in these swamps and forests; or, again, it may be shot—sitting, I apprehend— and in these tropical regions 'a day's iguana shooting' is a popular sport, comparable to 'a day's partridge shooting' here. . . . Now it may be that the iguana is no pleasant object to look at. Its small eyes, pail-shaped snout and shark-jaws, lined with a saw's teeth of steel, are, I know, repellent to many. Even the reptile's best friends, indeed, will be obliged to admit that at first sight it presents a somewhat case-hardened exterior, and that its saurian countenance bears an unpleasing expression, both sarcastic and ferocious. But it is good, *very good*, to eat: and its cost does not amount to more than the equivalent of a shilling; two facts which must both tell in its favour. The ways of cooking it are many, but the best seemed to me to be roast saddle, cooked with herbs, and served in a circle of its own eggs with a rich brown sauce, flavoured with madeira or port. The saddle is white and tender as the best capon, and the eggs, too, are a suitable, and even delicious, concomitant, once you have grown accustomed to the idea of them.

If, then, iguana, *sauté* or roast, is the great indigenous delicacy of Guatemala, *tortillas* and *tamales* constitute the country's most ordinary dish. You can see them everywhere, in market, hotel and restaurant, in house and hut. The sight and smell of them is as common in town and village and jungle settlement as is the music of the *marimba*, the liquid-tongued national instrument of Guatemala, which sounds out in *plazas*, in crowded streets, in wattle-built villages and in clearings between the jacarandas and flamboyant trees. . . . But the word *tortilla* is deceptive. First you must clear your mind of its Spanish significance, for here is no flattened-out omelette, sprinkled with strips of tomato and pimento, but a bastard pancake, resembling the sole of a boot fashioned of oatmeal, or some substance like it, instead of leather—though certainly leathery enough. *Tamales*, on the other hand, are more interesting: small, flat, hot, square packets of savoury maize, of a brown colour. The varieties are endless, but they are always very hot and aromatic, always square or rectangular, and always cooked and served in a neat green casing of banana leaf, which the consumer himself has to unwrap (this, perhaps, psychologically, is one of the secrets of all tempting food: it must give its consumer trouble, not make things too easy for him; that is why a cold lobster should never be separated from the shell except by him who eats it). In addition, *tortillas* and *tamales* seem in every instance to be permeated by a subtle and curious flavour, difficult to identify, but akin to the smell of incense—perhaps due to something used in the fires upon which they have been cooked.

In these two dishes I have just described, and in a very fragrant and sustaining paste, made out of *frijoles*, or black beans, the Indians of this country find their chief nourishment. Unfortunately the native liquor, also made from maize, which accompanies them, is a vile and brutish spirit, immature and immediately intoxicating. Two small glasses would overwhelm any European, and among these simple people, though more inured to it, the results are often distressing.

In the market you can see, too, the dried halves of armadillo that I have mentioned earlier (they have ribs, you will notice), which present a painfully smoked and desiccated appearance, and other food of the sort. Piled up, in a corner near by, are brightly coloured, juicy and often rather tasteless tropical fruits, mangoes or custard-apples—these last of many different kinds, but all with their dark and scaly skin, which seems to indicate that, as a dessert, they belong to the same order of dinner as does the iguana for roast, and all possessing a cool, very sweet flavour of mingled banana, pineapple, eau-de-cologne and turpentine. Custard-apples in mounds are rather beautiful, but not so effective as the hillocks of *serpoté*, many of them cut to display their yielding, flame-coloured flesh, and of grapefruit, tropical oranges with green rinds, and bergamots and limes, as refreshing and fragrant as they are decorative. . . . But you must turn away—it is time to leave the market now, being nearly eleven. Already the wings of the dust hang with a midday heaviness over the city. The peasants are furling their sails, putting their wares in boxes and packing up. Having eaten their meal in the refectory, others of them lie down in the most cool recesses of the cloisters, there wrapping themselves, head and body, in their home-woven blankets, preparatory to a siesta. It is time to go. Life in the market is dead—in the town outside, too, until dusk brings a revival, or until darkness brings the hour of pleasure. Tonight the *marimba* band gives a concert from under the arcade on the second floor of the Governor's Palace in the *plaza*. There are six of these long, wooden instruments, and two men play on each of them, by beating the keys with very flexible wooden gavels, thereby producing as liquid a music as that of carillons, or of falling waters or the tongues of fountains. Those peasants who have not far to go, and have not yet run home, sit on the stone benches of the garden, planted with strongly scented night flowers, or stroll about in the feathery shade thrown by arc-lamps spluttering above the fronds of the tall pepper trees which line the square and the diagonal paths that run through the garden. The concert lasts for two hours, tango after tango, rumba after rumba, and the audience sit, many of them, listening in silence, intently, as though they had never heard the instrument or tune before.

New York in the Twenties

WHEN I was in the United States in the spring of last year I met a friend who said to me, 'Do you realise that when you first came to America in 1925, Bessie Marbury opened her front parlour to give a party for you?' As I grasped the implication that by so doing she had paid me a particular honour, I wondered what other equivalent symbols I had then also failed to interpret. It had been in November, 1925, that I set off to discover America for myself—though, in fact, in the end I only explored New York.

In an English port, directly you climb on board an English boat bound for the United States, you enter America, for American habits and American prices prevail, and American passengers predominate. On the first occasion I crossed the mountainous waves that separated the two countries on the *Majestic*, which had been built as a yacht for the Kaiser just before the First War in order to show the world what a mighty monarch he was—but he had lost his throne before he could use his boat. The advantage of this ship for passengers was its immense size, which made it necessary, if a bad storm arose, for the captain to give orders to halt the engine in case the body of the ship should break in two. The reduced speed lessened the horrors of a rough crossing for the sea-sick, though, of course, it was apt to make the boat late in arriving.

As usual on such a journey, friends whom one did not know were on board continued to turn up on deck. Thus, after a day or two, Mrs Patrick Campbell suddenly materialised in a chair next to mine. Large but streamlined, she looked, with her big, dark eyes, more like an elegant and jaunty seal than a mermaid: and in contradistinction to her mellow and mellifluous speaking voice, her laugh, which sounded from time to time, resembled a seal's bark. Moreover, she proved to be as full of tricks as that playful sea-going mammal. She spent much of her time during the voyage in detailing a play about scientists that she said she wished me to write for her. . . . I recall on this visit to America going out to meet her at luncheon to which she had brought her New York hostess. At one moment this woman began to talk rather volubly. Mrs Campbell regarded her with calm contemplation, and then said, 'My dear, you are a very nice woman, but you are not fit to take out to luncheon.' I should prefer to record here an example of her good nature, so often at war with her sense of humour and her tongue. On the occasion of which I write, she was trying to sell for a young English artist two or three of his pictures to some rich American friends of hers. She accomplished this superbly, while, in addition, she gave a magnificent theatrical performance.

Dick Wyndham* was also on board. As he was travelling with me, that much I knew; but I did not learn till later that underneath, in the hold, was the immense Sargent portrait of his three aunts, the Wyndham Sisters,** which he hoped to dispose of in America. In fact, during this visit, he finally sold it to the Metropolitan Museum for the then very fine price of one hundred thousand dollars.

*　　　*　　　*

My visit coincided not only with the full tide of Prohibition but also with the full flood of the great Wall Street beano. Never had so many rich people been crowded together in so minute a space, for the island of Manhattan is small and has

---

* Richard Wyndham, artist and writer, 1896–1948.
** Mary Countess of Wemyss; Lady Glenconner, afterwards Viscountess Grey of Falloden; and Mrs Adeane.

therefore been obliged to develop vertically rather than horizontally. What follows in this essay relates to New York before the slump, when, in retrospect, the city was as innocent as Adam and Eve before the Fall. Sophistication showed already in individuals, but not in whole sections of the people as it does today. America had not yet grown used to her position as a great power.

To give an example of life in New York at that time, let me here record that in the Ambassador Hotel, where I was staying, lived a friend of mine, a professional photographer, not, by the standards of the time, a rich man. Except for getting up in the late afternoon to take a single photograph at an immense price, he stayed in bed all day, telephoning to Wall Street to buy shares on margin, but invariably got up in the evening in time for dinner—at which he always ate oyster-crabs neuberg, a speciality of New York—a much richer man on paper than when he had gone to bed the night before. Alas, this state of affairs was drawing to a close but nobody knew it. People then presumed that it would endure for ever.

When we arrived in New York some hours late, we found a day of extreme brilliance. It would be impossible ever to forget the first sight of the groups of slender towers that form the skyline of New York City, chanting hosannahs to a summer sky. English people who have not been there always presume that New York has a very dry climate, but, on the contrary, it must be one of the most humid cities in the world, though also that with the most changeable weather. In the two to three months I stayed there, I grew to know all possible varieties except extreme heat, because every day I would go for a long walk whatever the weather, stepping out fast beneath the cliff-like buildings. I used, for example, to walk from my hotel to Wall Street, or to the Battery. I would make my way through the Italian and Chinese enclaves and examine them at my leisure. Whenever I saw a bookshop I stopped and entered it and looked round, and I visited many picture galleries and museums. Thus I saw New York when it rained so hard that the water splashed back from the pavement. I saw it under snow, when, until the dust from buildings that were being destroyed takes possession of it—and in New York gigantic edifices are always being destroyed and re-created—it was as white and clean as the North Pole. I have seen it when the wind whistled knife-like round street corners, and I have heard the lion-mouthed thunder, redoubled by stone and cement, drown the hootings of the great liners; but I have never known a day more beautiful than my first, dry and crackling, and it enabled me to make a discovery of something of which no one had spoken beforehand: that in New York you receive a harmless electric shock when you ring the lift bell. If I asked for an explanation of the phenomenon, there would always be the same murmurs about 'static electricity'.

The first night I spent in New York I was taken to an immense dinner-party given by a great picture-collector and his charming and discerning wife. They were very kind to me and after dinner my hostess led me up to a chair, a cross between a camp-stool and a shooting-stick, but executed in wood, and said,

'This is our Dante chair.'

'You mean Dante sat in it?' I enquired.

'No, he was asked to, but refused,' she replied, 'and that is why we call it our Dante chair . . . I want you to sit in it on this, the night of your arrival in New York.'

Accordingly I sat in it and, as I did so, it crumbled into dust—albeit 'crumbled' is not the word to describe the process, since it carries no sense of immediacy, while this disintegration was instantaneous. When I had recovered from the shock—and I may say that my hostess was extremely kind about the incident, although I could not expect her to enjoy it—I found myself engaged in conversation with a fanciful lady of massive proportions, elaborately upholstered in green and yellow brocade.

'Let us talk about *you*,' she was saying. 'You Englishmen all wear armour.'

To which I countered, 'No. Let us keep the conversation to yourself.'

She replied: 'I'm just a wild Irish thing, just a li'l leprechaun.'

My first novel, *Before the Bombardment*, was about to be published in America, and George Doran, its publisher, gave a dinner in my honour for some twenty persons. Even at so comparatively small a party the American passion for oratory made after-dinner speeches compulsory. Among those present whom I recall were William Rose Benét, Frank Swinnerton, F. P. Adams and the biographer of George Washington, W. E. Woodward, a banker turned author, debunking but genial. In the middle of dinner he hissed into my ear, 'I have read your book, and I know you won't be taken in by this dollar business.' I reassured him. . . . In addition, I remember receiving a warning from a friend who was present that I should leave the party punctually at twelve, since that was the hour when the first alcoholic rows were liable to break out.

Liquor under Prohibition had become a national obsession. Love of liberty made it almost a duty to drink more, and worse, than was wise. In this respect, intellectuals vied with socialites. At the end of a ball it was not an uncommon spectacle to see smart young men who had, in the phrase of the time, 'passed out', stacked in the hall ready for delivery at home with the milk by taxicab or van. At any literary gathering there would be almost equally relaxed behaviour, because most festivities depended on supplies of synthetic gin and whisky, and the strength of these was formidable. . . . To show the ingenuity of purveyors, I remember Dick Wyndham ordered some champagne for a party he was giving —he had taken a studio at the Berkeley—and the next morning, while he was still in bed, the door was unlocked and a French couple entered with their luggage. There seemed a great deal of it. Dick kept on explaining to them that this was his room and that he was in bed in it. They appeared to be deaf, and paid no attention until all the luggage had been collected together. They then bolted the door, threw open their trunks, produced the champagne, presented a bill, received their money and left . . . Prohibition had some other curious, contradictory consequences. For example, at the hotel, where I was staying and which had large and magnificent public rooms, it was impossible in any of them, except the dining-room, to obtain even a glass of water, since no drink of any sort was allowed to be served.

One result of the current boom was a new development in the domestic-bird world. Rich old ladies bequeathed large legacies to their parrots, but so many of the human heirs were reluctant to take on the job of looking after these spoilt birds that a Parrots' Home, it was said, had been founded for accommodating only privileged, moneyed parrots, cockatoos and macaws, who were lodged and fed according to social position and income bracket. Accent and way of talking were taken into account. The parrots who had inherited ten thousand dollars a year and cultivated a Fifth Avenue or a Long Island voice would be given a better perch than the three-thousand-dollar-a-year birds, and would be entitled to more, and less mildewed, grapes. . . . What happened to these birds when the great slump came I never heard.

What I did discover on my voyage into that distant past was the existence of a completely unknown set of alternative literary figures: writers whose names were familiar to everyone in literary circles in America but of whom nobody had ever heard in England, and vice versa. Until I arrived in New York, I did not know the names of Heywood Broun, then at the height of his fame as a critic, of his wife Ruth Hale, of F.P.A., and of many others. What seemed more extra-ordinary still was that English novels—*romans à clef*—were in the United States fitted out with an entirely different and local personnel. If, for example, Desmond MacCarthy had been said to figure in an English book, in America this same character would be identified with Heywood Broun, and the figure of a woman writer of the time, say Rose Macaulay, would be replaced by that of Ruth Hale, and similarly, on through the whole volume. In short, there were two sets of characters, but if you explained that one of them was not an American but an Englishman, your statement would be received with incredulity.

One of my most pleasant memories of that time was of my first meeting with Marianne Moore, to whom I took a letter of introduction from my friend Mrs Bryher. She was then living with her mother in a trim red-brick house in a trim street in or near the Village. When I arrived punctually at four —and punctuality with me always means at least ten minutes beforehand (I have wasted as much time by this fault as another man loses by being late) Miss Moore had not yet returned from the office of the *Dial*, and I was received by her mother. Mrs Moore, like myself, greatly admired Dickens, and she talked to me of his tour in the States and told me of the towns where he had delivered his readings. After a little time Miss Moore arrived, a charming and very unpretentious young woman with the same quiet elegance and the same strong but merciful personality which has so finely developed throughout her life. In spite of her apparent simplicity, it was easy to discern beneath it a very definite, delicate and poetical nature. Though shy, she was able to take refuge behind an appealing and almost apologetic smile, but she was as full of character, both individual and national, as a swarm is full of bees.

Among the friends who gave parties for me when I arrived in New York, one of the first was Muriel Draper. (I remember with what amusement she told me, apropos of this party, that when she had sent a card with 'To Meet Captain Osbert Sitwell' written on it to Ford Maddox Ford, he had replied: 'You can't ask *Colonel* Ford to meet *Captain* Sitwell.' I had invented for him the name of 'Freud Maddox Fraud'.) This took place in her Gurdjieff period before she became a Communist, when she was still an interior decorator. There was much talk in her studio of furniture made of metal and glass, but this was before the nightmare became true, and culminated in the metal and chromium-plated tubes and uncured leather seats slung on three rods of steel that were to be the fashion many years later. . . . When I had been introduced to her in England some years before, we had immediately become friends. Much of her character is still visible in her book *Music at Midnight*, and thus can be recaptured, but her amazing gift of life and her entirely individual appearance are more difficult to record. I had first seen her remarkable head in the stalls of Covent Garden before the War. She seemed an embodiment of the American spirit and might well have been the figurehead of a new race. To talk to her was enchanting, for she combined frankness with the most extraordinary powers of minute observation. Everybody who knew her either loved or hated her. There was no middle way.

I also attended a party given by George Moore, not the novelist but the genial American financier who had previously shared a large house in London with Lord French of Ypres and who loved to provide amusement for his friends. He was now entertaining equally lavishly in New York. This was a noisy evening, with Cossacks giving toasts, and singing and jumping over their swords. It was impossible to hear a single word your neighbour said; so since I wanted to talk with Muriel Draper, who was sitting next to me, I proposed we should slip under the large supper-table and in that refuge finish our conversation; an idea which, accordingly, we put into practice. It seemed very quiet.

I do not know whether Scott Fitzgerald was in New York at that time or whether he was engaged in one of his alcoholic sprees on the continent of Europe. Indeed, no invitation to meet him was ever extended to me until many years after his death. It was in the autumn of 1951, after my sister and I had given a reading, that a very plump—and plump is a euphemism—unknown hostess came up to us in our dressing-room and said, 'I, Mrs Blank, am giving a cocktail party in your honour next Tuesday in my apartment. I have asked several notable writers to meet you—among others, Scott Fitzgerald will be present.'

This gave my sister and me rather a turn at the time. One day I mentioned the episode to my doctor. It turned out that he had been called in to attend the same lady to treat her over-weight condition, albeit he said that his advice had not been followed and that it was like trying to persuade a pythoness to bant when she was in sight of her prey.

One of the people I liked most in the New York of that time was Alexander Woollcott, who was both friendly and witty. The most valuable personal quality with which nature had endowed him was his so-obvious love of life and he showed no sign of the insolence with which his personality has been invested. I first met Woollcott, who was not then as famous as he became later, at Miss Elizabeth Marbury's; I have heard him be so funny in conversation that the taxi driver who was taking us to a theatre had to pull up at the side of the road because he was laughing so helplessly. (I have only known this to happen twice in my life; the second time was when I was driving with Leo Lerman in the spring of last year.)

Miss Marbury, with whom I began this description of life in New York in the twenties, was, mentally and physically, one of the remarkable figures of the time in New York. To write that she was large is an understatement. She was of such enormous dimensions that it was always difficult for her to get in or out of a motor, but this disability in no way discouraged her from going about, and usually caused her to laugh uproariously. Everywhere she went people were de-lighted to see her. Somerset Maugham had kindly given me a letter of introduction to her and I met her frequently just after I arrived in New York. On each occasion she watched and listened to me carefully with a frightening look of acumen. After this had happened four or five times and she had summed me up in her mind, she said to me: 'I should like to act as agent for you.' This was another honour from her, but one which, unlike the first, I fully appreciated at the moment.

I used to visit the 'château' on Fifth Avenue of Mrs Cornelius Vanderbilt, whom I had often met before in England. Indeed, on one occasion, at Polesden Lacey, I had said to her, 'What a lovely colour your dress is, Mrs Vanderbilt,' to which she in happy innocency had replied, 'Yes, I love blue; that is why in New York I am known as the Kingfisher.'

Her house was the social centre of New York. It was not lovely, but what was called, in advertisements of houses to be let or sold, 'well-appointed', large and luxurious, full of Louis Quinze furniture and of footmen, already a rarity elsewhere in New York. When the time came for me to say goodbye before leaving for England, I remember I asked if I could do anything for her when I reached London. She replied, 'Only give my love to the dear boys.'

I knew immediately whom she meant: His Royal Highness, the Prince of Wales, and their Royal Highnesses, the Dukes of York, Gloucester and Kent.

At this stage of her life, one would have said, certainly, that Mrs Vanderbilt was one of the most conventional people alive. Even her clothes, her invariable bandeau and her grey hair were a cliché, but as she grew older this characteristic faded, as I was to find out many years later when I sat next to her at a large luncheon party in the house of a friend in New York. She suddenly said to me, pointing to a well-known general who was sitting at the other side of the table talking in an extremely loud voice, 'That man is too noisy. I shall scream.'

Before I had time to reply, she had let out a yell, loud and fierce enough to have done credit to an American Indian out for a day's scalping. Undeterred by the sudden quiet that ensued, she said to me, 'Shall I scream again?' but this time I was able to dissuade her. . . . It is related that when Mrs Vanderbilt met the Soviet Ambassador for the first time, she began the conversation by saying to him, 'I was devoted to your Czar.'

When I first visited New York there was much entertaining going on and the descendants of the statesmen who had signed the Declaration of Independence still formed a society of their own. Now many of these families have disappeared. They then still constituted a kind of Domesday-Book society and, however poor some of the members of these families had become, they were always invited to and invariably attended the dinner-parties of their richer fellows.

The tornado of prosperity swept on. Coloured people offered hospitality as much as white, and one of the most memorable parties I attended was a ball given by Madam Walker, the heiress of that commodity *Antikink*, for two young nieces who were on this occasion to make their first appearance in black society. Madam Walker, who must have been a very rich woman, lived in one house and reserved another next to it for party-giving. The room where she received us was a tent room, carried out in the Parisian style of the Second Empire. She stood attended by a niece on each side, and by Doctor W. E. B. Dubois, who was known as the Negro Lenin. He had recently come back from Russia where he had seen Lenin, to whom, strangely enough, he bore some physical resemblance, rather like that of a negative to the print of a photograph. This remarkable man was the author of *The Souls of Black Folk*. He died at the age of ninety-five at Accra, Ghana, on August 27th, 1963. He had been one of the founders of the National Association for the Advancement of Coloured People, and was a member of the Communist Party. One curious feature of Madam Walker's party was that, when one arrived, no one would shake hands until he or she knew exactly where one had come from, and when my name was called out, they gave me a searching glance until I added 'from England'. Then they shook hands warmly.

Our hostess, a very large woman, was wearing an elephant-grey, tight Greek ball-dress and had braided her hair with a

Greek fillet in gold. When the time came for the dance to begin, Madam Walker asked me to go upstairs with her and talk. Downstairs we could hear the band start to play. Alleged Scotch whisky was the drink supplied below, but upstairs Madam Walker produced two bottles of champagne which she opened, and then proceeded to reveal to me her trouble: 'Twenty years ago,' she announced 'my feet spoilt my honeymoon—and tonight they're hurting me again, something crool.'

Though there was then no talk of integration, downstairs, one of the nieces, who was very sure of herself, was saying to Dick Wyndham, 'Excuse my asking, but are you high-class?'

He did not know what to reply. If he said no, he might have been asked to leave; if yes, he would probably be stamped as conceited, but in the end he judged it better to say yes; to which his dancing partner replied, 'I am so glad, because I have no colour prejudice, but I do think the classes oughtn't to mingle.'

The dancing was the greatest pleasure to watch. It was the year in which the charleston took the city by storm and most of the guests danced it beautifully. I sat there, interested and happy, until I grew very tired, and then realised that I had become the victim of an inverted snobbishness that was causing me to stay up longer than I wanted because this was a party given by coloured people. I knew then that it was time to go.

Harlem in 1925 was no hostile fortress as it is today, but a part of New York City, where coloured people welcomed the whites. It was an enchanting place to go at night. Whenever there was an occasion, Carl Van Vechten was always the white master of the coloured revels. I remember one ridiculous incident.... It had been announced that a hitherto unknown coloured singer, a mistress of exotic and nostalgic song, would make her debut shortly in New York at a well-known night club. Excitement had mounted for weeks and on the night in question the particular night club was crowded with people, standing as well as sitting. The artiste was very late in arriving and when she did appear had obviously swallowed more strong liquor than was good for her. However, when at last she stepped on to the stage, an expectant silence fell on the audience, but, alas, she began to sing in a lachrymose, ululant manner the whole of 'Auld Lang Syne', the words interspersed with her own hiccoughs and gusts of laughter from below.

I recall also with delight a comment made by a well-known Negro singer, Taylor Gordon, on my friend Aldous Huxley. Huxley always affected rather loose, shaggy clothes and wore his tie inside a ring. Muriel Draper had said to me, 'When you see Taylor Gordon, ask him about his meeting with Aldous Huxley.'

A few days later I saw him, fortunately recollected her words, and accordingly said, 'I hear you met Mr Huxley. How did you get on with him?' He replied, 'Mr Sitwell, when I think that that man comes from the capital of the world's tailoring!'

* * *

The New York theatre was in a state of great activity and vigour compared with its London equivalent. For example, the play *Broadway* was there to compete with the suburban comedies gone slightly off, then to be seen in London. It was easy to decide which was the more interesting. I found much pleasure and made many friends in the theatrical world. Clare Eames wrote to me a fan-letter about *Before the Bombardment* and asked me to have supper with her and her husband, the playwright Sidney Howard. We became great friends. They lived in a small house—even then a rare possession—and I often went there after the theatre and at two o'clock in the morning ate chicken fried by an excellent coloured cook. Clare Eames came of a famous theatrical family and was a niece of the well-known Madam Clare Eames. She would, I think, if she had lived, have become a great actress. Feeling for the stage was instinct in her every movement and expression, but she was the least affected person you could imagine. I saw her in her wonderful rendering of Katya in the dramatised version of *The Brothers Karamazov*. Alas, she died in London a few years later, and Sidney Howard died also before his time.

It was during this visit, too, that I became friendly with Charles Brackett, and the friendship happily still survives, as I found in Hollywood many years later.

*   *   *

In several directions American ways seemed to me to be old-fashioned. Thus I noticed that every time George Doran entered his enormous office full of people, the whole personnel would stand up until he had crossed the floor to his own glass pen. This procedure, I reflected, must have wasted a tremendous amount of time—say five man-minutes for one hundred people, which equals five hundred minutes, which equals eight man-hours and twenty minutes—but may have constituted one of the reasons why there was no unemployment in America at that time.

What I discovered in New York was a completely new range of friends and the most wonderful collections of pictures, both old and new. The Americans had been the first foreign patrons of the great Impressionist and Post-Impressionist masters who were now beginning to come into their own, but I noticed a tendency to treat the patrons who owned such works of art as if they had painted them instead of merely being the fortunate possessors; the tendency still continues today and resembles the flattering regard in which scientists are held, as if they had themselves made the phenomena they reveal. . . . All the same, the early American patrons deserve the greatest credit for their discernment and for having presented pictures of these Schools to public galleries. The most scintillatingly beautiful of all pictures by these painters, 'La Grande Jatte' by Seurat—a large canvas wherein top-hatted men and bustled women promenade by the shimmering water's edge in an eternity of light—was bought by an American patron and presented to the Institute of Fine Arts in Chicago. There is in France today no work by this great master to compare with it. Indeed, perhaps the only picture of his that is of equal importance is 'La Baignade' in the Tate Gallery.

From the welter of galleries and museums to which I submitted myself, a few stand out with a particular clarity, notably the Frick Collection with its individuality and splendour: the most beautiful Bellini in the world, for example —'St Francis'—a room of Fragonards, surely one of the most wonderful decorative rooms that has ever been painted; the 'Polish Cavalier'; and so many other treasures of the finest quality, in a perfect setting—a spacious and lovely house instead of an impersonal gallery. And there is the Spanish Museum, today not defunct but much changed. The chief memory of all is human rather than esthetic, a tragic experience which yet brought its own lesson of courage. . . . I was taken by a friend to visit the apartment of a great collector —mainly of Italian Primitives—who had gone blind, and whose chief pleasure it was to take people round his pictures, pointing out to them the particular beauties and subtleties of colour and detail. So well had he known them, so much had he loved them while he still retained his sight, that he never made a mistake; in this manner he kept alive and constantly renewed his memories.

*   *   *

I went home from my voyage of discovery by the southern passage, from New York to Naples, sailing on a great Italian liner, its interior designed and heavily furnished in the dark late Renaissance style prevalent in the most expensive Italian hotels. Here a phenomenon opposite to that to which I have called the attention of the reader as common to all English boats bound for the States, could be observed: you entered Italy the moment you set foot on board. The Italian voice, so beautifully modulated and so beautifully produced by the

Italian people—though often strident and shrill, equally among the rich and the members of the old ruling class—formed an animated background. The ship was celebrated for its parties, and I recall one lady from Boston had brought with her a grey silk dress that had belonged to her grandmother, which she was determined to wear when she presented the prizes at a fancy dress ball. An instance of such unsophisticated enthusiasm for fun of a modest kind would not be easy to find among her successors of today, a generation later: but it must be admitted that in this costume she looked very well, after the manner, no doubt, of the simple-souled Quaker lady for whom it had been made.

I also recollect that a New York dressmaker approached me one day after luncheon saying, 'Are you going to the Captain's party this evening?'

'No,' I replied, 'I haven't been invited.'

Whereupon she said, 'Well, I understand that he has asked everyone of any social consequence on board.'

We sailed through the Azores with its mists and, under them, its hills covered with hydrangeas, and stopped for a day and a night at Funchal, the capital of Madeira, that lovely island, a single mountain-top rising from a great depth in the middle of the Atlantic; an island full of fine nineteenth-century villas with their entrancing gardens of semi-tropical Regency and early-Victorian style, gardens in which orchids flourish as easily as Dorothy Perkins grows in England, together with solandra, their white buds so huge—several times the size of the flowers of a magnolia grandiflora—and if you pop them as you might a fuchsia bud, they make a sound like an old-fashioned motor-horn, and large paulovnia and jacaranda trees that can only blossom with this profusion in such a climate. All this floral exuberance rises on the foundations of the fortunes made from the wine that bears the name of the island. The members of the firms who live here in these villas are many of them descended from English sea-captains and non-commissioned officers who had spent some time in

Madeira in the course of their duties during the long years of the Napoleonic Wars, and had retained in their hearts such a love for this island, and, no doubt, for its wines, that they returned here to found their firms when peace came.

Perpetual early summer seems always to reign here. We left the island and sailed through estival seas, sportive with dolphin and porpoise nosing and jumping out of the Atlantic rollers, and with flying-fish sequining the green-blue lanes between them. Everything seemed propitious, but we rode straight into a tempest which hurled about the heavily-carved, massive pieces of furniture in the public rooms, injuring many passengers. I recollect the two celebrated Italian expert winter-sportsmen who were on board, returning in triumph to their land from receiving most of the prizes awarded at Lake Placid, and how terrified they looked as they raced past us on their chairs across the ballroom floor at a rate faster than they had ever attained on skate, ski or toboggan—travelling, indeed, though not of their own free will, at almost supersonic speed. However, after a day and a night the gale abated and life became normal again.

We disembarked at Naples, and, a few days later, I met in the street a very shrewd American lawyer to whom I had talked on the boat. It was his first visit to Europe and he observed to me, 'One thing I notice particularly; the people you pass in the streets here have a different expression in their eyes from what they have at home.'

What did he see in those magic mirrors, affording clues to the past and to the future, I wonder? In the past, the European triumphs of every sort, but specially in the arts, for century after century; the age-old dusty poverty, aggravated by war, of Naples, the last great classical city surviving to our own day? In the future, hints of the Civil War in Spain, that short rehearsal for the wicked struggle which was waiting for us round the corner; or the revival of the torture-chamber and the introduction of the gas oven in Germany? And what did he see in the eyes of his own countrymen when he returned to

New York? What *I* saw in the eyes of a generation ago, was infinite kindness and credulity, and the boundless confidence which enabled a great people to grasp the leadership of the civilised world, and then not know what to do with it.

Old Worlds for New

NOW that all the talk is of new worlds (whisper to me, you who are with me waking and sleeping, where I have heard such talk before, was it during the Trojan Wars, the Punic or the Wars of the Roses?), now, I was saying, that all the talk is of new worlds, I feel that I myself am bound for the old, a Columbus in a hurry to reach home. I have caught a glimpse of a new heaven and earth fashioned by Woolworth's and the B.B.C. from the wreckage of tanks and the spidery carcases of aircraft, and I prefer that which grew out of the fallen porphyry pillars of the Forum and of temples that had been cast down.

It is, you will tell me, a matter of taste, or, perhaps, of morality. The Common Man finds Woolworth's convenient, and therefore It Fulfils a Function, therefore the things it sells are not only useful, sometimes, and cheap, but a thousand times more beautiful than the antiquated products and goods —for there are no arts in this world of which I speak, but only products and goods—of Egypt, Greece, Rome, Italy and France in former times.

To which I reply, with rodomontade, that for more than twenty years I have collected and made worlds, both old and new: some that existed, some that existed only as I saw them— and for me alone until I gave to my generation the key—and some that I created. Of the worlds existing in the past, I saw one in Cambodia, and handed it to you floating upon the wings of kingfishers, another—or part of it—in the swamps and mountains of Guatemala, in those vast churches, dark and cloudy with incense, the floors of which are sprinkled with rose petals and glitter with stars of candlelight: vast churches built for the Christian chairman of a board of ruthless, obsolete gods, naked heathens—but that world I reserve for another occasion. Then there were the worlds, more familiar, of Spain and Italy, or the particular ancient Mediterranean world which is so difficult to focus, and which you can enter, for instance, through the Lion Gate at Mycenae, a world built momentarily anew by the same sky, and the same stream rushing with surly strength through that gully which cuts off every other approach; a world of vast bronze helmets, gold masks and echoing tombs. . . . But one of the oldest worlds of which for an instant I caught sight was at a garden-party given by Prince Pu-Ru in April 1934. Let me, then, try to catch that moment, though first we must have maps and charts and Chinese pedigrees, and generally become prosaic.

Prince Pu-Ru, a cousin of the former Emperor Hsüang-Tung—Emperor of Manchukuo—was, at the time of which I speak, the only member of the former Imperial Family allowed to reside in the northern capital. This forbearance on the part of the Republican Government and the City Elders was due to the esteem in which he was held throughout the length and breadth—and, in this connection, the phrase cannot be regarded as a cliché—of the whole country, as being the chief modern exponent of the art of calligraphy, the basic art of China, and the leading draughtsman of his day. The smallest fragment of his writing would change hands at public auction for several hundreds of pounds. He and his wife, also a member of the Manchu Royal House, lived in a palace—or rather the portion of one, since their residence had originally formed a wing of the Imperial City, until the Emperor Ch'ien Lung had severed it from the main body, and presented it to one of his younger sons; from whom the present owner is descended. And you must realise that the word *palace* here always denotes, not a single building, standing by itself, but

an organisation of groups of tiled and painted pavilions in a
series of gardens, and also that, because Peking is built of
houses of one storey, except for the Forbidden City and the
Gates, it covers an immense area. It contains huge thoroughfares—planned, it is said, by Kubla Khan—and innumerable
small, thronged streets, and then, suddenly, you will come to
some backwater; a broad *cul-de-sac*, it may be, where it seems
as though no one ever passed. The houses are ripe with age in
this empty sunshine. The grass grows between the cobbles,
there are no stalls for food or tea, no children, in their broad,
padded coats, stamping and tumbling in the dust, no piebald
dogs, no old gentlemen carrying bird-cages in which their pets
are waiting only to be uncovered before they start their song.
There are no street sounds, no echo of gong or wooden clapper
or bell or tuning-fork, no cries of the men who sell the
innumerable delicacies of the season: spring chicken, ducks
fattened in cellars, dumplings, smoked fish or the common
water-chestnut or sunflower seeds. . . . It was out of such a
broad and stagnant street, or *place*, as this that you entered
the palace of Prince Pu-Ru.

The Prince was not a rich man—there are few rich men in
China, except, it may be, for various atavistic missionaries and
their children, or the sons of former statesmen of the Dowager
Empress or the relatives of retired palace eunuchs, for graft
and favour, not commerce, brought the great fortunes of the
East. In consequence—and because the Prince was an artist—
the place had remained unspoilt. The right exterior painting,
vermilion and green, of the halls was dry and flaking, and the
ceilings and walls showed in places the ingenious, sombre
lacquering of the snows of this year and yesteryear, which
three times every winter roll a carpet of thick swansdown over
the flashing golden tiles of the Forbidden City, and the
herringbone-ribbed grey tiles of the Tartar and Chinese cities.
In the first room, in which we waited, I remember that two
pots, containing diminutive fruit trees in flower, stood between the windows; those dwarf trees that were grown in

Peking for house decoration, with the significant and distorted line of their small, crooked branches, and with blossom—cherry or peach—the precise counterpart of that which you see in a Chinese painting. Soon the Prince came in, and I was presented to him. He was a sturdy figure, in a dark-blue robe, with a face broader than the ordinary Chinese face, and thoughtful and kind in its cast. He talked to me for some time, through the friend who had brought me, and who now interpreted, albeit, indeed, the exquisite courtesy and dignity of his manner needed no translator. Before long the Princess joined her husband and helped him to show us—for my friend was a celebrated connoisseur—some of his treasures; small bronze vases of great antiquity, and a huge carved emerald which had belonged to that great collector, Ch'ien Lung. This stone had a rippling surface like that of water, green water, containing a lost unfathomable depth of light. Of the purest colour, it was the size of the Princess's foot—remarkably small, though the feet of Manchu ladies had never been bound. ... All this time, from behind a pane of glass in the wall—the windows, of course, were of oiled paper—a very beautiful Chinese girl, her face painted in a florid, extremely stylized manner, and wearing an elaborately embroidered Chinese robe of blue silk, was watching us. But presently, when tea was brought, she came in to wait on the Princess. ... At the end of the interview the Prince told us he was giving a garden-party the following week; and invited us to be present.

The importance, as it turned out, of this function was that it proved to be the first Manchu social event that had taken place since the Marshal Feng Yu-Hsiang's troops, doubtless at their leader's inspiration, had forced their way into the Forbidden City, and the young Emperor had been obliged to escape, some ten years before. And, when the afternoon arrived, it seemed as though, in itself, it might have been worth waiting for through a whole decade. Certainly, in England, it would so have seemed. But in the climate of northern China such a day at such a time is to be confidently expected. The seasons are unbelievably regular in the incidence of their weather. Each fall of snow in the winter, each gradation, almost, of temperature can be predicted. Thus, at the winter solstice, it is customary in Peking to make a 'Nine-Nines Chart of Lessening Cold', composed of nine patterns and eighty-one small circles, or else to paint a plum branch in outline, bearing on it nine blossoms with eighty-one petals, so that a circle or a petal can be struck off each day before the fulfilment of the spring. . . . But now the Feast of Excited Insects (on the morning of which day, it is said, the herons return to the moat of the Imperial Palace, leaving for the south again about five months later, on the evening of the Lantern Festival) was long over, spring had come, its Feast of Ching Ming, or Pure Brightness (when all good citizens wear circlets of willow, sweep the graves of their ancestors and burn coloured paper money on their behalf, so that they can purchase little luxuries beyond the tomb), had gone by. Each day seemed finer than the last, and the effervescence of spring was everywhere to be felt, in the fairs held within temple precincts, in the streets, in the broad roads or in the quiet lanes, by the lake of Pei-hai, by the moat, by day and by night.

The advance of the year was so rapid you could almost hear the branches of apple and quince and wistaria creaking with the life within them, almost see the sticky buds first appear, and then unfold and open into their spice-breathing cups and tongues and turrets. And, since the object of this party was to see the crab-apple trees in bloom, no afternoon could have been more fitted, more consecrated by Nature herself, to this purpose. It might have been fashioned solely for men to savour the scent and essence of such trees in flower, and the gay, sheepskin clouds, flecking the blue dome of the sky, were translucent as the clustered petals themselves.

We drove to the palace in our rickshaws, and were kept sitting therein for a minute or two in the deserted space outside, while—and this time I noticed them particularly since on the last occasion, too, I had seen them and had asked my friend from a lodge each side to open the stout wooden gates. They stood now, as we passed through, hanging on to the doors in order to have an excuse to scrutinise us minutely, staring at us with a curiosity of so intense a nature as to proclaim that it had not been properly satisfied for many years. The whole troupe consisted of about twenty persons, ten on each side, and they were dressed in long robes of vellum-coloured cloth. They were tall, a few of them inclined to fat, but one thing they all shared in common: their rather colourless faces, on which many lines were deeply incised, bore an oddly weazen look, like that of green and wrinkled apples. I had been sure, when first I set eyes on them, that somewhere, not long before, I had come across beings of this same order. ... And then the memory had come back, of the tea and gossip—albeit incomprehensible to me—that I had enjoyed with the ancient inmates of the Ancestral Hall of the Exalted Brave, an almhouse for retired eunuchs in the Imperial service which I have described in a chapter of *Escape with Me!* But the youngest of those pensioners had been at least fifteen or twenty years older than these, the last recruited eunuchs of the Forbidden City, who now confronted us. Hither they had fled from impending massacre—although they had first made sure that their young royal master had also eluded it—on that terrible night in 1924; here, in this palace that seemed to stand forgotten in its large grounds, off the main ways of the city, they had found a sanctuary with Prince Pu-Ru's father. And, though now they could discover no means, as formerly, of making great fortunes, though now they were not living in the lavish grandeur in which for so long the people of China had been obliged to keep them, this curious and artificial sept perpetually recruited from the ranks, nevertheless they at present constituted its only living representatives in the whole of China; anomalous beings who were actually still pursuing their duties, which were the same as those of the eunuchs who had guarded the divine thrones, ever since they were set up, of Babylon and Ur, the Indies and China, Byzantium and Turkey.

The gardens seemed immense, as we got out of our rick-shaws and began to walk. Inside the boundaries of their walls, crowned with yellow tiles, were groves of old cypresses, the frond-like arrangements of their leaves lying upon the air as though they were layers of blue-green smoke, there were eighteenth-century water-gardens, now dry but full of wild flowers, and there were the sunk gardens wherein flourished, with gnarled, rough trunks, the crooked and ancient fruit trees which constituted the chief pride of their owner. As we approached the pavilions, we noticed how many guests had already arrived. And although there was nothing political about this gathering in intention, the atmosphere was heavy and strange, laden with feeling for the old régime, for here, today, within this green domain, walking slowly as tortoises, hobbling, waddling, trudging, a few of them almost crawling, were all those who had come through from one world into another. Most of them, indeed, appeared to be very old. Some had been in hiding ever since the death of the Dowager Empress, some since the first revolution, some merely since the flight of the young Emperor; none, you would have pronounced with certainty, had ventured out for at least a decade.

Looking at them, it was at once possible to see that these Manchu nobles, in spite of their infirmity, and though very different from their ancestors, the simple warriors, with their outlandish ways and barbarous foods*—that belonged more to the tents of tribes wandering through the vast plains of Manchuria and Mongolia, and over the wild mountain ranges,

---

* These foods survived in perhaps a modified and more civilised form until lately. A Manchu civil servant, who wrote just before 1900, has left in a book he wrote (*Annual Customs and Festivals of Peking*, by Tun Lich'en, translated and annotated by Dr Derk Bodde. Henri Vetch, Peking, 1936), an account, for example, of a delicacy called Manchu Cakes, made of sugar and koumiss, this last being a fermented liquor made of mare's milk and a typical food of the nomads of northern Asia. These cakes, he tells us, 'are cooked during the night, when the weather has become extremely cold. Their pure whiteness is like frost, and when one has them in one's mouth, it is as if one were crunching on snow. They have a special flavour of the north. They are made into the shapes of plum flowers, or that of squares joined at the corners. . . .'

than to the inhabitants of palaces—were yet incontestably the members of a ruling caste. Though they approximated now to the Chinese, in the same manner, let us say, that the English families settled in Ireland came to resemble the Irish—nevertheless, their faces were heavier, their noses more emphatic, they had all the air of those in whose blood existed the capacity and inclination to command. Old, old men, their beards thin, their benign but resolute faces wrinkled round the corners of their eyes by the hot suns of the Chinese summers and by their bland smiling through several scores of years, they had, since the collapse of the Imperial power, remained in the discreet seclusion of their households and ancestral temples. Today they had come out, and their famous names and titles, now forgotten in the city outside, had been announced with a renewed flourish. Many of them supported their weight on sticks, many leant on the arms of younger relatives, and a few were so frail that they had to be aided, or even carried, by two men. But they had come out, and they all wore proudly the robes of maroon and mulberry and puce that belonged to their race, and—though this last was an indictable offence in modern China—some of them, or of those who supported them, boldly paraded pigtails.

The Princess was the only woman to be seen, and as she and the Prince went the round of the guests, obeisances were low. A certain feeling of sadness, it is true, permeated this almost ghostly congregation. The very welcome, even, which the eunuchs at the gate had accorded to each guest well known to them, the shrill cries of recognition and enthusiastic squeaks of greeting, contained, too, something of a nostalgic quality. In this enclosure, this oasis of the past, a lost world revived. The hoarse, ritual shouts of the Eight Banners as they greeted the Son of Heaven, moving through the courts of the palace as the sun moved—so it was held—through the sky, seemed to be audible again in the distance to sentient ears. These old men could recall so vividly the precise unique walk, a kind of conventional totter, as though upon stilts, decreed by the usages of antiquity for the Emperor of China, and the unique Imperial voice, inhuman—and so, godlike—loud and high, of which the very recollection was dead (though once I was fortunate enough to hear an imitation of it, given by a Russian who had been received in audience by the Dowager Empress—but he was rather drunk at the time, and nobody except myself would listen). Outside, each man was a stranger: outside, each man was a shadow belonging to the past. Now, it was only within the compass of these walls that there existed yet a sense of relative importance, that everyone could chart with exactitude the identity and position of each man present. Outside, there was nobody to whom to talk, nobody who remembered *anything*. . . . And, kindling in this new warmth, the guests, after greeting their host and hostess, passed on, beyond the pavilions, in the direction of the orchards.

Perhaps they could scarcely be termed orchards, because the trees, being grown for their blossom rather than their fruit, were irregularly disposed, and were fewer to the given area than is our custom. Bent, contorted with age as the old men who were now on their way to inspect them, they must have been planted some two centuries before. Each of them might have been shaped by the green fingers of a Chinese God of Growth, each was as exquisitely placed upon the green turf as any figure upon a scroll by the hand of a great artist. Perfect in their balance and grotesque posture, some inclined, at the precise angle best calculated to display their unexpected and singular grace, while one tree, even, lay on its side and blossomed on the ground.

Slowly, painfully, the old men hobbled along the crooked, paved paths that zigzagged to these trees. When they reached them, they were conducted up small flights of stone steps, so fashioned that, saving where the steps showed, they seemed natural rocks that had cropped up through the turf or had fallen from the sky. These flights, their tops level with the tops of the trees, are thus placed near apple and pear and peach and quince and cherry, so that the connoisseur can obtain a perfect view of the blossom. Even to a newcomer, inexpert in the flowery lore of the Chinese, from each different plane, the particular view of the tree for which the step had been constructed offered a revelation of a new world; of the same kind as when first you fly in an aircraft above the clouds, and look down upon their fleecy humps, white and golden—except that clouds disperse, are opaque, and do not favour an ordered development.

To the Chinese amateurs of the garden, however, these steps offer even more than to someone, like myself, who was fresh to them. In consequence, the old gentlemen persevered —for it was difficult for them to ascend such crags. Many of them took a long while over the process, and only gained the summits by the help, as it were, of guides. Next year, one felt, they would require ropes as well.

Once there, they would remain for a full hour, matching in their minds the complexion and fragrance of the blossom of previous years with that before them. Then, after the general examination of the crop, came the more intimate tallying of one branch, one flower, one bud, with another, and finally it was necessary again to consider the entire grouping and design. But the bees, inordinately busy and managing, behaving as though they were old women in a market, got in the way, and even the less industrious butterflies obscured the view with their gaudily decorated sails or dragged down a petal too heavily when suddenly they perched upon it. . . . Critical appreciation of this high order could not be hurried. After all, it was better fully to use now the powers of judgment with which the years had enriched them, and to apply their trained abilities in this direction, for, in the order of things, they could scarcely hope to see many more of these flowery harvests.

So, they stayed on. . . . But, alas, it was time for us to go. We said good-bye to our host and hostess, and turned away towards the gates, towards the new world of Salvation Army shelters and American Mother's Days, of corrugated iron and cocoa. But, as I looked back, I could distinguish in the distance the tops of the trees, so old, yet so intensely alive, producing these living hives of fragrance, living translucent clouds of snow and roses, dusted with powdered gold, and on the top of every flight of steps I could see, too, a decrepit dignitary of the extinct Empire, his robes of maroon or burnet causing the blue of the sky to vibrate more intensely. Each old man stood, outlined, motionless above the blossom, staring down at its frothy intricacies, waiting there with a certain solemnity, it seemed, and a proper sense of the occasion—for even tomorrow this perfection would be tarnished and it would be too late to form a considered opinion, even one day would have made all the difference; each old man waited, thus quietly under the immense blue dome, as though he were a watcher on a tower, or the guardian of an ancient shrine calling the faithful to worship.

Lord Grey de Ruthyn

THIS chapter is not to be placed against the London background I have so far adumbrated, but against a scene of combined rusticity and industry, with tall plumes of smoke rising from huge chimneys, and against woods and substantial stone houses, red-tiled, and stone walls that run round fields. It would be of no avail to try to place the subject of this portrait against a London background, for he would have left the city before you had spotted him.

It was at the time of the raids on Sheffield that I first met Lord Grey de Ruthyn, though he was so near a neighbour, living in the village of Barlborough some two miles away. We quickly became friends, though my father and mother had somehow contrived to wound his rather delicate susceptibilities and I had never even seen him, until he had become Chairman of the Renishaw bench of magistrates. He never told me what my parents had done or failed to do, and to this day I am ignorant of it. I am, however, grateful to them for this act of omission or commission, because the result of it was that here, so close to me, was a fascinating human being to explore, a man of warm and kindly nature, of a simple character, albeit with many fantastic traits and convolutions, enough to make him of continual interest, I hope for the reader as much as for myself.

I first met Lord Grey, then, at the magistrates' court after a particularly bad night of it. (A bomb had fallen just inside the Eckington Gate of the Park, but no one had been hurt.) The magistrates had collected early that morning and were occupied in keeping stiff upper lips. At the stroke of the clock a door opened and a rather red-faced figure in a blue serge suit and carrying a dome-like bowler hat entered and said in a loud voice as he came in, 'Good morning. I don't know what you all felt about last night, but *I* was absolutely terrified—and I can tell you so were my geese. They gave the alarum; such intelligent birds.' These words, said plainly but with conviction, let us all down badly: stiff upper lips began to thaw. And this sentiment was typical, as I was to learn later, of the speaker, who was entirely honest and without cant. To elucidate further his words I must explain that he was very fond of geese and kept a flock of them, the leader of which, a bird of dignity and sagacity, he had named after himself: Goosey Grey de Ruthyn. He was, moreover, impressed by their power and also their divination. He did not allude on this occasion to the classic instance of it, when the geese on the Capitol gave the alarm of invasion by the Gauls climbing the hill, in time for them to be hurled back. No doubt this passed through his mind, for he had been given a good classical education at Mount St Mary's, the Jesuit School nearby. His education led him, indeed, to think of the emperors of Rome as his contemporaries, so that when I used to ask him what he was reading, he would make some such reply as, 'I am just reading a new book by Suetonius about the emperor Tiberius, dear heart: some shocking stories have come to light about him, I am sorry to say,' or, similarly, he would allude to a later date and remark, 'I am reading such an interesting chronicle of the Wars of the Roses.' When a friend of ours was staying at Renishaw and Lord Grey came over to tea and in the course of conversation was asked by our friend if he had read a book which had just come out about the recent escape of a nun, he replied, 'Yes, I remember it very well—in Alsace, at the time of the Franco-Prussian War.' But that was very late for him; for, in fact, he had a great love of history—though not of the kitchen-sink variety, since he was more interested in the individual than the masses; but as a rule the latest date which roused his interest was that of the Dauphin, the son of Louis XVI, and he would say, 'I've often wondered what became of him?' He had read everything that had been published on the subject. At this point I must interject that his knowledge of history, for which he had a passion, was better than his geography. I remember his receiving a postcard of Taormina, which he confused with Tasmania, that being the name more familiar to him.

Another of the effects of his Jesuit education was that to him Latin was a living tongue, a medium of communication. Thus, when we were together on the governing body of the same grammar school and attended a meeting, he would pass to me a note written in Latin, and he always refused to believe that I could not answer him in the same language, or even read it with ease.

His appearance was remarkable and had you first seen him in a train you would have wondered who he could be, but would not have found an answer easy. He might have stepped out of a suit of armour, and it was easy to picture him looking out from under a raised vizor, so that it was not difficult to believe that he possessed a hereditary right to carry the Gold Spur at the Coronation. When he was interviewed by the reporter of a daily newspaper, who asked why he did not claim this right, he replied that he could not afford to go to London, whereupon the employees of the local bus proposed opening a subscription list to pay all his expenses at the Coronation, but this he refused. There must, however, have been few people to whom such an offer would have been made. He led a very simple life, but this may have been, and almost certainly was, from preference. If he were poor, he did not particularly show it, nor do I think that he felt it.

He seldom left his native village even for a night, or went away at all, except for rare festivities in other Catholic families which, as a young man, he had attended, and he had once spent a week in Venice. Then he would occasionally go to London, but only for the day, to preside over a meeting to abolish blood sports or to protect animals against scientists.

It was, however, thought that he was poor, and certainly the roof of his gate-house attracted the attention of people on the road passing above, and led one to form this opinion. There were enormous holes in it. But rich or poor, it did not worry him. His family had been rich and powerful in the thirteenth century and thereafter at intervals. The barony of Grey de Ruthyn, which had come to him through his mother, dated from 1328 and had eventually become merged in the dukedom of Kent, which died out in the eighteenth century, leaving behind it a great many ancient baronies and, as a monument to itself, the magnificent garden at Wrest, now demolished. Lancelot still retained some eighteenth-century characteristics, and I recall that, on the first day we met, as we were walking away together from the magistrates' court, he said to me—for I had on my hair a rather strong-smelling lotion—'I like your scent.' It will be remembered that scent was a common feature for men in eighteenth-century drawing-rooms.

The chief reason, I apprehend, that he chose to lead so simple a life was that he had a simple nature—or rather a nature both simple and complex. Indeed, he often reminded me of a character in a nineteenth-century Russian novel. There was, for example, a suggestion of Oblomov—though Oblomov would never have bothered to attend so many committee meetings. His local enthusiasm was very strong, and when he said 'Didn't you see it in the *Times?* he was always alluding, not to *The Times*, but to the hebdomadal *Derbyshire Times*. He seldom, as I have said, went to London. Indeed, he seemed only to gravitate in a latitude from Barlborough to Skegness and Lincoln, completely neglecting the longitude from London to Edinburgh which others followed. (To be taken over Lincoln Gaol was one of the treats he held out to his friends.) As for Skegness as a health resort, he was enthusiastic about it to such a degree that he had been known to take a house there for a fortnight in August.

In aesthetic matters his taste had remained under-developed. The quality of his surroundings meant, obviously, little to him, though he was much attached to them. He claimed to be fond of music and I remember him saying to me one day, 'Yes, I'm musical, dear heart'—this was one of his old-fashioned ways of speech—'I like listening to one of those Beethoven sympathies.'

However that may be, it can be conceded that the visual arts meant little to him.... He offered other treats besides Lincoln Gaol. For a long time, he had said: 'I've a friend who lives at Winter's Edge. He collects. You *must* come one day and see his collection.'

'What does he collect?' I enquired.

'Oh, the most wonderful things. You'll see,' he would reply. So, one day—and it proved to be one of the strangest days in my life—we set out for Winter's Edge, a colliery village about ten miles from Barlborough. The house, a square box, stood in the High Street; its owner turned out to be a grizzled old Negro doctor, a West Indian with a passion for East Indian objects, especially, apparently, if they had been made in Birmingham. Benares brass, rather than as one might have expected, Benin bronze, was the lodestar of his life. In those days, I must confess that to see a Negro doctor in a mining-village was a rare thing, for the Empire had not yet begun to invade us. As for the collection—and collection it undoubtedly was—that was rarer still. It would have been impossible to imagine. The spare hours of a long and busy life—he must have been seventy—had been spent in amassing over half a century this gleaming accumulation of trays and jugs and bowls and idols and ashtrays and temple fittings, and we had to sit among them, making polite conversation. Lancelot had quickly made friends with my sister. At first when he came to tea with us, he would arrive in a bowler hat, like an African head of state. It somehow conveyed the idea of a chieftain . . . One day I had gone out for a walk and had just reached the gate of the Renishaw drive, when Lancelot appeared, approaching it from the road. He was wearing a black cap instead of the familiar dome, from which I gathered that whatever he was going to do was of an informal nature, but—and this puzzled me—he was carrying what seemed to be an enormous bouquet of flowers, done up most carefully in cellophane. He said to me, 'Good evening. I am just going to leave this at the house for Edith; she said the other day that she liked them, and I was given this one. I wonder if you'd take it up for me, and then I can catch the next bus. It will be going in five minutes' time.'

I was just going to say, 'What lovely flowers!' when I looked again, and saw that what I had taken for red blossoms was really marks of blood on a pig's head, carefully done up in cellophane. 'You don't mind carrying it up for her, do you, dear heart?' he asked. It would have been churlish to say I objected, but, I reflected, what an odd gift to make to a poet. I said: 'Of course I'll take it,' and turning back, I shouldered my grisly burden, and Lancelot just caught his bus. But my adventures were not over. Unhappily, I had chosen a short cut through the Wilderness by which to return home, and climbing up a precipitous hill-side, I slipped and fell, still clutching my burden. I remained for some minutes unable to get up, cheek by jowl, the pig's eye gazing into mine with silent reproof.

If Lancelot's tastes in food, then, were rather medieval, nevertheless when you went to tea with him, it was always lavish. There would always be a plentiful supply of scones, sandwiches, cakes both large and small, disposed on tiered trays. There would be no experiments. There was, I apprehend, an element of danger in his experiments. And I like to remember his saying to me one day: 'I love oysters, don't you? My housekeeper always gets them at the Shambles at Sheffield. They're very good—and so cheap.' The Shambles is a market at Sheffield worthy of this name, only lately rebuilt.

. . . Lancelot was interested in medicine and fond of simple remedies which he would discover in neighbouring chemists' shops. But I doubt whether, for all his pharmaceutical array, he could have coped with the results of such oyster-eating.

Lancelot's voice was clear and loud. He spoke as one quite sure of himself. When you went to see him, you could tell, by the volume of barking coming nearer, whether he was approaching the door himself or whether his maid would open it. If it was himself, the barking was always louder, and he would be carrying one dog in one arm and somehow restraining another dog with the other arm. It was like a conjuring trick, as it seemed obvious that one of them was bound to escape, but it never did. His voice sounded loud above the barking, reiterating that two such angels (but the angels were striving and eager for the first bite), would never really hurt anyone. . . .

I remember his telling me of how, once, when he had opened a garden-fête for charity at Barlborough, after his speech was over, he asked one of the Committee who was on the platform whether his speech had been audible. He received the enthusiastic reply, 'Yes, they loved every word of it, and so they did at Clowne—some two miles away.' Incidentally, his voice was apt in speaking, to show a local northern inflection and intonation, albeit this was not to be wondered at, when you remembered that he had practically never left his native village—partly, of course, because he had never felt the urge, and partly, as I have said, because of his devotion to his dogs. When he came to Renishaw for tea, he would leave the dogs behind him, out of respect for our cats, but otherwise they were always with him, and the chief reason that he had not taken his seat in the House of Lords was that he would not be able to take them with him, for if they saw him in his robes, there was no knowing into what furies they might not be transported.

Lord Grey was very much liked in the village, and people would come to consult him at all hours about their affairs.

I recall a pleasant incident at the Renishaw Court. Lord Grey was in the chair, and a very loquacious and rambling old woman was giving evidence. At one point, she complained, 'I tried to tell the whole story to the police, but they wouldn't listen,' whereupon Lord Grey lent forward and said to the witness, 'That's all right, my dear. You come up one afternoon and tell *me* all about it. I'll listen, I promise.' I forgot to ask him what happened, but I am sure that she went up and had the time of her life, talking herself out.... In consequence of such an offer as this, people would turn up at all hours to ask his advice.

One night at about twelve, he thought he heard a noise downstairs, and going down to the drawing-room, he turned on the light, and then he saw a young man carrying a torch. Lancelot, thinking he might have come to consult him, had said, almost automatically, as he turned on the light, 'Good evening! What can I do for you?' Upon which the prospective burglar—for such he was—(if he had succeeded in his plan, I could not help reflecting that he would have been sadly disillusioned with his haul, unless he were collecting for some small auction of china objects of unimaginable use with 'A present from Skegness' or 'A gift from Blackpool', written on them)—the prospective burglar, I was saying, scrambled up the wall and out of a high window. He got away, but was found a day or two later, and appeared in court at Renishaw. There he explained that he had been spoken to with such kindess that he had been unable to go on with the burglary or to attack Lord Grey, and had abandoned the whole matter.

When Lancelot was very ill with pneumonia, his house-keeper was also very ill and there was nobody to see to him in the night if he wanted anything: whereupon the fathers of the village deputed a sixteen-year-old girl to sleep on a couch at the end of his bed, but at right-angles. This was quite a new application of the *droit de seigneur*.

Lancelot's whole world consisted mainly of local events. He showed a great knowledge and grasp of the life and customs of the village of Barlborough and the neighbourhood generally. He was invited to all the weddings and funerals, and I remember him telling me of one wedding reception he had attended in a village near by, where the bridegroom was a young butcher. His mother-in-law, a substantially-built person, had consumed a great deal of drink under the strain of emotion. The family had first experimented with the effects of taking off her shoes and stockings and squirting soda-water from a siphon on her naked feet, then of blowing on them (shades of T. S. Eliot's 'Mrs Porter and her Daughter'), but her condition had not improved, until finally she lost consciousness and passed out and the butcher had been obliged to carry her upstairs on his shoulder. Then he threw her down on a bed, saying as he did so, 'Luckily I'm used to heaving the sides of great beasts.'

Every fine day Lancelot would go for the same walk between Barlborough and Clowne—if it was not too hot: he hated hot weather—for it was almost flat, and paved, and so easy to walk, even with the dogs playing round his feet. It was a ceremonial walk—known as 'taking the dogs for a walk' and for it he would wear his bowler hat, and he could be heard a long way off booming greetings to friends and acquaintances. . . . When you went up to see him, he would no sooner be in than out again, for he would say at once, 'You don't mind, do you, if we go to see someone?' and you found yourself engaged in visiting the sick, afflicted and crippled, for it was his belief that nothing did so much good as suddenly to introduce a complete stranger into their rooms.

Lancelot was very superstitious—or psychic, if you prefer it. On several occasions he saw apparitions and I remember he used to see wraith-like presences floating above the churchyard which was just across the road from his house. His own house was haunted, he would tell me, and his mother had seen the ghost several times. Its chief object was to warn the household of the death of any member of the family, and his mother had seen it the night his father had died suddenly. His house was plainly very ancient, but it was impossible to tell how old it was or what panelling might be hidden under the ordinary wallpaper. There were several narrow steep staircases and most of the rooms led into one another.

I remember Lancelot telling me that during the war a Canadian soldier had been found guilty of murder in England. Lancelot had never seen him but said that night after night the soldier kept on bothering him to have a mass said for him. Eventually he did this and the nuisance stopped.

His divining powers seemed to work best with bridges. There was one occasion at Eckington when the Great Central Railway, as it was then called, refused to stop a train for him. He was going up to London for the day to preside over one of the Societies for the Prevention of Cruelty to Animals of which he was president. He said to me, 'You'll see, the train will have to stop,' and sure enough the bridge broke down just outside Ecklington. The train was stopped in time. . . . When I went first to Montegufoni after the war, he warned me, 'Be careful of bridges, most careful.' After a night-journey, I looked out in the morning and saw that we were just crossing a wooden bridge which seemed most dangerous. All the bridges between Bologna and Florence were similarly perilous, for all of them had been destroyed and makeshift ones had been run up temporarily in their place.

The last time I saw Lancelot was on a summer evening in 1963. The weather had suddenly turned fine for a few minutes and there was a burst of sunshine. In this apotheosis he suddenly arrived in a motor driven by a friend. I had been away for nearly a year and had not seen him. In the meantime he had been ill and his appearance had altered. He had grown much thinner and his high colour had gone. The gothic lines in his face had asserted themselves. He would not come into the garden, as he complained of the heat—he must have been the only man in England that year to do so—but came to the library and talked. He could only stay a few minutes, he asserted, and said he was much better. That was the last time I saw him. About two months later he died on the eve of his eightieth birthday. But I can never traverse the stretch of flat road from Barlborough to Clowne without expecting to see him, his bowler hat looming up suddenly out of the fog that so often envelops that part of the world, and I only wish it could be so.

London 1943

For H.L.D.

FOR the last four years, London, especially during autumn and winter nights, has seemed to many of its citizens a place they had never seen before. Yet to others it may have revived memories of a London of which they have read; of London in the age of Elizabeth, or at times during the seventeenth and eighteenth centuries. In the words of Dekker, as 'soone as ever the sunne was gon out of sight . . . darkness like a thief out of hedge crept upon the earth', and 'the Banckrupt, the Fellon and all that owed any money, and for feare of arrests, or Justices Warrants had like so many snayls kept their houses over their heads all the day before, began now to creep out of their shels, to stalke up and downe the streets as uprightly . . . as if they meant to nock against the starres with the crownes of their heads. . . . The serving-man dare walke with his wench: the Private Punke (otherwise called one that boords in London) who like a Pigeon sits billing all day within doores, and feares to steppe over the threshold, does then walke the round till midnight, after she hath been swaggering amongst pottle-pots and vintner bags.'

During all the war period this great city has been at night a secret, apparently deserted, hive of darkened streets, of glimmering torches that dare not give so much light as Dekker's candle; of corners where footpads, too brutish to be conscious of their ancient ancestry, lurk once more, and where the prostitutes are bolder again in the pursuit of their dreary trade, jostling, laughing, talking loudly in broken English.

Looked back on, it seems that the nights have always been dark and cold, with a soaking, all-pervading drizzle. People hurry down the streets as if they were haunted. They appear with a startling suddenness out of the darkness, and are swallowed up again by it as swiftly. Shapes are discerned for an instant, but not faces, unless a passer-by strikes a match for his cigarette. Even the searchlights, those glittering instruments that continually probe the darkness of the sky, reveal to us nothing; great domes in the sky, certainly, and golden roads of light, changing, shifting patterns, effected with diagonal lines that afford strange revelations of perspective, making us realise the immense distances above us in the heavens, so great as to have no distance; but nothing here, nothing down here below, on our own creeping level, as we scurry along, borne on a keen wind. The last buses, with their small blue lights, are starting—they seem always to be starting—and a perpetual bleating sounds from the pavements and the black doorways of apartment houses and hotels: Taxi! Taxi! Taxi! But not a single cab answers the call; each one approaching is watched by anxious groups on each side of the road; but it speeds on through the mud, unheeding. Sometimes groups of men and women in uniform, wardens or members of the A.F.S., stand in the dark gulfs that are the openings to houses, watching the interminable calculations of the searchlights, thinking of the end of their term of duty, wondering perhaps when the war will finish, and what London will be like in the years that follow.

Even as I write, London is changing again; a different sort of city, very confident of victory, has been brought into being before our eyes. Its people walk with a new ease and swagger. Many buildings have gone—yet this could be no city but London. . . . And it is at least appropriate that the background should vary, for the essence of London is change, and, in turning my half-century, I have seen and can remember at least five Londons. . . .

The earliest was the London of the late nineties, when I

was a small boy; a London of vast railway stations for ever full of golden fog; a London to which the trains that came were lit by little yellow gas-flames flowering like *immortelles* beneath an inverted and steamy glass bowl. Outside, the carriages, the omnibuses, the hansoms, waited in line: but the 'growler', or four-wheeler, with the inevitable smell of oats and beer and leather within its mouldy interior, was the chief method of conveyance. First came the drive through the endless mean streets, and then the West End, the old Regent Street, lying in front of us, gas-lit, with the curve of some sickle-bay in a Greek island. . . . At night there was little traffic, the clop-clop of an occasional cab, the bells of a hansom and the forlorn and desultory whistling that served as its enticement. The daylight, when—and if—it came, revealed a city of yellow plaster houses, continually repainted, a modest city of crumbling caryatids and vases—though always, of course, there existed as a background and a culmination the splendid exteriors of Wren's churches, to show to what heights of genius, and even of magnificence, the English art of good manners and the plain statement of humane facts could rise. It showed, too, a city of paint and varnish and of glitter, transient in its impeccable finish. The brief winter sun flecked its red-gold on every kind of shining object, brass plates, plate-glass windows, elegant balconies, newly painted and varnished doors, and upon the royal coats of arms, and supporting lions and unicorns that embellished certain favoured shops, and drew out of them, though in a subdued and most respectable manner, a thousand muted sparkles. In spite of the high lights, there was no ostentation. The top-hats of the wealthy and of the hansom-cab drivers, with their polish and dark shining glitter, might well have stood for the symbol of this world now perished; but the clothes of the women, rich and poor alike, were complicated, fussy, designed for richness rather than for beauty or for smartness; fashions that remained the costume of Cockneys on gala days even until the outbreak of the present war. This London that I first remember was the capital of the world, whither the Thames bore its tribute of the spices of the East; delicacies responsible for as many wars as, since that time, has been the gold of South Africa—also conveyed here regularly, and over which hostilities were even then about to break out. Cattle from South America, leather from Russia, endless objects from China, wheat from America and Canada, all were brought hither, while some of the cargoes, no doubt, were of the most unexpected and almost fabulous character— humming-birds from the West Indies, hundred-year-old eggs from China for the colony in Limehouse, sea-shells from the coastline of Arabia, fruit from South Africa, turtles for Lord Mayors' banquets brought from the South Sea Islands or the islands of the West Indies. And the great fortunes that resulted from the commerce in these and other outlandish goods were to be lavished on such temporary, homely things as paint and varnish in a city so dark and foggy that one could seldom see the effect which they were attempting; thus the little sparkle that could be obtained ranked as a moral, rather than a material aim.

The next London I knew was the city of stilted Edwardian baroque, when the full tide of riches and materialism was sweeping over Victorian London, submerging it. The old Nash houses of Park Lane, so modest in their luxury, many of them rising to no more than two storeys, country villas set down on the most expensive sites in the world, were making way for riotous excesses, for flights in the Chinese Gothic manner, and for fantasies in the Hindu and Arabian styles; the capital of England was becoming a cosmopolitan city. Everywhere you looked the stucco houses were beginning to be torn down, and the monotonous, swollen palaces of commerce and of the newly created bureaucracy were replacing them. Only the lodging-houses and the slums remained the same. London, formerly, in the last century, renowned for its dullness and decorum, was now the pleasure capital of the world, and for the first time conscious of its mission. Triumphal roads, arches, stone balustrades, had been constructed. Blore's old plaster front of Buckingham Palace, chocolate brown, and with the statues of Britannia and the Lions decorating its roofline, was soon to be hacked down, and a rather mean and featureless Portland-stone façade, a kind of gigantic prophecy of prefabrication, was to be erected in its place. Portland stone constituted an ideal, to be worshipped rather than used. This was now a city built for processions, called into being to challenge the Rome of the Emperors; these great streets were built for visiting monarchs and for semi-captive princes to ride down, potentates who must be cheered enough, but not too much, on their way to Guildhall banquets. The Guildhall itself, and those who governed it, were still unique in their civic consequence, as when Dunbar had praised them five hundred years before:

> Thy famous Maire, by pryncely governaunce,
> With swerd of justice the rulith prudently.
> No Lord of Parys, Venyce, or Floraunce
> In dignytie or honoure goeth to hym nye.
> He is exampler, loode-ster, and guye.

At night, as during the day, the din of motors, of lorries thundering along the roads, was overwhelming. In the daytime, horse traffic had almost disappeared, except for the vans of a few obsolete, obstinate tradesmen, yet clinging to old ways and deathlessly determined to block the traffic; though at night the slow, clumsy market carts, with the carter asleep, still lumbered along Piccadilly. But by 1912 there were not more than a hundred hansoms left; one of them was the only three-wheeled cab in London. In addition to the two enormous wheels of the ordinary hansom, it boasted a small third wheel tucked underneath it, the purpose of which remained obscure. This cab was owned, and had been invented, by its driver, who wore a black bowler hat and a black beard. He was a man of marked originality, and a delightful and untiring conversationalist, and I used much to enjoy a talk with him after the opera, for normally he plied outside Covent Garden Theatre.

The hotels, previously discreet and even muffled places of comfort, given over still to muffins and stone hot-water bottles, had now blossomed out into cosmopolitan centres, created in a universal Louis-Quinze style, and each, despite the impossibility of telling it from the next, famous throughout the globe. The opera was the most celebrated in the world, mounted on an unusually extravagant and ugly scale, until Sir Thomas Beecham came to reform it. But even if the stage often left something—or rather less of something—to be desired, the audience was certainly the most astonishing spectacle in Europe. The glitter of the jewels and the general splendour could not be matched elsewhere, and the talk, during the music, was louder—if not more entertaining. (The story of the well-known hostess who cancelled her opera-box on the grounds that she had a sore throat, belongs to this period, though it is said to have occurred in later years.) Indeed Edwardian London rivalled for gaiety that of Elizabeth I or Charles II.

Nevertheless, in this genial Edwardian climate, the arts too were beginning to be respected, and there were among the rich some who had begun on occasion to wonder whether the clever were not more amusing than the dull. They would perhaps experiment, invite one or two of them to their houses. . . . Indeed a ferment was to be felt in the art world. Shaw's plays were beginning to be popular; Augustus John's vast and impressive pictures of gypsies squinting in their camps were attracting much attention, and, finally, Russia, represented by Diaghilev and his band of painters and dancers and musicians, had taken artistic London captive with a genius for music, dancing and stage spectacle new to Western Europe. Russian ideas now influenced fashion and spread even to house decoration. The ballet *Scheherazade* alone was responsible for innumerable lampshades and cushions that blazed in barred and striped splendour from the shop windows; and a more exotic style began to banish the drawing-room wall-papers trellised with roses and water-lilies, and the early Edwardian wood-panelling, that had seemed created as a background for long cigars, or perhaps even fashioned out of the fabric of their boxes. For the rest, in the warm long summer evenings, dance music prospered in the golden air of the squares, and striped awnings rose like mushrooms in the night to shelter the international herds of the rich. For more rich people congregated here than anywhere in the globe; and more poor—but the poor now had their diversions, mammoth football matches and cricket matches, and newspapers which, on Sunday, served up at great length every species of moral delinquency in order to shock the intense and abiding sense of respectability and responsibility, dwelling still in the hearts of the majority of the citizens of London.

This glittering city of lights ended on August 4th, 1914, and for the next four years a different London, a London in transition, came into being. . . . Now it had become a place devoted to officers and to men on leave. We were perpetually surprised at the way in which this darkened city, ever bleeding from the immense losses in process of being suffered just across the water, kept up its spirits. Lights were low, and bombs—though few and feeble compared with the bombs that fall on cities today—were yet sufficient in number and strength to be intimidating; but the cheerfulness was maintained, even when there was no manifest reason for it. Indeed, the First World War came in and went out in a blaze of popularity. I saw the vast crowds cheering it in front of the Palace in August 1914; I saw them dance it out in every paved square and open space on the night of November 11th, 1918.

Within a few years of the Armistice, one London the more had come into being—a new city which largely depended on the ruin of the old. The clouds of dust, rising from street and square, now added the same peculiar glory to London sunsets that the volcanic dust from the erupting mountain of Krakatoa was previously said to have produced. The age of destruction, which had originated in 1914, was continuing. Concrete was beginning to replace Portland stone; and the country itself, within a radius of thirty miles, was becoming part of London. A vast new economic class had been called into being, and the individual members of it were being housed in the red bungalows and villas on the city's edge. There was a new tendency to extravagance in life and morals, and the acts of a few rich young people, who, endowed with an idiot persistence, set themselves to enjoying life in their own manner—culminating in the celebrated exploit when they, literally, 'set the Thames on fire'—attracted more attention than the steady conduct of the mass of reputable citizens. But the mass of reputable citizens loved, nevertheless, to read of these antics in the papers.

The ferment in the arts continued, but there was never quite the same feeling as had existed in the former decade, that we stood at the edge of a great art revival. The fact that the stupid had been once again proved right—for they had been the only people to foretell the war—had set a further premium on general stupidity. It became the rage. . . . All the same, in spite of the complacency, in spite of the smugness, in spite of the vulgarity, it was an epoch of hope and accomplishment. People were happy. . . . But at the end of the pleasure-loving twenties, a difference was to be sensed in the air, a certain imponderable dullness, typified by the new fashion in house decoration; there was, it seemed, a rush for the vacuum, for negation, for nothingness, for beige and cinders and ashes; for white, and more white, and white on white, and near-white.

Now came the desolate London of the thirties, a disconsolate and apprehensive city; the City of the Slump, when all wondered what lay behind the curtain—for everyone could feel that it was on the point of rising. An intense and dreary earnestness blighted the arts. The new buildings were less vulgar but more boring. There must be no trimmings. Life was to be a matter of wrestling with facts in a continual struggle, and economics began to take the place of religion.

(Soon it would be impossible to distinguish the speeches of an archbishop from those of Lord Keynes.) Wren and the great builders had not, it was felt, looked life in the face, or come to grips with it. A wave of spiritual desolation engulfed literature, architecture and painting, and the voice of Lord Elton began to be heard in the land. I am not trying to say that the painters were not in themselves good, but a nightmare brooded behind their minds, and poetry—leaving even the marvellous world of nightmare aside—became acrostical, argumentative, a matter of addition and subtraction plus moral fervour. But artists are always right, always initiate, always inspired ahead by the years to come. . . . Outside, apart from the looks on the faces, which had indeed altered, the life of the West End remained much the same, except that hotels were fuller, the food in them richer and worse, the motor-cars more numerous. And when a reigning monarch—so much rarer a figurehead now than in the London I have previously described—came to visit us, he was still received in a style with which no other place could vie. . . . At night, though, a difference was to be detected. There were lights, neon lights and electric signs. The news, nearly always bad, wound itself in letters of fire round the squalid cornices of large Victorian buildings, yet, in spite of the greater illumination, the life of the streets had grown less vivid, partly, perhaps, because of the various purity campaigns, fiercely supported by the police, and partly because the suburbs offered the same form and quality of entertainment. The night was dull.

The London that followed was the darkened, sublunar London that we know today, and that I have attempted to describe at the beginning of this essay. Yet, as I have said, this war-time London itself has varied widely enough. . . . Compare, for example, the city of dropping bombs in September 1940 with that of 1943. Both are alike only in their darkness. On the second night of the 'blitz' I walked from Charles Street, Berkeley Square, to my home in Chelsea. It took me half an hour, and I passed hardly anyone on the way except

constables on duty, in steel helmets. There was no traffic; a
few buses, dark, black and deserted, drawn up in small lines
at the sides of the roads. The noise then came from falling
bombs, not from our gun-fire, for, in those times, we had
few guns with which to fire, few aircraft with which to give
battle. That kind of night has gone; only the black-out
persists. . . . Now, as I write, the long summer evenings are
beginning, and we are no longer confined to the primitive
darkness of the Stone Age. The streets, during the long
twilight, are crowded with soldiers of every nationality, French
and Dutch, Greek and Polish, American and Norwegian. Some
talk gaily, others are musing, thinking perhaps of the vast
endless wheatfields of Canada or the States, that roll their
golden waves over a whole continent, covering it with the
sign of the sun; others are remembering sadly the tobacco-
stained air of the cafés of provincial towns in France, the quiet
talks and the games of chess, or the inns, where workmen sit
outside under a trellised vine, above a river, and drink coarse
red wine. Others, again, recollect scenes in Poland and
Bohemia, pictures that suddenly flash into their minds, memories of their families, a chanting in a church, a bear trundling
out of a wood into the snow.

In the day-time the city blazes with life, in spite of the
ruined buildings, now tidied up and finished off like newly
made graves. The flat lawns of water, installed where once
were the basements of houses, reflect the light, and people—
because of the deadness of the winter nights—cram into these
hours of summer daylight an unimaginable pressure of life.
The parks, too, trampled and without any railings, are fuller
than in peace-time. Airmen, sailors, soldiers are lying and
sitting on the grass, sunning themselves, and in some parks,
where formerly duels were fought, groups of sturdy young
Americans are playing baseball. The streets round Piccadilly
teem with men in uniform, especially Americans. Everything
is very bright, flamboyant and sure of itself. And the spring
of 1943 provided an unequalled setting for this gaiety; it

favoured the Americans, who must have been granted almost
as many hours of sunshine here as they would have enjoyed at
home. Flawless day followed flawless day, alike in its golden
rind, until finally, in April, the whole city burst into flower;
apple and cherry blossom, prunus and peach and lilac, in a
thousand delicate, egg-shell varieties. The suburban gardens,
the gardens of Hampstead and Chiswick, and such outlying
districts, became comparable to tropical jungles. You could
scarcely see the walls dividing them. The new shrubs introduced into common use some twenty years ago—and every
Londoner is a gardener—had now grown up. Never had there
been such a profusion of blossom. Even in China, even in
Central America, with its jacaranda and coral and flamboyant
trees, even in Spain, during the spring, when in the orchards
of Andalusia, almond, peach and orange burst simultaneously
into bloom, never have I beheld a scene which suggested an
equal force of flowering.

It was such weather as caused you to look out of window
every instant, and called on you to walk whenever you got the
chance. . . . I used every day in those weeks to go by the Green
Park, and thence into St James's Street, making my way there
by means of what had formerly been a dark, narrow passage,
pressed between high walls of old and grimy yellow brick
but was now open to air and sky. On one side, below a wall
a foot high, I passed every time, a floor of white marble, with
an inlaid circular pattern, in the antique manner, of porphyry
and serpentine; a floor now identical in appearance with those
from which originally it had been copied a hundred years
before, those pavements that have been uncovered by archae-
ologists in the Roman Forum, or in the Golden House of
Nero. Thus one night of modern high explosive can be seen
to have produced the same effect as the rolling past of two
millenniums, including numberless incursions of old-fashioned
barbarians, and numberless outbreaks of old-fashioned wars.
. . . But what imparted to this floor for me a particular interest
arose, I deduce, from my egotism: this was the hall floor of a

house in which I had often dined; it was here, standing on
these designs in inlaid marble, that the butler and footman had
waited deferentially to take the top-hats and coats of the guests.
On the staircase above had stood the majordomo after dinner,
posted there to call out the names of those who were arriving
for the ball; names that he called portentously, as though
trying to evoke an echo out of a tomb. The rooms that lay
beyond were, when I knew them, always full of people, gay
with flowers and pictures, and with tapestries that seemed
from their colour to have been fashioned from rose petals. . . .
When next I see the floor of a villa uncovered in some meadow
or by the classic sea I shall be able to picture better than before
the life of which it is the surviving token. And the smaller
floors, those wooden miles of flooring that have gone, completely vanished; they meant as much, and are no less our gage
that London shall be rebuilt, and yet remain her own self,
only more splendid.

Of all the cities in the world, the future calls upon London,
when the hour strikes, to rise from her ashes with a magnificence transcending even her own tradition in that respect.
For, indeed, ashes are nothing new to her; like the Phoenix,
she soared up from them once before, in a splendour born
from flames. This historic city, already of 'high renown' in
the Middle Ages, bore in it, even then, the traces of a legendary
past and the seed of a no less fabulous future. Moreover, it
was the prototype in Europe of the great modern cosmopolitan
centres. As early as the first years of the Hanoverian dynasty.
it possessed—apart from Naples—the largest population of any
Western city, and by the middle of the eighteenth century
it had come to contain its enclaves of Chinese, French, Indians,
Italians. And this fact, more than any other, illustrates the
nature of London. As with Imperial Rome before her, the
very character of the place is complex in its essence, varied and
variable. And we must, therefore, be most careful not to
rebuild it in a way that will restrict it to one particular facet
of its genius.

London 1943

London, then, is not one city, but a noble group of cities, united by the waters of a river—the Thames, that tranquil and seemly river which, with its dark, quiet flowing, has made our capital one of the world's treasures.

Above all ryvers thy Ryver hath renowne

wrote Dunbar, for the importance of the Thames was recognised from the first moment that London began to flower, and, instead of trying to hide it, we should undoubtedly strive continually to lay emphasis upon it. It is the Thames that quickens London every day with a breath of sea-air, and the Thames through which the blood of the Five Continents beats. These unsensational waters, with their typical lack of glitter, with their effects of beauty dependent upon surrounding mists and darkness, and a sense of purpose, are yet more important than any of the great historic rivers of the world. The Thames is, indeed, the one permanent feature of a shifting scene, for London changes with each decade. It was always a lavish, always a spendthrift city, tearing itself down and building itself up, apparently with no purpose but commerce and a love of change. We Londoners have destroyed, or allowed to be destroyed, even in the last two decades, far more of our historic heritage and architectural wonders—take the great squares of the West End alone—than the Germans could ruin in several years of war. During each raid that I experienced in London I was able to thank Heaven that we had been permitted to enjoy the sensation of destroying these things ourselves, and that if, for example, the Germans were blowing up the present Regent Street, at least the damage to the arts would be negligible. Nor must we forget that the clearing process effected by the German planes has, esthetically, its good aspect. If it has destroyed little of military value, it has rid many of the classical churches of their hideous Victorian coloured-glass windows, which defaced entirely the interiors of some of them. Similarly, in certain instances, the glass roofs of buildings have been injured, and we can see how unsuitable they were and are. Those condensers and preservers of fog and darkness are no longer apropos. Time, moreover, heals the wounds of a great city very quickly, and, for example, many who knew Paris intimately would be amazed if they realised how much of it perished in the Siege and the Commune, how much has been patched, mended and renewed. The unforgivable scars in that city, the boulevards and the vulgarisation, were the work of the inhabitants themselves; Haussmann's wholesale reconstruction, regardless of tradition, made Paris hard and mean and featureless, and long ago, moreover, its great arcaded alleys had become the centre of the world's traffic congestion; which nullified their whole purpose.

What sort of city, then, are we to build to make a capital worthy of the people of London? (. . . I do not intend to write about London here from the angle of hygienic housing, but from the esthetic point of view, for bad housing will no longer be tolerated. Moreover, one cannot live in one's bath; we must have a perspective outside it.) . . . First, let me offer a word of advice.

Never trust architects; they are the most untrustworthy of artists, and have now become entangled with interior decoration and the various stages of fashions. Some would like to make the City of London into a garden suburb; others, under the spell of a tardy but grandiose Edwardian ideal, into the sort of thing we have lately seen at the Royal Academy; others want a cement hive for busy bees, a Middle Western city or mid-European, a concrete cobweb of flat-faced, flat-roofed houses. But we must avoid constructing a city in which each house resembles an airplane. There is no need for it, any more than there was a need, in the nineties of the last century, to build a city in which every house resembled a bicycle. The airplane is only a method of conveyance. We want none of these schemes, no excesses, old or new. . . . What we want is a new *London*, not just a new city.

Therefore the characteristics of the place, inherent in the

nature of the various districts and its inhabitants, must not be
denied. . . . London is, and must continue to be, a conglomer-
ate city, what in botanical terms is called a composite. We must
uphold the ancient—what little of it remains—as much as
build another London. Modelling our new capital we must
yet take as a model the old. Above all, we must remember
the classical tradition, the hundred spires and shell-like
turrets of Wren and Hawksmoor, so dignified and beautiful,
and so unlike any other system of architecture in the world;
a London that could only be London, austere and solid and
reasonable, for all its imagination. We must never again
haggle for years over the rebuilding of a bridge, but build with
certainty, create bridges that are a hundred times more lovely
and more effective than those that stand today.

Let us examine the proposed semi-Edwardian scheme, for it
has the greatest popular support since it entails the spending
of the most public—by which is meant private—money. We
saw plans and models of gardens and fountains and arcades
built with arches too wide apart to give us shelter from the
delights of our climate. . . . Fortunately, London is London;
even when we abolish a great part of the fog by abandoning
the use of coal fires, it—thank God—will still be a lovely and
a foggy city. . . . I imagine that, when the first Romans or the
first Britons came to the site of this great metropolis, what
they beheld on the marsh each side of the river banks was—
a London fog. That, too, is what our most remote descendants
will see.

It is a special and a very lovely robe of pearly smoke and
mist in which our capital thus arrays herself. It possesses every
attribute of poetry, and has been lauded, in their various
mediums, by artists as dissimilar as Dickens and Whistler. It
may not be easy to breathe, but it is the native atmosphere, and
so there can be no purpose in introducing into it those vistas
created for sunlight in Florence, Paris or New York. London
should—and always will—be a Gothic city, true to its soil, a
place of surprises, in which you come upon things suddenly,

and not a town in which you can see at great distances. In Rome the superb twin colonnades of St Peter's enclose, above its fountains, stretching high over domes and towers, a vast arena of blue sky, piled with Roman clouds, like the trophies of conquered nations; but here, in London, we should not, if we are wise, plan to see too much of the sky, or it will fall on us in rain and snow and soot. We need arcades, certainly; but to protect, and not to expose, us. If you open up a vista of St Paul's, what you will see will not be St Paul's, but more fog, and, perhaps, a policeman looming up out of it from near an island. . . . The people of Bologna created, against the rain and cold of their winter, a special city of narrow arcaded streets, giving shelter. We must, similarly and obversely, be true to the tremendous fogs that have been granted to us as a birthright. We must remember that both Inigo Jones and Wren, though it was then a so much smaller city, understood London. They gave it those precise towers and spires round which London fogs wreathe themselves with a peculiar splendour, suddenly releasing, as it were, the vision of them, so that they are unexpected, magnificent. We must remember that Nash's stucco and Wren's Portland stone were the most admirably suited mediums for building in this atmosphere, for the first could be—and must be—continually repainted, and the second acquired, from being smoked, a perfect texture and colour. We must try to invent new building mediums with the same qualities. We must never seek to emulate other cities, but only to transcend our own. We must not, for example, embank our river (alas, it has already been done), hemming it in as if it were some paltry ditch, because continental cities have treated their rivers in this way. We must avoid making another and more heartless cosmopolis; a poorer edition of some South American city copied from Paris or Vienna. We must remember that the people of this city are a people full of heart—and that is what the teeming irregularities of London have always shown and represented.

The seasons may vary, and with them the aspects of

London; a fresh London may grow up and disappear, but the character of its inhabitants never changes. They are, indeed, the citizens of no mean city, and prove themselves worthy of it every day; royal in their politeness, ostentatious—even the poorest—in their generosity, unequalled in their courage, unsurpassed in their originality. In spite of the immense foreign influence brought to bear on London for so many centuries, the people are the very essence of the country. Rich and poor are alike in their courage, in the continuity of their conduct and in their determination. The rich accept countless inconveniences without a murmur, resolved to bear, without flinching, everything to which they are accustomed—bad food, little food, cold, walking in wet streets for miles, no servants, disagreeable servants—all because the war must be won. You can almost hear them repeating under their breath the public-school commandments: 'Do not let the side down, you can't do it, don't-yer-know.' The poor remain equally steadfast, working harder than ever, and taking little advantage of the position in which they now find themselves. Like those formerly more fortunate than themselves, they have little to which to look forward, but they are as resolute, unbeaten and unbeatable. And although the rich members of society may be more staid in demeanour, there is a feeling of irresponsible gaiety and *élan* about true Cockneys, as can be remarked during any Bank Holiday on Hampstead Heath. City-bred, they have the country-man's humour, identical, sharpened only by an additional tolerance and quickness. An immense love of liberty, a feeling for the best of life, inspires them. In their humour there is a sort of wise gravity that no other people knows, a consciousness, too, of the sacred idiosyncrasy of every human being that is typically English.

In this connection, I often recall an occasion before the war, when I heard a Covent Garden porter, as the crowd was coming out of the opera, hail a taxi in the street for an elegant young man in white waistcoat and top-hat, and open the door for him with the words 'In with you, Norman!' ... Or, again, I think of the time when I passed some navvies in the now destroyed Lansdowne Passage. One of them dropped a paving stone as I passed, with a tremendous crash, and, noticing that I jumped at the noise, remarked—with a true observation of character, for he plainly deduced that I was not a devotee of night life, but an artist, possessed of a delicate nervous system—'There, sir! . . . That's the worst of them night-clubs!' . . .

What a mistake Hitler made to provoke these people, the inhabitants of this city, let alone of Great Britain and of the Empire! . . . How is it possible not to love Londoners, with their understanding of life, their want of envy?

The Magnasco Society

[UNFINISHED]

My brother and I had been two of the founder members of the Magnasco Society. My brother—it may be remembered —had, some ten years before this, at the age of twenty-one, published *Southern Baroque Art*, a book which had done much to focus interest again on the then almost forgotten painters of the Italian seventeenth and eighteenth centuries. The name 'Magnasco' had been chosen by the Committee because the bearer of it was at the time one of the least considered of the artists of that period, albeit in his own time a famous artist of the Genoese School. This choice of his name may be thought rather captious, for during the time of his great popularity, he was known universally by the nickname of Il Lissandrino. Or should one say the pet-prolongation of his Christian name, Alessandro?

Magnasco's influence continued to be felt after his death, since his work had influenced Giambattista Tiepolo. He himself showed the influence—though, of course, at several removes—of El Greco. Against a murky sky, lit solely by a patch of vivid blue, his elongated figures twisted round a crucifix still call to mind the Cretan master, while his romantic landscapes, with equivocal forms lolling in or strolling through them, sometimes contain a prophetic hint of a very different master, Fragonard. He resembled his contemporaries, such as Luca Giordano, only in being compelled at times by want of money to copy old masters, which were easily mistaken for the original paintings, though it is hard to see how he could

159

divest himself of his own very particular and personal style in order to paint with the glow of a Titian or the dusky but effulgent convolutions of Tintoretto.

The object which the Magnasco Society proposed for itself was to restore Italian seventeenth- and eighteenth-century Italian painting to the position which it formerly occupied in the esteem of western man, before the gradual setting-up of new standards in aesthetics—the vogue and publicity of Egyptian and Chinese art, and of Mexican, with its peripheral sub-species—had ousted it from its proper place. In the catalogue of the first exhibition of the Society we find its aim well defined:

> The Exhibition of seventeenth and eighteenth century painting held in Florence* in 1922 was one of the most important artistic events of recent years, and it directed the attention of art-loving Europe to a period which, in this country at least, has suffered during the last seventy years from a most unmerited neglect. This neglect is especially deplorable since the schools now under review are exceptionally well represented in this country.

Many of the painters of this period, such as the Caraccis, Guido Reni, Carlo Dolci, Salvator Rosa, Solimena, Luca Giordano, Bernardo Cavallino, Francesco di Mura, Matteo Preti, and Magnasco himself had for a time been almost forgotten, in spite of the innumerable large and often start-lingly original works still in the places of honour in which they had been placed at the time they were painted. Thus the vast ceiling of the Escorial Chapel and that of the pro-cathedral in Valletta, both by the hand of Matteo Preti, very different though they may be from the near-Ribera pictures of bearded and hairy saints. Then, typical of its period, is the great picture 'Belisarius', which I was fortunate enough to see and to buy at Christie's; it is an enormous picture, some twenty

* The Pitti Palace.

feet high, representing Belisarius stripped of his honours and blinded by order of the Emperor, begging in the streets of Rome: a quite apocryphal scene, but none the less splendid. This work had been presented to the first Lord Townsend, the English Minister in Berlin, when he left, by Frederick the Great, and on its superb baroque frame is the crowned eagle of Prussia. When it arrived in England it was hung in a room specially built for it, and named the Belisarius Chamber. Of this picture, however, I have written elsewhere.

Salvator was, of course, a man of genius; yet his painting, musical compositions and poetry scarcely conferred upon him as much fame as did his revolutionary politics and the fact that after Masaniello's revolt he was obliged, in order to be safe from arrest, to live with gypsies in a cave. In his epoch, painters do not seem to have been able to sublimate all their revolutionary fervour, as in later times Cézanne and Van Gogh were apparently able to do: they had, as well, to expend their energies in politics.

Generally speaking, then, it can be said that only the Venetians, by the brilliance of their renaissance in the seventeenth and eighteenth centuries, managed to escape oblivion; the Tiepolos, the Riccis, the Longhi, the Canalettos, Piazzetta, Pittoni, the Guardis, and others continued to retain, to a certain degree, their popularity. Apart from them, Caravaggio alone of his period was admitted to shine as an international star with his own lustre. Nevertheless, visitors to Italy and Spain had only to look round them in the churches and palaces to see that there were others.... But we wander away from the Magnasco Society.

Members of the Magnasco Society held an annual dinner-party in the summer of each year at the time of the exhibition. The dinner took place at the Savoy in a private room which was always decorated for the occasion with pictures of the period. Then, during the meal, there would be music—not strictly of the epoch, because very little Italian music of that time was known in England, before the B.B.C. had chosen to enliven our evenings with the music of Vivaldi. (I never remember hearing any composition of Salvator's played anywhere.) The music, then, had been selected because it was thought to belong in spirit to the time; Rossini's *Stabat Mater*, and various quartets of Mozart, for example . . . The food and wine were always delicious, being chosen on the advice of our fellow-member, the well-known gourmet and connoisseur, the late Richard Temple.

The warm human element which gave life to the Magnasco Society was supplied by Doctor Tancred Borenius, a Finnish friend of ours, who, in addition to being a recognised authority on European painting in general and Italian in particular, had filled several diplomatic and difficult posts for his native country since it had gained its freedom after the Russian Revolution. He was a man of the widest interests, and always interesting and amusing to talk to. When he was a boy of ten or eleven, living in St Petersburg, his father noticed that he took a more than usual interest in pictures, and thereafter, on every possible occasion, deposited him, with a packet of sandwiches, at the Hermitage when it opened, and called for him just before it shut. It was after this fashion that he added his great knowledge to his natural taste. He had written many books, the best known of them being *Italian Painting* and *Later Italian Painting* and *The Painters of Vicenza*. Some of his books were published when the author was in his early twenties.. . . Let me here give an example of his *expertise*. I happened to be in Paris, and by chance met Tancred, who was going round the galleries. He suggested that I should accompany him, and I eagerly accepted. At last we entered a gallery, and the proprietor hurried forward and said, 'Oh, Doctor Borenius, you're just the person I want to see. I've got a painting here on a panel, which I bought in Vienna, but I think it is Italian. I can't think who painted it.' He produced it, a panel about eighteen inches high and three feet wide. Tancred surveyed it for several minutes, and then said, 'If it is painted on a panel of pine, it is by Rubens, painted during the two years he spent in Italy as a young man.' It was painted on pine-wood, and the dealer rejoiced.

Tancred was a devoted adherent of lost causes. I apologise here for repeating a phrase that, in spite of its truth, is all too frequently repeated—of lost causes which always end by winning. Societies such as the White Rose of Finland at once appealed to his loyalty and claimed his interest. They could be sure of his enthusiastic support. After the Russian Revolution he and his wife settled in England. About his appearance there was something very northern, a quality almost cetacean. In the evening he always carried a gibus or opera hat, almost the only article of clothing which puts modern merchandise in touch with men's clothes; perhaps it was his devotion to lost causes which prompted him to cling to it, and certainly the sound of it when opened was very familiar.

During his last years, his mind was clouded with melancholy. He had devoted himself, heart and soul, to working for the Poles, and their fate at the end of their courageous and unsuccessful struggle made him overwhelmingly sad.

Another to whom the Magnasco Society was greatly indebted was Lord Gerald Wellesley, later Duke of Wellington. His enterprise and enthusiasm did much for us. For example, he obtained for one of our exhibitions, through the kindness of his brother, the fifth Duke, the loan of Giovanni Paolo Parini's 'A Fête in the Piazza di Spagna', a battle scene by Salvator Rosa, and Ribera's 'John the Baptist'. These paintings had been among those captured at the Battle of Vittoria in the carriage of Joseph Buonaparte and subsequently presented to the Iron Duke by King Ferdinand VII of Spain.

The reason why the Magnasco Society was able to achieve so admirably its ambitions rested chiefly, however, on the quality of its exhibitions, this in its turn being due to the number and quality of the pictures of our period in English collections: they had been judiciously bought and well chosen at the time. Thus in March and April, 1925, we were able to show, among others, Caravaggio's then newly-discovered

'Boy With a Lizard' from Lord Harcourt's collection; a fine Magnasco and a Pittoni lent by Sir Herbert Cook; a painting by Bernardo Strozzi from the National Gallery of Ireland, and a Bellotto lent by the Earl of Powis. Again in 1929, for the exhibition limited to the works of Canaletto, we were fortunate enough to be lent by King George V, some magnificent paintings from the Royal Collection which demonstrate the quality of this artist at his best more clearly than do any other of his pictures. These superb paintings had been bought from Joseph Smith, a famous collector and crypto-dealer, who filled the post of British Consul in Venice from 1740 to 1770 and, being on the spot in those most fruitful years, was able to induce painters to work for him. In addition to these transactions, King George III bought Smith's library from him.

One dinner of the Magnasco Society comes back to me from across the years with particular clarity. Who was there? Lord Gerald Wellesley in the chair; Tancred Borenius, of course, Harold Acton, Peter Lycett Green, David Horner, Colin Agnew, William Walton, my brother and myself. The late Lord Carisbrooke was the guest of honour, and made a well-worded and tactful speech. He was followed, to our delight, by Walter Sickert, another guest, who made a brilliant oration. In it he praised greatly the pictures round the room, a Ribera, a Domenico Tiepolo, a Sebastian Ricci, a Salvator, a Magnasco and many others. Afterwards, we found the subject of his speech difficult to define, albeit it contained a whole repertory of imitations from Sir Henry Irving down to Little Tich. I remember walking away from the Savoy to the river and along the Thames Embankment in the last moments of daylight on that rarest of all occasions, a fine summer evening in London, and noticing how the sky and water picked up the very translucent tints of the Venetian pictures we had just left—white, red, blue, and plum and peach and light green, in that glow that comes before darkness.

Moving House

───────◇───────

To move house after a lifetime is a harrowing and hair-raising experience. One of the many extraordinary things about it is the number of forgotten objects and events that are then salvaged, as it were, from the past; the manuscripts which had been lent and with which Time had walked away; the pictures which had been shelved, or rather floored. When I first took the house in Carlyle Square in the spring of 1920, most of the few objects I possessed went there by taxi. When finally the lease ended, it was necessary to have two large vans loading and unloading, shuttling to and fro between the house and my new flat in Kensington, and the operation of removing took not less than ten days, by which time I was so muddled that I nearly got removed myself. To make the process of dealing with material possessions easier for me, however, I suffered two burglaries at about this time. During the first, the burglars had been interrupted, and in their sudden flight had left on the floor a sackful of objects all ready to spirit away. After this, the house was naturally in disarray I remember that a representative of the press telephoned to me and revealed several fixed ideas, one of which was that I must have been giving a large party at the time of the burglary, whereas, in fact, I was ill in bed.

'Were you entertaining?' he enquired.

The hopelessness of trying to get any sense into his head led me to reply, 'I hope so. I have always tried to be.'

The next day he gave an account of my supposed party.

Among the pictures found was one by the first abstract painter in England, which had somehow been mislaid. There were books, too, everywhere, which threatened, and still threaten, to overwhelm the living person, and there was a debris of machines which I had never used and the working of which I could never understand—dictaphones, electrical adaptors, coils of wire and india rubber, and curious antiquated stoves.

There were objects which seemed far too heavy to be lifted, even by the numerous stalwart, aproned men who had turned up to carry out the job, and pieces of furniture so bulky that they appeared to have grown where they stood and would never pass through the small doorways and up and down the narrow, twisting stairs by which they must have entered the house forty years earlier. Nor had I realised before that smooth marble, exposed to heavy torrents of rain, becomes so slippery that it is almost impossible to handle. To move a large piece of marble statuary of the Goddess of Liberty from the minute garden at the back of the house required techniques used—and now forgotten—in building the Pyramids, and took about half a day. I had found an ideal position for this statue in my new flat: a lead roof, surrounded by distant trees, that lay outside the French window of my bedroom. Fortunately, at the very last moment, I discovered that not even a bowl of daffodil bulbs could be placed there without the permission of the landlord and, as I had left it too late to obtain this, the goddess had to make the long journey to Renishaw and now stands in a cold stone passage, waiting for a position to be found for her in the garden there, which had already some years earlier given shelter to another refugee. I had come home from a sojourn abroad to find that a friend of mine had given me Sir Hamo Thorneycroft's Muse of Fame, removed by the authorities from the top of the Poets' Fountain, which had stood outside Londonderry House. She had presided over the figures of Dante, Chaucer and Shakespeare, before they had been destroyed in a fit of planning ardour. The Muse could not enter my London house owing to the great span of her golden wings. Now, almost entirely concealed by luxuriant rhododendron bushes, she blows her trumpet to the empty air in the solitude of my Renishaw garden.

The kitchen had developed its own gallery of pictures and had become one of the nicest rooms in the house. It was there, in a cupboard, that we at last found, lining the cat's basket, a manuscript of a play—the only copy in existence—written by a journalist, who insisted on leaving it in my house, though I had warned him not to. It had disappeared at once, though for years we had sought it, until the cat's basket was about to be destroyed.

During the removal, I had occasion to be dismayed by the way in which objects crumble at a touch. Things which had appeared solid, stable and beautiful, and which had efficiently served their purpose for forty years, suddenly disintegrated before one's eyes. I am thinking in particular of a small ornate console table in my dining-room. The top was a fine piece of veined verd-antique marble, which rested on intricately carved supports with large gilded masks of baroque brutes, part lion and part some mythological animal. When the removal man tried to lift it, the heavy marble crashed to pieces, crushing the beasts, which were found to be eaten away by woodworm and to have the consistency of that light, porous sweet known as Edinburgh rock. Had no one tried to move it, no doubt the table would have stood up to life for another forty years. As it was, there it lay, a sorry mass of sawdust, splinters and marble, and I had to pay for this rubbish to be collected and consumed.

On the whole, the dining-room stood up nobly to the squall. One heavily-framed mirror had fallen long ago, but so gently had it slipped from the wall that it broke none of the delicate shell furniture beneath. It has been fixed more firmly and survives to hang in my new dining-room: its seven playful black cupids, naked except for neat gold pants patterned in green, and wearing gold caps on their curling hair, are gaily climbing up festoons of lacquered wood.

My dining-room was a very dark room and since the darkness could not be dispelled, I had tried to accentuate it. With its rich blue and silver tapestry wall-coverings, its shells, and its shell and dolphin furniture, the room resembled a grotto under the sea. Now all these objects, though not the shell chairs, stand exposed in my new flat to the full glare of daylight, thereby acquiring an entirely different appearance.

When moving house, many pictures have had to be separated, but I have been able to keep together three of my favourites, which now hang in my dining-room: firstly, Giambattista Tiepolo's 'Rinaldo and Armida', in which Rinaldo, clad in pink coat-of-mail and golden cloak, lies sleeping at the edge of the blue Mediterranean, while Armida leans over him, and a mermaid, emerging from the sea, looks on; secondly, a youthful 'St John the Baptist', variously attributed to Raphael, Sebastiano del Piombo (referred to in a letter from the insurance company with which I deal as Sebastino Pimbo Jumbo) and Giulio Romano, the only Italian painter to be mentioned by Shakespeare; and finally a beautiful picture of the Judgment Day, painted on wood by Breughel, in which hosts of delicate white skeletons are carrying off flesh-and-blood human beings to a doom that is certain, though its nature is less sure, and are gloatingly playing havoc with the happiness of man.

The large dining-room table had remained firm. It is a sumptuous affair and its history is this: I bought a sample, a slab of French marble from a monumental mason's yard, and hoisted it on four bronze lions that had come from a chiffonier in Carlton House Terrace. This might have supplied a regular skeleton at our feasts, but somehow it did not. If the table could acquire the habit of name-dropping, there would be an impressive list. Taking at random the names of friends who have sat round its soft gold and peach-coloured surface, it would murmur, Arnold Bennett, W. H. Davies, Maurice

Ravel, Serge Diaghilev, Maynard Keynes, Lydia Lopokova, Walter Sickert, Clive Bell, Roger Fry, Virginia Woolf, Léonide Massine, George Gershwin, Harold Acton, Arthur Waley, T. S. Eliot, and many others, not to mention William Walton who lived in the house and members of my own family.

As I left the dining-room for the last time, my mind went back to an earlier occasion, a Christmas Eve celebration in 1920, when twenty-four people dined at three tables arranged on three sides of a square. One of the guests, Sydney Schiff, chose to wear the pink coat of some obsolete and forgotten hunt, looking exactly as if he had just come from a hunt ball. When I asked him why he was wearing it, he explained that it was to give people a good idea of England. At a later stage of the proceedings, the Icelandic poet, Harmer, known to his friends *tout court* as 'Iceland'—no doubt to balance the painter Guevara, who was known as 'Chile'—was missing. Eventually he was found in a room at the top of the house staring intently in a looking-glass. When asked what he was doing, he stated that he was fixing his image in the glass; so that his image, too, has now been moved to my new flat.

Poor man, his life was short. He died some two years later after a singular episode. He came to see my brother, and complained that his landlady was putting electric currents through his mattress and that people kept on climbing up drain-pipes to the fourth floor of a house in Doughty Street in order to peer into his room and threaten him. What was he to do? My brother counselled, 'See a doctor.' We persuaded him to go to our own doctor, who lived nearby in Oakley Street. His chief complaint, however, was neither of electric currents nor of people peering at and threatening him, but of a man carrying a black umbrella who would frequently come up to him in the street and murmur some indescribable message in his ear. Through fear of danger from this man, Iceland always carried a revolver. We got him safely into the doctor's consulting room and waited for him outside. In a little while the doctor invited us both to come in. We entered and he turned to us and said, 'Mr Harmer now admits that what he thought he saw was, all the time, an illusion.' The doctor then persuaded him to give up the revolver and we left. Suddenly I noticed that I had left my stick behind and went back to fetch it. When I returned, my brother and I, to our surprise, saw a man carrying a black umbrella come up to Harmer, speak in his ear and then shuffle off into the twilight. Harmer looked at us in a distracted manner and exclaimed, 'Now you see for yourselves!' And from that moment until his death there was nothing more to be done for him.

The material difficulties of moving are innumerable and often appear insurmountable. I had to chose from the accumulated possessions of forty years what I could take with me and what would have to be sent away to be stored or sold. The choice was agonising, yet oddly enough difficult to remember, so that I am always being surprised at something not being here that I had thought to see again.

I found myself in a world of red tape and misunderstandings. Whenever I stirred, I was tripped up by the invisible barbed wire of rules and regulations. The frustrations were mitigated by an apparently amiable, willing and efficient body of men and women who remained untiringly anxious to 'carry out all your requirements with the maximum of attention'. Nevertheless, good-humoured men (always in pairs) turned up at the new address at the wrong hour to fix the gas-stove before it had been disconnected at the old address, and the telephone engineer came across a tangled cluster of wires which have no purpose but cannot be extricated from behind the walls. Perhaps many years ago the flat had been used by a spy who had been obliged to leave in a hurry, and certain rooms had been specially wired to trap the words of the unwary.

In every room in my house—and now in my flat—there is a piece of furniture, a picture or some ornament with a memory. Ethel Sands decorated a wardrobe for me, and on the outside she painted a replica of the inside, shelves of ties, collars, shirts, shoes and shoe-trees, a shiny black tall hat and a long cane with a tortoiseshell handle. I also possess two curious glass bottles with Negro heads. They were given to me by a remarkable charwoman in whom I had at once recognised a likeness to various members of my family. She had exactly the look and bearing of several relatives of mine, and suffered severely from gout. A week later this newcomer came up to me and said, 'I'm sorry that gout compels me to leave you, but I've brought you these two bottles as a present. They were given to my mother by your great-uncle.'

I seldom entered my drawing-room without there coming to my memory a winter's evening in November when the rehearsal of William Walton's *Façade* was in progress; it was subsequently given its first performance in that house. The rehearsal was peculiarly exciting. The cold outside was terrible and, in spite of two large coal fires, the players had to be brought to by copious draughts of sloe gin. As I listened to the subtly-constructed melodies evoked by popular songs, there was borne in on me the realisation of the touch of genius already manifesting itself in the work of my talented friend, although he was still so young.

As I prepared to leave my house for the last time, the air was full of the names of friends, and I was aware that ghosts were watching my departure from the windows. I was going to stay in a suite at the Ritz while the removal men destroyed what had been my home in order to construct it elsewhere. I recalled a night when I had been a young man of about thirty and was returning to my house after a concert. As I got out of the taxi, I noticed that the driver was dressed in a somewhat unusual way. On his head was a large, broad-brimmed sombrero, and he wore round his neck a voluminous, dramatically-coloured and patterned necktie. I was paying him the fare when he said to me with assurance, 'You are a writer, aren't you?'

I acknowledged this and enquired, 'How did you know?'

'Oh, I often drive my taxi at night on the astral plane and I sometimes see you there,' he answered casually.

I wonder whether fellow-travellers on the astral plane may not still see me darkening the door of my former house and fumbling for my latchkey. Forty years is a long time.

W9-BCZ-117

"Two of the most wonderful friends that God ever gave my wife and me were Johnny and June Cash. Now that they are both in Heaven, we miss our times together with them. During one of our vacations together, I watched Johnny working many hours on a book he was writing. He had done extensive research and study of the life of the apostle Paul, and amazed us as he talked about Paul and we shared the Scriptures together.

Johnny's book is a novel based on Paul, entitled *Man in White*. When it was first published several years ago, my wife and I both read it—then read it again! Now that it is to be reprinted, I hope that its new audience will enjoy the novel, and be challenged to also read the entire biblical account of Paul, the great follower of Jesus Christ, the Man in White."

—Billy Graham
May, 2006
Montreat, NC

A Novel About the apostle Paul

JOHNNY CASH

WestBow
PRESS

A Division of Thomas Nelson Publishers
Since 1798

visit us at www.westbowpress.com

Published in Nashville, Tennessee, by WestBow Press, a division of Thomas Nelson, Inc.

Publisher's Note: This novel is a work of fiction. Names, characters, places, and incidents are either products of the author's imagination or used fictitiously. All characters are fictional, and any similarity to people living or dead is purely coincidental.

ISBN 978-1-59554-237-3

This book is dedicated to my father, Ray Cash,
1897–1985, veteran of World War I.
Discharge: Honorable. Conduct: Good.

The friends of the Nazarene became united
And I became enraged
And led a slaughter zealously
I found their secret places
They were beaten, they were chained
But some of them were scattered
Justified in fearing me.
Then the Man in White
Appeared to me
In such a blinding light
It struck me down
And with its brilliance
Took away my sight
Then the Man in White
In gentle loving tones spoke to me
And I was blinded so that I might see
The Man in White

INTRODUCTION

It is highly unlikely that, having taken years, and with a lengthy period of respite from writing *Man in White*, I could possibly name everyone who, in some way or another, directly or indirectly, purposely, incidentally, accidentally, unknowingly, unwillingly, unintentionally, uncaring, unwanting, or eagerly, hopefully, helpfully contributed to the completion of this publication.

Many don't remember, as I may not, nor do they realize the vital role they played in this work, and I regret that I failed to give due credit to those whose contribution fails my memory.

Thanks to Irene Gibbs, my secretary, who typed, retyped, retyped, and retyped.

To Roy M. Carlisle of Harper & Row San Francisco, who, after reading the first draft, said, "Come on now, John. Give me a break. Put a little more prayer and thought into the first scene depicting a Christian worship service, then write it again, please?"

Thanks also to the agnostics, the atheists, the unconcerned, and the uncaring. These may have been among the most inspiring and encouraging by providing the negative force I needed against my determination.

I'm a traveling man, and I meet a lot of people. I have, on occasion, had the opportunity to talk to people of diverse persuasions. I introduced myself to an Orthodox Jew at the Newark Airport baggage claim area. Reluctantly, he shook my hand. He took a step backward in hesitant awe when I asked him, "Could you please tell me a little about the Feast of Weeks, as it was celebrated around AD 60?"

He finally warmed to the subject and supplied me with insight into that period.

I had numerous dinner-table discussions (sometimes confusing) with conservative synagogue members about first-century Temple life. I was instructed by Jewish associates in ethics, traditions, customs, and actions from the old school, the new school, and the unschooled.

I went to a Western store in Los Angeles and bought saddlebags that I carried over my shoulders for the last five years of my travels. In the bag was my "book." Also the Thompson Chain-Reference Bible; the New International Version; the Catholic Bible; and from time to time, *Everyday Life in Jesus' Time*; *Foxe's Book of Martyrs*; *A History of the Early Church*; *The Twelve Apostles*; *The Twelve Caesars*; the *Jewish Encyclopedia*; and the writings of the Romanized Jewish historian Flavius Josephus.

June read each and every page and in her painfully honest way let me know what she thought. I listened, waited, prayed, and then acted upon my own judgment, as I did with other, less outspoken critics.

✠ ✠ ✠

A reporter asked me, "What is this about a new book you're writing?"

"It's called *Man in White*," I replied.

"Neat idea. *Man in White* by the man in black."

I nodded, waiting.

"What's it about?" he asked.

"The apostle Paul's conversion, before and after," I explained. "It's a novel."

"Nothing about yourself?"

"No, it happens in the first century AD."

"Really, a novel? Anything about prisons?" he laughed.

"Yes, as a matter of fact, Paul sang in prison. He sang a jail-breaking song."

"Really. What was the song?" he asked.

"I don't know," I said. "He and a guy named Silas sang a duet, but they never recorded it."

Others I've talked with about it were excited, or at least intrigued.

"Is it written from the Baptist Church's angle?" one asked. "You are a Baptist, aren't you?"

"Paul was not a Baptist," I replied. "He admonished those whose doctrinal tenets focused on John the Baptist."

"Then you're a Catholic, maybe?" he asked.

"Maybe," I said, "since *catholic* means 'universal.'"

"But not the Roman Catholic Church?" he asked.

"No," I said. "Paul was a Jew. He was a doctor of the Law."

"Then it's written from the Jewish viewpoint, right?"

"No, mine," I said.

"But you're a Baptist."

I finally settled on a fundamental answer. "I, as a believer that Jesus of Nazareth, a Jew, the Christ of the Greeks, was the Anointed One of God (born of the seed of David, upon faith as Abraham had faith, and it was accounted to him for righteousness), am grafted onto the true vine, and am one of the heirs of God's covenant with Israel."

"What?"

"I'm a Christian," I said. "Don't put me in another box."

There was a long pause, and then he said, "Really, Adolph Hitler was a Christian."

"He was not," I argued. "There was nothing Christlike in what he did."

"How do you know?" he asked.

I thought for a minute. "I don't really know," I said, "but Jesus said, 'By their fruits ye shall know them,' and I've seen his fruits."

"Where?" he asked.

"At the Holocaust Museum in Jerusalem," I said.

✻ ✻ ✻

Thanks to Ken Overstreet, Jay Kessler, Dan McKinnon, and all at Youth for Christ.

Thanks to Dr. David Weinstein, chancellor of Spertus College of Judaica in Chicago, for his invaluable contribution.

Karen Robin, wife of my agent, Lou Robin, is a diligent student of Christianity, and in recent years a convert to Judaism, in which she has dedicated herself to studies in the Law and tradition, ancient and modern. She most graciously caused me to search out and prove numerous Hebraic pieces of my narrative. To her, I am indebted, as I am to her husband, Lou, who confirmed, or at times added with a few words, a feast of food for thought.

To Stephanie Mills, to Chet Hagen, and to Judy Markham. To Marty Klein, head of the Agency for the Performing Arts, with whom I have been associated for fifteen years, who listened to parts of my story from time to time, and who greatly encouraged me to express this work in my own words and imagery.

✻ ✻ ✻

When June and I were married in 1968, we read a lot. We found much common ground in our tastes for books.

I had just come off seven years of addiction to amphetamines and other prescription drugs. I had been a devastated, incoherent, unpredictable, self-destructive, raging terror at times during those years.

Now with a lot of love and a lot of prayers and that madness behind me, we spend a lot of time reading great books. Having been on vacation to

Israel, we love everything we read relative to that land, especially about it during the time of Christ—*Ben Hur, The Robe, The Silver Chalice, Dear and Glorious Physician*, and *The Source*.

June's father, Ezra Carter, left me his religious-historical library when he died. He had talked to me about some of his favorite reading, books about the early church fathers, the post-Nicene and ante-Nicene councils. He kept telling me before he died, "You're going to love Josephus and Pliny and Seutonius and Gibbons and Tacitus."

At first I found Josephus slow, plodding, and hard to read, but the more I read, the more excited I got, seeing Josephus's Roman world as the earliest Christians saw it. I eventually got into them all and bought many other books related to first-century Judea. Those dusty old books came to life.

For example, do you know about the world's first recorded "mooning"? Mooning is a bit like "streaking," where a person suddenly appears naked and runs through a public place, but in mooning, only his backside is bared.

Flavius Josephus, writing around AD 80, tells us that it was during the reign of Augustus Caesar that Roman soldiers caused a near riot by marching past the holy Temple at Jerusalem bearing their banners and holding aloft the imperial-blazoned eagle. Angry over the presence of such an engraved image, the priests and elders of the Temple shouted insults and threw stones at the standard. As the column of soldiers passed by, ignoring the Temple and its priests and elders, according to Josephus, "a centurion stopped and faced the Jews. He then, turning in the opposite direction, raised his tunic, lowered his loincloth, bent over, and bared his hindmost parts to the priests and elders." The first known recorded mooning.

For three years, June and I took correspondence courses in the Bible from Christian International in Phoenix through Evangel Temple in Goodlettsville, Tennessee, which was the church we belonged to at the time. We worked on assignments at home, on the road, on the bus, on planes, and sometimes in a quiet spot like a cabin in the woods near home. Whenever we had a few minutes or a few hours, we would work on our lessons; then we'd mail them in and await the next course.

In 1977, three years from the time we began, we got signed, wax-sealed certificates from Christian International. We never hung them up for display. "This is only the beginning," I said. "All my degree means to me is that I am now qualified to study the Bible."

That last course I had finished I couldn't get off my mind—"The Life and Epistles of St. Paul" by Conybere and Howson. I started reading books about Paul, the novels, and there are some very good ones, especially the ones by Sholem Asch and John Pollock. Then I got into the commentaries on Paul by Lange, Farrar, Barnes, Fleetwood, and others. I started making notes and writing my own thoughts on Paul when I saw so many different opinions in so many areas. Tons of material has been written about his differences with Peter and Mark, but I discovered that the Bible can shed a lot of light on commentaries.

And for ages pulpiteers have speculated on the physical makeup of his "thorn in the flesh"—how big it was and where it stuck him. Why didn't he pull it out? He couldn't, and that's probably why he had a doctor (Luke) traveling with him. He was probably an epileptic, someone said. Was the thorn symbolic? He craved young women, said another, and so on and so on.

Well, I decided, if theologians can do so much speculating and make it interesting, I might throw in my two cents worth. After all, Paul had become my hero. He was invincible! He made it his life's mission to conquer and convert the idolatrous, pagan world over to Jesus Christ. And he did everything he planned that he lived long enough to do.

He smiled at his persecutions. He was beaten with rods, with the lash, with stones; he was insulted, attacked by mobs, and imprisoned; his own people hated him. Yet he said, because of Jesus Christ, he had learned to be content in whatever state he was in!

As an old man in prison in Rome, in his last days, he wrote of things he still wanted to do, one of which was to evangelize Spain! He always had a great plan and he always carried it through; then he made journey after journey to go back to the cities he had visited to make sure people were running things the way he taught them to.

I started writing about Paul in a kind of documentary way, but right up front there wasn't much to document. He suddenly appears at Stephen's execution, and the Bible says that he had cast his vote against him. The people who killed Stephen laid their clothes at Paul's (Saul's) feet. *Why?* I wondered. I had to know. I found out why.

When he said he zealously persecuted the Christians, I wanted to know what he said, what he did. How long did he do it? What did his own people think of him? As a Pharisee, what was his relationship with the high priest? Was the high priest happy to give him letters to go to Damascus because he was glad to get him out of town? Maybe so. He had really disturbed the peace in Jerusalem.

The Roman Empire had its own little thorn in the flesh—Judea. The most undesirable appointment for a Roman officer would be to be sent to "govern" Judea. It was a remote, miserable outpost. In the time of Tiberius Caesar, governors or procurators such as Pilate and Marcellus soon learned that the Jews governed themselves, with the Temple to their one God as the center of their religious and social life. The high priest was their top man, no matter who Rome sent.

Rome was forced to allow them to mint their own money, for the Roman coins with their idolatrous images were forbidden in holy places. Jewish coins were simply designed and crudely struck. A shock of wheat or a pomegranate tree might appear on one side and numbers signifying the number of years since the last rebellion against Rome on the other.

The followers of Christ were at first considered by the high priest and most of the general population to be just another Jewish sect, of which there were many. But of all the sects, this was the most despicable. They worshiped a dead Galilean preacher who couldn't even keep himself alive. He died the most shameful death the Romans could devise. It was said that his friends stole his body after he was buried—grave robbing, a most depraved crime, punishable by death.

The horror stories grew. His friends said that he rose from the dead, walked with them, then ascended to heaven before their eyes. After he was gone, it was reported to the high priest that the followers of the Nazarene had kept some of his blood and drank it whenever they got together. To drink blood, according to the Law of Moses, was abominable. And how about his flesh? Yes, they even told how he had left them pieces of his flesh to eat in remembrance of him. Cannibalism!

So it was not just the Temple theocracy in Jerusalem that considered the Christians enemies of God; the whole flood of public opinion was against them. They became a closed society to survive. And the man who would later write fourteen books of the New Testament was their most hostile persecutor.

Jesus Christ told us how to live. The apostle Paul showed us how the plan works. Jesus Christ told us how to die, unafraid, with an eternity of peace following, and Paul showed us how to prepare for it.

It was Saul of Tarsus, the persecutor of the followers of the Nazarene, who left Jerusalem bound for Damascus to find, arrest, bring to trial, and execute those who worshiped that "Name."

And it was Paul, the apostle for Jesus Christ to the world, who entered Damascus a few days later.

Jesus had died, been resurrected, and ascended to heaven, according to his disciples, and they expected his eventual second coming. They looked anxiously for the promised return. Every convert expected it. No one, especially Saul the Pharisee, authority and expert on Mosaic Law, expected him to appear in the middle of a clear day and to have a one-on-one conversation with him.

As best I can time it, not accounting for any pauses in the exchange of dialogue between Jesus and Paul and according to Paul's writing in his Letters, the conversation lasted approximately one minute, maybe a few seconds less. Yet a world was changed because of that one-minute conversation. It was one great paramount minute in the history of humankind. That minute determined the destiny of countless millions of people yet to be born. No event short of the birth of Jesus Christ himself has affected the life of humankind on this earth as powerfully as the commands given and accepted in that one minute. But what we know about Saul/Paul from three years before that minute to three years after that minute, we can glean from only a few versus of Scripture.

I lay awake nights back in 1978 and 1979 thinking about Paul—the amazing transformation, how he turned that zeal for persecution and slaughter around and immediately went forth with the same zeal for Christ. That six-year period intrigued me. The more I studied, the more I wrote down my own thoughts on Paul. In my mind, he took on character and personality, and I wanted to give character and personality to the high priest who sent him to Damascus. I wanted the people he persecuted and slaughtered to have names, and I wanted to see them and hear them in those earliest Christian worship services.

Someone said a religious novelist can be "God's liar"; that is, by novelization of the activity and reality surrounding a tiny grain of truth, great truths can be illuminated and activated. I have not and do not claim to be a novelist, but I suppose that is the form my writing about Paul has taken. I found a story to tell in those few verses, and the story I tell around those verses is my own.

Of course, the Scriptures dealing with the six years we're zeroing in on don't need further illumination by me—truth is its own illumination. In studying them, I began to glimpse the unfathomable depths that lay there.

What exactly was Paul seeing and hearing that instant he went blind on the Damascus road? I suppose I was trying to see beyond the great void, to perceive just a flicker of the divine brilliance that struck him down. One of the days I was pondering this, it wasn't meant for me to get a flicker of divine brilliance, but it *was* meant for me to be struck down.

An ostrich tried to kill me. I was trying to look across the abyss between heaven and earth and put some of it in words at my cabin in the woods, which is near my home in a fifty-acre fenced-in area stocked with wild game. I got up to take a walk and relax when I met this eight-foot-tall ostrich in the path. He had lost his mate in the winter freeze and had become hostile. I was thinking of Paul being struck down on the Damascus road by a binding light when I was suddenly struck down by the two big feet of an ostrich.

As soon as he hit me, he ran off into the woods. I picked myself up, examined myself, and realized that I wasn't hurt, so I walked on down the path.

After I had taken my walk and started back toward the cabin, there stood that ostrich on the path again. He spread his wings and hissed at me. "I think I'd better show you who owns this land," I said, picking up a long stick. Then he attacked. I swung the stick at his long neck, which is just what he wanted me to do. He jumped straight up out of my reach and came back down on me feetfirst. He broke three ribs when he hit me, and only my belt kept his big, dirty claws from ripping me open.

Like Paul when he was struck by the Light, I fell flat on my back, but unlike Paul, I broke two more ribs on the rock I fell on. The ostrich ran and left me lying there. I finally managed to get back home and to the doctor.

Painkillers led to sleeping pills. Sleeping pills led to "uppers" again, and soon I was back on that mood-altered, not-so-merry-go-round. My story about Paul got stuck away in a closet. Only occasionally would I take it out and try to write. Mood-altering drugs vex the spirit, and if inspiration comes to a writer while under the influence, it's usually distorted, meaningless, and senseless by the time it gets on paper.

I had to let Billy Graham read "my book," and every time I talked to him, he asked me if it was finished. I'd say, "Too busy on the road," or give some other excuse. The truth is I wanted to see more of what Paul saw on the Damascus road and thereafter, and it wasn't happening. I had no vision. I had no inspiration.

I tried several times to "get away to write" in Florida or Jamaica, but I couldn't get away from myself. The fire and the spirit were gone because of medication I was taking. I began to wish I'd never let Billy Graham, or anyone else, read anything I'd written. But I had.

John Seigenthaler of the Nashville *Tennessean* had read it and in April 1982 wrote a long critique on "my book" for me, greatly encouraging me to finish it and saying that it was an important story. I carried John's letter in the back of the rough, ragged, would-be manuscript from that time on, and though I didn't respond to his critique, I must have read it a hundred times.

June noticed that I wasn't writing anymore, and of course she knew why, so I didn't have to explain it to her.

From the pulpit at a crusade, I heard Billy Graham tell his listeners that Johnny Cash had written a book about Paul called *Man in White*, and he thought it was one of the best writings on Paul he'd ever read. I was embarrassed and ashamed. *Man in White* was about half-finished, and Paul was stuck indefinitely on the Damascus road. I could not "see" Paul's experience. I decided that I had taken on more than I could handle. The love of writing was gone. I even forgot most of what I had written. After all, seven years had gone by since I had started it. *I've changed my mind,* I thought. *I can't write a novel. Why did I ever think I could?* I resented the obligation I had saddled myself with.

During the excitement of my early writing, I had talked to everyone about it. "Just a few more months," I'd say. "I'm still working on it." But I wasn't. By 1983, I had stuck it away in a closet somewhere and tried to forget about it. I kept it out of my sight for three or four months at a time, but I couldn't forget about it. I'd drag it out, go over my notes, and try to write. Time after time I wrote dozens of pages while under the influence, but when I read them afterward with a clear mind, I burned them.

In October 1983, I was packing for a tour of Europe. There in the corner in the back of my closet lay the "Man in White" briefcase. I pulled it out and laid it with my suitcase.

"Are you going to finish your book?" June asked.

"I don't know if I can," I said.

"Yes, you can," she said. "It's important. You'll have lots of spare time on airplanes."

I had only recently had another accident. I had fallen on my knee and broken a kneecap. So I loaded up on strong painkillers, enough to last for the tour, and of course sleeping pills in case the pain kept me from sleeping, and of course "uppers" to kill the hangover from sleeping pills when it was time to perform.

I carried "my book" with me on the tour, but I never once looked at it.

The combination of medications gave me blackouts. We performed in fourteen cities, but I only remembered four.

My physical as well as my mental and spiritual condition quickly deteriorated. I went home and into the hospital, bleeding internally. The pills, so many of them day and night, had burned holes in my stomach. By the time I had been given fourteen units of blood to replace what I had lost, the doctors had no choice but to operate. Surgery lasted seven hours; they took out half of my insides, and they gave me nine more units of blood by the time it was over.

Now the painkiller morphine was given to me intravenously around the clock, day and night, for many days, and I remember terrible hallucinations. I saw people coming at me to kill me. I threw things and screamed. The terrors lasted as long as the morphine was going in. I was as close to death as you can come. I saw, in hallucinating, old friends who weren't really there, but they were talking to me, and every one was like a farewell conversation. They were saying things like, "Well, at least you can say you've lived a full life," or "June and John Carter will be taken care of."

In my half sleep, I heard the doctors talking beside my bed. "His chances aren't good," one of them said. Another one said, "His heart stopped once. I can't see how he can fight it much longer."

Many times I opened my eyes to see June's face and the resigned expression. She was telling the rest of the family I was going to pull through, but her confidence didn't show. Many times I was aware enough to pray, and many times, in my pain and mental terror, I felt the warm presence of the Great Healer, and I always knew that I would live, that I wasn't finished for him yet.

Once when I was unconscious, I suddenly became aware of a gentle hand on my forehead, and I heard my mother's voice. "Lord," she said, "you took one of my boys, and if you're going to take this one, he's yours to take, but I ask you, let him live and teach him to serve you better. Surely you still have work for him to do." Though I was allowed no visitors, my mother got through.

Love and care poured in from everywhere. I began to be aware for a few minutes each day, then for an hour or two.

Waylon Jennings sent me a note in intensive care. The nurse read it to me. Waylon said, "I can't imagine a world without Johnny Cash. Get out of there." Every day I got a message of some kind from Waylon. I began looking forward to it each day. Once his message said simply, "Let's get the show on the road."

I began to feel alive again, and every day I was inspired, remembering Waylon's line, "Can't imagine a world without Johnny Cash." I had been to the bottom of the pit, and God sent loved ones like June, Waylon, Jessi, Billy, and my parents; they were doing so much more to pull me out than the medical care I was getting.

My family was there when I came out of intensive care. The room was full of familiar faces, all but one. A doctor from the Betty Ford Center was there with them; he had called them together to explain my situation.

Because I had been on morphine for a long term and had other narcotics administered to me as well, the doctor suggested that as soon as I was able to travel I should go to the Ford Center in California as a volunteer patient for drug withdrawal and rehabilitation. It was going to be rough, but it would be the only way I could survive, and the education I would get on my problems of chemical dependency would help me in the future to guard against any use of mood-altering drugs.

We talked a long time. My pastor, Rev. Courtney Wilson, was there and prayed about it. I volunteered to go.

When June was packing my things a few days later, I called her, told her where my manuscript was, and asked her to pack it. After two weeks at the Betty Ford Center, I read over my manuscript. I saw the story clearly now—where I would take Paul and how it would end.

For almost two years, I labored over it whenever time allowed. But since I had missed so many months of work—recording, concerts, television, and so forth—and a large staff of people were depending on me, it went slowly. The real problem, however, was the chapter on the Damascus road experience. I prayed for a vision. I prayed for a revelation, some glimpse into the "forbidden," a look at the heaven-and-earth connection like the one that came to Paul.

✻ ✻ ✻

Dreams have always played a role in my affairs from time to time. For instance, a few times I have dreamed I heard new songs never before sung, and I'd wake up and write them down. Some of them I recorded. As a child, I dreamed an angel came to me to tell me my brother Jack would die, but that I must understand that it was God's plan and someday I would see that it was. Jack died two weeks later. I had another forewarning in a dream of a close friend's death. I called his home the next day, and he had been killed in an automobile accident the night before. On Christmas night 1985, I had another visionary, dreamlike experience.

My father had died, and that day I had been to the funeral home with the family. He looked so handsome in that fine blue suit and burgundy tie. His countenance belied his eighty-eight years. After months of suffering he seemed to be so much at peace. The church and military funeral would be the next day. Loving words by Rev. Courtney Wilson and a twenty-one-gun salute at the cemetery would leave the old World War I soldier at his rest.

My father had always bought us kids fireworks for the Fourth of July and Christmas. It was one way we waved the flag and praised the Lord. Back in October, hoping my Dad would be home for Christmas, I bought a large assortment of fireworks and planned to shoot them in his front yard so he could see them through the window.

I came home from the funeral home around sundown on Christmas evening and dropped my mother off at her house. Her grandchildren, great-grandchildren, and other friends and loved ones were there to be with her.

I went home to change clothes, and there in the corner of my closet was that big box of fireworks I had bought in October. I picked it up and showed it to June.

"I was going to shoot these tonight for Daddy," I said. "In his front yard."

"The children would like to see them," she said. "And Grandpa would want you to."

I hesitated, then finally came up with that old corny line. "What will the neighbors say?" Then I burst out laughing. "He'll see them better tonight than ever before," I said. "He's no longer got cataracts on his eyes."

I set them up in a row across the middle of the front yard of my parents' house—skyrockets, Roman candles, sparklers, colored fire fountains, bursting stars, rainbow cones, everything that would shine, sparkle, pop, spurt, and glow. My mother watched from the window, and the children laughed and squealed at the beautiful display of fireworks. There was a constant stream of multicolored fire across the yard, and a lot of laughter. I kissed my mother good night, reminding her of what time I would be there tomorrow to go to the funeral.

I went to bed early, but it must have been three hours or more before I fell into a deep sleep. I dreamed that I was standing in front of my parents' house, facing the road as if I was waiting for someone. I was there alone, and my mother was somewhere inside.

A long, bright silver car came over the hill and stopped at the curb, which was about fifty feet directly in front of me. The car had no driver, but the left rear door opened and my father got out and started walking toward me. He had on that beautiful blue suit, white silk shirt, and burgundy tie. He was smiling as he approached me, walking with the stride of a young man. His clear eyes sparkled; they were not covered with the dull film of age I was used to seeing, but were clear, bright brown eyes. His teeth, when he smiled, were like a young man's, and his gray hair was full, with as much dark hair as gray.

"I was waiting for you to come home," I said. I reached out my hand toward him to shake hands. His hand reached out toward mine, and we were only a few paces apart when suddenly a long row of light streamed up from the ground between us. He smiled a knowing smile, dropped his hand, and stood looking at me. The steam of light between us widened, grew in brilliance, and became an unbreachable gulf. His face smiled at me across the chasm, and I knew that I could not touch him.

I looked behind me through the window. I couldn't see my mother but knew that she was inside. I turned back to Daddy and asked, "Are you coming inside? Mama would like for you to."

Still smiling, he said, "No, Son, I'm afraid it would just cause more pain for everyone."

The light was streaming between us. "You really look great, Daddy," was all I could say.

"Tell your mother," he said softly, "that I just couldn't come back. I'm so comfortable and so happy where I am."

"All right," I said, and I knew it *was* all right.

"I just don't belong here anymore," he said.

The light grew in intensity and I couldn't see him though it. Suddenly the light was gone, and so was he, and there was no bright silver car at the curb. The only thing in the yard were the spent fireworks from that evening.

I awoke and looked at the clock; 1:00 a.m. I had slept only a few minutes. I got up and walked the floor most of the night, troubled by such a vivid dream. It had been unlike any dream I'd ever had. I felt that I had lived it. Day was breaking and I was sitting by the window looking out at the lake when I finally found peace and understanding.

The burden of grief was lifted that day, even at the funeral. When I went to pick my mother up, the house was full of people—family, friends, and loved ones. I took my mother aside, and in private I said, "I had a God-sent dream last night, Mama," She smiled, believing. "I dreamed about Daddy, and he asked me to tell you something."

"What?" she asked, holding on to my hand.

"He asked me to tell you that he's comfortable and happy where he is. Besides, he said that he doesn't belong here anymore."

I explained the whole dream to her, the silver car, the blue suit and burgundy tie, and the deep gulf with light between us.

She cried, then she laughed. "God still has his hand on you," she said.

We both felt great peace that day. She sang along to "Amazing Grace" and led the whole family clan out of the church with a smile of joy that comes from knowing a loved one is at peace and with God.

I was never privileged to have an experience like Paul did just outside Damascus, but on Christmas night 1985 I had that visionlike dream and saw a light that was unearthly and much more beautiful than the whole box of fireworks.

The glorified Christ is described in the book of Revelation in imagery of flame and fire. Also fire, water, and wind are sometimes symbolic of the Holy Spirit; so are tongues. It all helped to spark my imagination.

I went to work. Once again, I found joy in writing. I've "finished" *Man in White* several times since my father died. I'm never satisfied that I didn't leave out something important or put in something meaningless. If the publisher hadn't finally said, "Enough," I'd still be writing.

If no hidden grain of truth is illuminated in this book, it will still have served its purpose. It kept me going back to the Bible—searching, meditating, envisioning, and talking about it for the better part of ten years. My disclaimer is that it's only a novel. Other than that, it's something I should have been doing anyway.

Please understand that I believe the Bible, the whole Bible, to be the infallible, indisputable Word of God. I have been careful to take no liberties with the timeless Word. Where the Word is silent and for my story's sake, I have at times followed traditional views. Other things, some characters, some conversations, and some occurrences are products of my broad and at times strange imagination.

Perhaps a few of the things I have written, I humbly suggest, resulted from a tiny flicker from God's great storehouse of brilliance.

I dedicate this book to my father, Ray Cash, whose face I saw in that tiny flicker.

John Cash
Bon Aqua, Tennessee
March 21, 1986

PROLOGUE

He had been called Cephas, the Rock, by the Nazarene. His actions were anything but stonelike. His hands moved from one outstretched hand to another in the crowd. They called his name and pleaded for him to touch them. His touch left many in ecstasy. Some fainted; some looked toward the sky and uttered words of praise at having been so fortunate as to be touched by the big fisherman.

He moved slowly eastward across the Tyropoean Valley and on up the street toward the steps that crossed the southern porch of the Temple compound. He was dressed in a one-piece homespun robe made of goat's hair, and he wore sandals he had made himself. He was a tall, robust man, with a square face and strong nose. Dark eyebrows shadowed the kind, deep pools of his black eyes. His thick, unkempt hair was a copper color, and his full red beard had never been cut.

He moved among the people with a loving, gentle grace. He was followed by many little children, some of whom pulled at his robe. He reached down and, smiling, picked up a boy in one arm and a girl in the other. He held them close against his face, rubbing his coarse beard against them and leaving them laughing with merriment.

At the foot of the steps surrounded by a large group of people were James and John, the sons of Zebedee from Galilee. John was speaking to the people, quoting some of the sayings of Jesus. "I am the bread of life. He who comes to me shall never hunger, and he who believes on me shall never thirst."

"Give to me this bread of life," shouted a man with palsy. His hands reached out, shaking uncontrollably. John grasped them to hold them still and said, "In the name of Jesus of Nazareth, be whole." The man held his steady hands before his face and wept unrestrained.

From Jericho and Bethany they came. From Samaria they came, the poor, the sick, the blind, the infirm. Their numbers clogged the thoroughfares in and out of Jerusalem. By the hundreds they came, by the thousands they came. Undaunted by the heat and the dust, they hobbled along on makeshift crutches or were carried on litters by their loved ones. One man crawled on his hands and knees from Bethlehem. They all had a common destination in mind—Solomon's Porch, the spacious, open, colonnaded area on the side of the Temple compound. It was here that Cephas, or Simon Peter, preached at three o'clock every afternoon. Hundreds already gathered on the porch. Hundreds more were on the steps, and countless more streamed from every direction to try to see the fisherman Cephas.

A man with twisted feet and hands cried out to Peter, "Let your shadow pass over me and I will be healed." Peter's shadow covered the man as he stopped and smiled down at him. Then he moved on, leaving the ecstatic, weeping man behind him.

He moved to the steps, and the people parted to make a pathway for him to ascend. They fell in behind him and moved up with him. The steps became a mass of humanity, moving toward the great quadrangle, which opened into the Court of the Gentiles.

With the crowd gathered around him, Peter began to speak.

Across the Temple compound within the Court of Israel the council was in session. Caiaphas, Jonathan, Alexander, and Theophilus, the kinsman of old Annas, the high priest, sat with the Sanhedrin.

Jonathan was officially high priest and wore the vestments of that office, as did Annas's nephew Caiaphas. The younger Alexander was somewhat of an embarrassment to Annas because of his Greek name. It had been heard said in the Court of Israel itself that Alexander's election to the high priesthood would bring shame upon Israel. The words "Father Alexander" would taste bitter in the mouth of a son of the Covenant.

It was a strange situation. Jonathan had been readily accepted and served well. Yet for a people steeped in history, the four hundred years since the Macedonian Greek Alexander the Great had sacked towns and slaughtered the children of Israel was a relatively short time.

Alexander's time, however, would come.

When the balding, white-haired Annas decided to sit on the seat of the high priest, his family took secondary seats close to yet lower than his.

Annas ruled not only the Court of Israel; his worldly power, influence, and wealth extended throughout the immediate area. Toward Bethlehem he owned a vast parcel of land upon which his shepherds raised the snow-white lambs to be sold in the courts of the very Temple where he was high priest. His dovecotes in Bethany and on the Mount of Olives housed thousands of the cooing white birds, which were purchased by the very poor as an acceptable sacrifice. His wealth had grown at an amazing rate. His Greek wife, Athaena, supervised the operation of stalls in the Temple compound. His personal hoard of foreign silver and gold coins was fabulous.

Annas glanced up at the gold water-clock on the balcony. The scales of justice hung evenly from the clock, which now showed that the tenth hour of the day was past. "Is there any further business for this court?" he asked his sons and nephew.

From his seat in the council, Saul the Pharisee, the newest and youngest member of the Sanhedrin, sprang to his feet with his left arm raised.

"Yes?" said Annas, tiredly eyeing him, then the clock again.

"The Lord has brought over us a deep sleep," Saul said, paraphrasing the quote from the prophet Isaiah. "He has sealed our eyes and covered our heads."

Annas regarded Caiaphas, then Jonathan, questioningly for an indication of what the fiery Pharisee was speaking about. They shrugged their shoulders, and Annas asked, "What are you talking about, Saul?"

Saul paused to give his coming words impact, then said boldly, "This council stands in danger of sacrilege. The very laws and sacrifices it protects are mocked within the Temple courts."

Annas did not move; he sat waiting with his eyes on Saul. The other priests looked toward Annas, anxious as to how he would handle this confrontation.

Saul continued, louder and bolder than before. "The chief apostles of the carpenter-rabbi from Nazareth are now preaching and healing on Solomon's Porch. Their leader is one called Cephas, the same one who was brought before this court and admonished to teach no more in the name of the Nazarene." Saul's temper rose. "He proclaims in the Nazarene the power of resurrection of the dead."

Annas sighed deeply. He looked down, then up at Saul. "This Cephas is again teaching in that name?"

"Yes," shouted Saul, "and his hearers multiply."

Annas paused a moment and sighed again; then with the golden baton he held in his hand, he struck a loud cymbal. "May the Most High be praised by the judgment of this court," he said.

Immediately seven Temple guards entered the room and stood before the high priest. The chief guard stepped forward.

The high priest said, "Use all care not to bring unrest to the people of Solomon's Porch, but at an opportune time arrest Cephas and those of his party who preach and heal in the name of the Nazarene, Jesus."

The chief guard raised his left arm in salute to the ruler of the Jews.

"Imprison them," Annas continued, "and bring them before this court tomorrow morning."

✳ ✳ ✳

The air was foul, and the prison stank. The chatter of rats was constant. It was long past midnight, and Peter and John sat on the damp floor with their backs against the wall. They had talked long into the night, sharing the joys of suffering for their Master's sake. The murmur of their voices had made the two guards sleepy, and they nodded. They sat on each side of the heavy iron door and slept.

The voices of the apostles fell silent, and they, too, would have slept— except for the light. The light seemed to come from nowhere, yet everywhere. A white brilliance covered the jail door, and the iron bars vanished. There appeared an angelic form where the bars had stood.

The brilliance of the angel was blinding, and Peter and John closed their eyes and fell to their knees. The angel reached out its hands to the apostles, signaling them to rise to their feet.

"Go stand in the Temple," said the angel, "and speak words of life to the people."

Peter and John rose, and a warmth and a joy engulfed them as they walked toward the light. They walked on through the light and out of the prison. Then as quickly as it appeared, the light was gone. The iron door appeared again, locked, with the guards sleeping beside it.

The next day they were arrested again as they were leaving the Temple after preaching to a great crowd in the southern court and brought before the high priest. Annas eyed them coolly. "You have obviously gained great favor with the people of this city," he said to the fishermen. Then cynically, "The news of your healing the cripple at the Gate called Beautiful has been broadcast to every ear. You have gained many followers."

"The stone the builders rejected has become the cornerstone," said Peter.

Annas ignored Peter's quote from the Psalms, refusing to equate the psalmist's prophecy with the coming of the Nazarene. "We gave you strict orders not to teach in the name of the Nazarene," he said. "You seem determined to make us guilty of this man's blood."

John spoke up for the first time. "We must obey God rather than men."

Peter, fully in command of the defense, raised his hand. He looked kindly upon the young John, then taking up from John, he said, "The God of our fathers raised Jesus from the dead."

A ripple of low murmuring went through the Sanhedrin. Saul of Tarsus murmured to himself, but loud enough to be heard, "Abomination of desolation."

Peter ignored him. "He whom you had crucified God has exalted to his right hand as Prince and Savior, that he might give repentance and forgiveness of sins to Israel. We are witnesses to these things, as is the Holy Spirit, whom God has given to those who obey him."

Gamaliel was an honored teacher of the Law. He raised his hands, and the room became quiet.

"Father Annas," he said, "it is improper that these men stand before this court, if this court is going to debate their fate at this time. I move that these men be taken to a secured chamber in this hall until such time as judgment is pronounced."

Annas motioned for the captain of the guards, and Peter and John were gently but quickly ushered from the room.

Annas motioned for Gamaliel to come forward and address the Sanhedrin. When everyone was quiet and all eyes were upon him, Gamaliel said, "Men of Israel, consider carefully what you would do to these men. These are not the first in Israel to draw the people after them. Some time ago a man called Theudas appeared. About four hundred people rallied to him. He was killed, and his followers were dispersed.

"Now again," said Gamaliel, "hundreds, even thousands gather daily to hear these fishermen from Galilee. By their works it appears to one that they are not promoting rebellion against Israel or against Rome. By some power the cripple was healed who has sat for forty years at the Gate called Beautiful. This court examined him, and the whole city knows of this miracle.

"And may I remind you," continued Gamaliel, "in the days of the census,

Judas the Galilean led a band of people in revolt. He, too, was killed, and his followers were scattered. Therefore, I advise you, leave these men alone and let them go. If their activity is of human origin, it will fail. But if it is from God, you cannot stop them. You will be fighting against God."

Saul dropped his head in submission. Such a statement by Gamaliel before the high priest was tantamount to an ultimatum to and a decision by the Sanhedrin.

Annas had Peter and John brought back in and said to them, "You shall be taken to the Hall of Flagellation. At least the scourge will remind you that this court is still the ruling body of the Jews and that this Temple is the dwelling place of the Most High. You should remember that our traditions and our holy laws are not open to individual interpretation. Should you return to your former ways and preach in that name, you will be brought before this council for your final judgment."

The sound of the lashes echoed in the stone chamber. Peter and John stood facing marble columns with their arms stretched around the cold stones and their hands tied tightly. The lash cut their backs as it came down time after time. Though the whip cut the skin and drops of blood ran down their backs into their loincloths, Peter's expression of ecstasy never changed.

This gruesome scourging was the one thing the Sanhedrin borrowed from the Romans. Garments were ripped down the back, exposing the flesh to the requisite thirty-nine stripes.

Halfway through the ordeal, John moaned in pain. Peter shouted, "Bear up, John! Count it glorious that we are privileged to suffer for the Master's sake."

Saul stood beside the door silently watching. He had never felt such hatred. *What idiotic fanaticism!* he thought. *It would be better if all Israel were rid of these religious lepers . . .*

ONE

THE VOW, AD 37

Sometime just before dawn, Saul was awakened by a sound in his room. He heard nothing at first, then, again a *crunch, crunch,* like feet walking on straw. Then it stopped. He looked around the room in the dim light and saw that he was alone. *Maybe it was my imagination,* he thought and dozed off into a light sleep again. Then he heard the sound again and a light bumping noise. He looked slowly and silently around his room, first at the wall and the window, then, straining to see his door, he noted that it was still bolted. Nothing there. He looked at the back wall where the loom stood. He saw nothing unusual, yet there was the sound again. It was coming from the area of the room where the cubical stood that held his scrolls of Scripture. His eyes remained on the spot as the morning light slowly revealed the scene. The velvet covering had fallen to the floor. His scrolls were all in their place, except for one. It was pulled out a few centimeters and was being gnawed and eaten by a large rat.

A low moan started in Saul's throat, and as the sound became audible, the rat stopped eating and raised its head, turning its black eyes upon Saul. Saul got up slowly. The rat didn't move. Saul reached down to the floor and picked up one of his sandals. He raised it over his head and with a grunt threw it at the rat. The rat leaped to the floor and disappeared. The sandal knocked another one of the scrolls to the floor.

The rat was under the loom now, and Saul crept across the floor, pushed the loom over, and leaped with his bare feet down on the hard rock floor where the rat had been. He looked around the room, trying to decide where the rat had hidden. His cloak lay on the floor by the bed. He danced upon it, but the rat wasn't there. Embarrassed at himself, he turned again to survey the room. The vile rodent had to be near the basket and spindle. He slowly crept up and kicked the basket. The rat jumped out, but out with it came a mass of fibers its feet had become entangled in. The rat leaped left and right, sideways and upside down in a frenzy to free itself, but it only succeeded in entangling itself more. Saul watched it squirm as it bound itself in a web of cotton. He slipped on a sandal and pressed the rat down on the floor with his foot. The monster shrieked and clawed, trying to free itself. He looked down at his head with hatred, deciding just how to kill it.

Just as he was about to take its life, he remembered. "The filthy thing has shreds of the sacred Scriptures in its stomach," Saul said aloud to himself. He paused. *It must die,* he thought, but still he couldn't crush it, thinking of the precious scroll. "What a horrible visitation upon me," he whispered, standing on one foot and holding the rat down with the other. "What, O Lord, is the meaning of this?" he moaned. "I spend all my waking hours on your holy Word, and a messenger of Satan, a . . . a veritable demon of hell steals in while I sleep."

He stood thinking for a long time, then finally reached down and put his thumb and fingers firmly behind the rat's head. He picked it up and broke it and its wrapping free from the rest of the mass. He opened the door and flung the live rat, tied just as it was, far out into the street. He didn't watch to see if the rat escaped from its bondage; he just closed the door and bolted it.

The room was a shambles. First Saul picked up the scroll that had fallen to the floor and examined it in the light under the window. It was the book of the prophet Isaiah. Unrolling its two rollers, he discovered that there was a bend and a small rip in the parchment where his sandal had hit it. *I could have it repaired by a Torah scribe,* he thought. He had copied the scrolls himself years ago, writing with a stylus on parchment. The ink he had made by mixing cypress with lamp black. If he had only remembered to use oil of wormwood in the ink mixture, the bitterness would have discouraged rodents and insects from eating the scrolls.

He examined the other damaged scroll carefully and saw that the rodent had indeed eaten a part of it. He opened up the scroll of Chronicles and laid it across the table. Even though some of the text was missing, Saul knew the passage well. The words were a thousand years old—God's promise to Solomon—"If my people which are called by my name shall humble themselves, and pray, and seek my face, and turn from their wicked ways, then will I hear from heaven, and will forgive their sin and will heal their land."

God made these promises to Israel during the Feast of Tabernacles at the dedication of the Temple Solomon had built, the first great Temple that had stood where the greater Temple now stood. Accompanying these promises was a warning: "If you observe my statutes and my judgments, I will establish the throne of your kingdom . . . But if you turn away . . . and serve other gods . . ."

The rat had done more damage than he thought as he unrolled the scroll further, gently pushing the parchment across the table. "This house which I have sanctified for my name will I cast out of my sight. And it will be a proverb and a byword among all nations . . . Because they have forsaken the Lord God of their fathers, which brought them forth out of the land of Egypt . . ."

He moaned at the desecration of the Holy Scriptures, the horrid toothmarks on the scroll.

"The holy Temple of the Most High shall never fall," he said. "His service and his house are my life, my daily portion, my daily service."

He rolled the scroll back up and placed it carefully and lovingly back in the cubicle. It took awhile to put the loom, basket, and spindle back in order. Having done this, he went to the basin and washed himself all over, brushed his hair and his beard, and put on a clean loincloth and tunic. He faced in the direction of the Temple, where the sun rising over Mt. Nebo was beginning to bathe its pinnacles in a golden glow. Then he began his morning prayers. It was to be a long, troubled day.

✠ ✠ ✠

Jonathan ben Annas, the high priest, looked down at the young Pharisee who stood before him. He was a small man; his hair and short curly beard were auburn, but his dark eyes under heavy black eyebrows were alive and piercing. Saul of Tarsus had brought before the Sanhedrin another prisoner charged with blasphemy. Only forty-two members of the Sanhedrin were present. Many had excused themselves, claiming other business rather than hearing the case against and deciding the fate of yet another follower of the crucified Nazarene.

Since the last days of Herod, the Temple at Jerusalem was watched over by what the Jews called "the evil eye in the sky"—the perpetual presence of Roman guards who stood watch atop the fortress Antonia at the northwest corner of the Temple complex. This fortress could barrack as many as a thousand soldiers. Adjacent to one side of the fortress were stables for the soldiers' Syrian horses. The Roman governor, Marcellus, was afforded every luxury that his office and position allowed. His hall of justice was on the main floor under the tower with business offices and chambers around it. Underneath the justice hall was the prison, a dark, musky, vile-smelling nightmare almost as large as the barracks itself. Into this dungeon were thrown the rabble of Jerusalem, the drunks, thieves, and rebels, anyone who wouldn't bow to Roman law, and captured Zealots, those awaiting trial for active organized resistance to Roman rule in Judea.

On a balcony on the side of the great hall that touched the Temple wall were two huge iron doors at which ten Roman soldiers always stood guard. Beyond these doors was a hallway through the wall, a no-man's-land forty cubits long that led to another pair of huge iron doors that opened into the Temple area. The hall through the Temple wall was cut by Herod, and the pious spat in disgust at the sound of his name. They could never forget that the holy Temple of God was defiled on the northwest corner by the presence of the hated Romans. Their tower could even be seen from a portion of the open sacrificial court. Inside the second pair of iron doors was a large balcony from which seventy wide steps descended into the Court of the People and onto the Temple complex.

On feast days and other holidays, this giant Temple rectangle accommodated enormous throngs of pilgrims. Its outside walls were eight hundred cubits long. Made of precision-cut white stone blocks, the walls were eighty cubits high and forty cubits thick. The Temple in Jerusalem was the center of worship and sacrifice, yet very few people were ever in the area of the steps that led up to the guarded doors. A Jew would consider himself unclean if he set foot on the pavement of the fortress Antonia.

The Temple building nearest to these steps was the hall Gazith, the Palace of Hewn Stone, or the council chamber of the Sanhedrin. The Jews wanted to believe that the Sanhedrin was the highest court of all, but there was no denying that Roman officials had supreme power, even over routing Jewish affairs if they chose to become involved. The installation of a high priest as head of this council was automatically approved by the Roman governor if the man elected was willing to adhere to Roman military and civil policy.

The Sanhedrin sat in session daily except on the Sabbath and holy days, governing the religious order of Jews; its decisions and pronouncements were adhered to not only by the Jews of Judea but by those dispersed throughout the empire as well. In this chamber the seventy-two members voted to, or not to, allocate funds from the Temple treasury for various projects and charities. Malefactors were judged before this body of men; suits were decided and judgment pronounced.

Behind Saul stood a man called Stephen. He was barefoot, and apparently the only garment he had on was the rough goat-hair robe he wore. He stood perfectly still, and though his beardless chin was caked with dried blood and a large blue bruise was evident on his cheek, his face was expressionless, his blue eyes staring blankly ahead. The presence of the high priest and the supreme court did not intimidate him; his mind was obviously elsewhere. His curly hair was cut short in the Greek style and framed his face like a halo. He was tall and stately, with wide shoulders; long, muscular arms; wide, full lips; and an aquiline nose. A very handsome man, he had the bearing of a man of wealth and position. He had, in fact, come from a wealthy family, but had forsaken it all to promote the cause of Jesus of Nazareth.

Jonathan wanted to be done with the whole matter of the Nazarene, because his followers had been a constant problem ever since his death. It was evident that this sect was not dying out.

"Saul of Tarsus, who is this man, and what is the charge against him?" the high priest asked solemnly.

Saul was glowing with triumph. His dark eyes, under heavy curling eyebrows, were piercing.

"His name is Stephen," Saul said. "He is a Jew from my own country of Cilicia, but unlike myself, he has the heart of a Gentile. I know his kind well, Father Jonathan. He was trained from youth to pollute the Law, and now, here in the city of God, his perverted religion has reached fruition. He teaches radical doctrine in the name of the Carpenter. He is one of the chief followers. He has publicly blasphemed Moses and the Law and vilified this very Temple. I have brought two witnesses against this man."

"Let them speak," said the high priest.

One of the two stepped forward, reluctantly. He, like the other, was unkempt, ragged, and dirty, one of the street rabble always on the lookout for a way to make a piece of silver for services rendered. He moved with a slight limp; his foot twisted outward, and he favored that side as he shuffled forward.

"Speak up," Saul whispered as he stepped up beside him. The man stammered at first, standing in great awe of this august body of judges and the high priest himself.

"My brother here and I," he began, "have heard this Stephen vilify this Temple. He said that Jesus of Nazareth will destroy it!"

A murmur arose in the Sanhedrin. "Jesus of Nazareth is dead," said the high priest.

"This man claims he is alive again and is coming back to destroy this Temple and to abolish its sacrifices," the man replied.

"Have you actually heard him say these things?" the high priest asked the man.

He looked at his brother, then at Saul, and then, nodding to the high priest, he said, "I have."

The second man had only one eye; it stared wide to compensate for lack of the other. Shy and fawning, but ready to be a part of the action now that his brother had spoken out, he came forward and, with his head down to hide his deformity, said, "He prays to that Jesus." He paused as all eyes were upon him, then stumbled on ahead. "He perverts the worship of the foreign Jews newly come to this city. We've heard him speak to hundreds in the language of the Greeks. He gathers all those of the Synagogue of the Libertines about him, and those of the Synagogue of the Isles of the Sea, desecrating this holy Temple."

The first witness, wanting to get back into the act, piped up, "He goes about working magic, deluding the people by giving honor to that Jesus for cures that are supposedly wrought by his hand."

"What tricks and what cures does he claim?" the high priest asked.

The man became perplexed and nervous, embarrassed at the direct question. "I . . . I . . ."

"Speak up," Saul said to him sharply.

"Saul, would you please be seated until these proceedings are completed?" said Jonathan. Saul reluctantly moved to a bench nearby, turning as he sat down so that he was facing Stephen and his witnesses.

"He has no more power than the Egyptian magician who came through Jerusalem deceiving everyone," the witness began.

The high priest interrupted. "We are not to be concerned with your personal opinion of this man. He is charged with blasphemy. Were you a witness to such?"

"There was a beggar who sat at the Damascus Gate, claiming to be blind. Everyone knew he could see as well as I. But he was lazy, so he begged from strangers. I watched this Stephen as he was entering through the gate. It was very crowded, and he knew that many people would be convinced that he had miraculous powers. He stopped and laid his hands on the beggar's eyes. When he took his hands away, the beggar shouted, 'I can see! I can see!'"

The high priest stopped him again. "We are not here to examine the validity of Egyptian tricks or miracle cures. We are assembled to decide whether or not this man has committed blasphemy."

The Sanhedrin was becoming restless. One of the judges beckoned for a servant to fill his goblet with pomegranate juice and wine. Many of the judges sipped the fruit-wine drink during court.

At this point the teacher Gamaliel raised his hand to be recognized. "May I ask the witness a question, Father Jonathan?" he asked quietly. Jonathan nodded, and all eyes in the chamber were upon Gamaliel.

The stately, handsome Gamaliel was one of those people whose presence filled a room. He was tall and slim as a willow. What little hair he had left could be seen in silver gray under his Pharisee turban. His face had a kind, fatherly countenance. He took a deep breath and held his hands together in front of himself, the fingers of one hand slightly touching and tapping those of the other. His gracious manner had a calming effect on the man he addressed.

"What is your name?" Gamaliel asked.

"I am Shemei of Hebron, Master Gamaliel," he answered.

Saul sat up straight and turned toward Gamaliel. Very rarely did his old teacher and friend speak out from his seat in the Sanhedrin. Whenever he did, it was worth hearing. He was the most loved and revered teacher in Jerusalem.

"Shemei," Gamaliel began, "this council spends much of its time in session, hearing charges against the exponents of the doctrines of the Nazarene.

Concerning these so-called miracle cures, we have heard enough about people claiming various powers from various sources. Now I would like to ask you something," he continued.

I know what he's going to ask, Saul thought triumphantly. *Now we're going to convict this man.*

"Shemei," Gamaliel asked, "did this Stephen invoke the name of a divinity when he supposedly performed this cure?"

"No, Master," said Shemei. "He did it in the name of the Nazarene, Jesus."

There was a rumble in the chamber. Someone said, "Stone him." Another said, "That's the end of that." The Temple guards lining the walls of the closed council chamber were tense. High Priest Jonathan raised his hands for silence.

Stephen stood still, his eyes still straight ahead, but he appeared to be somewhere else. Faint traces of a smile were upon his face. Many curious eyes were upon Stephen, but Gamaliel was not finished. Looking at the second man, he asked, "And your name?"

"I am Cononiah, also of Hebron, Master," he answered.

"Cononiah, were you with your brother when he heard the accused invoke the name of Jesus the Nazarene?" Gamaliel asked sternly and slowly.

"I . . . I was there, Master. I was coming through the gate just behind my brother," he said.

Gamaliel asked patiently, "Did you hear the accused speak?"

"No, Master," he replied, but added quickly, "I heard the blind man claim he had been cured by Stephen."

Gamaliel sat down with a sigh. "Thank you, Father Jonathan. No more questions," he said.

Saul anxiously stood up to be recognized by the high priest, who nodded his assent.

"Master Gamaliel," Saul said, "for many years I studied at your feet. Through you the holy Torah was opened up to me. You, Master, taught me to love the Law! You have filled my heart and mind with the oral traditions of our fathers. I treasure the years you gave me. There are three things that are important in my life: our people, our Law, and our traditions. Our Law we received directly from the Most High. I see the authority and the integrity of the Law threatened by the vile sect." Saul's voice was rising. He was waving his arms, and his eyes were blazing. As he continued talking, his hands sliced the air, chopping up imaginary victims. "I have been responsible for the arrest and trial of many of them. Fortunately, I have seen justice done in many cases. But this Stephen"—Saul was shouting, pointing at the accused—"this apostle of the so-called dead messiah, I have carefully watched, and he is a great prize. Hundreds every week are breaking the Covenant of our fathers and banding with this corruptible clan. This man is a ringleader! He must die!" Saul sat down. Sweat dripped from his face, and he was trembling. Opening and closing his fists, he stared at Stephen.

Gamaliel was of the highly respected group called Pharisees, as was Saul. The Pharisees had begun and flourished when national power and spirit were endangered by pagan influences, resulting in a necessity for men to protect the true faith of their fathers. Hence, a devout band organized in rebellion against the contamination of the Jewish spirit and called themselves Pharisees. They exerted a powerful moral and spiritual influence on people.

Another group, the Sadducees, was also represented in the Sanhedrin. Many of these men sat in the Sanhedrin because they belonged to families of wealth and power. Though they helped maintain worship in form, they were worldly and cared little for the strict rabbinical interpretations of the Law they helped enforce.

The high priest spoke up before Gamaliel could respond to Saul's tirade. "We do not have the authority to carry out the death penalty without Roman approval," he reminded Saul.

Saul forced himself to calm down before responding to the council chairman. "What the Romans do not know about will cause us no pain, Father," Saul said. "Many times they have turned their backs rather than become involved in our affairs. I personally have meted out justice to some of these insects in certain situations where I caught them in abominable acts against Israel, and I intend to do everything in my power to bring them to justice."

He was furious and ached with other things he wanted to say, but dared not. He knew that the high priest communicated closely with the Roman procurator, Marcellus. He knew also, but dared not say, that the reason the Romans looked the other way on many Jewish affairs was because of tacit agreements between Marcellus and Jonathan. The high priest controlled the people, prevented rebellions against Rome, and counseled toleration of the unfolding of the Roman standard at the games. In return, Marcellus gave Jonathan free reign in the exercise of Temple worship and religious rules, which included the trying of those accused of heresy and blasphemy. This was supposedly a secret agreement, though many, like Saul and other members of the Sanhedrin, knew of the understanding between the high priest and the governor. In order for this arrangement to continue, though, it had to be kept quiet; such subversion could never reach the ears of Tiberius Caesar, so no one appeared to know.

"Saul," the high priest said sternly, pointing a long finger at him, "*You* are not the Law. Justice will be determined by a vote in this Sanhedrin."

"Yes, Father," Saul replied resignedly.

Cononiah raised his hand for permission to speak once more.

"Yes?"

"Father," began the witness, "the same day that my brother heard him use the name of Jesus when he touched the blind man, we came by later and heard this Stephen speaking in Aramaic to a crowd of people near the gate."

"What did he say?"

"He said, and . . . as he spoke, he pointed to the Temple, even the inner parts, the Holy of Holies, and he said . . ."

"What did he say?" asked the high priest calmly.

"He said that Jesus would leave the right hand of God's throne to return to destroy the Temple and abolish the sacrifices," the man stammered.

A roar went up from the Sanhedrin. Several Pharisees stood, grasped their robes at the neck with both hands, and tore them to the waist as a display of shock and disgust at hearing blasphemy. A smile of victory appeared on Saul's face. Now that both men had testified that they had heard Stephen speaking of Jesus' claim, Stephen was doomed. Many of the Sanhedrin were talking wildly, pointing to Stephen. Some were beating their own chests in protest against the blasphemous accusation. They would stop their own hearts from beating rather than hear more abominable words of sacrilege.

Saul, upon seeing that Stephen was unmoved through all this, began to seethe. *The man stands in this holy place,* he thought, *near the very dwelling place of the Most High, and he appears to be proud of the evil things he has spoken and done. He stands smiling to himself about it all. I should not have brought him before this council, knowing for sure of his guilt. I should have killed him myself. He is wasting my time, and I need to be about the work to which I have been called.* Saul's mind was raging now. He could hardly remain in his seat. *How has he preached of his dead messiah? Countless generations of my people have lived and died with the glorious hope I pray for daily—the true Messiah!*

Near to bursting with anger, Saul sprang to his feet. "This man stands convicted," he shouted to the high priest.

An affirming cry went up from the assembly. The high priest began banging on the table. "Silence!" he shouted again and again.

Gamaliel had remained seated during all the commotion. He knew the prophesy of Jesus concerning the Temple, that it would be destroyed, that not one stone would be left upon another. Jesus had spoken these words to his disciples shortly before his death, telling them of terrible things to come and signs of the end of the age. When the shouting stopped and all was quiet, Saul, red-faced with fury, realized that all eyes were upon him, especially the quiet eyes of Gamaliel. Saul reluctantly took his seat.

Stephen still stood unmoved, his expression unchanged. There was a strange, unearthly air about him—he seemed at peace in all this turmoil, even seemed to emanate a sort of joy.

The two witnesses now crouched near the tall double doors. The high priest gave them a stern look, and a Temple guard pushed them back into the room. The doors had been kept closed at Saul's request. Many of Stephen's companions had wanted to come into the council chamber, but Saul had kept them out and closed the hearing to them. The room became quiet, and the high priest spoke to Stephen. "You have been accused of speaking in the name of Jesus the Nazarene. Your accusers have also heard you say that this same Jesus will destroy this holy place. Are these things so?"

Stephen blinked and finally seemed to become aware of his whereabouts. He turned and looked at Saul—a look not of malice but of kindness. It was met with a hostile glare. He glanced at his accusers, who dropped their eyes, unable to meet his. He looked around at the faces of the Sanhedrin, and then he began in a surprisingly powerful, authoritative tone. "Men, brothers and fathers, hear me," he said. "The glory of God appeared to our father Abraham when he was in Mesopotamia before he moved to Canaan, and God said to Abraham, 'Leave this country and your people, and go to a land which I will show you.' He came out of the land of the Chaldeans and lived in Haran. He was sent by God to this land where we now live."

What is this ploy? Saul wondered. *What does the story of Abraham have to do with his answering the charges against him? Does he hope to prove his innocence simply by telling the story of our people? His eloquence will not nullify his blasphemous words.* He looked anxiously toward the high priest, but Jonathan, seeing Saul's impatience, made a motion for Saul to remain silent.

Stephen continued. He talked for many minutes. He recounted the history of Israel from the call of Abraham, telling of how the Jews were a people set apart and chosen by God to deliver his word and his salvation of humankind. He correctly related the stories of Isaac and Jacob, of Joseph and his brothers, and of Moses. He told how Moses talked with God, how God gave him his oracles, the Ten Commandments. He spoke in articulate Hebrew, and his words filled the hall. The longer he talked, the more Saul's hatred for him burned within him.

Saul's mouth was dry. *My tongue would cleave to my mouth,* he thought. He snapped his fingers for a Temple servant to bring a tray of refreshments. From the silver tray, Saul took a cup of the red fruit juice and wine mixture, poured a little honey in it, and rattled the mixing stick loudly as Stephen continued. *He's well schooled in oration,* thought Saul. *A typical Greek god himself. A polluter of the Covenant. He has no right to call himself a Jew. To remain silent while this man stands here and tells stories of our people with the high priest and the Sanhedrin for an audience after he has blasphemed the very name of Israel . . .* Saul sipped his drink as Stephen related the times of David and Solomon and the building of the first Temple.

When Stephen mentioned the Temple, Saul sat alert. *Will he trap himself? Would he make those claims again about his Jesus being able to destroy this sacred sanctuary?*

Stephen, however, quoted the Prophets. "The Most High does not live in temples made with hands."

He's trying to impress us with his knowledge of the Scripture, thought Saul. *No one will be taken in by this traitor.*

"'Heaven is my throne and earth is my footstool. What houses will you build me?'" Stephen continued, quoting Isaiah. "'Haven't my hands made all these things?'" Stephen paused.

Saul clutched his drink hard in both hands.

"You stubborn and jaded in heart and mind. You do not have the spirit of holiness just as your fathers did not. They killed the prophets who told of the coming of the Just One," Stephen said loudly, pointing his finger at the high priest. "You were given the Law by divine dispensation, and you have not kept it. You are betrayers and murderers."

Saul was up on his feet instantly. He flew at Stephen, bellowing a death cry. His heavy silver cup was drawn back in an upraised hand when he left his seat. It struck Stephen on the side of the head with a heavy, dull sound and sent him sprawling backwards.

The high priest shouted, "You, Saul, a master of the Law, have struck a man who still stands in judgment—an unlawful act!"

But his words went unheard as others rose to follow Saul's attack. The elders came out of their seats as one and, amid shouts, attacked Stephen. Cononiah and Shemei joined in, relieved that the hearing had gone in their favor. The high priest called for order, and finally, Saul, most of his fury spent, stood up and held the others back. "Take him out and stone him!" he said to no one in particular but to everyone present.

"Stop!" the high priest shouted. "The man has not been found guilty. Saul of Tarsus, you have no power to give an execution order!"

Saul was seething. He whipped around, eyes aflame, to face the high priest. "Call a vote!" he shouted.

Jonathan ben Annas's eyes turned from Saul to the agonized body of Stephen, who was trying to raise himself up. He felt a strange kind of pity for him. *What a handsome man this Stephen is, and how different from the dozens of other ragged rabbis, some of them gathering great groups of followers, who were reinterpreting and often discovering new beauty in the Scriptures.* His interpretation of the Scriptures, though, had evidently gone beyond illumination to become heresy.

Jonathan, addressing the Sanhedrin, said, "All judges who find this man guilty as charged of blasphemy stand before me with left hand raised." They all stood except Gamaliel, who was carefully meditating on Stephen's speech. Four or five Sadducees who didn't care one way or the other sat unmoved.

"This tribunal finds this man, Stephen, guilty as charged," said Jonathan ben Annas.

Suddenly, before they could lay hands on Stephen to take him out, he sat up on the floor, opened his eyes, and looked straight ahead in Saul's direction. His eyes were glazed over, and a smile played on his bloody lips; his hands were raised in a gesture of praise. The expression on his face shocked everyone into silence for a moment, and in that moment, Stephen said joyfully, "Look, I see the heavens open, and the Son of man standing at the right hand of God."

Everyone faced the direction Stephen was looking. Saul, finding that all the eyes were turned toward him, quickly glanced behind him. Then, embarrassed at being stopped by an obvious trick, he quickly said to Cononiah and Shemei and the Temple guards, "Remove him from this place!"

Stephen was taken by the Temple guards, servants, elders, and other onlookers, including the two witnesses, out of the Temple and down the streets to the gate that is called Golden. As they hurried the bruised and bleeding Stephen out of the city, many of the curious street rabble joined the mob, shouting at him and kicking him, happy to be a part of the excitement. Many who followed, however, were of the sect of the Nazarenes and had been waiting outside the council chamber praying for Stephen's deliverance. Now they openly wept as they trailed along behind the mob led by Saul.

On the brow of the cliff overlooking the Valley of the Kidron directly across from the Mount of Olives, they threw Stephen off the rocky ledge and watched as his body ripped and crashed its way to the bottom. Bruised, broken, and near death, he managed to pull himself to his knees, look up at his accusers, and cry, "Lord, do not hold this sin against them."

"What's he saying?" screamed Saul. "What's he saying?"

Most of the elders and the Temple guards had now left the scene and returned to the Temple. Saul sat on a boulder looking down at Stephen.

"He is praying to his Jesus," said Cononiah.

"What shall we do?" asked Shemei.

Saul turned to an elder and two guards and said, "Take off your Temple robes and lay them at my feet." With none of the executioners wearing the raiment of Temple elders, no one could later prove that this execution was carried out with Temple sanction. They removed their outer garments and dropped them at Saul's feet.

Saul looked up at the fortress Antonia. Roman guards with bows and arrows in hand were looking down upon them. They were too far away to be of any threat to Saul now, but he hated this fortress, this all-pervading Roman presence, imposing itself upon the affairs of the Jews. He did not fear the Romans in the least, he himself being a Roman citizen by birth, but living with the Roman soldiers' presence had caused him lifelong pain. He would never have peace of mind so long as they were in his beloved Judea, but he would never fear them.

Saul stood up and raised his fist defiantly at the Romans, then spat loudly on the ground as an indication of his disgust at their presence. The soldiers turned away from what they knew was about to be another Jewish execution and ignored Saul and his companions.

Saul pointed to Stephen and said sharply, "Kill him!"

The first stones missed; then a large stone hit his shoulder and broke it. Still Stephen was upraised, his face covered with blood but his countenance joyous. Cononiah held a large, sharp stone, and as he raised it to throw it, Stephen cried, "Lord Jesus, receive my spirit!" The stone found its mark, crushing the skull, and Stephen was dead.

I've never seen one die like that, thought Saul. For a long time Stephen held his attention. He hardly noticed as his companions reached down at his feet, picked up their robes, and left silently. Saul was alone, and disturbed. *There was something different about this one,* he mused. *The man almost appeared to be happy about dying. He held the smile until his last breath.* Saul's thoughts were broken by the appearance of people on both sides of him climbing down into the Kidron. Men and women ran to Stephen's body lying facedown in the dirt. They fell upon Stephen weeping and wailing.

Saul's anger rose again. "Where did all these Nazarenes come from?" he wondered out loud. "The caves along the Kidron? The Garden of Gethsemane? They're everywhere! Hundreds of them!"

They were now lifting Stephen's broken body and carrying it away from the Kidron. Poor and ragged men and women fell in behind, forming a long, mournful train as they carried Stephen's body away. Some of them cringed in fear as Saul stood up and shouted at them with clenched fists, "Hear, O Israel: The Lord our God, the Lord is one!"

A voice behind Saul said softly, "But you, O Lord, are a God full of compassion and gracious, long-suffering and plentiful in mercy and truth." Saul stood and turned to see the ancient, white-bearded face of Master Nicodemus, a senior member of the Sanhedrin. Immediately Saul resented this retort, and without wavering he returned, "Thus saith the Lord who created the heaven ... I am the Lord and there is none else!"

Nicodemus answered without pausing, quoting from Leviticus. "You shall not avenge nor bear any grudge against the children of your people, but you shall love your neighbor as yourself. I am the Lord."

Saul held his temper. Nicodemus had not been there today when Stephen was convicted by his own words.

"This man has been found guilty of blasphemy, Master Nicodemus," said Saul. "Had you been with the Sanhedrin in session today, you would have cast your vote for his death." An ironic smile played at Saul's lips, for he doubted his own words—Nicodemus had never sat in on a hearing against one of the Carpenter's disciples.

Although Nicodemus was officially retired from the Sanhedrin and was the Temple Minister of Waterworks, he occasionally sat in with the Sanhedrin to be among his old friends. Most of his duties as water supervisor he delegated to stewards and priests. He received a daily report on the purity and abundance of water flowing into the Temple's many chambers and courts by way of the aqueduct from Solomon's pools on the Hebron road.

Saul stood his ground with Nicodemus. He quoted again from the Book. "He who blasphemes the name of the Lord shall surely be put to death and all the congregation shall certainly stone him." Saul spoke the last sentence slowly and bitingly. "Can the Scriptures be any clearer than that, Master Nicodemus? Is there any liberty to debate those sacred words?"

With a sigh Nicodemus sat down on a stone a few feet away from Saul. His kind eyes looked upon Saul with pity as he spoke. His shoulders were stooped. His hair was a shock of white, flaring out like a halo under his head covering. His face, especially at the corners of his eyes, was greatly lined. His hands trembled slightly. Out of respect for his age and his office, Saul again sat and waited to hear what the old man would have to say.

"No, I would not have cast my vote for that man's death," Nicodemus said. He glanced down into the Kidron, which was empty now. The only evidence of the execution was a few scattered stones and a dark shadow in the sand where Stephen's face had fallen. "I would not wish such a death for any man, Jew or Greek, bond or free. These eyes have seen much death in their time, and upon reflection, I must say that men would do better if they ceased taking it upon themselves to bring about the suffering and death of other men."

"It was this man's crimes against the Most High that brought about his death, Master," said Saul.

He had scarcely spoken to Nicodemus in the five or six years that he had known him. Nicodemus had personally known Jesus the Carpenter and had been overly tolerant of him. He had spoken with him on numerous occasions, he had listened to him preach, and he had not approved of his death when he stood convicted before Caiaphas and the tribunal.

As he thought on these things and listened to Nicodemus's grandfatherly speech, his anger began to rise again. "Tell me, Teacher," Saul said testily, "did not the Galilean claim to be the Son of the Most High?"

Nicodemus waited a long time before he answered, then said gently, "He did not make many claims of himself, Saul. He gave God as the source of all earthly power."

Saul did not need to question Nicodemus to know what Jesus had taught. He knew the words of Jesus almost as well as he knew the words of Moses. Many times over the past few years, he had heard Jesus' teaching expounded and discussed. He had been filled with disgust when he heard those self-righteous fanatics proclaim their independence of the Law and their salvation by mere faith in Jesus. These people were defilers of the Law, the sacred Law. The holy Torah was Saul's everything. The Word, the richness of the Word, was something to be delved into deeper and deeper, something upon which to grow old and gray, something to make new joys burst upon the mind every day. There was no better pursuit in life than the study and contemplation of the Book. Though Saul knew that perfection was an attribute of God only, his aim had long been set for the ultimate life's achievement—the goal of fulfilling all 613 commandments and observances of the Law. Impossible or not, this was the height toward which he would strive. For one to be a complete Jew, Jewish sentiment was not enough—practice and observance were required. The customs, feasts, rules, and traditions of his people were engraved in Saul's soul. He could only love the Law more as he grew older.

His total fulfillment came from the joys of inspiration that study of the Scriptures brought; his spiritual satisfaction, which suppressed his human needs, was found in that and in the practicing of the customs, feasts, and traditions of his people. He had no time or place for a family, and worldly wealth had no appeal to him.

When my hair is white like Nicodemus's, thought Saul, *I will not sit on the fence in confusion over my covenant with God. I will live and die by the Law, and I will carry the Word and the Law in my heart all my days.*

Saul stood and faced Nicodemus. Calm now and sure of himself, he lowered his normally high-pitched voice, but his words still had bite.

"Teacher," he said, "the Shema, proclaiming the oneness of the Lord, is the first thing I memorized as a child. To worship the one God is our first commandment. The Carpenter's people, in baptism, in prayer, and in ritual, worship three Gods—the Father, the Son, and the Holy Spirit. For this reason, if for no other, I find these people an affront to all I hold sacred. The sword of his Word pierces my heart to think of their claims. God's Son crucified by the vile Romans! Does the Creator of heaven and earth need help from a man who cannot keep himself alive to finish his work?" His voice was pleading now for Nicodemus to understand. "Are we to allow people to live among us and call themselves Jews who go about proclaiming the divinity of a Nazarene who died a shameful death by crucifixion? Was the one promised for hundreds of years meant to come and go like a bad mistake?"

Nicodemus looked at Saul with compassion.

"And the third deity which they claim dwells within them is the Holy Spirit," Saul continued. "Master Nicodemus," Saul said, slowing up a little, remembering that, after all, even though he had no feelings for the man, Nicodemus was a chief priest and leader in the Sanhedrin, "the Holy Spirit of the blessed God of Israel was the divine inspiration of our patriarchs and prophets. May I ask you, Teacher," he continued, "can weak, corruptible flesh contain the very Spirit, the Holy Spirit?"

"God is a spirit, Saul," said Nicodemus, "and those who worship him must worship him in spirit and in truth."

He's quoting the Nazarene, thought Saul bitterly. *A master of the Temple of God sits before me quoting a dead rebel . . .*

"You will excuse me, Master," Saul said, hurrying away.

Nicodemus sat with his head bowed. "Vengeance is mine, saith the Lord," he said weakly. He gathered his robe about himself and, taking one last look at the bloody spot where Stephen had lain, turned and walked slowly, with a heavy heart, back toward the city. He must go to the family of Stephen and offer words of consolation. A chill ran through Nicodemus as he remembered the fiery look in Saul's eyes. A new round of bloodshed was just beginning.

Saul took great strides back along the eastern wall of the Temple. The farther he walked, the faster he walked, his long, muscular arms swinging in time with the determined paces of his short legs. He was a fearsome, formidable sight, his cloak waving behind him, his dark eyes staring straight ahead, his long, curling eyebrows shooting up to almost touch his turban. His attire alone was enough to make people stop and stare. His headdress and robe signified his position in the Temple, but over his shoulders was a vest of mail, and on his feet were heavy sandals like those the Temple guards wore, with wide leather lacings strapped up to the knees.

He moved furiously toward the entrance of the Temple. Now he was firmly resolved! He would destroy the congregations of the Nazarene. He solemnly believed it to be God's work, and he had a deep personal interest in the task. He had always strived to please God. Still, he always felt that he hadn't done enough, that he fell short of fulfilling God's wishes in his tribute to him. He never found perfect peace in any accomplishment. He was never satisfied that his personal work for God was all he could do. Now here was his chance to recompense, to really please God in this splendid service to his people. This thought gave edge and energy to his zeal. *God's plan for man was revealed at Sinai,* he thought. *For centuries the Torah has stood in its richness and glory, holding a promise of the Just One, the Anointed One, who will descend from heaven in glorious splendor. These promises will stand against all the false prophets and fake messiahs who try to force themselves upon the people.*

Jesus of Nazareth must not be preached any further. Men like Stephen, who are trying to connect him to God as a son, as a deity in a triune godhead, must be silenced. The Nazarene, thought Saul, *is not any new truth that God has tacked on to Sinai as an afterthought.*

✻ ✻ ✻

Jonathan ben Annas was of average height and medium build. He wore his clothing proudly and had the bearing of a king as he strode about his chambers. He wore a heavy gold chain around his neck, a gold seal ring on his left hand, and a large ruby ring on his right. He was a strikingly handsome man with auburn hair and a deep, ruddy complexion. He had great bearing, yet at times he appeared rather aloof because his face was hard to read. He greeted everyone with the same placid expression, perhaps as a shield against the endless stream of visitors. He never let down his guard by showing his emotions, yet he wasn't prepared for a private visit from the zealous Saul of Tarsus.

He was dictating letters to a scribe, who wrote slowly and carefully on the parchment with a stylus. A guard stood just inside the door as Saul burst in, his face red and perspiring. The high priest raised his hand to stop Saul as he continued speaking to the scribe, determined to finish what he was writing before he lost his train of thought. No one entered unannounced into his private chamber; the guard was embarrassed that Saul had entered without his knowledge and confused as to whether he should allow him to stay. Saul, however, ignored him and stood waiting for the high priest to recognize him. Finally, having finished writing the letter, the scribe gathered his scrolls and rose to leave.

"Ask him to stay," Saul said to the high priest. "I require his service if you will grant my request." Saul realized he was intruding, but in his mind nothing could be more important, no task could be more vital to the sanctity of this Temple than the one he was about to embark upon. Jonathan was angry and didn't try to hide it this time. He stood with his face inches from Saul's.

"It is late in the day, Saul," said Jonathan ben Annas, anticipating that whatever it was Saul wanted could wait until tomorrow. "This day has seen enough trouble to stress the virtue of any good man. Tomorrow, Saul, tomorrow. Tomorrow's evils should be confronted tomorrow."

Saul, however, would not be turned away. "The Nazarene apostle Stephen is dead, Father. His friends are now mourning over his remains. Word of his execution will be on the lips of all of them soon, and they will scatter. I request a letter of official sanction of the Sanhedrin to find them wherever they are and bring them to justice."

The high priest studied Saul carefully before he spoke. "You would personally go about the task of destroying the community of the Nazarenes?"

"Yes," Saul answered quickly. "God wills that the heirs of his Covenant shall not suffer this degradation in our midst."

Jonothan fingered the lengths of chain in his necklace and held his temper. "The business of the Nazarene is behind us," he said softly. "God wills?" he asked louder, and again louder. "God wills? After years of our striving to deal with these people, the solution is suddenly revealed to you? You are blessed with the knowledge of God's will?"

"The Law of God is my motivator, Father," Saul retorted. "As the psalmist said, 'I delight to do thy will, O my God; yea, thy Law is within my heart,'" Saul continued. "The wrath of God is stirred up within me, Father Jonathan. There is no greater lover of the Law, nor one who has tried harder to be a better keeper of the Law than I: therefore, through the love and knowledge of the Law within me, I am called to do this work which I know to be his divine will."

Jonothan was raging. "You are called? You are called? Did you hear his voice, or did he appear to you personally? In a burning bush? How are you called?" he screamed.

Saul didn't answer. He only held his head higher, prouder. "I am called," he said.

The high priest was astounded. He stared, unbelieving, at the young warrior before him. *To know the will of God,* he thought to himself. *How many lives for so many centuries have fervently sought the will of God in their actions? Saul, the Benjaminite, has just pronounced that he knows the divine will!* He shook his head, rejecting what he had heard. He returned to his chair. He took a long time responding. *He is dangerous,* thought Jonathan.

"Your zeal will consume you like a burning fire, Saul," said the high priest calmly. "Fanatics are always at the fringes of society, no matter what the fanatacism is—and most always they go over the deep end into the abyss."

"Father Jonathan," said Saul sharply, "had it not been for fanatics like Elija the prophet and Ezra the scribe, there would be no Israel. I pray that I might be compared with such fanatics after I have fallen into the abyss."

"Saul," said the high priest finally, "do you not agree with Master Gamaliel that if the Nazarenes are heretics and practicing outside the will of God, as you say, then they will die out trying to exist side by side with the worshipers of the one true God? Why should a man of the Law such as yourself embark on a mission of violence and destruction?"

"God wills it," Saul said simply.

This man will cause me much trouble, thought Jonathan.

"Many people will die, Saul. They are of your own race, your own blood, for the most part. They aren't all Greeks or pagans. They are of the twelve tribes: your own kinsmen."

Saul paused before answering. "He who has separated himself from the Covenant is cut off from the vine of Israel. I shall glean the vineyard."

The high priest heaved a deep sigh, realizing that further conversation with this man was useless. He would go after the Nazarenes with or without the sanction of the Sanhedrin. Better that the Temple exercise some kind of authoritative control over his actions along with its sanction; at least a letter would get Saul out of the city. Still, he must be watched and stopped in some manner should he prove to be an embarrassment or a danger.

"Have the scribe write the letter. Then I will study it and sign on behalf of the chief priests, should I judge it to be a safe and proper thing to do," said Jonathan ben Annas.

Saul turned to the scribe, who unrolled a new parchment.

FROM THE CHAMBER OF THE HIGH PRIEST
TO THE SYNAGOGUES OF JEWS IN JUDEA,
SAMARIA, PHOENICIA, SYRIA,
AND ALL SCATTERED ABROAD.

This letter serves to introduce the bearer, one Saul, son of Benjamin, a Pharisee, and an exalted member of the Sanhedrin at the Temple of the Most High in this Holy City, Jerusalem.

This same Saul is hereby commissioned by this tribunal to examine the doctrine expounded in any synagogue or other place of assembly, and should he discover heretical teaching and practices of the sect called "The Nazarenes" or "The People of The Way," he shall arrest and bring to trial exponents of Jesus of Nazareth, the same being deceased, having been crucified by the Romans under Pontius Pilate.

These apostles are commonly known to preach, teach, and proselytize the divinity of Jesus of Nazareth, claiming his resurrection from the dead and ascension to heaven, where, they say, he sits on the right hand of the Most High. These and other such defiling precepts are contrary to the Law of Moses and the Order of this Holy Temple.

Saul, son of Benjamin, should be afforded such license as is necessary to properly halt the growth and spread of the sect of the Nazarenes.

Jonathan ben Annas
High Priest

The scribe melted wax and poured a few drops on the parchment and laid it before the high priest, who pressed his ring into the wax and handed it to Saul. At that moment Nicodemus entered the chamber.

Saul bristled. The odor of his own perspiration mingled with that of lemon oil and cedar from the rich chamber. Feeling suddenly as if he were being followed, then caught in the act of something unquestionable, he said, "Do not fear, Master Nicodemus. The Temple sanctions the work I am about to do. A few days here, then I will no longer be a bother to you."

Saul had reached the door when Nicodemus said, "Remember the words of Zechariah, Saul. Execute true judgment, and show mercy and compassion every man to his brother."

Saul smiled wryly and said as he was leaving, "I know who my true brothers are, Master. They are in no danger."

"Saul," commanded the high priest, "those you arrest you will bring to this council of elders to exact judgment."

"Am I not of this council?" Saul shouted back. "My witnesses, the Hebronites, will prove me." Jonathan watched in anger as Saul turned on his heel and left.

When he was gone, Nicodemus turned to Jonathan. "What is he going to do?"

"I pray that he will soon leave this city," said Jonathan. "Until then we will watch him."

"And then?" asked Nicodemus.

"And then he will still be watched," said Jonathan.

"But the man is obsessed, Jonathan," said Nicodemus.

"Enough of this man this day!" shouted Jonathan. "I'm going home to my family."

Jonathan felt a certain relief at the thought of Saul's impending departure. After all, he had asked for no money from the Temple treasury. This was a personal endeavor he was embarking upon. Thanks to the careful wording of the letter, the Temple was still protected. The man would be solely responsible for his actions.

✠ ✠ ✠

Saul crossed the wide-open pavement of the court of the Gentiles. Though it was late afternoon, the Temple complex was still crowded and noisy. There were thousands of people in this gigantic open area. He passed the many money changers' stalls. Only coins minted in Judea by Jews were accepted for donation into the Temple coffers. Roman coins and coins from all other provinces had to be exchanged for locally minted Jewish currency. The money standard for Temple donation was the bronze half shekel. Even silver shekels were traded for these lesser coins. The money traders took whatever profit they could get in these exchanges. Haggling was going on at every booth. People were shouting at each other, hotly arguing the exchange of their coins. The operators of the stalls were among the wealthiest men in the city.

Saul walked past them in disgust, going through a maze of dealers in birds and animals. There were pigeons, brown doves, and snow-white doves, which were more expensive. There were rams, ewes, lambs, and all kinds of goats— a great menagerie. The very poor usually bought two pigeons or possibly two doves for a sacrificial offering. Those who could afford it bought a snow-white lamb without blemish to be killed on the altar. Then again, the purchase depended on which holy day a certain sacrifice was required or upon a person's individual duty for a particular offering.

As he walked, he uttered the thirteen divine attributes, asking God's mercy on the transgressions of Israel. "The Lord, unchanging, almighty, merciful, gracious, slow to anger, abounding in kindness and in truth, remembering loving-kindness for a thousand generations, forgiving iniquity and transgressions and sins, and giving pardon to the penitent." Then he said, fully aloud, "Praised be the name of the Most High."

Saul finally made his way through the commercial madness, out of the Temple compound, and on toward the quarter where he lived.

"When the Messiah comes," he said to himself, "he will purge God's Temple of these lovers of money. The prophet Malachi said that he shall come to this Temple and sit as a refiner, purifying his people, purging them as gold and silver that they may offer to the Lord an acceptable offering. Purge and purify me now, O Lord. Sanctify me and steel me for the work that I must do."

He passed beneath the giant water-clock, or *Clepshydra*, as the Greeks had called it, whose one hand pointed to the eleventh hour. "It is the eleventh hour for the Nazarenes," he thought. "Their time is short."

The clock arose above the walls of the Temple and could be seen from almost anywhere in the city. Its water supply was by gravity flow from Solomon's pools. The mechanics of the clock were simple but very accurate. A gold chain hung from a cogwheel that turned the hand. The chain was attached to a giant copper bulb floating in the lavoratory that comprised the lower half of the tower. A valve was precisely adjusted to allow exactly the right amount of water to run from the lavoratory. As the water slowly went down, it lowered the copper bulb, which pulled the chain, which turned the clock's hand.

Every seventh day, on the evening following the Sabbath, the tank was refilled and the valve adjusted if necessary. To the faithful such as Saul, the clock was a familiar sight. The large bronze bell in the clock tower rang every three hours, audibly marking time and calling for prayers.

TWO

THE FAST

Sarah set before her brother Saul the second course of the evening meal. He finished his goblet of Carmel wine, broke off a piece of the round, flat bread on his plate, and dipped it into the chickpea and grain mush mixture. He offered it to his four-year-old nephew, Jacob ben Levi, who sat comfortably on his lap. The child ate with relish.

Jacob was a lively, intelligent boy. He loved his uncle Saul, and Saul dearly loved him. *He has many of his mother's better features,* thought Saul, *and fortunately so. Thanks be to the Most High that he shows little similarity to his father, Levi ben Lamech.*

Sarah served a bowl for Levi and refilled the wine goblets. "Eat, Saul," she said, sitting across from him. "Jacob can feed himself. It's you who need nourishment."

"Yes, Mother," Saul said to his sister, smiling, but he continued to feed his nephew.

Levi sat silently eating. He said very little during meals, which was very well with Saul. Levi was a lawyer, a civil lawyer, and Saul had little in common with him. No one in his family had ever had such an occupation; it was a dishonorable one in Saul's eyes. Levi was a deliberator, a referee in public suits in which sons of Israel were pitted against each other. *Such civil squabbles brought disgrace upon the participants*, Saul thought, *and diminished Jews in the eyes of non-Jews.*

"I'm waiting for the next course," said Saul. "Do I smell roast goose?"

Smiling, his sister arose to go to the oven.

Levi put down his empty goblet for the third time and opened up the subject that had taken much wine to get around to discussing. "So today the Sanhedrin judged the apostle of the Nazarene Carpenter, the Greek called Stephen. Is this true, Saul?"

"It's true," Saul answered, not looking up from his food.

Levi, a big man, was perspiring heavily, although the evening was cool on the rooftop where they ate. The lighted Temple heights were framed around Levi's head from where Saul sat. In the candlelight his fat jowls were red and flushed. A perpetual leering grin made his face even wider, and his lips were wet with the wine. Strands of his twisted black hair stuck to his forehead.

Saul felt his own face flush with anger at the conversation Levi had launched into.

"I trust that the scribes are keeping count of the cost and time spent in determining judgment on the countless numbers of followers of that sect," said Levi ben Lamech.

Sarah returned with the steaming platter just in time. Saul could feel his anger growing—the subject of the Nazarenes always put him on edge—but he ignored Levi's statement. He would not argue with his brother-in-law in the presence of his sister and the child.

Sarah sensed the tension, however, and looking first at Levi, then at Saul, she said, "You will eat now, Saul. It isn't every day that I cook a goose." She moved Jacob to a chair of his own and served the meat. Sarah was a vibrant, slim woman, by nature a cheerful person, with large, friendly eyes. The top

of her garment bore delicate embroidery, and her thick, dark hair was taste-
fully arranged on the back of her head.

Saul ate a few bites without speaking, but he could contain himself no
longer. He had to respond to Levi ben Lamech's remark. "Time and money
have no limit compared to the priority of preserving the unity of our religion," he said.

Levi ben Lamech ignored Saul's sharp tone. He leaned back in his chair,
feeling quite expansive. "Seven years have passed since the execution of the
Carpenter," he said. "His followers continue to multiply. With another trial
of just one of his apostles, isn't the Sanhedrin spitting against the wind?"

Saul didn't answer. He turned his attention to his food.

Levi ben Lamech continued. "I witnessed the recording of the death of
the Nazarene in the records of the people. 'Death by execution. Crucifixion.
Jeshua ben Joseph, carpenter of Nazareth.'"

Saul turned to Levi and, holding his temper, said, "It should have said
'crucifixion by Romans.'"

"Are we not Roman citizens?" Levi ben Lamech asked Saul. "And why
does the issue of the fact that he was crucified bother you so?"

"Levi," Saul said calmly, "I am a guest in your home, and I am honored
to sit at your table, but I must say . . ." He paused, thinking to carefully
choose his words. "Yes, we are Roman citizens by birthright, but first and
last we are Jews. Crucifixion is foreign and pagan to me. The very thought
of suspending a human body from a crossbeam to die in agony is archaic,
yet the Nazarene deserved death, and he is dead. So that is that."

"Is stoning more humane?" retorted Levi ben Lamech.

Saul looked directly into his brother-in-law's eyes. "For our people it has
long been traditional for the execution of malefactors," replied Saul.

Levi laughed again. "One would think you are a Maccabee, championing
the independence and purity, as you say, of our religion. Times have changed,
Saul. Roman gods and Latin superscriptions are on the coins we spend to buy
bread. There is a centurion and a Roman post in every town and village of
any import."

Saul was boiling, and that made him also fidgety and restless. Each small bite of food seemed to expand in his mouth before he could swallow it.

A rumbling sound came from Levi's great stomach, and he wiped his hand across his mouth.

"I do not need a lesson on the recent history of this land," said Saul coldly. "It has been almost a hundred years since the Roman general Pompey invaded our land, but we still freely worship and sacrifice in the holy Temple. The Most High has not turned his back on his chosen."

"Still, I cannot understand," said Levi ben Lamech, "why after seven years the great ruling body of this nation is so concerned with those who remember just another rebel."

"They don't just remember him," said Saul. "They worship him. Some even call them the 'Synagogue of the Nazarenes,' and this the Sanhedrin cannot condone. Not here. Not in Jerusalem." His voice was rising slightly. "Not in the shadow of the holy Temple, the dwelling place of the Most High."

Levi smiled at Saul. "My dear brother-in-law," he said as he leaned forward, "you have the whole pagan world against you, as we, as a people, have always had. Will your zealous efforts on behalf of the people ever really mean anything?"

Saul's face flushed, and Sarah interrupted just in time. "Levi, please do not discuss this at supper."

Saul wanted one last word. "Yes, Stephen was tried, found guilty, and executed."

"Spitting against the wind," said Levi, pouring himself a fourth cup of wine.

Saul had stopped eating and was sitting with his hands folded.

"You're not finished, are you?" Sarah asked.

"Yes. Thank you for dinner. I must go as soon as we have recited the benediction."

Jacob didn't seem to feel the tension; he continued breaking off pieces of his meat and eating them. Sarah sat with her arms folded, trying not to look at her husband, who sat with a bleary stare, holding his cup in both hands.

✳ ✳ ✳

Saul's place of abode was a cavelike basement room beneath a synagogue. The room was very sparsely furnished. On the left against the solid stone wall was a washstand with a basin and pitcher of water with a cloth over it to keep the water clean. On the right, under the one narrow, dim window, but facing toward the Temple even though it couldn't be seen out the window, was a stool and a small rough table with a tiny oil lamp and quill and inkwell. On the far side of the room was the ledge carved out in the rock where Saul slept. A single goat-hair blanket that he had made himself and a straw mat for a mattress were his only bedding. It was impossible to sleep comfortably on the rock ledge, but Saul had long ago forced himself to become accustomed to it. He only reclined when he was exhausted and ready for sleep. The ledge was always cool and dark. On the floor beneath this ledge was a small rug Saul had made from the wool of a lamb that had come from Hebron—Hebron, where lay the bones of Abraham, Isaac, and Jacob.

Against a fourth wall was a large vertical loom on which he wove the goat's hair or wool he had spun to make cloth for the rabbi upstairs. Saul had made a sturdy black awning to cover the front entrance to the synagogue. As pay for his room, Saul had made every item that Rabbi Baanah ben David had even casually suggested a need for—a covering for the table of shewbread, a rich lamb's wool cloth with a golden border, a multicolored tapestry to cover an unsightly area where an old door had been walled up, a floor mat for just inside the door, and even a pair of soft warm shoes for Baanah ben David when the weather was cold. Saul also helped Baanah care for the synagogue and its equipment.

Saul loved the old rabbi, and he loved Saul. He couldn't remember when Baanah ben David had not been at this synagogue. He realized that it had been more than seventeen years ago that a letter had come to Baanah from his old friend Janus, a tentmaker in Tarsus, telling him that he was sending him the thirteen-year-old Saul, a son of Benjamin. Janus was Saul's *sandok*, his godfather. The young man, said the tentmaker, had an eager, open mind and was free to travel. Saul's father had died and his mother would live with a brother, allowing Saul to devote his youth to the study of the Scriptures.

Saul often thought of his birthplace and his childhood home, Tarsus, a beautiful city of more than three hundred thousand citizens. There were three classes of people in Tarsus—the very wealthy, who lived in fine homes in the city and villas in the mountains or along the seashore; the very poor, who lived in squalor along the eastern bank of the Cyndus; and the Jewish community, who lived in crowded but comfortable two- or three-story brick or stone buildings on narrow streets on the western bank.

For half a millennium, Tarsus had been a great prize and a strategic point for the warring nations to the north and south, east and west. During the time of Alexander the Great, the Greek elite considered Tarsus a barbarian city. Its buildings were mostly of mud-brick and wood. The poorer lived in countless lean-to houses made of straw. Some lived in tents made of black goat's hair called cilicium. When Alexander reached Tarsus on the Cyndus, the city was burned, then rebuilt mostly of stone, the most imposing of edifices being styled after classic Greek ones.

A mint was built and the coinage bore Greek superscriptions. Greek was the common language of the people of Tarsus, yet after its conquest by Rome in the second century BC, Latin became fairly common. The Jews, however, also spoke Hebrew, read the Scriptures in Hebrew, and taught it to their children.

Saul, living in Tarsus, had mingled with Syrians, Cilicians, Pisidians, Cypriots, Cappadocians, and travelers from far and strange lands. He had seen the caravans come in from the East laden with oriental merchandise, silk of every color, lace, furs, ivory, teakwood, and rosewood. Some caravans continued on to Egypt to trade for brass, Ethiopian jewels, and the grain that grew abundantly in the verdant delta of the Nile.

To the great harbor of Tarsus came ships from every country, and from over the steep Taurus mountain range to the west came the caravans of traders and travelers upon the Roman highway. Roman roads, which traversed every province or country that became part of the empire, connected every corner of the captured world to Milepost Number One, which stood in the center of the city of Rome.

He remembered working with his father as a child. It was mainly in this harbor that Saul learned his trade as a tentmaker. He remembered the great rolls of hemp, cotton, or cilicium and his father's approval as he, small and agile, climbed as swiftly as a cat up the ropes to repair a torn sail, using his father's needles, pliers, and hooks.

After a time Saul's father decided he had advanced enough that he could send him off on his own. Day after day he rose early and, carefully wrapping his father's tools, left the city by foot and followed the Roman road to the foothills of the Taurus mountain range.

It was on these slopes that nomadic shepherds tended their flocks. Their lives revolved around their flocks, and when the flocks needed fresh pasture, the herdsmen and their families took down their black tents, folded them, and lashed them to travoises pulled by donkeys. They and their goats moved on. Saul followed the herdsmen and sometimes joined in helping pitch the tents. If he had to mend a torn tent, he always amazed the nomads by the speed with which his fingers flew with the tools and cilicium thread, mending and reinforcing the tent fabric.

He often dined with the nomad shepherds. The food was wholesome, but not truly to Saul's liking. Each midday meal was always the same—a stew made from goat's meat, leeks, garlic, and whatever vegetables or wild edibles were available. The flat unleavened bread was passed around, and each person broke off a piece large enough to hold across four fingers to dip into the communal pot. The child Saul silently gave thanks to God as he began and as he finished a meal. He ate very lightly, just enough to please the shepherd host. To decline the food would have been an insult to the host.

He neither received nor expected any pay for his services. He went from tent to tent, politely inquiring if he could be of service in repairing or restoring old or damaged tents. This apprenticeship gave him practical experience as a tentmaker. When he was barely twelve years old, his father died and his mother turned his father's tentmaker's shop over to him.

He mastered his craft, and then it was time to take up the matter of further education in the Law. It was suggested he go to the Holy City of Jerusalem to study under the revered Gamaliel. "Jerusalem!" said Saul aloud when he heard the news. The City of God! How often he had longed to see the City of God as it had often been described by those who had been there. How many countless numbers of his people had lived and died yet never seen Jerusalem? Every day he knelt and bowed toward the direction of Jerusalem and the Temple when he prayed. Now he would see them!

The Holy of Holies was the greatest fascination. There, behind the veil, dwelt the presence of the Divine One. Saul knew that he would never enter the Holy of Holies, but the prospect of seeing the Temple walls and the parapets of the Temple reflected in the sun made his heart leap for joy. "Jerusalem," he said. "I shall see Jerusalem."

Memories of his childhood would not leave him now as he sat in his dim room beneath the Jerusalem synagogue. He suddenly remembered a shepherd king named Zeno of Ephesus. Zeno had told him an amazing story of migrating geese and the fierce eagles that lived in the rocks and crags of the cliffs atop Mt. Taurus. The story was a lesson on when to speak and when to be silent.

"Every year," Zeno had said, "with the coming of winter for as long as people have handed down stories to their children, they tell of the smooth river stones that fall from the sky upon the hills of the Taurus which go down to Tarsus and the Cyndus.

"Look to Mt. Taurus. Its craggy peaks reach nearly a mile into the sky. In the lofty crags of the peaks of Taurus, many fierce eagles nest.

"Beyond the mountains, in the fertile valleys of Cilicia, Phrygia, Bithynia, the Pontus, and the Black Sea, great numbers of geese feed through the summer and autumn. With the onset of winter the geese know that it is time to migrate southward to the warm, rich delta land of the Nile in Egypt.

"In the darkness of night the eagles in the rocky peaks of Taurus listen for the flocks to fly over. They plan to attack the honking geese, kill them, and take them back to their nests. But surely it must be the hand of God which compels the geese to do what they do.

"Before they leave the ground for the long flight which takes them over Taurus, each goose goes to the riverbed and in its beak takes a smooth stone, not too large, but large enough to fill its mouth. Then they fly southward, climbing slowly but untiringly in the darkness. By the time they fly over Mt. Taurus where the vicious eagles await to kill them, they are thousands of feet above its summit. With stones in their mouths, they fly silently and are not likely to make any noise that will attract the killer eagles. Then, having safely passed the eagles, they open their mouths and drop the stones. Then they fly safely on to Egypt.

"Remember the geese and the eagles," Zeno had said. "There is a time to speak and a time to be silent."

Saul came out of his childhood reverie a little troubled. *Now more than ever,* he thought, *I need to remember the lesson of the eagles and the geese: when to speak and when to be silent or refrain from action.*

He put on his prayer shawl, lovingly fingering its bright fringes. He turned toward the Temple, closed his eyes, and began praying. "Consecrate me, O Lord, for your service," he cried. "To you, O Lord, I lift up my soul! Let integrity and uprightness preserve me, for I wait upon you. Redeem me, O Lord, and prove me. I have walked in truth. I have hated the congregation of evildoers. In your synagogues I will glorify you, O God. Your enemies roar in the midst of your holy Temple. The foolish people have blasphemed your name. Who is so great a God as our God?"

He prayed loudly, as though he would reach out with his voice from the basement and attract the ear of God on high.

"You have established a testimony in Jacob and appointed a Law in Israel, that your children might know the Law and set their hope in you and keep your commandments. But the heathen have come into your inheritance; they have defiled your Holy Place. Let me pour out your wrath upon them. Let them come before you as prisoners, crying, and let them be punished sevenfold for their offenses. Your enemies shall perish, Lord, and under your hand I will destroy the wicked of the land. I will rid your Holy City of these evil ones."

The vow of the Nazirites was an ancient one, and Saul reached for the scroll of the Book and read again God's direct order to Moses about its observation. For seven days Saul would fast, pray, and sleep. He would drink no wine. He would neither see nor speak to anyone. He would not leave this room. He would separate and consecrate himself for his task ahead. At the end of seven days he would go to the Temple and complete his vow with sacrifices. "Hear, O Israel: The Lord our God, the Lord is one," he prayed again.

He would go beyond the requirements of the vow. Nothing else mattered save the accomplishment of this work. In his mind he prepared himself to give up even the few simple pleasures he enjoyed. It was true that he believed God created all things for man's pleasure and fulfillment, but there was a time for everything—a time to laugh, a time to cry, a time to feast, and a time to fast. This fast was going to be his most severe, however. In appealing to God for a double portion of stamina, perseverance, and thoroughness, he was going to offer more than a double portion of sacrifice. He would meditate upon God with an attitude of joy and gratitude for the privilege of serving him with all his heart, body, and soul.

He lay down on his sleeping ledge without lighting his lamp. He would arise before the light and say his morning prayers, but sleep didn't come for hours. The day had been a stimulating one, and Saul couldn't keep the day's events out of his mind. He thought of death, death by stoning. Remembering the face of Stephen, he forced himself to stop thinking about it. But again his mind came back to death, death by crucifixion this time, the common way of Roman execution, a most cruel and unnecessarily prolonged way to die. Many of his people, even some of his friends, had been executed by the Romans.

He remembered on one occasion nearly a hundred had been crucified at one time, just outside the city walls, but in plain sight for all to see. A group of young men from a house of learning had gathered outside the fortress

Antonia to shout protests against the erection of the Roman standard over the Damascus Gate. Soldiers were dispersed to contain the shouting demonstrators. When the students began throwing stones at the soldiers, more soldiers were called out. With their shields and swords they hemmed the young men in against the north wall of the Temple, then beat and cut them into submission. Several lay dead against the wall, and the rest were later crucified.

This memory disturbed him, and he tried to erase it from his mind. He thought again on the Scriptures. With his eyes wide open he began reciting, but each time he finished a prayer or a verse, his memory returned to that day.

He had been out of the city when this happened, buying cotton and fleeces from a rural merchant on the Bethany road. Upon approaching Jerusalem, coming around the Mount of Olives, he saw the crosses being raised on Mt. Scopus. He ran all the way to the terrible scene and walked along the row of dying students, ignoring the hostile stares of the Romans. Looking up at the pain-stricken faces, he suddenly saw one he knew. He let out a heartbroken cry when he recognized Michael, the eighteen-year-old son of his neighbor Nathan, the cheese-maker. Michael had always been a quiet, shy boy, definitely not a leader in such rebellion against the Romans, but evidently a follower; or maybe he had just gotten caught up in the excitement with his friends. At any rate, he now hung dying on a Roman cross with long spikes driven through his hands and feet. Saul had kneeled beneath his writhing, twisting, groaning body and prayed for him. In his agony, Michael looked down at Saul and recognized him.

"I'm thirsty," he whispered through clenched teeth.

Saul arose, went over to some women, and begged a sponge filled with drugged wine, which family or friends of the victims were allowed to give the dying. Saul put the sponge with the opiated wine on the end of a long pole and raised it to his friend's face. Michael opened his mouth, took the sponge between his teeth, and squeezed the liquid out of it. Soon his groans diminished from the effect of the drug, and he looked down with thankfulness at Saul.

"Why, Michael?" Saul asked. "Why did you join such an insane rebellion?"

"For you," Michael whispered. "And for Israel."

Saul was sorely grieved and perplexed. The Roman soldiers approached and motioned for Saul to leave. He ignored them.

"But to die?" Saul shouted up at him. "What cause is worth dying for?"

"Survive, Saul. Survive if you can. But a brother is worth dying for," said Michael.

The flat side of a Roman sword knocked Saul to the ground, and he felt the heavy, nailed Roman sandal kick him in the ribs. He lay still until the soldiers moved along. When he felt free to move, he looked up again at his dying friend.

Suspended from the crossbar, from time to time Michael put his weight on his nailed feet to lift himself up to breathe. By now the weight of his body pulling on his chest and shoulder muscles had so weakened them that he was actually suffocating. Without occasional support from below, the crucified man was gasping to get just a little breath in the crowded air passages.

At this point, as an act of mercy or, more likely, as a move to get the job over with, a Nubian slave of the military came with a heavy hammer and with two blows to the shins broke the legs of the victims. Saul's friend screamed, then gasped. Being unable to fill his lungs, he did not take another breath. Michael ben Nathan was dead.

"O God," cried Saul from his sleeping berth, "renew my mind. Cleanse it of all evil and trouble and let me think only of you and your will." Still, it was hours before Saul slept, and then he slept fitfully that first night. His memories drifted into dreams, disturbing dreams of Stephen, of Michael, and at times of the Nazarene himself.

He did not remember his dreams clearly at first light. He washed himself thoroughly, then stood facing the direction of the Temple and began his morning prayers. He refused to allow himself to think of his dreams of death when they attempted to crowd themselves back into consciousness. "Sanctify me for your service, O Lord," he prayed.

After the third night and day, Saul was no longer hungry. He began to feel light-headed and as if he were "above" his body. His mind was clear, and, beginning with his evening prayers on the fourth day, he stood in a state of prayer, moving back and forth on his heels reciting the Scriptures he had known from youth. He repeated a promise from Isaiah, and as he spoke the words aloud, he felt that the prophet must have had him, Saul of Tarsus, in mind when he wrote them: "Fear not, for I am with you; yes, I will help you; yes, I will uphold thee with the right hand of my righteousness."

He was interrupted by a knock at his door. His room was dim. He had not lighted an oil lamp. He quietly moved to the edge of the window by the street and looked out. The street was at eye level, and there, an arm's length from his own face, were the feet of a Pharisee standing at his door. The golden hem of the fine linen cloak told him so. Leaning a bit and looking up, he recognized the man who was knocking at his door a second time—Master Nicodemus.

What does he want? thought Saul, moving quietly across the room to hide in the darkness. Nicodemus knocked again, louder. *Go away, traitor,* Saul thought, almost aloud. He stood still. Nicodemus did not knock again but slowly turned away from Saul's door. *He knows I'm here and won't see him,* Saul thought. *Maybe then he'll know how a true son of Israel feels about the polluters of the faith of our fathers. His face fairly shines with the same self-righteous piety as Stephen's and the other Nazarenes'. All is not peace and joy in the Temple of God. His wrath will work his vengeance on all who oppose and betray him. Not one will be spared. Not even Nicodemus.* "Hear, O Israel: The Lord our God, the Lord is one!" Saul said aloud with a clenched fist held high in the darkness of his room, alone against the wall with no one but God to hear. Had anyone been in the room, he would have seen the fire in Saul's eyes.

He paced the room flaring in anger, yet he was undeniably a little curious as to why Nicodemus would have been calling upon him. To admonish him more for certain, but he might have been able to force Master Nicodemus to admit to being active in assembling with the Nazarenes. This Saul had long suspected, and this thought made Nicodemus smaller still in his eyes. Imagine this Judean sage sitting part of the time in the highest council of the Jews and then sitting in the dirt with the wild Nazarenes the rest of the time! He had to stop thinking of this man; else he would be ill. "Renew my mind, O God," he cried. "Prepare me for your service."

His bed seemed harder than ever that fourth night. He had not lighted his lamp for fear that Nicodemus would return. He renewed his vow to speak to no one for the entire seven days of his self-exile. He tossed back and forth on the woven straw mat covering the solid rock ledge. His room was black, and each time he turned his weakening body toward his room, he could see through his one small window a handful of stars in the clear, moonless sky. His mind was a whirling machine. "Where are you, God?" his mind cried out. "I love to do your will. I live only to serve you, yet you are so far from me."

Is God up among those stars? he wondered. *Surely the Creator is greater than his creation.* Somewhere out there above the earth lived the one true God. Yet this was another mystery. Did not God command that the wilderness tabernacle be built according to his own specifications in order that he himself could dwell among man? Was not his divine presence in the Holy of Holies in the Temple? And did not God dwell in the heart of man? In the mind of man? In the soul? He often felt God's presence, but it was fearsome. Could the goodness of God abide with the evil of man—with Saul himself? No matter how committed, no matter how dedicated Saul was, would God manifest himself in Saul's life?

His doubt plagued him. Frail mortal that he was, no matter his sacrifice, no matter his dedication, would, could, the Omnipotent be manifested in his weak human flesh?

He was suddenly ashamed of his lack of understanding of the person of God. He is omnipresent and omniscient. The prophet said he is in heaven above and in earth beneath, and the psalmist said, "He is in the very substance that made me." In the wilderness tabernacle had he not indicated his presence among them with a cloud by day and a pillar of fire by night? How big is God? How small is God? He is everywhere, yet Saul could find no peace in him anywhere. "Let me labor in your service, O Lord," he cried. "In this noble task which you have appointed unto me, let me find peace. Let me find joy. Let me find you!" But Saul was not to be comforted. After the night was half-gone, he fell into an exhausted, troubled sleep. Then the horrible dream began.

He dreamed he was in a whirling flood of water. The rain was pouring down and the day was half-dark. Saul reached out for the shrubs and vines that grew along the edge of the water, but the force of his body in the raging flood pulled the plants up by the roots. He went under, then he was back up, then under again, then back up. He saw a large stone jutting out from the bank and with clawing fingers grasped it. It was solid, and if he could only hold on, he could pull himself out of the flood. He strained every muscle in his body; his fingers were raw and sore as he groped around the large stone, trying to hold on. But a sudden wave opposed him and washed him back toward the rock, and as he realized he was going down in the water, he awoke himself with his own cry for help.

He sat up trembling and sweating in the cold, dark room. "I understand the dream, O Lord," he muttered. "The psalmist said 'The Lord is my rock, my fortress and my deliverer.' And I know, Lord, that the flood signified your enemies, my enemies, all the ungodly men. But in the dream, why could I not hold on to the rock? O God, don't forsake me. Don't let me be washed away. I have a service to perform for you."

After a long time trying to silence his troubled mind, Saul finally drifted off to sleep again and the dream continued. He dreamed he was walking on the shore beside the raging floodtide. He was wet and cold. He was conscious that he was dreaming in a not-too-deep sleep, watching himself in his own dream. It was a strange feeling. He knew the fasting was partly responsible for his mental state, yet even aware enough to realize this, he couldn't wake himself. He saw himself shivering from the cold, and all of a sudden he was cold, but he was falling into a deeper sleep now and could not come out of the dream. He twisted and turned on his ledge, in a sweat.

Cries seemed to come from the water, and there appeared to be many, many people in the water, but he couldn't recognize any faces. Voices were pleading and moaning now, and the river became a sea he could not see across. Thousands of people were in the water, and their voices were strange, foreign. He still walked along the dry, rocky shore, but it was getting darker and he didn't see the small stream until he stepped into it. The stream was just a rivulet, and as it ran into the sea, he could hear voices laughing and weeping with joy. Some seemed to be singing and praising. It seemed that the water from the rivulet in which he stood was working some kind of magic on the pleading souls in the water. The people were struggling to move in his direction. He heard some of them call his name. Why were they calling to him to save them, and why were they trying to reach this particular spot where the stream ran into the sea? He trembled with fear. The water in the stream had a strange, musky, sweet odor, and for the first time he realized his feet were warm where he stood ankle deep in the . . . blood. "It's blood," he screamed, and he awakened.

Dawn was breaking, and the knock on the door seemed to pierce his temples. He covered his ears with his hands, and with his head down and his eyes closed, he tried to keep out the world outside and go back into his dream. He was confused and irritated by the interruption. Even though the dream was frightening, he had to think, pray, and immediately interpret its meaning before any of it was forgotten, but the interruption persisted. Rabbi Baanah ben David knocked loudly at his door and called out now, "Saul, Saul. Open up."

Saul sat still for a long time, for it was a few minutes before the rabbi gave up and left his door. *Maybe he will forgive me when he realizes that I have taken a vow,* thought Saul. *He will understand. Maybe even now he understands and is praying for me.*

He walked across the room and looked at himself in the polished metal mirror. His face was ravaged from the torturous night of little sleep filled with nightmares. He poured cold water from the pitcher into the basin and washed himself thoroughly. As he washed, the words of the psalmist flowed out of his lips as the dream replayed in his mind. "Save me, O God, for the waters are come in unto my soul . . . I am become a stranger unto my brethren . . . the zeal of thine house hath eaten me up . . . I chasten my soul with fasting." He was very weak. The ordeal of standing and washing himself was exhausting, but the mirror showed a brighter face. He brushed his hair neatly. Saul studied himself, hoping that he didn't appear to be fasting. He wanted strength to be reflected in his face, but his eyes showed confusion. "The blood," he said. "A symbol of sacrifice, but what blood? Whose blood? The people in the water were calling my name in foreign tongues. I wish I could just forget this disturbing dream."

By midmorning, he was beneath the window with the scrolls of the Law and again found himself at peace in the Scriptures. He read the book of Exodus, and his brilliant imagination took him along with Moses through the wilderness wanderings. He was with Moses on Sinai. He, in his mind, helped build the tabernacle. He could see the priestly garments of Aaron as clearly as if Aaron stood before him. He saw the Ten Commandments, carved in stone by the hand of God. He heard the children of Israel in wickedness and idolatry and admired Moses's righteous anger. Saul cherished his precious scrolls of the Scriptures and fingered them lovingly.

He noticed again the tattered, rodent-eaten ends of the scroll of Chronicles. It was still not repaired. Maybe he would replace it—he would make a new scroll. Yes, he would get new parchment and copy it himself. He would throw away the defiled scroll. He would restore those words of the Most High. "This Temple which I have sanctified in my own name, I will cast out of my sight . . ."

Troubling words, but an unspeakable thought in Saul's mind. The destruction of the Temple? The destruction of the very Covenant? Never. The heirs of the Covenant had failed before, for Solomon's Temple had fallen, but never would it fall again, for men such as Saul would always consecrate themselves and protect the Law and the Covenant. The dwelling place of the Most High in this, his city, should never fall.

It was dark again on the fifth night when he rolled the scrolls up and, without lighting a lamp, stored them back in their niche in the cubicle, dropped the velvet covering over them, and lay weakly down upon his mat.

He had not allowed himself to think of the dream in the past few hours, for somehow he had the feeling in the back of his mind that the dream somehow concerned the Gentiles. He had not allowed himself to give any thought to the vile, idolatrous Greeks or to the despicable Romans, even though he knew that some of them would be harboring his victims when he started his work of preserving the unity of the religion of his fathers in just two days. The Romans were generally tolerant of any and all religions, even in Rome, the city of Caesar, itself. They didn't really believe in their own gods, so how could they be expected to take seriously the God of the Jews and the proper worship of him? The Macedonians and Cilicians were even harder to understand. They worshiped everything, including their own bodies. They had a god for everything, for every sin, and couldn't understand a Jewish God who wasn't worshiped through love's sensual pleasures. *It is the mentality of these cultures that weakens and waters down our religion when they live among us, these polluters who would worship a poor, wandering, crucified Galilean rabbi. Such a one was Stephen,* Saul thought in self-consolation.

He realized that his mind was wandering back to the Nazarenes, and he stopped himself. "Two days hence, the obliteration of the sect of the Nazarenes will be my task," he mused, "but for now, O Lord, let me meditate on your Holy Book." In his mind he was walking through the parted waters of the Red Sea, and he finally fell asleep.

The sixth night and day passed, and Saul became weaker. There was not one ounce of fat on his already-slim body. He felt light-headed, and as he walked around his room the sixth day, he could barely feel the floor. Even wide awake he felt that he was above his body. It was a pleasant feeling. He was not the least bit hungry; he hadn't thought of food after the third day. He read the Scriptures for short periods of time, then meditated upon them for longer periods. He sat for hours beneath the window. He was one day from beginning his work of destroying the Nazarenes, and the Word of God was all that filled him. He was more reassured than ever that he would accomplish his task. Reciting aloud from Joshua, he felt a personal message in the verse. "This book of the Law shall not depart out of your mouth, but

you shall meditate upon it day and night, that you will observe to do according to all that is written there, for then your way shall be prosperous and you
will be successful."

Just before the seventh night began, Rabbi Baanah ben David knocked at
his door again. Saul moved quickly from the window and into the gloom.
He would not break his vow, though he was lonely and would have loved to
talk to his old friend. Baanah was one of the few people he talked to at all.
Saul hadn't many friends, but he loved the rabbi.

He had spoken to him before about his feelings toward the Nazarenes,
once becoming enraged over the subject. The old rabbi had cautioned Saul
sternly about his wish to destroy their congregation. "There has been enough
bloodshed in this city, Saul," he had said in a fatherly tone. "The soil of Israel
cries out not only from the blood of the prophets, unjustly murdered, but
also from that of the many simply poor and downtrodden. Be careful that
you do not shed innocent blood."

"Saul," Baanah ben David called more loudly. "Why won't you see me?"

Saul stood quietly still until the rabbi gave up and left his door. He sat
down upon his sleeping ledge. He suddenly realized that he was very, very
lonely. He wanted to share his heartfelt convictions with his friend. Surely
Baanah would understand now that the Nazarenes had to be destroyed.
"Defilers of the Law are not innocent, Master," he had said. "These 'People of
the Way' would destroy the Law. They claim that faith alone in their dead
Carpenter gives them sanctification and salvation, even eternal life."

"Many offshoot sects of Judaism have claimed such things before, Saul,"
the rabbi had replied. "God laid out his plan for humankind centuries ago
in no uncertain terms. A few hundred, or even a few thousand, malefactors
at this late date are not going to alter it or change God's mind. Let them go
their own way. God's truth is its own protection."

"God calls his people to action, Master," Saul had responded with final-
ity. Now weak and alone in his room, he would have liked to tell his friend
his plans, share his dreams with him, but he must not. He must meditate
on the task at hand tomorrow.

Saul lay down for his seventh night. He felt faint, and it was a few moments before his head stopped spinning around. He knew somehow that the dream was going to recur. His thoughts were spinning as well, and he was into the dream even before he was sound asleep. He heard the voices in the water first. They were Gentiles, he recognized in astonishment, crying out to him in Arabic, Cilician, Greek, Macedonian, Latin! They were calling his name in their own languages. "Help us, Paul! Save us, Saul! Paolo! Pol! Paulus!" cried the multitudes of voices in the dark, whirling sea at his feet. As a child in Tarsus, Saul had often been called these names, but he had always responded negatively to hearing himself called "Paul," the Gentile equivalent of the Hebrew "Saul."

On the dark horizon, he could see no end to the faces and upraised arms. He walked along the seashore confused and troubled that so many cried for him, yet he actually felt no need to help the strangers, those Gentiles who cried out his name in so many tongues. He didn't see that rescuing them from their plight was his responsibility, yet they seemed to need him.

Again he didn't see the red stream until he had stepped into it and felt the wetness. Knowing it was blood this time, he awoke himself with a cry. He lay slightly trembling, staring at the stone ceiling. "The interpretation! The interpretation!" he whispered to himself, searching his mind as he rethought the vivid dream. No interpretation came to him, and he began trying to force it out of his mind.

I will not continue the dream when I go back to sleep, he thought. *I will meditate on the Word of God.* His sharp memory recited the call of Abraham, word for word as it is written in Genesis. His mind dwelled upon Joseph's bloodstained coat as he retold himself the story of Joseph and his brothers. Blood again. And with that his mind was back on his dream and the blood was on his feet and hands. "No, I will meditate on the Word of God," he said silently, becoming sleepy and dreamy again. In his mind he saw the scroll of Exodus and was well into it before he fell into a faint sleep or a sleepy faint, whichever; he did not know or care. He was quoting a verse of Scripture about the Passover of the Israelites, which became a transition from awareness to the continuation of the dream. ". . . and the blood shall be to you a token upon the houses where you are. And when I see the blood, I will pass over you . . ."

"The blood! It is all over me," he cried in his dream. He turned from the sea and began clawing up the hill, following the stream and climbing toward a light at the top. Something was drawing him toward the light. It was frightening, yet there was something beautiful about it. He stumbled, and reaching to catch himself, he fell upon the bloody forehead of the smiling Stephen. Again aware that he was dreaming, he tried to awaken himself, but the light at the top of the hill held him in the dream. Weeping as he ran, fell, crawled, and stumbled over countless bodies all wearing the face of Stephen, he at last found himself lying in the stream of blood with his arms around the foot of the crucifix. He pulled himself up to look at the face, although he did not expect to see Stephen or his friend Michael. The light emanating from the man blinded him, but he could see the sign. The Nazarene!

He woke himself screaming and found he was standing in the middle of the room, disoriented for a moment. Then as he realized he had redreamed the terrible dream, he sat heavily on his ledge. He was concerned that he found himself asleep on his feet. *I must reason this out,* he thought. He meditated for a long time, and nowhere in the Scriptures, nor the Law, the Prophets, or the Writings, could he find the revelation of the dream in scriptural reflections. He could not rationalize the crying Gentiles or the thousands of Stephens. And why should he dream of the Nazarene? He had never seen Jesus of Nazareth. Yet in his mind he had. He had heard him described and had a mental picture of his face. And it was a Stephen-like face—not in the physical features, for the Nazarene had a beard—but in the expression of joy, that curious bliss.

And the blood flowing from him? Against his will he interpreted the rest of the dream. The blood flowing from the Nazarene was offered as a sacrifice for them, and Saul on solid ground was to offer to rescue them through the blood sacrifice of the Nazarene.

Saul shook his head and paced the floor. "No!" he said. "No, this is what the heretics believe, not what I believe."

"Forgive my being tricked by the Evil One," he said.

He lay back down to think. His mind. His mind was fairly alive with words. Words from the Scriptures. He could not close out the words. Thousands of verses of Scripture ran through his mind, and as he lay down again, the words took wing. A prism of colors flashed under his eyelids, and he was content as he recycled the Law through the machinery of his marvelous mind. He fell into a sweet, deep sleep.

Following his morning prayers, he surprised himself by having slept soundly until the sun was an hour high. He could not remember having ever slept this late. But then, last night had not been ordinary. The dream had exhausted him emotionally, and his body, being denied sustenance, was weakening. For the first time in seven days, he allowed himself to think of food. Later today he would purchase a couple of barley and date cakes and some cheese and wine from the bazaar. *I will forget the dream,* he thought. "The dream was put there by the Evil One to trouble me. I will not despair," he whispered. "To despair in a complicated or tragic situation is to deny God's compassion for his creatures." Saul praised aloud, "Merciful are you, O God, who gives me courage in adversity."

He put on a clean loincloth and tunic; he cleaned his sandals, put them on, and wrapped the leather lacings up to his knees. He put on his girdle and Temple cloak. He stuck the letter from the high priest inside his tunic.

He stood before the mirror and placed his head cover on the back of his head. The small, round, bowl-shaped cap with its distinctive design and trim identified him to all Jewry as being of the tribe of Benjamin. Then, on second thought, he took it off and crowned himself with the conical headdress of the Pharisee. So adorned in his strange mixture of ecclesiastical and military clothing, Saul of Tarsus, lean and hawklike, ended his seven days of self-sacrifice and preparation and strode out for the Temple of God with his cloak flying behind him.

Inside the Temple sanctuary was the Most Holy Place, and inside the Most

Holy Place was the Holy of Holies, the dwelling place of the Most High. The room was without furniture of any kind, and the entrance to it was not a doorway but a heavy golden curtain or veil. The only person ever to enter the Holy of Holies was the high priest himself, and then only once a year on the Day of Atonement. He entered upon his knees and burned incense, "a sacrifice of sweet-smelling savor," to the Most High. The rule of total exclusion of all others was so severe that the high priest entered with a rope around his waist in the event that he should faint or die while in the Holy of Holies. No one would be worthy to enter this inner sanctuary to bring the high priest out in such a case. The rope would be used to retrieve the body.

From the Most Holy Place, there arose a perpetual column of black smoke from the endless number of lambs, rams, ewes, and doves that were killed as blood sacrifices and burned at the altar. On a clear day, the smoke could be seen as far away as Mt. Tabor in Galilee, eighty miles to the north. On windless, damp days such as this one, the smoke hung like a pall over the city. The pungent smell of burning hair and flesh permeated every house in Jerusalem. People who left the city from time to time discovered that their hair and clothing often smelled of the smoke from the Temple sacrifices.

It was a pleasant smell to Saul. He had spent much time in this area, in the halls and courts beneath the enormous towering columns adjacent to the Most Holy Place. In reality, here he had spent many of his days from the time of the beginning of his instruction in the Law. He loved to share his own interpretation of certain Scriptures, and he loved to hear other students and masters of the Law expound their views.

But he was always very selective about whom he chose to debate with. He had never taken seriously any of the poor wandering rabbis. The Temple courts were full of them, and small and large groups gathered everywhere to listen to various preachers expound various views. Saul, upon recognizing Galileans or foreigners such as Cilicians, people from his own country, steered clear of them. The Greek and Roman influence outside of Judea was sometimes damaging to their faithful practice of their religion. Saul saw this as evil, these new innovations in modes of worship.

None of the foreigners were more despicable to him than the Galilean Jews. They had made up the nucleus of the Carpenter's following. He even hated their dialect—the way they distorted the language of his fathers with their coarse speech angered him.

But now he was happy, joyful, even ecstatic as he approached the sanctuary. He passed under a marble beam held high between two columns. Carved in the stone in Hebrew, Greek, and Latin in large letters were these words:

JEWS ONLY: ALL OTHERS PASS UNDER PENALTY OF DEATH.

Saul passed through the large Corinthian brass gates and ascended the fourteen wide marble steps. The gates were so heavy that twenty men were required to close them for the night. He felt as light as air. He fairly flew up the steps, and when he reached the level of the sanctuary, he was faint and would have fallen, had not a Temple guard caught him by the arm. It was not an unusual thing, however, for the Temple guard to see one of the faithful faint from fasting.

He regained his balance and walked to the right of the great burning altar where the sacrifices were being made. Dozens of priests were in the area with hundreds of people who had come. A great variety of services and sacrifices were performed by the priests. Here the vows of the Nazirites were consummated. Here the animals were slaughtered. A great truth of his religion was "Without the shedding of blood, there is no remission of sin."

With the progressive decay and degeneration of worship and the growing emphasis on ritualistic form, a lucrative business had presented itself a few years earlier to the old high priest Annas. The business was now carried on by the retired high priest, his nephew Caiaphas; and the present high priest, his nephew Jonathan ben Annas.

Most of the land between Jerusalem and Bethlehem had been owned by old Annas. In these fields, shepherds bred and raised the snow-white lambs to be sold for sacrifice. Most of those slain at the Temple altar came from those fields.

In one of the many booths adjacent to the great altar—booths provided to afford a semblance of privacy for the final part of the Nazirite vow—Saul sat down before a low table and spoke quietly to the priest who stood by. "One he lamb of the year without blemish for a burnt offering; one ewe lamb of the first year without blemish for a burnt offering; and one ram without blemish for a peace offering. Also a small basket of unleavened bread and wafers anointed with oil, and cakes of fine flour mingled with oil." As Saul spoke, the priest marked the amount of each item on a slate.

"What is the purpose of your vow?" asked the priest, more as a matter of routine than as a question to obtain information.

"To publicly testify of my dedication to the Most High," Saul said proudly, "for a service which I am about to perform for him."

The priest, knowing he required no payment from Saul in advance, then turned and showed the list of sacrifices required to an attendant, who left to get them. Saul paid his tithes regularly, and at the same time added enough to pay for his frequent sacrifices. His lack of worldly possessions and spartan lifestyle were partially necessitated by his generous contributions to the Temple, which came out of a fairly modest income he derived from his trade.

The priest wrapped a towel around Saul's shoulders, then, taking a bottle of scented olive oil, poured it slowly on his head. He gently massaged his scalp, working the oil in with his fingers. He faced Saul and gently rubbed the oil into his beard, then his eyebrows.

He took a razor from a golden box and honed it carefully on a leather strap. He began at the top of Saul's forehead and shaved straight back all the way down his neck, being careful to catch every one of the curly, wiry hairs and stuff them in a container. He shaved each side of the head until Saul was completely bald, his head smooth and shining from the olive oil.

Saul sat very still with his eyes closed in a highly spiritual, prayerful state. The priest continued his work. He shaved the upper lip next, then the face. Now the only hair left on Saul's face were the eyebrows. The priest shaved off first the left, then the right one, putting every hair into the container.

He then folded small pieces of parchment with portions of the Law as found in Deuteronomy 6 and 11 and placed them in a rectangular black leather box. He laid the box against Saul's forehead, then attached the leather straps around his head to hold the tephillin in place. Another set of scriptural passages was placed in its leather protection and strapped to Saul's left wrist.

The young attendant had hung the three small animals by their tied hind legs from a rope stretched from the booths to the altar. Saul followed the priest as he slid the animals along the rope to a pole at the edge of the altar. The priest quickly and painlessly cut the throats of the animals with a razor-sharp, two-edged ornamental knife. He was so adept at this work that the animals never let out a cry. The main arteries of their throats poured out most of their blood in a few seconds, and they died quietly.

Saul stood before the priest, praying loudly as the blood ran into the furrow beside the altar and down into an opening in the ground. The priest slid the three dead animals down the rope to two young priests waiting at the tubs. They quickly opened the animals' stomachs, removed the intestines and all the fat, and began washing the entrails in a large tub. Then the priest, seeing that the young priests were completing their work, picked up the container with Saul's hair in it. Saul stood just behind him now as he dropped the hair into the fire. He took the three animals' intestines from the boys and dropped them into the fire with the hair. Saul prayed, "Receive, O God, this as a memorial to my penance, to my sacrifice and dedication to your service."

The sun was down, and the giant brass gates were being closed as Saul walked back out through them.

Baanah ben David recognized Saul by his walk as he came through the gates. He stood at the Court of the Gentiles watching Saul talk animatedly to the captain of the Temple guards. Saul was gesturing and speaking sharply. He saw him hold up six fingers and point to the fortress, Antonia.

"Six Temple guards, and four Roman soldiers to oversee the mission," thought Banaah aloud. "Plus his two Hebronite witnesses. There is no stopping him," he added weakly.

The captain of the guards had not nodded assent, so Saul quickly pulled out the letter from the high priest. Upon seeing it, the captain turned on his heel and left to procure the contingent Saul required. The Romans, however, would furnish ten soldiers. They would insist on outnumbering the Temple guards in Saul's contingent.

I will pray, then eat, and an hour from now the service for which I was born will begin, Saul thought as he turned to cross the Court of the Gentiles.

"Saul," said Baanah as Saul was passing without seeing him, taking long steps in his hurried walk to make up for his short legs.

"Baanah, I hope you understand . . ." he fumbled.

"Yes, it's all right. I was just concerned about you. So were the others. Nicodemus asked about you."

Saul turned his eyes away.

Baanah added quickly, "Your sister, Sarah, knows about your vow, and we determined that just about now you would be ready to enjoy a nice hot meal."

"I'm sorry, Baanah," said Saul. "I have no time for dining. The Temple torches are lit. My preparation has ended."

The Temple was even more beautiful at night than during the day. It was well lit by great torches that lined the outer walls and inner building and columns. Actually the torches were great tubs on pedestals. The tubs contained a kind of pitch, large blocks of hardened petroleum and turf chopped from the asphalt pits near the Dead Sea. The pitch burned brightly, leaving no shadows in the Temple compound.

"Saul," the rabbi demanded, "we need to talk now."

Saul looked steadily into his friend's eyes and past before he answered. Baanah was a man of middle age, tall, of medium build; he wore a simple homespun garment under his long black cloak, which seemed to have a habit of whirling about as he walked or even as he stood. He was slightly bent at the waist, his own frontal phylacteries the most imposing thing about him. Baanah's quiet dark eyes searched Saul's face.

"My heart and mind are set steadily upon my task," Saul said. He raised his left arm slightly to show the phylactery. "My determination to do the will of God is burned into my mind by the power of his commandments which I wear between my eyes. And this hand will do his work of deliverance from the infection of the Covenant as surely as Moses delivered our fathers." He raised his wrist before Baanah's face. "What else is there to talk about, Master Baanah?"

"Saul," said the rabbi, "during your isolation many things have happened. The city has trembled at the news of Stephen's execution. The Nazarenes have scattered in every direction like ripples from a pebble tossed in the water. The 'ripples' think of you as the 'pebble.' Few of them are left in Jerusalem. A few congregations still are going to synagogues, but for the most part the 'Synagogue of the Nazarenes' has gone out of sight. Only small, quiet groups are meeting at the Temple."

"I will remove the residue of them from this holy city, Master," said Saul. "I will find them. I will bring them to justice. Then I will follow the ones who have flown," Saul paused. "I fully expected this."

"You're pale, Saul," said Baanah. "You're down to bones and leather. Do not our own dietary laws for everyday living and eating impose sufficient restrictions on the body?"

Saul changed the subject. "Did my sister come to see you?" he asked.

"Yes," said Baanah. "She had your old friend with her—Jemimah of Jericho."

Saul diverted his eyes. The mention of the girl from his youth disturbed him. He turned in anger to Baanah. "Your comments about my health—were they at my sister's suggestion?"

"She wants to see you, to cook you a good meal," said Baanah.

"She never gives up!" shouted Saul. "It's Jemimah she wants me to see. I want you to know, all of you, finally, that I have no interest in that woman anymore!" He turned his back on Baanah and was seething. "I will not go."

"Where will you go?" asked the rabbi quietly.

"I have work to do tonight," said Saul menacingly. "And there is no place in it for Sarah or Jemimah, or even you for that matter."

"What work? Where?" he asked.

"You will hear," said Saul, leaving. "You will hear."

THREE

THE PURGE

In the Synagogue of the Isles of the Sea, a man named Barnabas of Cyprus was addressing the congregation of "the People of the Way."

"I stand before you boldly in this place to speak to you of the grace and mercy of our Lord Jesus. In him there is no fear. We have not been given the spirit of fear, but the spirit of power in his name. Therefore, we appeal to him for mercy, and through him we find grace to help in time of need."

The gathering was made up mainly of men, but many wives were present, sitting among them with a few children on the floor at the feet of Barnabas. All of them were very attentive, listening carefully to the words of this great speaker.

"I would not have you harmed by the persecutors," Barnabas continued. "The Lord has not led me to call people to martyrdom, but to repentance and to his service. His kingdom is not of this world," he said. "His kingdom is to be established in your hearts. The Holy Spirit will guide you, will comfort you in your fears.

"Let Stephen's death be considered a further sacrifice. If you must suffer likewise, so be it, and find the peace of the Prince of Peace in whatever befalls you. But we must strive to labor for him. We must not tremble in fear at the thought of what the Romans can do, nor what the Temple authorities can do. The lips of the Pharisees in the Temple do God's service, but their hearts are far from him.

"The Holy Spirit promised by the Lord Jesus will lead us into all truth. We experienced the infilling of that Spirit on the day of Pentecost. That promise was fulfilled. We must pray for the constant communication and instruction of the Spirit. Let us go forth in his name with boldness, in the Spirit of his holiness. Do not fear. Speak of him. Tell of his wonders. Do not deny him in any condition, that you will not be denied before the heavenly Father."

Saul came quietly in the door, followed by Cononiah and Shemei, the Hebronites. They followed him from the Temple steps, ready to be useful against the Nazarenes again, Shemei dragging his clubfoot on the cobblestones as he shuffled along and Cononiah walking alongside with his one good eye, wide and piercing. Saul represented the Temple, and to them the Temple meant money. A few pieces of silver now and then was better than the few coppers they might get begging. They sat unnoticed near the back of the room, listening and watching the service of the Nazarenes. The Temple guards and Roman soldiers waited outside the door, to be called upon to make their entrance at Saul's command.

Barnabas continued, "I was one of the seventy disciples whom Jesus sent to preach his word. Another brother and I went to Caesarea Philippi to work in the regions around about. My companion, Aristotle of Crete, knew the Lord's close companions James and John, sons of Zebedee, as well as Cephas, who is called Peter. There are those of us who have been given a heavenly dispensation. It is an honor, a blessing, this dispensation, yet it carries with it an obligation, an obligation to share the precepts of God's plan of salvation for humankind. In our receiving and sharing these insights from firsthand experience with the Master and his friends, we also share with you the peace and consolation I just spoke of. For your instruction and for the further edification of the Lord Jesus, I introduce to you my friend and brother Aristotle of Crete. Aristotle was there at the village at the foot of the mountain called Hermon the day the Lord came back with his inner circle of disciples. I will ask Aristotle to bear witness of certain things concerning the Lord to you at this time."

Barnabas sat down, and as he did so, he noticed the Pharisee sitting in the back near the door. *It's the persecutor Saul of Tarsus,* thought Barnabas, *and he is looking for another Stephen.* Barnabas, however, made no indication of recognition. He slowly closed his eyes in prayer as Aristotle began to speak.

"I will get you sooner or later," Saul said to himself, thinking of Barnabas and studying him. "A heavenly dispensation? Does that mean a divine directive? Their distortion of the true worship is so diversified now that their total abandonment of the Law is their natural course. Well, not in the synagogues of God!" he breathed, clenching his fist. "Not even in the Synagogue of the Isles of the Sea. I will hear out this Aristotle, then I shall winnow this congregation." He looked around at his two witnesses. The Hebronite brothers were attentive as the tall, lean Cretan began speaking.

"Brothers and sisters," began Aristotle, and when he said "sisters," Saul noticed the women sitting among the men near the front of the congregation. His rage increased. *There is no area of synagogue service that they aren't practicing in a heretical manner,* he thought.

The speaker continued. "I have witnessed the miracles and heard the words of the Master on many occasions. I followed him and his disciples for many months, as did many other men and women throughout Galilee, Samaria, and Judea. I longed to be among his close disciples, to work only for him, to live only to serve him. For, from the very first, I was convinced that he was more than a man."

Saul's hand opened and closed on an imaginary sword handle. Just outside the door the guards had swords. The prophets spoke of God's sword cleaving for righteousness and justice.

"I am armed for the stroke of your judgment, O Lord," he prayed.

Cononiah and Shemei looked back and forth from Saul to Aristotle, waiting for the moment Saul would conclude this speech. But Saul would hear the man out. The more he spoke, the more damaging he would be to his own cause.

"Barnabas and I and many other of the followers were instructed by the Master to wait in Caesarea Philippi while he and Peter and the sons of Zebedee went to Mt. Hermon. No one knew why he chose only the three to accompany himself, but I was certain that it was for a very special reason.

"When they returned from the mountain, there was dissension between James and John over trifles such as who would be greatest in the Lord's kingdom. These arguments were founded on a lack of their understanding his words.

"The Master brought them to a speedy understanding of their position with himself, however, by the use of a simple illustration. He took a little child in his arms and said to them, 'Whoever receives this child in my name receives me, and whoever receives me receives him that sent me.' Then," said Aristotle, "he dissolved the conflict with one sentence. He said, 'Whoever is the humblest among you shall be the greatest.'"

"Rubbish," said Saul under his breath. "The philosophy of a half-witted do-gooder."

"I noticed a marked change in Peter from the time he came down from the mountain," said Aristotle. "He even *looked* different. And he didn't engage in the petty arguments with the other disciples. He looked upon the Master with a new kind of wonder. I asked some of the others what had happened on the mountain, and they couldn't tell me. They only said that Jesus had told Peter, James, and John not to speak of it for a while. It was later, on the way to Jerusalem, that James and John confided to me the miracle on the mountain."

The miracle on the mountain, thought Saul. *More Egyptian sticks to impress the rabble.*

Aristotle continued. "They were praying, the four of them on the very top of the mountain, when suddenly Jesus' countenance was changed to an unearthly beauty. They stood away from him, trembling with fear, and watched as his whole being became glorified. Even his clothing was changed. His robe took on a radiance and whiteness that no cloth on earth has ever had. A mantle of gold appeared around his chest, and the hairs on his head turned pure white. His hands and his feet shone with a heavenly glow. The disciples looked upon him with wonder."

The high, thin air on Mt. Hermon, the cold, and the wind, thought Saul. *Come now. Tricks, delusions, and illusions. I want to hear what you really have to say, you Greek dreamer.*

"Then," said Aristotle, "as he stood glorified before them, there suddenly appeared with him Moses and Elijah."

Saul gasped and sat up straight. Moses! Elijah! Cononiah and Shemei looked questioningly at Saul. His face was flushed in anger. Realizing that his assistants were looking to him for a sign, he contained himself. He shook his head and held up his hand for them to wait.

The suppressed consternation of the persecutor was not lost on Barnabas. From his seat near Aristotle, he silently observed Saul's response at the mention of Moses and Elijah. He then closed his eyes and listened prayerfully as his friend continued.

"Moses, Elijah, and the Lord Jesus conversed at great lengths as the three disciples stood off watching and listening to the miraculous manifestation. Jesus was speaking to Moses and Elijah of his coming death, burial, and resurrection. The three listeners did not understand most of what they heard. But part of what Jesus was saying they took to mean that when he died, his spirit would go into the world of the dead and he would free the souls of the righteous, of the faithful to the Covenant, and bring them into paradise."

Saul shook his head, trying to follow the meaning of this mad dialogue. *They have gone to great lengths of desecration,* he thought. *This is far enough.*

Aristotle continued, and again Saul paused before calling in the guards and soldiers. The little children were paying rapt attention. They had moved closer to the speaker and were listening in awe. No one in the congregation made a sound.

"Suddenly," said Aristotle, "a bright cloud covered the three glorious beings, and the voice of God was heard to say, 'This is my beloved Son. Obey him!'"

Saul was instantly upon his feet. "Blasphemy!" he shouted, pointing at Aristotle. Saul stepped out into the aisle and walked halfway through the congregation as the guards and soldiers came in the door behind him. The children were terrified and ran to their parents, some of whom were praying, some of whom stared at Saul in fear.

Barnabas also was on his feet. Saul stopped when Barnabas pointed his finger at him and said sternly. "Saul of Tarsus, you, as a master of the Law, know it is improper to interrupt a guest speaker until he has finished."

Saul shot back, "He was finished when he stood in this synagogue and related that abomination. He equated the Carpenter with Moses and Elijah, then proceeded on to further verbal desecration by claiming God's voice was heard, calling Jesus his Son." Saul started to turn to the soldiers, but Barnabas spoke more loudly.

"Let him finish. You will do what you will do, so let the speaker finish what he has to say."

Saul screamed at Aristotle, "Speak, then, blasphemer. Seal your conviction." He stood in the aisle with his legs spread, his hands on his hips.

Aristotle was calm. He had not moved from his spot, but because he had been distracted by Saul's outburst, it took him a moment to continue his story. Barnabas sat back down, and the children clung to their parents, watching the man in the aisle.

"When the cloud disappeared," said Aristotle, "Jesus stood there alone and appeared again to be in human flesh and blood. The three disciples were afraid and confused, and Peter, running to the Master, was so overcome with what they had just seen and heard that he stumbled over his own words. He said to Jesus, 'It is beautiful here.' Jesus didn't answer immediately, so Peter, trying to say the proper thing following such an inspiring experience, said,

'Let us build three tabernacles, one for Moses, one for Elijah, and one for yourself.'"

Saul, thinking Aristotle was finished, took a step forward, but again Barnabas stopped him. "Before you proceed, Saul, son of Benjamin, I would like to comment briefly upon the words of Peter concerning the tabernacles."

Saul waited, staring at Barnabas.

Barnabas continued, speaking kindly and quietly to the congregation, as if Saul were not there. "Whether or not Peter knew it at the time, his spiritual eye was seeing Moses as the Law, Elijah as the Prophecy, and Jesus as the fullness and fulfillment of both. The chief prophets of the Most High and the Son."

"Are you speaking on behalf of this man or for yourself?" Saul screamed at Barnabas.

"Neither," said the Cypriot. "I speak with the authority of the Holy Spirit."

"Tie that man to a column and scourge him!" Saul shouted to the soldiers, pointing to Aristotle. Then standing where Aristotle had stood, he addressed the congregation. "Deny your allegiance to Jesus of Nazareth and go free. Stay and witness the punishment of this blasphemer and then go to prison and to trial with him."

No one moved at first. The people looked at one another and at Barnabas. Saul shouted again as the first lash of the Roman soldier's whip cracked against the naked back of Aristotle. His wife screamed and fell at his feet.

The children were under the benches, cowering and crying. Aristotle shook his wife with his foot and said, "Take the children and go." The lash struck again.

The woman shook her head, refusing. "I will stay with you," she said.

People were beginning to leave the synagogue. Some of them took the children with them and hurried out. The ones who remained, more than half the congregation, moved forward at Barnabas's beckoning and came as close as they could to Aristotle. Following Barnabas's example, they knelt and began praying as the lash continued to fall on Aristotle's back.

The Roman scourge was severe punishment. Thirty-nine times the whip was laid to the back and shoulders. The instrument was made of a short handle to which were attached long thick strips of leather, pointed at the end and tipped with small sharp pieces of flint, which cut into the flesh with each blow. The reason for thirty-nine blows was the saying, "Forty lashes are enough to kill a man, so if he dies from only thirty-nine, it is his own fault."

The soldiers and Temple guards had the kneeling congregation surrounded by now, and when the man's punishment was completed, they would all be taken to prison. Aristotle would be tried and executed as Stephen was. The rest would there be scourged as this man was.

The woman on the floor raised her head and screamed when she saw blood running down her husband's legs from the cuts of the leather and small pieces of flesh torn out from the flint. Saul leaped over and kicked her in the stomach, shouting, "Stand away from the condemned!"

Barnabas was instantly on his feet. "Leave the woman alone," he commanded. Saul took a sword from the guard and, with the tip of it in the hollow of Barnabas's throat, backed him onto the altar and against the wall.

"Do you really want to die also?" Saul asked bitingly. The tip of the sword had slightly pierced Barnabas's skin, and a drop of blood ran down the sword. "You shall," said Saul. "You shall, but in due time, when I have used you to bring all your friends and followers of the Beggar Rabbi out of hiding. When I have obliterated your congregations, then you will have finished your part in God's plan for me. Then you shall die also."

"I do not fear you, Saul of Tarsus," said Barnabas. "Do what you will with this body. My soul is with my Lord."

Saul clenched his teeth and continued to hold the sword at Barnabas's throat. With the pain of the sharp point piercing his skin, Barnabas shouted out without moving his head or even his eyes, "It is with much tribulation that we enter into the kingdom of heaven! Aristotle, bear up under the whip! God give you grace and strength."

"Keep your mouth shut," Saul said to Barnabas, his trembling hand causing a larger cut on Barnabas's throat.

"Have courage!" Barnabas cried to the congregation. "You will overcome this world in him who overcame for us!"

Saul drew his sword back and swung the heavy weapon with all his might, striking Barnabas on the side of the head with the flat of the blade and instantly knocking him unconscious.

The last of the thirty-nine stripes were laid on the flayed back of Aristotle. "Drag him out of here," said Saul to the guards and soldiers. "Take all these people with him! Every one of them! Men and women! Out!" He slapped the sword across the back of the bleeding body of Aristotle and the backs of the others as they passed through the door; they were all being prodded and abused by the soldiers as they went.

Saul looked around. The place was empty except for the unconscious Barnabas on the floor and an elderly man who still knelt in prayer toward the back. He had been missed by the guards. Saul walked back to him and nudged him with his toe. "Get up!" he said. The old man only leaned farther over, continuing to pray. "Get up!" Saul said again, louder. The man remained in prayer.

Saul became furious. He slapped the man sharply with the sword. When the man still refused to rise, Saul plunged the sword deep into the man's hip. As he drew it out, the man moaned and fell over on his side. Saul took the man by the foot and dragged him to the door, leaving a trail of blood from his bleeding hip. Pulling and kicking him out into the street, Saul called to a guard to come back and get the man. The guard carried the whimpering man up the street to join the group on their way to prison.

Saul paused a moment, looked back into the synagogue, and observed that Barnabas was still unconscious. He looked down at the floor at the blood, then at his own feet, and saw that he was standing in the blood. A chill passed over him for a moment, and he trembled. The blood! "The stream of blood," he said almost aloud, and his mind went back and locked in on the dream. He paused in the doorway, and for a moment the terror of the dream flooded over him. But just for a moment. Then he steeled himself, raised his left hand, and shouted into the empty room, "Hear, O Israel: The Lord our God, the Lord is one."

✼ ✼ ✼

The traumatic dissemination of the congregation of the Nazarenes from the Synagogue of the Isles of the Sea was followed by similar incidents in other synagogues over the next few days. So successful was Saul's mission that finally after two weeks the followers of the Carpenter of Galilee were not to be seen in public worship. For a great deal of that fortnight, he tried to catch Barnabas conducting public service again, but Barnabas did not return to the Synagogue of the Isles of the Sea. Neither did any of the other Nazarenes.

Aristotle died in prison the day following the scourging. It was reported that two of the women arrested also died before they could be tried. One of the women was the wife of Aristotle. Some were scourged and released. No one knew how many more of them died.

Thereafter the services of the followers of Jesus were held in various homes of the believers, sometimes a hundred or more locked away in a basement out of sight and sound of the persecutor. At times they gathered in the evenings on a rooftop of some friend of the People of the Way. A few of the Pharisees and even some of the Romans gave refuge to them. It didn't take the Temple rulers or the Romans long to see that these poor, peaceful people were no threat to anyone. The Laws of the Sanhedrin did not change, but the general attitude of public opinion began to turn more toward tolerance.

The high priest would have liked to ignore them and proceed with business as usual. Their injuries and deaths in the Roman prison had begun to become somewhat of an embarrassment.

✼ ✼ ✼

The Feast of Weeks, the holy day Sharvoth, was upon Saul before he realized it. Coming to his room one afternoon, he saw Baanah ben David in the open door of the synagogue with sheaves of wheat in his hands.

"Shalom, Master."

"And peace be with you, Brother Saul," said Baanah. But Baanah's face showed pain, not peace.

"What's troubling you?" asked Saul.

"The high priest wants to see you," said Baanah. "It seems that one follower of the Nazarene died from scourging, and another almost died from a concussion and infection of a cut on his throat . . . from a sword," he stammered.

"I will go to the high priest," Saul said, ignoring the inference. He stepped past Baanah through the doorway.

Saul looked thinner. He had missed many meals and many nights' sleep. He was pale, and his eyes lay in deep, dark holes. His face and head with two weeks' growth of hair reminded Baanah of the head of one of the wild weeds that grew in the wilderness; before him was a prickly burr with two black eyes.

"Are you using the synagogue for a storehouse of grain?" Saul asked jokingly.

Baanah laid the wheat on a table just inside the door. The table was almost covered with all sorts of grain as well as baskets of beans, radishes, cucumbers, leeks, onions, berries, melons, and pots of honey.

"Tomorrow is the sixth day of Sivan," Baanah said, smiling. "Doesn't that fact tell you something?"

Saul was embarrassed. He had lost all track of time in his work. "Of course," he said. "It's the Feast of Weeks."

Baanah sat down on a bench, wiping sweat from his face.

"Tell me what to do. I'll help," said Saul.

Baanah paused, then bowed his head, understanding that Saul would not discuss his "mission" that was bothering him so very much. "Wherever you like," he finally answered. "The lamps need oil, and the ceiling has cobwebs in the corners."

"Rest, Master," said Saul, striding into the large room furnished with the bare necessities. There were benches for the congregation of men on the main floor and a half balcony for the female worshipers above. At the opposite end of the room was the ark for the holy scrolls, covered with a rich, golden-bordered, velvet tapestry, the only expensive thing in the building. In front of it were the platform and the reading table. Some of the benches were moved to the side, and the floor was still wet where the rabbi's wife had mopped it.

Saul placed flowers in vases that hung from the balcony columns. Suddenly he started singing:

> When the Lord turned again
> The captivity of Zion,
> We were like them that dream.
> Then was our mouth
> Filled with laughter,
> And our tongue with singing:
> Then said they among the heathen,
> The Lord has done great things for them.
> The Lord has done great things for us,
> So we are glad.

Baanah, sitting on his bench at the door, smiled to hear Saul's song. *Possibly the man can find some joy in his life,* Baanah thought. *Even though he cannot sing, at least he is trying. His countenance has been only fierce and foreboding up until now, so let him sing.*

Saul walked to a storage room and brought out a large jar of olive oil. He went to each of the hanging lamps and, pulling them down by their adjustable brass chains, dipped a cup into the jar and filled the lamps. He sang more loudly:

> Turn again our captivity, O Lord,
> As the streams in the south.

> They that sow in tears
> Shall reap in joy.
> He that goes forth weeping,
> Bearing the precious seed,
> Shall doubtless come again with rejoicing,
> Bringing the sheaves with him.

Saul finished filling the lamps. He then moved past Baanah, singing with armfuls of grain and fruits and vegetables, loading them into a cart at the door. His song being finished, he now began joyfully reciting Scriptures appropriate for he occasion. The everlasting covenant:

> While the earth remains,
> Seedtime and harvest
> And summer and winter
> And day and night
> Shall not cease.

Having loaded the cart and seeing that the room was becoming darker, he took the tinderbox from the niche just inside the door. With the flint and steel he lit a tiny lamp, with which he proceeded to light the hanging lamps. He chanted:

> Moses stretched forth his hand
> Toward heaven,
> And there was a thick darkness
> Over the land of Egypt three days.
> They'd not see one another,
> Neither did anyone arise
> From his place for three days,
> But the children of Israel
> Had light in their dwellings.

Saul returned the hand lamp to its cubicle, then looked back into the room. The lamps were beautiful to him. He stood gazing at the rich tapestry covering the Torah.

> And the Gentiles
> Shall come to thy light,
> And kings to the brightness
> Of thy rising.

He noticed the cobwebs on the ceiling, and as he began erasing them with a broom, he thought again of the children of Israel in bondage in Egypt. They had been held like the moths in these cobwebs. *The all-powerful hand of the Lord delivered them,* he thought as he jammed the broom into a corner of the ceiling.

Tomorrow, the forty-ninth day after the second day of Passover, was the celebration of the giving of the Ten Commandments on Sinai, as well as the sacrifice of firstfruits. In his mind as he worked, Saul saw the finger of God write the commandments in stone—the Decalogue, the fountainhead of all Law. He recited the commandments as he worked. "I am the Lord your God. You shall have no other gods before me. You shall not worship idols. You shall not take the name of the Lord your God in vain. Remember the Sabbath day, to keep it holy. Honor your father and your mother . . ."

"You shall not kill," the voice of Baanah ben David interrupted Saul. A chill went up Saul's spine; then he felt a quick flash of anger.

Baanah stood searching Saul's face for . . . for what? He didn't know.

Perhaps some explanation that all the death and destruction reported to him recently had not really been at Saul's hand.

"What else can I do for you, Master Baanah?"

The old man turned and went to his bench. As he sat down, he said, "The high priest sent a steward looking for you three times in the last day."

"What does the high priest want with me?" Saul asked.

"The steward said he wants to talk to you," said Baanah.

Saul said, more to himself than to the rabbi, "What does he want to talk with me about?"

Baanah paused. "Probably the same thing I would like to talk to you about."

Saul's eyes became cold, defensive. "And what is that?"

"Go to the high priest," said Baanah. "You should go now."

✠ ✠ ✠

Saul took with him to the Temple Cononiah and Shemei. The two were faring better with Saul's successes. They wore new robes and sandals. Cononiah sported a large lapis lazuli ring on his finger. The finger in it, however, was still dirty. They stood grinning behind Saul as they eyed the elegant office chamber of the high priest.

"You sent for me, Master Jonathan?" Saul asked.

The high priest arose from his couch and paused before speaking, looking first at the two Hebronites, then back at Saul. "Yes," he said. "Sit down." He indicated a comfortable, linen-covered armchair. Then after a pause and a nod in the direction of Saul's attendants, he added in a light manner, "It will not be necessary for your companions to stay. I am not going to interrogate you." Saul motioned for the two to leave the room as the high priest resumed his seat.

He studied Saul before he spoke. He tapped his fingers on the arm of his couch and looked his visitor up and down. "You look ill, Saul," he said.

"I am quite well," he replied.

"Pardon me for playing the concerned father, but you have lost weight, your skin is yellow, and your hands are trembling."

The high priest paused, then continued. "Piety is a principal virtue, Saul, but I must remind you that the sages call a pious fool the man who endangers life and limb in strict self-disciplinary measures."

Saul sat up straight and faced his host, holding his hands together between his legs. "Thank you for your concern, but I am more than thirty years old. I have always managed to fend for myself." He paused and looked down at his hands. They were trembling slightly. "I confess to you, though, that I have lost sleep and meals in the constant deployment of my mission."

"Your sister came to see me," said Jonathan. "She is worried that you will be ill, pushing yourself to the limit of endurance in all undertakings. She asks that you visit her again for some food and rest."

"Sarah would be a mother to me also," said Saul. "Between the two of you, I am well looked after." He paused, then added, "I suppose a good night's sleep after a bowl of Sarah's hot soup would be a good thing."

"Your sister is your kerovah, your nearest relative," the high priest mused. "She feels that she bears a special responsibility of love and support for you. And, Saul," he continued conversationally, "perhaps it is the mothering instinct in her, but in her goodness she feels obligated to help you in whatever your endeavor. To not do so, she would feel guilty and cruel."

The high priest had much to talk to Saul about, and he relaxed on his seat, hoping that Saul would do the same. Saul did not, however—he remained sitting up with his hands clasped between his knees, ready to hear what this meeting was about. Jonathan ben Annas took his time. *I must be careful with that temper,* he thought. *A man needs all his wits about him to deal with this one.*

"Your sister," said Jonathan, "had a friend with her when she came to see me at my home."

Saul stared at him inquiringly.

"Jemimah is the daughter of an innkeeper from Jericho," he continued. "A strikingly beautiful woman. She appears also to be a modest, retiring woman, virtues indicative of strength and piety. All these qualities in a woman are much to be desired by a man of such true Jewish spirit as yours."

He waited.

Carefully Jonathan continued. "I understand that at one time you were going to marry her."

"There was no betrothal binding us," said Saul.

"A man needs a wife," Jonathan said boldly.

"God did not will that I marry Jemimah of Jericho, Father," Saul said. Then suspiciously he asked, "Does Jemimah have anything to do with my invitation to a hot meal and a bed? Is she a guest of my sister?"

"No, I don't think so," he replied. Then quickly, "Saul, do you not find it in our traditions and ethics to marry and propagate our race?"

Saul bristled slightly. "I find it in the Law, Father, to serve God with all my body and spirit. I have always known that the good fortune of most men of marrying and raising children is not mine. There is no share of time in my life and work for a family." He finally smiled at the high priest, to the latter's great relief. "So you would be matchmaker, would you, as well as father to me?"

Saul relaxed and leaned back, for it appeared that Jonathan was going to take his time getting down to business.

The high priest was unrelenting. "I believe, Saul, that God's work can be accomplished better by a man whose needs are taken care of at home between workdays. There is no substitute for the means to fulfillment in a man which is the duty and joy of a wife. To be more specific, conjugal relations are necessary for the overall health and well-being of a man; they give a man more self-esteem and respect for his own body, which attains satisfaction, thus freeing his spirit."

Saul paused, carefully weighing his words before he answered—he wanted to make a simple, straightforward reply that would end the conversation on this subject. Finally he said, "Father Jonathan, I learned these things from the time of my induction into divine service. But from that day I have known that God was not to allow me such luxury. Such comforts as you describe are for yourself and others. I do have female companionship in one area of my life, although I cannot seem to control it, and that is in my dreams. But then if I begin to tell you of my dreams, it would require days." Saul stopped, then focused back in on the thing he hoped would be his final response on this matter. "I shall never attain position, prominence, and importance such as you have as high priest, over all Jews, but as sure as the sun rises in the east, I am sure that God has set me apart for a special work. Now," Saul said, pausing, "now I feel like I have begun that work for which I was born. Nowhere in my consciousness do I find a wife and family a part of that plan."

When the high priest didn't answer but only stared as if meditating upon what he had just heard, Saul concluded, "In the practical course of working his way in my life, the Most High gives me power and consolation to overcome my human frailties of temptation. I find peace in his Word and fulfillment in his service." Saul was finished. With that he relaxed a little and looked away from Jonathan with an attitude of final release from the subject.

Jonathan slowly arose and paced in front of Saul, glancing down at him. Finally he shook his head and sat back down, facing Saul. "Celibacy," he said, "is part of the Naziritic vow. Obviously you have made that vow."

Jonathan became a little uncomfortable, and a little angry. This man was a stone wall. They sat silently, staring at each other for a while, then finally Saul relented.

"I will afford myself the luxury of a bowl of hot soup and a soft bed tonight, Master. Thank you for transmitting the invitation." Then he added thoughtfully, "The food for sure, but the soft bed only if Jemimah of Jericho is not a houseguest of my sister."

Saul waited. The high priest took a chalice of fruit wine mixed with honey from the tray brought in by a Temple servant only seconds after he rang a tiny bell on his desk. Saul politely declined the offer of a drink.

"Saul," said Jonathan, "my information sources tell me that death and serious injuries resulted from your arrests in the Synagogue of the Isles of the Sea."

"Whose death, Master?" Saul asked.

"The Greek Aristotle died from your flogging. One Barnabas, a Cypriot, is recovering from a sword wound, and another, an older man, will die from a sword wound. This information has been investigated, and its source is a Greek physician in Bethany."

Saul paused for a moment, then asked, "Are you asking me if this is true, Master?"

"No," said the high priest. "I was simply stating what was reported to me.

I was also led to believe that you personally inflicted the wounds on these two men."

"People resist, Master," said Saul. "Force is sometimes necessary to accomplish the arrests. I did not arrest the Cypriot Barnabas. I let him go so he would lead me to others of this sect. His illness explains why he has not been seen." Saul paused thoughtfully. He decided to go no further in explaining the incident in the Synagogue of the Isles of the Sea.

"Justice cannot be effective unless tempered with mercy, Saul," said Jonathan. "Mercy is indispensable to justice."

"Compassion is at times a strange sentiment to manifest," Saul replied angrily, "especially when I am being assisted by a contingent of barbaric Romans. Hereafter, Master, I shall require no assistance from them in the discharge of my mission. I shall take with me only Temple guards and servants."

"The Romans would find a Temple contingent moving through the streets of this city highly suspect," warned Jonathan, his voice rising also. "You *shall* cooperate with the Romans."

It's his money and position and his own precious skin that he is concerned for, thought Saul. He felt his own face flush in anger, but he managed to control himself.

"Our forays will be done at times and in places not frequented by them, Master," Saul reasoned. "This sect has gone underground; they gather in private homes of converts or sympathizers."

"The majority of them have dispersed to other cities," Jonathan replied, calmer now, "to cities of the Decapolis. Following the death of Stephen, they went into Samaria and throughout Judea. I was notified that within a very few days they joined other assemblies in Antioch, Damascus, and Alexandria. The sect of Jesus will gather wherever synagogues are open to them." He paused. "For some reason, Damascus seems to have a community that welcomed them into brotherly love. An ambassador of King Aretas of Arabia informed me that the disciples of the Nazarene number in the hundreds there, and the congregation is growing daily."

Saul was breathing deeply and his hands were visibly trembling again. He stood up, bowed to the high priest, and, groping for words in his distress from the news just related, said, "In these cities where my fellow Jews are taking unreasonable liberties in public worship, they shall become corruptible liberties in public worship; they shall become corruptible even in the eyes of the Gentiles. When a Gentile finds a Jew unworthy, he misjudges the whole household and faith of Israel. Our people in all these cities should strive to live the kind of life that brings no disrespect to Israel and thereby to the Holy Name. I shall go to Damascus, then to Antioch and Alexandria, to every city that harbors these defilers."

The high priest slowly arose. "You are more determined than ever, aren't you?" he asked.

"More so," said Saul boldly. "More so!" He bowed again, and then he was out the door.

Jonathan smiled and sipped from his chalice of fruit wine. *A good man has gone into the abyss of fanaticism. At least he will be in Damascus,* he thought.

Out of the city walls, across the Kidron Valley, and up the slopes of the Mount of Olives, Saul marched with his raiding party of Temple guards, servants, and the two witnesses, Cononiah and Shemei. Through the ancient olive trees his witnesses now led him into Gethsemane, which means "the place of the olive press." Here much of the oil used in the city's lamps, stoves, and kitchens was rendered. Oxen hitched to a long pole walked in an endless circle, turning the large stones that pressed out the oil. After going through a refiner, it was poured into six-gallon stone jars and stored in a warehouse.

These groves, the mill, and the warehouses, all of which covered half the western slopes of the Mount of Olives, were owned by a man named Joseph from the Judean town of Arimathea. Joseph was a member of the Sanhedrin, an upright and godly man, well loved in spite of his wealth. Joseph had sat in council on that early dark morning a few years ago when the Nazarene was tried and turned over to Pilate.

In Joseph, the Nazarenes had found a friend. They worked for him occasionally at the olive press and in the warehouses storing and loading the oil for shipment. And they gathered in the warehouse of the Arimathean for worship services. It was fitting for them that a place of worship covered the very spot where Jesus was arrested. This was the place where his disciples had abandoned him, fearing the Romans and the Temple guards.

Joseph owned a cargo ship that docked in Joppa. Every season his ship, laden with oil, plowed the waters of the great sea, westward and out through the Strait of Gades and Tingis, through the Gates of Hercules, up the stormy Atlantic coasts of Hispania and Gallia, across the Channel of the Engels to Brittanium. There the olive oil was sold or traded for tin ore. Great carts of the ore were freighted down to the harbor from the tin mines up the river and loaded onto Joseph's growing wealth. Each year upon the return of his ships, his tin ore was eagerly awaited by the tinkers on Jerusalem's street of the tinsmiths.

The group of Nazarenes who met in Joseph's warehouse had not been hard for Cononiah and Shemei to find. They had suspected certain ones, and they knew that Jesus had often met with his disciples at Gethsemane. They had hidden behind the giant olive trees and, as evening approached, followed them and watched them go into the warehouse. It was at the door of this building the witnesses now stopped and, pointing to the door, said to Saul, "They are here!"

A crude wooden carving of a fish was nailed to the doorpost. "A secret sign," Saul muttered angrily. "In place of the mezuzah, I find the symbol of the Galilean fisherman! This is a meeting hall for the polluters who would bring Israel down." He took a sword from a guard, ripped the wooden fish from the doorpost, and chopped it to pieces on the ground.

He pushed open the door and walked in. Many stone jars had been moved against the walls, clearing a large area where benches were made by setting the ends of boards on the remaining oil jars. At the far end was an altar, made by laying several boards together across some jars. Saul was somewhat surprised by the large number of people present as he listened to them recite a prayer, men, women, and children together. "Our Father, who is in heaven, holy is your name. May your kingdom come . . ."

Their heads were bowed, and they didn't notice the persecutor walk silently in. To one side he saw men and women apparently washing each other's feet in the small tin pans used in the refinery work.

Joseph of Arimathea carried a basket of round, flat bread through the congregation. Each person he approached broke off a piece of bread and ate it. A young girl followed Joseph carrying a chalice and a pitcher of wine. Each person ate bread, then accepted a sip of wine from the silver chalice the girl kept filled from the pitcher.

Saul started to approach Joseph but was ignored. Instead, the Arimathean began speaking to the worshipers.

"We do this in remembrance of him," said Joseph. "This bread is a symbol of his body which was sacrificed for us." He paused, glanced at Saul, but continued, "This wine is a symbol of his blood which was shed for us for the remission of our sins. As he ate and drank with the disciples on that Passover eve, so do we now commemorate that consecration."

Saul shouted at Joseph, "This entire congregation is under arrest by the authority invested in me by the high priest." Everyone turned toward Saul, but no one seemed afraid. "You are charged with heresy, blasphemy, and abominable acts against the Law, the holy Temple, and the Most High."

The congregation became very still and quiet as Saul raved. He pointed to the people on the benches. "Praying in pagan tongues and reciting the Holy Scripture in heathen dialects!" Then he pointed to Joseph. "And I charge you with sacrilege! You desecrated the feast of the Passover by using certain of its courses as a memorial to the Carpenter on an improper date."

Joseph smiled at Saul and walked toward the door. "Hold him," Saul said, shouting to his guards. Two from the Temple contingent took Joseph by each arm roughly. "Take them all to prison," Saul shouted to the other guards, indicating the whole congregation. Then he turned back to Joseph.

To the two guards he said, "Remove his robe and scourge him." The robe was ripped open down the back and dropped to the floor, leaving the man standing in his loincloth. He turned his back to the guards to begin and, facing Saul, said, "May God have mercy upon your soul, Brother Saul."

Suddenly Saul recognized him. He had never seen Joseph of Arimathea in clothes other than his priestly Temple garments. Here in the dim oil light and in his homespun robe, he had looked like any of the rest of the rabble.

For a moment Saul weakened and trembled. *What am I about to do?* A fellow member of the Sanhedrin, and he was about to punish him . . . But as he looked around the room again, blinding anger took control of his senses.

"Scourge him!" Saul said, and at the same time he took his own tunic and rent it from the neck to the waist with a cry. He paced the floor in a circle, moaning, "Blasphemy! Abomination!" and beat himself on the chest with his fist as the whip landed on the back of Joseph. Joseph never once cried out.

Saul kicked over the pans of water used for foot washing. He turned over the chalice and bread basket and crushed with his heel the pieces of unleavened bread on the floor. With his foot on the bread, he stopped, for a thought struck him. He remembered the rat, the rat he had caught eating his scroll of the Scriptures that night. He looked at the man being whipped. He could crush out this man's life as easily as he was crushing the unleavened bread. He had not killed the rat, for it was innocent in its hunger and it had the sacred shreds in its stomach. This man's life was worth less than the rat's.

As he strode to the door, the guards were laying on the last of the stripes to Joseph's bleeding back. Saul only glanced at him in passing, but a shocking chill overcame him for just a moment at seeing the man's upraised face. He wore the same expression that the executed Stephen had worn. *From where comes an expression of peace and joy out of agony?* he asked himself.

As Saul reached the door, Joseph cried, "God go with you, Brother Saul. And may you come to know the Lord Jesus."

Saul hurried away toward the prison to finish the night's business. "This is enough in the City of God," he said. "I surely must have them all here. Imagine, Joseph of Arimathea! Let him bleed. Let his scars remind him that he transgressed. My cause is just. I shall no longer debate with my own. I shall no more argue my cause with my own high priest. I gave my calling, and I must continue. I shall go on to richer gleanings." He shuddered in the unseasonably chilly air of the early summer night as he rushed through the darkness.

The morrow was a long time coming, for he barely slept that night. Arriving at his room well after dark, he remembered that he had missed supper again. The only food he had in his room was a bowl of figs and a few nuts. Rather than go back out in the night, he would let that suffice. He turned toward the Temple and offered a prayer of thanks for his meager meal.

He sat at his table alone, staring into the lamplight and thinking. He was deeply troubled, and this was not the feeling he had expected, considering his success in his mission so far.

Had he fallen out of favor with the high priest? This much he knew. Jonathan ben Annas wanted him out of the city. Was no one on his side? Was their faith so weak that everyone but him would tolerate this evil in their midst? Baanah ben David, and certainly Nicodemus, had tried to discourage him from fulfilling his task. Was the high priest suggesting that he abandon his work by emphasizing mercy and compassion in that last conversation? The high priest had given him authority on behalf of all the chief priests and elders. How many of them would still stand with him against the Nazarenes?

His letter had not been rescinded. He would take his retinue and proceed toward Damascus tomorrow. He stood and prayed again. "I delight to do your will, O Lord."

He felt a slight relief as he snuffed out his lamp and lay down upon his mat. Many gains had been made. There was no visible evidence of public worship of the Carpenter anywhere in the city. *The Most High is with me,* he thought, closing his eyes and turning his face toward the wall.

An image appeared in his mind's eye of an upturned face with an expression of peace, joy, and resignation. Who was he thinking of? Stephen? The Greek Aristotle? Joseph of Arimathea? No, none of them, but all of them. They were the same. Why the same expression? And why didn't the punished cry out from the lash?

He had to admit to himself, though it troubled him, that such strength and inner peace at such a time were admirable. They had claimed the indwelling of the Holy Spirit. This idea, in addition to being abominable, was pure rubbish! By the power of the Holy Spirit had come timeless oracles of God—the Law, the Prophets, the Writings. From the mouths of the Nazarene's followers had only come blasphemous statements about the Carpenter.

He tried to reason it out, and the human spirit, when caught up in lofty ideas, can become quite formidable. Had the popular delusion and extraordinary madness surrounding this character Jesus given these people a false, superhuman spirit? Maybe that was the answer. They were caught up in a fascinating new idea—a god-man in beggar's clothing who would stop and talk to them and even touch them, one of their own kind. And the healings allegedly wrought by his hand? Deluded belief. The people were healed simply because they believed strongly enough that they would be. But there were other questions. How could they so readily believe in the idea of a god-man? Thousands had been converted. Surely the true Holy Spirit would intercede and help stop this madness. Meanwhile, he must move ahead.

The night moved so slowly. He was anxious to be up packing and getting ready to leave for the trip tomorrow, but he knew he had to rest, had to sleep. But the face kept reappearing in his mind. He turned over again and again, trying to close it out. He could not, and he could not sleep.

He would think of something else—the trip, the six days' journey north to the Syrian capital. He would go through Samaria. Maybe he would stop in Shechem and rout out any of the People of the Way who may have congregated there. The ancient city of the prophets must not suffer this sect in its midst. He would cross the lush green Jordan Valley just south of the lake, the Sea of Galilee. He would go around the eastern shore rather than pass through Tiberia, the Roman city built on the western side. He would not defile himself by walking on the soil of Caesar's puppet, King Herod Antipas, that incestuous, idolatrous, Romanized half Jew. He would follow the caravan route past the lake over the lower western slopes of Mt. Hermon and across the watered plain to Damascus. There would be plenty of food along the way, with the early harvest having begun—grains, berries, melons, anything and everything from the fields. "The earth is the Lord's, and the fullness thereof," he quoted and said a silent prayer of thanks for the strengthening food that the Lord would provide on the journey. He, his guards, and the witnesses would dine on fish on the eastern shore of the lake. The melons would be ripe in the fields below Hermon.

Earlier the peasants had planted those fields just as they had done for a thousand years, two thousand years, with a simple wooden plow and an ox. The plowman used one hand to steer the plow and carried a goad in the other hand, a long pole with a sharp end to prick the animal when it slowed every few steps. The dumb animals would kick at the goad every time they were pricked, but it was to no avail; they had to move forward.

It was pleasant contemplating country life. The six-day trip, seeing affluent travelers by the thousands headed for everywhere in the world, would be a welcome relief to Saul, who had spent the last few weeks dealing with those he considered simpleminded and disillusioned.

With that thought, the face presented itself again in his mind. *Stephen. That smile! That joyful submission to death! They're all insane,* he thought. He began reciting Scriptures and contemplating the Law, then the Psalms. "I will not think of their faces. I will sleep now with the sacred words of the prophets singing in my mind." And finally, he did sleep. For a while.

He dreamed a variation of an earlier dream. He was standing on a hill looking down into the endless sea. The light was behind him now, and his back was turned to it because his eyes couldn't stand the brightness of it. The stream of blood ran near his feet and on down the hill. Among the bodies ran the stream into the dark sea. He thought he heard his name again coming from the water, and moving toward the water, he could hear it more clearly. They were calling him. "Saul! Paul! Paulus!" It sounded as if the people of all the world were calling to him in many languages. "Why are you calling me?" he cried in his sleep. "And *what* are you calling me? I am Saul of Tarsus. Of the tribe of Benjamin." Still they called him.

He feared the dark waters, and he turned and began climbing back up the hill. He had to reach the light. He fell on the face of Stephen. Or was it

Aristotle? Or one of the women? They all had that angelic countenance. For the first time he saw that they were not all Stephen, but they all were dressed in the common garments typical of Jesus' followers and looked as if they had died in ecstasy. Rushing on up now, for some reason he felt he had to reach the light. Groping and clawing, he finally fell at the base of the cross and found the terror gone. But he refused to look up, fearing the sight of the crucified Nazarene. He touched on the ground something with his hand, and looking down, he saw the sign of the fish, the splintered board that he had cut with his sword that night. He raised himself, and straining against the brightness, he again saw the sign nailed over the head of the crucified man. The Carpenter was hanging upon the cross, but because of the light Saul could not look upon him. He awoke with a moan.

For the first time, he felt pangs of guilt. For the first time, he thought of the one who had died as a result of his purge. Then he thought of Damascus and the other great cities and how many, many more would die in the exercising of his vow. The road of Damascus suddenly seemed like a long, arduous journey.

But he turned over and admonished himself for the weakening thoughts. He would not let himself think on these things. He would not be distracted. The preservation of the unity of the true worship had to be accomplished. The Most High himself had decreed death for blasphemers. Saul had to be strong; he had to be sure of himself. He could not allow unjustified pangs of conscience to alter anything. Trying again to go to sleep, he whispered, "Tomorrow, Damascus."

* FOUR *

THE ILLUMINATION

Saul looked straight ahead at the approaching city of Damascus. His body was weary, but with his destination in sight he was anxious to conclude his journey and rest. He was in desperate need of sleep. The house of Judas the Pharisee would provide a comforting refuge from the long, weary road. And he hoped the hospitality of Judas would help ease his troubled mind. Perhaps Judas would give him encouragement. Fears and doubts had plagued him for the last six days and nights.

Damascus was a big city and a strange city. Even armed with his letter from the high priest, he felt ill at ease. If he felt no sense of triumph in his accomplishments in Jerusalem, would this be any different? The purging of the Nazarenes in the City of God had brought him no real satisfaction. No one had offered support, no one except the Roman soldiers. They had been hard on the prisoners because they knew no one would care how cruelly they treated Jews condemned by their own people. He regretted the suffering of his victims at the hands of the Romans. Perhaps it would be better in Damascus. No Roman soldiers accompanied him. But the treatment of his captives in the Syrian prisons would probably be just the same. The Damascus stockade was infamous for its cruel treatment of the prisoners.

I must not let my mind dwell upon these things, he thought. He had forced himself to suppress his doubts and fears every evening as he and his companions had stopped at inns to sleep. But sleep was always slow in coming. Then the dream. Every night the dream, the same dream. The face of Stephen in a blissful smile. The people calling to him, crying out to him. Nightly now he also dreamed of the man in the warehouse who had said, "May you come to know the Lord Jesus, Brother Saul." The man wore the countenance of Stephen. It didn't matter who he saw, the dream—the joyous expression—was always there.

There was a strange love in these faces. A radiant love when they had died in torture. They looked at him as if they loved him. Why? Why did they love him? He didn't love them. He hated everything they were doing to the true religion of his fathers. But did he hate them personally? He thought so. He couldn't be sure. But he knew he didn't love them, he told himself.

Was that love from God? If it was real love, it must be. All goodness is of God. God is all goodness. But these people were an affront to God, opposing God. Still . . . love? Their apparent expression of love lingered until their last breath. Was God trying to tell him something through these people? Should he abandon his mission? How many would die in Damascus in the fulfillment of his task? The thought of the dying men, women, and children overwhelmed him, and he was almost sick to his stomach, but he came to his senses. *The Evil One is working against God's work in my mind,* he thought. *I will never be divided between two opinions. I am tired. A fatigued body is fertile ground for forces opposing God.*

And the noonday sun—the heat was exhausting. Homes, farms, and flocks were numerous now alongside the road through the irrigated plain. Cattle rested in the shade of the scattered trees. Not a breeze moved. The crops in the fields beside the road stood motionless. No birds were in the sky. They were all in their nests somewhere waiting for the passing of the heat of the day.

The earth shuddered. Or did it tremble in fear and wonder? The ground shook; the stones moved. Limbs fell from trees, and dust quickly arose from the ground in every direction. Before he could cry out, he was overwhelmed by pure light. The awesome brilliance of a light far greater than the sun burst through the gulf between heaven and earth. The Shekinah glory streamed with such force that Saul and his companions fell to the ground. The nucleus of the light's power appeared before his eyes in such splendor that instant prostration was the result. One moment he was on his feet; the next he was on his back, his face blistered and his hair singed. Though the center from which the light emanated had been before him, he felt its heat all over his body. He quivered in shock.

The light, the beautiful, horrible light. And there before his eyes, manifested physically in glorified reality, for just a split second, was the figure of the Man in White. The Man, carried to the earth to appear before Saul in a stream of wonderful, dazzling beauty, a flowing stream of divine substance, came in a white so white, so pure, so brilliant that his eyes were seared and scaled over.

He raised his head from the ground to try to look again at the Man in White, but he was blind. On the back of his eyelids was a negative of the Man. He would never forget the image. In startled wonder he recalled the magnificent sight that struck him blind. The man's bare feet shone like gold, much, much brighter than the polished brass lamps that hung from chains in the synagogue. There was a well-healed wound on the arch of each foot— even the wounds sparkled and shone.

His robe was long and flowing and whiter than any earthly fuller could make cloth. It appeared to be a one-piece robe, hand-woven of linen, but what wonderfully white linen! Around his chest was a golden mantle. *Signifying what?* Saul wondered. Certainly a priestly piece of apparel. Or covering . . . what? The gold, a symbol of God's purity covering bloodstains that had fallen from his brow, which was banded with a golden crown. He knew, but would not, could not yet accept the fact of the identity of the Man in White. His arms were outstretched, and on his beautiful hands were wounds, one in each palm.

Saul could not distinguish the features of the Man's face. The light had prevented it. But his hair was as snow-white as his robe. His mouth was open, ready to speak. The man's eyes pierced through the light and touched Saul to the depths of his being. Eyes of love. Eyes of sorrow. Eyes of compassion, of understanding. Terrible, captivating eyes.

The light bridged the void, the unbreachable time-space from heaven to earth, and in the instant that Saul had seen all this, he saw also that around, above, and for endless reaches of space behind the Man in White were angels—thousands of angels, tens of thousands of angels.

Saul had once heard that Jesus of Nazareth had claimed that he could call down twelve legions of angels to assist him if he so desired. He had made that statement to the Temple guards the night of his arrest in Gethsemane. There were more than twelve legions of angels accompanying the Man in White. Seventy thousand? There were more, countless more. As if seventy thousand were a small number. It was. For the angels ascended through the breach, in the void all the way to the infinite reaches of holy heaven. There was an endless, countless number of them beginning at his feet and ascending as his train through timeless time and endless space. He lay on the hard ground of the Damascus road, thinking he was dead, that he had been cast into everlasting darkness. Then the sound began—the sound of water. *From where comes the sound of running water on this hot Syrian plain?* Then he knew that this sound was coming through the breach between heaven and earth where the Man in White had stood before him. He realized then, in his blindness, that the unworldly, celestial experience was continuing and the sounds he was hearing were not of this world. He was in the presence of divine direction, and he lay dazed but transfixed upon everything that came to him. This was the ancient sound of the creative work of the water that divided the land masses when the earth was created. It was the sound of the water that parted to make way for Israel to

cross the Red Sea. This was the sound of eternal water, living water, the
water that flowed from the rock at Moses' hand. The roaring and rushing
fury grew in intensity. Ocean waves crashed on rocks. He heard the sound
of heavy seas rolling, the rippling and whirling of streams and rivers. The
water fell, splashed, churned, and boiled in sheets, sprays, funnels, and seas
of water.

And along with the sound of water, he heard the voices again calling his
name, "Saul! Paul! Pol! Paulus! Paolo!" The Gentiles of all the earth were
calling him.

He was wide awake, he knew, for he could feel the hard, hot stones on his
back where he lay and trembled in greater fear. Then he sensed the warm
presence flowing over his senses, the glory of the Divine filling his very
being, touching him, yet he could still feel the spiritual gulf between this
world and the higher one. Then the presence spoke to him.

The soft, loving voice spoke to him through the sound of the water, and
it was meant for his ears only. It was a stern but kind voice, piercing yet
consoling. It was a friendly voice of love, of familiarity, of brotherhood and
compassion. A voice as ageless and endless as creation, coming all the way
from the divine dwelling place, through the gulf, bridging the eternal with
the temporal, came to the ears of the persecutor.

"Saul," it said.

He listened. He tried to raise his head, but he could see nothing. He
wanted to cry, "I'm blind," but would not attempt to shout over the roar of
the water. He could not yet speak.

"Saul," came the kind voice again, calling his name in Hebrew. Not in ages
had the Voice called to a mortal man from the dwelling place of the Most
High. He trembled so much that he could not answer. He waited, unable to
reply.

Could it be the echo of the Divine Voice, the Bat Kol? he wondered. *I am
not worthy to hear the echo of the Divine Voice.*

But the Voice was not an echo. In childlike loving-kindness, warm and
pleading, it said, "Why do you persecute me?"

And then he knew. Although he asked, "Who are you, Lord?" he knew. It was the glorified human voice of the living water, the resurrected and ascended Son.

The answer came quickly, and any lingering doubt ended when the Man in White answered conversationally and kindly, "I am Jesus of Nazareth, whom you are persecuting. It is hard for you to kick against the goad."

At first Saul did not understand the statement, "It is hard for you to kick against the goad." Then slowly it was revealed to him. Jesus had often taught in parables. Saul had been kicking against, resisting something he could no longer resist. True, there had been indications that such resistance to the truth would do no good. He had had pangs of conscience and doubts and regrets concerning the continuance of his mission. There were the ill feelings he had had when he thought of the ones who were suffering under his hand and the inner cry he had heard on his victims' behalf. He remembered the resigned, worried attitude of Baanah ben David and his plea for tolerance, his spirit of goodness. He remembered the high priest's attempt to reason with him and Nicodemus's opposition.

But mainly he had kicked against the pleading of his own conscience, the spirit of good within himself. The Spirit of God within himself! The . . . Holy Spirit within himself? Pleading for tolerance, for peace, for righteousness? The Holy Spirit working through others even?

The sound of waters continued in his ears, in his mind, flowing into his very soul. The Voice had said, "I am Jesus of Nazareth," simply "I am Jesus of Nazareth, whom you are persecuting . . ."

Is it him? thought Saul. "Jesus, the Son of . . ."

He was far too frightened to put into words the many questions he wanted to ask. Though his companions had arisen and watched in confusion as Saul still lay upon his back, he knew he was in communication with some presence not meant for them to share.

Finally Saul managed to ask, "What do you want me to do, Lord?"

"Arise! Stand upon your feet," came the private order.

Instantly, in response to the command, Saul struggled to his feet. His companions took him by the arms to hold him up, for he was, at first unable to stand alone.

He was a fearsome sight to the men who now observed him. He looked as if he had never walked before. His face was scorched, his eyes glazed with a smooth, white, scalelike covering. His parched lips were open in a futile attempt to speak. The men held him on each side and turned him toward Damascus. They called him by name, but he did not hear them.

He heard the sound of the water, and then of a rushing wind. The fire of the Light had seared his face and formed scales over his eyes. Now along with the sounds of water and wind, he heard the crackling and roaring of the flames. Fire and wind are symbols of the Holy Spirit. And angels sang, countless glorious voices sounding out in praise. Through these sounds came the Voice.

"I have appeared to you for this purpose," the Voice continued, "to make you a witness of these things which you have seen and of those things which I shall reveal to you, delivering you from your people and from the Gentiles to whom I now send you, to open their eyes and to turn them from the darkness to light, and from the power of Satan to God, that they may receive forgiveness of sins and inheritance among them who are sanctified by faith in me. Go into Damascus, and there you shall be told all things that are meant for you to do."

The channel between heaven and Saul was suddenly closed. The Voice did not wait for a response to its commands. Saul knew only that he must obey. He was conscious that his feet were moving and that human hands were guiding his movement.

"What happened to his eyes?"

Someone whispered, "He can't see."

Tears began trying to force themselves out of Saul's eyes, and in a short while they were flowing from beneath the scales covering both eyes. His parted lips still made no sound, but inside his soul a shout was rising, a shout proclaiming unspeakable joy.

Yes, his mind answered. *I am blind, blinded in order that I might see.*

"Let the blind man pass," cried Cononiah, leading Saul by the left hand. His brother, Shemei, held Saul by the other as they made their way under the great Roman marble arch that framed the eastern gate into Damascus and was the beginning of the wide, colonnaded street called Straight. Beggars and sleepers sat under the arch in the midday heat. The Temple guards and servants preceded Saul and the two Hebronites to clear the way to the house of Judas the Pharisee. The street was virtually empty, as all the shopkeepers closed up for two to three hours of respite from the sun and the heat in the middle of the day. By midafternoon the street would again be alive with the activity of buying and selling, bartering and arguing, the perpetual shouting matches held over most transactions. A dealer in brassware would know the exact price he was willing to pay. The seller, however, would not want to sell without an argument. He would want to have a chance to show the buyer that he was a charitable man and would suffer a loss in order to let the buyer have his fine brass pot, rather than allow him to go to the next shop where the goods were of a poorer quality.

As Saul passed these shops, led by his companions, he was not aware of his whereabouts. His mind was still on the Man in White. He was still speechless from the vision, and though his eyelids were open, he could see nothing except the afterimage of the figure imprinted on the scales that covered his eyes. But that image, he knew, was stamped upon his mind, for he was indeed blind.

The house of Judas the Pharisee was a spacious, columned, Greek-style home set off a ways from the street Straight behind a beautifully manicured garden and court. A Temple servant rattled the ornate door knocker three times before there was an answer from inside. A servant opened the door just wide enough to see the strange group of men who stood under the portals of Judas's front door.

"The master is asleep," said the house servant gruffly.

"Tell him Saul of Tarsus is here. He is expected," said the Temple servant.

"Open the door and let him come in," came the voice of Judas from inside the house.

The door swung open, and the Hebronites entered leading Saul; the others remained outside.

Judas didn't recognize him at first, and when he did, he was shocked at what he saw. "What has happened to you, Saul?" he asked.

Saul did not answer.

Cononiah said, "He is blind, Master. We were all struck down on the road just outside the city by a terrible light. The light was in front of his face, and it was like lightning, except that there was no sound. We don't know where the light came from, but he heard a voice as he lay on the ground; he conversed with someone none of us could see."

Judas looked at Saul thoughtfully for a moment, then said, "He has looked into the midday sun too long. That would blind anyone." To his servant he said, "Go to the physician. Tell him to come right away."

Saul spoke for the first time. "No physician," he said. Then quietly and kindly he added, "Master Judas, if you have my room ready, I would like to lie down and be alone."

"No physician?" asked Judas. "Saul, your eyes may be damaged from the sun."

"Not the sun," said Saul. "May I . . . may I go to my room?"

Saul took a coin purse from his belt and handed it to Cononiah. "I will not need you in Damascus," he said. "Here is what you would have been paid. Go back to Hebron or Jerusalem. Tell the guards and servants that my mission here has been abandoned."

The Hebronites looked at each other questioningly, then at Saul. They shrugged and backed out the door, counting the money and dividing it among themselves.

Judas took Saul by the hand and led him through a door that opened to a canopied walkway; they went past a formal inner-court garden, up a short flight of stairs, and through a polished lemonwood door to a spacious, cool room. He led him to a bed and sat him down on the soft cotton mattress. Saul covered his face with his hands.

"Thank you," he said.

Judas looked down at his friend for a moment, then said, "Rest until the evening meal, and after you've eaten, if you haven't . . . if you aren't feeling better, I shall send for my physician."

"Thank you, Brother Judas," said Saul. "I will have no evening meal. I must think . . . and pray."

Judas stood helplessly for a moment, then said to Saul, "You are abandoning your mission? At the news of your coming I sent word to the high priest that as chief rabbi of this city I would assist you."

"I can no longer destroy and slaughter, Brother Judas," said Saul.

"What will you do?" asked Judas.

As Saul lay back, the letter from the high priest dropped to the floor, and Judas picked it up.

"You may destroy that letter," said Saul.

"May I read it?" asked Judas, seeing the seal of the high priest.

"As you please," said Saul. "I have a new mission."

Judas went to his private chamber. When he had finished reading the letter, he muttered, "A new mission?" He paced the floor thinking, debating. Then he came to a decision. "I must send news to the high priest. We could be in for a great deal of trouble here."

Alone now, Saul covered his face with his hands to hide the tears of joy. From deep inside his soul had come these tears. He wiped them from his face and said, "Thanks be to God for his unspeakable gift." He wept openly. A flood of relief and release came over him. Then he quoted aloud to the empty room from the prophet Isaiah. "With joy shall you draw water out of the wells of salvation."

Most of all, he felt enormous peace at actually having said, "The mission is abandoned." He felt fulfillment in humble submission to the will of the Man in White.

He tried to pray aloud, but he couldn't speak. He could not take his mind off the vision—he relived it. The Lord had said, "I am Jesus of Nazareth, whom you are persecuting. It is hard for you to kick against the goad."

"Now I understand," he whispered aloud. "I have tried to resist the goad-ing of the Spirit of goodness, the very Spirit of the Most High. The Holy Spirit!" He paused, then whispered softly, "I no longer kick against the goad."

The joy filled him again, and for a while he could do nothing but praise. Then he realized that this was a part of his religion he had practiced in form only. Now, meekly and childlike, he said, "O Lord, I offer to you a sacrifice of praise." And he remembered he had heard Stephen quote Jesus, "Except you humble yourself as a little child, you cannot enter the kingdom of heaven . . ."

"Create in me a clean heart, O God, and renew a right spirit in me," said Saul. "Do not cast me away from your presence, and do not take your Holy Spirit from me."

A warm, peaceful presence filled Saul's being, and he lay still and let the power take control. The presence he felt was the same ominous presence he had felt at the vision of the Man in White. This time he saw no vision, but the comforting presence was there, and this time he felt no fear.

Now the presence, the Comforter, was speaking to Saul's inner mind, his heart. "I will not leave you comfortless. I will bring to your mind all my words, and you will, in due time, hear those spoken to all my apostles. And as I taught them, I shall teach you, Saul."

"I submit, Holy Spirit," said Saul. "I shall remain in constant submission."

"No," silently whispered the Spirit. "You are flesh and not sinless, nor shall you ever be free from the war the Evil One will fight for your soul. Daily, hourly, reaffirm your receptiveness to my love and counsel. I will not fail you. I will speak through you when the words fail you. I shall bear up your countenance when you would show despair. I shall strengthen the very fiber of your muscle and bone. You shall see much persecution and affliction, but nothing shall separate you from the love of the Anointed One, so long as you are faithful to your calling."

Saul opened his eyes suddenly and tried to look around the room. The scales were still there; all was black. For an instant, a chill swept over him, and he was on the verge of being afraid again. "I will fear no evil," he said aloud. "Your rod and your staff, they comfort me."

A glorious revelation came to Saul. God's rod and staff—the Messiah, his

Holy Spirit—the Man in White. The resurrection. The fulfillment of God's plan for humankind. The sacrificial lamb of God. The love of God in human form. A man to see, to listen to as a man speaking the words of God. The God-man, whose hands and feet and side were pierced, who was crowned in mockery with a crown of thorns and adorned with a royal robe, a visage of glory. By this sacrifice we see the unsearchable riches of the love of God. This is God's Messiah! His only Son given in death to bring us to him through faith in this, the new covenant; justification through faith.

The Messiah, thought Saul. *Will he not deliver Judea from the Romans? Will not the Messiah sit upon the throne in Jerusalem?*

The Comforter replied, "God did not send his Son to condemn the world, but that the world through him might be saved."

Saul's mind was quiet for a moment, then again he was quoting the prophets. "And a virgin shall conceive and bear a son. It speaks of you, Lord?"

The Counselor again entered Saul's reasoning. "So how can you count the miracles of God? And why do you marvel when any miracle with God is only a drop of mist from the floodtide of his overflowing divinity? Therefore, the seed of David does indeed sit on the throne at the right hand of the Most High, born of a woman to sacrifice the blood of atonement, his blood."

Weakened in body from such highly stimulating spiritual experiences, Saul lay back on the narrow bed, his arms hanging limply off the sides. He breathed deeply, and after a few moments he was quiet and peaceful again.

Someone entered the room, and he heard the clatter of dining utensils. Then he smelled the food. "Take it away, please," he said kindly. "I shall not eat."

"Yes, Master," said the young woman who had brought the food. She quietly left the room with the tray of food, leaving the odor of broiled fish behind. But it was spiritual food Saul hungered for, the Spirit of Truth, the Spirit of Wisdom.

He then became aware of another odor, an earthbound odor, the pungent, musky odor of his own body. He realized that he hadn't washed. He arose immediately and with outstretched arms made his way around the room until he found the washbasin. He found the bowl and the pitcher of water. In a small dish he found the round ball of soap made from lamb's fat, ashes, and pumice. He bathed himself thoroughly with the perfumed water and, having finished, slowly turned in a circle until he felt he was facing the general direction of the Temple at Jerusalem. He prayed fervently and sincerely, more praise than prayer. In his blindness, he poured out his soul to God in a prayer of praise and thanksgiving.

Having finished his prayers, Saul sang softly from the Psalms while feeling around again for his bed. Reclining, he said, "What is man, that you are mindful of him? Blessed is he whose transgression is forgiven, whose sin is covered."

Now, O Lord, he thought, *let me be receptive to the voice of your counsel.*

The Voice said, "You may study under every human teacher, read every written scroll, and learn all the theology of the ages. You may intellectually understand all the statements of truth, Saul, but until you realize the indwelling of the Anointed One in your life, you can count it all as meaningless. The Spirit of Truth, the Spirit of Love must abide within you, that you yourself may become a source whence childlike goodness and love spring forth as living water." From the sacred writings of Isaiah came these words to Saul that the Voice now spoke. "I will give you the treasures of darkness, and hidden riches of secret places, that you may know that I, the Lord, who calls you by your name, am the God of Israel. For Jacob my servant's sake, and Israel my elect, I have called you by your name.

"I proclaim to you anew the hallowed commandment," continued the voice of the Teacher, "that you love your neighbor as yourself."

"But why me? Why did you choose me?" he asked.

"For this purpose have I called you, to be my apostle, to carry my gospel to all people."

Saul answered, "I am not handsome, Lord. My features are not those that appeal to the eye. I am no orator. When I have tried to address those in my own synagogue, my speech is weak and contemptible. No one will listen to me. You need a stronger vessel than me to pour out your living water."

The Voice answered simply and kindly, "My strength is made perfect in your weakness. You shall be my minister and a witness both of things which you have seen and of things which are to come. I shall give you power in oration. When you stand to speak my name, it is I who shall speak through you. I will bring to your mind everything I would have you speak. My power shall be manifest in your acts, in your words, and in your countenance."

"Your will be done in my life," said Saul, waiting, wondering what would happen now. The Voice had implied that Saul was going to see into the future. Such honors, such gifts had been given only to the prophets of old, the seers of God. He could not fully grasp the import of the idea. He had always been wary of "seers" and false prophets, but this was something different, something real. A marvelous thing was happening to him, and he was eager and anxious for the next words. But there was silence for a while, and no voice came, no revelation.

Saul sat up on the bed and opened his eyes. Darkness. He stood up and reached out his hands, taking a few steps. He made his way around the room, feeling the walls, the doorway, the window, and the furniture. The Voice remained silent. He found his bed again and sat back down, trembling and slightly chilled. His hands were cold, for his thoughts were frightful. He remembered suddenly the faces of Stephen and the others. He panicked in his blindness as he thought of the innocent women and children who had suffered at his hand. He remembered the pleading words of Baanah ben David and the pain his old friend had suffered in seeing Saul dedicated to violence in the name of God. He felt shame in recalling the last meetings with the high priest. Saul had demanded the high priest's blessing on his mission. And his sister, Sarah, and the young Jacob—what pain were they suffering because of his infamous acts?

He cried out, "O Holy One . . ."

Before he could say anything further, the warm, comforting presence touched him, and the Voice said, "Purge your conscience of dead works and prepare to serve the living God."

"But I am guilty of shedding innocent blood. With great zeal I have persecuted beyond measure pure-hearted seekers of truth," said Saul.

"You have confessed your sins," said the Voice, "and he is faithful and just to forgive you, cleansing you from all unrighteousness. You have been given a new commandment. The end of the commandment is charity out of a pure heart, a good conscience, and a faith unfeigned."

The Teacher spoke to Saul for a long time, and his mind opened up to greater and greater truth. He was overwhelmed by the fact that he was chosen to be the object of such divine love. He remained in total submission to the Teacher's voice. It soothed him and lulled him into a light sleep, yet even in sleep the Teacher continued to speak to him, to tell him things, and to show him things that he would always remember. His mind, in sleep, was receptive to the wisdom the Voice of love imparted.

A smile formed and stayed on his face. Laugh wrinkles appeared in the leathery skin around his sightless eyes.

Pictures were forming in his mind. The afterimage of the Man in White appeared in Saul's mind's eye, and he heard the precious yet fearful Voice say, "I am the Alpha and the Omega, the beginning and the end."

"The first and last letter of the Greek alphabet," Saul said. "What does it mean?"

"I am Alpha, the source," said the Voice. "I am Omega, the fulfillment. From the source, from Alpha, you spring forth as my elect. To Omega, I will go with you and glorify you. Omega shall be Alpha. The end shall be the beginning. I am Alpha and Omega. You have your beginning in me who has no end.

"See now, Saul. Now come certain revelations to you," said the Voice. "The fellowship of the mystery which from the beginning of the world has been a secret of God. He created all things by the Son. Without him nothing was made that has been made."

"Hear, O Israel: The Lord our God . . ." Saul began, but he stopped, for the Voice was explaining the very thing Saul found confusing.

"God spoke in times past through the prophets. In these last days, he speaks through his Son, who is heir of all things, and you are joint heir with him through his atoning blood. Through the atoning blood of the Son, the kingdom of heaven.

"God's covenant with Abraham is everlasting, and now out of the seed of David has come the new covenant of faith, the new testament of God. His gift to all humankind, the sacrifice of his Son as propitiation for all sins, the fulfillment of the Law.

"Nothing shall destroy God's chosen, so that his plan may be fulfilled. They shall be scattered. They shall be persecuted. They shall be killed and gleaned on every hand. The remnant of the chosen shall survive genocides as in the days of Mordecai and Esther. The remnant shall multiply and scatter again and again. Inquisition and holocaust shall come. The hearts of the chosen shall at times wax cold in the belief that God has forgotten the covenant with Abraham, that he has neglected to send his Promised One. But God is faithful and is not lax concerning his promise.

"In due time the Anointed One came to establish the cornerstone of his church to be gathered in these last days. A jaded people failed to recognize in him the Spirit of the Most High. The Holy Spirit now begins a work in chosen men such as yourself, Saul of Tarsus, to gather the bride together, faithfully preparing her for the return of the Bridegroom. You shall go forth to the Jews scattered abroad and to the Gentiles, declaring the gospel of his salvation to all men. Doors shall be opened to you, and doors will be closed to you. Not your will, but the will of God shall direct you. Through deliverance of the message of the love of the Son, of his sacrifice and resurrection, shall the remnant of Abraham's seed be finally gathered together."

"I am afraid," Saul said silently. "I am flesh and blood. I am a man as any man."

"The incorruptible mind of the Holy Spirit shall live in you," breathed the silent Voice.

After a moment of silence, the Voice again spoke to Saul, and through his blinded eyes he again caught a glimpse of the glory of God. "Now," said Jesus, "I shall show you what great things you must suffer for my sake."

Saul suddenly lost awareness of his own body, of the room, of the scales on his eyes. He saw a great sea in his vision. In the sea were voices calling to him in every tongue. "Paul! Saul! Paolo! Paulus!" they shouted. "Come and help us. Teach us."

Saul felt a closeness with the Counselor, the Teacher. The holy Voice said, "This is the meaning of your dream of the voices in the water. To the many isles of the sea you shall go, preaching in my name. To your own people you shall first take my gospel, to the synagogues out of which you shall establish congregations. The salvation of God is revealed to all men. He has other vessels like yourself. Many are called, but few are chosen," said the Teacher. "Those Gentiles who became one with God through the indwelling of his Spirit through his Son shall become engrafted into the vine of Israel. The vine shall be pruned by the husbandman of the vineyard until perfect fruit is borne. Many shall believe in me, yet many shall reject me. You shall suffer severely for the cause for which you have been called."

Saul saw himself moving swiftly in a matter of seconds from Damascus to Arabia to Jerusalem. From there he saw himself in Judea, Samaria, Syria, Cilicia, Macedonia, Greece, and Italy, city after idolatrous city. "Look down upon the task for which you are given. Those minds are totally opposed to the gospel which you will deliver, yet those souls hunger for its substance. Observe your lot."

He saw terrible scenes of torture, of floggings and stonings—all kinds of verbal and physical abuse. He saw himself age in a moment, his head becoming bald and his back bent. Upon his own face, he saw that Stephen-like countenance of joy. He saw that he was not alone, that various companions accompanied him wherever he went, and that his joy increased with his suffering.

In each strange place in which he saw himself, he saw other companions and followers, faithful men who shared his sufferings with him as well as his moments of joy. Crowds followed him as if he were a leader, yet at times he saw crowds hostile toward him. He sensed that the Spirit of the Man in White was always with him.

"Come," said the Voice. "I will show you many things. Some mysteries you are to keep locked within your heart for all time. Other truths you are to share, and there are things which shall not be revealed even to you. See and hear now what is yours to witness."

There was a deeper darkness about Saul, and he felt weightless, suspended in the air somewhere above Damascus—no, farther—somewhere out of the environs of the world. Then he saw the stars, and farther away still he found himself looking at the streams of stars, swirling as if from a wheel. He was seeing a galaxy. The galaxy of millions of stars or suns, billions of suns, with great distances between each. He saw worlds that shone and sparkled with colors and light that he had never known before.

"The Lord God has made the heavens and the heaven of heavens. See how he hangs the worlds upon nothing. The Lord God has numbered and named all the stars and all the worlds in his creation. He calls all the worlds by their names. The Lord rejoices in his works as a little child."

Saul saw that there was no end to space, and no beginning. *Beyond all these works,* his mind asked, *what lies there?*

For an instant, beyond the outer reaches of space, he saw a light, a fierce, overpowering light. The light was not part of the glitter of galaxies strung out endlessly throughout the blackness of space. The light was outside all this wonder of creation and of an intangible nature. The magnificence of the light appalled even the spiritual mind and being of Saul, and he realized that this light was the Light of creation, which was on a different plane of existence from the countless stars and worlds. He felt suddenly that there was an unbreachable gulf between him and the Light.

The Light! This was the Light from which the Man in White had come to him, across the chasm between himself and holy heaven. "Am I seeing heaven?" he asked, and he pleaded to the Voice to let him see more. "The dwelling place of God?"

The Voice sang to him, and he recognized the sweet words from the psalm: "Your Lord is clothed with honor and with majesty. He is covered before you with light as with a garment. He walks upon the wind, and he makes flames of fire to be his ministers.

"See the earth now through the eyes of the Creator, a precious blue and white marble spinning in a sea of darkness. You are to bring his light to those in spiritual darkness."

He was looking again at the afterimage of the Man in White in his mind's eye. He was aware that he was lying upon his bed in the house of Judas, yet he felt the channel still open to the Voice.

"Do not marvel at the things that you have been shown. Though he creates countless worlds, he shall now live within you—but only when your own self is diminished, when you shall become as a little child. The author of the magnificence of all creation desires to abide in you in childlike purity. Not a sparrow falls that he does not see. The Creator of suns observes the death of a butterfly.

"Consider the love of the Lord; see how it is manifest in all creation. He separated the land masses of this world and formed the seas. He commanded the sunrise to know its place and time. In love he brings rain upon the earth, to satisfy the desolate ground. He causes the tender herb to spring forth. He knows the ordinances of heaven. He brings the constellations forth in their own season. He brings the wind. He holds treasuries of water and snow and brings them forth in season. He provides the raven its food. He marks the time when the wild goats in the rocks bring forth young; he knows the number of months till they bear. He gave the beautiful wings to the peacock. He hardens the heart of the ostrich against caring for her eggs; she turns her back on her young, for many of them will go to feed other creatures. He gave the horse strength and put thunder in its neck; it goes into battle in fierceness and rage. The hawk and the eagle mount up as he has made them to do. But of all creation, the apple of his eye is man.

"In love he created man, and he would have no man suffer, but that he should come to know his love and come to him. To man he gave dominion over all the earth. His covenant with him has not been forgotten. The heirs of the covenant must restore it and show fulfillment of it through belief in his Son. This is your task.

"You have been shown your sphere of ministry in order that you might know the significance of your calling. Study to show yourself approved of God, a workman who must never be ashamed but boldly speak his truth."

The sound of rushing waters, the living waters, returned to Saul's spiritual ears. Behind the scales of his eyes a face took form, the bearded face of a young man. Then the Voice spoke from out of the waters, "When next you open your eyes, you shall see this face. This is my servant Ananias, who is sent to minister to your needs. He has been faithful to his calling, and you shall find in him a kindred spirit."

Saul studied the face in his mind's eye. The joy of the Nazarene radiated from it. He thought of Stephen and of Barnabas.

The vision and the Voice were gone with the sound of the door opening.

"May I come in?" asked Judas.

"Yes, Master," said Saul.

"There is a man outside to see you," said Judas. "He says he was sent to you but will not say who sent him." Judas paused, but Saul did not answer. "He wears a homespun robe and old sandals," Judas continued. "I suspect he is one of the followers of the Nazarene."

Saul almost smiled. "Why do you suppose he is?"

"What does it matter?" Judas asked. "You can see no one, can you? Can you see at all yet?"

Saul smiled. "I can see eternity."

"I do not want those people in my house, Saul," said Judas.

"Why?" asked Saul.

Judas was angry. "I sent a message to the high priest that you have abandoned your mission. I am waiting for instructions from him."

Judas paced the floor. Saul raised a hand, and Judas looked down at him. "What is the name of the man who has come to see me?" he asked his host.

"His name," said Judas, "is Ananias. Do you know one here by that name?"

Saul paused before answering. "He is my . . . physician," he answered haltingly.

"Your physician?" Judas exclaimed. "He is no physician; he is dressed in homespun and carries neither medicine nor physician's instruments."

Saul sat up on the bed and turned his sightless eyes upon Judas. "Please allow him to come in if you will, Master Judas. He has been sent to me."

Judas went back into his chamber and called in a scribe. "The letter I am about to give you to the high priest," he said, "must have the highest priority. Couriers must stop neither day nor night until it reaches his hands."

Saul stood up when he heard the approaching footsteps. He was in a state of prayerful expectation as he felt a kindred spirit enter the room. The footsteps stopped just in front of him.

"Saul of Tarsus?" asked Ananias.

"Yes," he answered.

"The Lord Jesus has appeared to me in a vision," said Ananias. "He has told me that you have been shown things that you will suffer for his name's sake."

"I have seen the Lord," said Saul.

"I have heard of much evil that you have done to the People of the Way in Jerusalem, and that you came here on authority from the chief priests to arrest the saints in this city."

"That is true," said Saul, "but I have seen Jesus."

Ananias stepped closer to Saul and, raising his hands, placed the ends of his fingers over Saul's eyes. Saul felt the warmth of the Spirit in the hands of Ananias; he raised his own hands and placed them gently upon Ananias's hands. Ananias said, "Brother Saul, the Lord Jesus who appeared to you as you came to this city has sent me to you that you might receive your sight and be filled with the Holy Spirit. The God of our fathers has chosen you that you should know his will. You shall hear the voice and see the face of the Just One."

"I have heard his voice and was blinded by his countenance," said Saul. His knees weakened, and he sat down.

Ananias continued. "The Lord said that you are a chosen vessel, to bear his name before the Gentiles, before kings, and before your own people, Israel."

Ananias's hands shook under the warmth of Saul's. The scales fell away from Saul's eyes, and he looked into the face he had seen in the vision.

Saul looked around the room, then back to the Stephen-like face of love. "Take me and baptize me, Ananias."

"Let us thank your host," said Ananias. "Then we will go to my home."

Judas met them in the courtyard as they came out of the room. "You can see," he said to Saul.

"Yes," said Saul.

"Where will you go?" asked Judas.

"Into the world," said Saul. "Thank you for the lodging. I have no money to pay, but I have a precious gift for you if you will believe."

Judas was anxious for them to be gone. He knew Saul had been blind, but now he thought he was insane, conversing with the unseen and with himself.

"Believe what?" Judas asked testily.

"That Jesus of Nazareth is Lord," said Saul.

Judas turned to Ananias, disregarding Saul. "Where will you take him?"

"To my home," said Ananias, "but we will be at Synagogue Moriah on the Sabbath."

"I will be looking for you," said Judas as he watched them go.

Leaving his cloak with the golden fringes and the Pharisee turban behind, Saul left with Ananias. His legs were shaky from the momentous experiences at the house of Judas. Holding on to the arm of his friend, he struck out down the street called Straight. His formidable countenance was Stephen-like; yet it was not as one dying but as one having just been born.

✠ ✠ ✠

Saul sat in the preacher's seat of the Mount Moriah Synagogue in Damascus. Prayers had been offered and the Law had been read and commented upon by the Rabbi Judas.

Saul had asked, as guest speaker, to read verses from the Prophets and to comment upon them. He was dressed in a simple, dark, seamless garment, with a prayer shawl over his shoulders and the Benjaminite skull cap upon his head.

He read haltingly from the scroll, not as if he was unsure of himself, but as if he wanted to be sure that he was heard and understood. He took his time as he read and looked straight ahead into nothingness when he did take his eyes off the scroll of Isaiah.

He continued reading more loudly. "You shall be my servant to raise up the tribes of Jacob and to restore the preserved of Israel. I will also give you a light for the Gentiles, that my salvation may go to the ends of the earth. So said the Lord, the Redeemer of Israel and his Holy One, to him whom man despises, to him whom Israel abhors."

He closed the scroll, inserted it into the ark, and dropped the golden coverlet over it. He stood and faced his audience.

"The Holy One, the 'servant' just spoken of, is the Messiah. He has come."

Saul waited as his audience murmured and shuffled their feet, then continued. "I have realized the beauty and the unsearchable riches of a word which only recently I found despicable. The word is 'Christ,' the Greek translation of 'Messiah.'" He spoke more loudly as the audience's murmur rose in volume. "To the Gentiles who never had such a promise as we have had in the Messiah, the word 'Christ' takes on glorious connotations. Our Messiah has come to us and to the Gentiles."

Judas the Pharisee arose. Saul stood facing him, silently challenging him to interrupt. After a while Judas gave in and sat down to hear him out.

"In Christ," said Saul, "we have a new high priest who does not require new daily blood sacrifices, because for the propitiation of our sins he offered himself up as a sacrifice for us all. He returns to us now in the Spirit of the Comforter and Counselor. All who receive him and his love are made joint heirs with him in the kingdom of heaven."

Again Judas stood up to speak, but Saul raised a hand to stop him. "I will debate with you or answer questions when I have finished, Master Judas," he said. "For a few moments now I have more to say."

Again Judas sat down and with a red face turned and looked in another direction. *How did it come to this?* he asked himself. *A new high priest indeed! What will happen when Jonathan ben Annas hears of this heretical dissertation in my synagogue?*

The worshipers were restless. The members of the synagogue were in various stages of surprise and hostility. They looked anxiously at Judas, expecting the preacher to be stopped.

Saul stood straight and, it seemed, taller than he had ever been. He raised his face to search out the receptive faces in the congregation, and his countenance took on that glorious Stephen-like serenity. When he began speaking again, it was as if the Voice were speaking through him. He felt like a man renewed, a man refilled with power, invincible and unafraid. His voice echoed the flowering fruit of the Word that filled his mind.

"The psalmist asked the Lord, 'What is man that you are mindful of him?' He cares enough in that he sent his Son to die at our hands, and for us he died a human death. And to those who sought after a sign, he gave the sign of the prophet Jonah. He lay in the grave three days, then by the power of the Most High, he arose from the dead and now sits at the right hand of the Father."

People continued to stir and mumble, and Saul's voice grew louder to rise above the noise. Rabbi Judas sat with his arms folded, sternly awaiting Saul's conclusion.

"The Messiah, the Christ himself, said his kingdom is not of this world, yet having been of this world for our sake, he here shed his blood for our redemption.

"It is appointed for men to die once, and after this, the judgment. So Christ died once, never to die again, yet in the self-sacrificial offering, he died to bear the sins of any who call upon his name. So it is that without the shedding of blood, there is no remission of sin. The Lamb of God is our final blood sacrifice. Without the cross there is no crown of glory, but by his crucifixion and resurrection, if we come to him and live in the bond of his love, we are joint heirs with him in the kingdom of heaven. By faith we come to him. By faith in him we are justified. In our faith in him, we will live according to his blood covenant, and our seed of faith shall bear good fruit; therefore, by our works we shall be known.

"The new blood covenant, the new testament of Jesus of Nazareth, does not make null and void the Law of God as given to us by the men of God of old. Faith is the substance of things hoped for, the evidence of things not seen. Jesus is the fulfillment of the Law."

Saul paused. Judas was slumped in his chair, his eyes turned away from Saul and locked upon some imaginary spot on the wall. Some members of Synagogue Moriah followed Judas's attitude and sat with courteous disinterest as Saul concluded his sermon. But Saul smiled at those who listened in rapt attention, spellbound by the self-assured speaker.

"The prophet Isaiah has said, and it is written, 'Who has believed our report? To whom is the arm of the Lord revealed? The people who walked in darkness have seen a great light.'"

Saul paused again, remembering the glorious light that had temporarily blinded him outside Damascus.

"I have seen that glorious light," said Saul in conclusion.

After the benediction all eyes were upon Saul. Ananias came to him and said, "Sit and wait for the congregation to leave. You will face much hostility among some of these Damascenes."

Well, thought Judas, still studying Saul, who remained in hushed conversation with Ananias, *he brought his message to his kinsmen, and at the expense of a tumult in this house of worship.*

Ananias and Saul stood up as Judas arose and approached them, pulling his waistband up under his robe. Judas was gray-haired with a long, sharp beard, which was prematurely white. Judas's stern, highly intelligent eyes twinkled.

"Tell me, Brother Saul, how is it that in such a short time you have gone from the chief persecutor to chief authority on the teachings of the Nazarene? Your status in the holy Temple came from lifelong study and contemplation of the Law. You wore the head covering of a Pharisee. Now you seem content in homespun and the prayer shawl of a peasant. The only vestment of your religion and race is the Benjaminite cap you wear." Judas was sincerely puzzled, and though he had been offended by Saul's sermon, he earnestly sought the answers to the puzzle of Saul's about-face in his religion. "Where and how did you so quickly learn the doctrine of salvation through faith in the dead Nazarene?" Judas looked at Ananias, but Ananias dropped his eyes.

"I have seen Jesus," said Saul. "He appeared to me on the way to Damascus." Then Saul added with a kind smile, "And while I was a guest in your home, he taught me."

Judas's face flushed, and he stammered, "The Nazarene in my home?"

"His Spirit," said Saul. "I have seen him, and even still this day his counsel of truth teaches me, and through me he speaks."

Judas stared at him for a long time, at a loss for a retort to such a presumptuous, outrageous statement. "I warn you," he said. "Go your way in peace, and speak no more in public in the name of Jesus of Nazareth."

"Why, Master Judas?" asked Saul.

Judas paused, studying the bright, clear eyes of the Benjaminite. He sighed deeply, then softly said, "You have publicly proclaimed a high priest other than Jonathan ben Annas in Jerusalem. You may not leave this city alive."

Saul paused, then calmly said, "Perhaps I shall if the Lord leads me to do so. I do not fear what men can do to me, nor can I help but preach Jesus. Thank you for your hospitality, Master Judas." He raised his hand in a salute. "Now I must go with Ananias to meet with the People of the Way."

Judas slowly followed Saul and Ananias to the door and was as unsuspecting as they were when the stones started flying. Seeing Judas's display of consternation during Saul's speech, a dozen or so of the men of the Synagogue Moriah had gathered outside the door to wait for Saul. He had taken no more than a couple of steps outside when he saw the men. As he glanced to his right, he barely had time to glimpse the stone that struck him squarely on the head. He saw only stars before his eyes as he fell. He was unconscious just for a moment, and then he realized he was being carried, not by those who would kill him, but by Ananias and the other Nazarenes. They were fighting for him. Stones were striking him even as they were carrying him away.

Judas was shouting for the mob to disperse. "He has been admonished and will return no more. Let the man go."

"Yes, I will return, Master Judas," said Saul as he blacked out again. His friends carried him away.

A horseman, riding hard, came upon the scene just as they were taking Saul away. Judas, standing at the door of the synagogue, recognized him as the courier from Jerusalem.

"A letter from the high priest," said the man to Judas as Judas reached up for it. He walked back inside and sat down to read it.

To Judas, Chief Rabbi of Damascus
Praised Be the Most High.
Greetings:

Place Saul of Tarsus under arrest and bring him in chains to this holy Temple. He is to be charged with blasphemy, murder, and certain other traitorous acts and will be tried before the Supreme Council.

> Jonathan ben Annas
> High Priest
> Seal affixed

At the house of Ananias, his wife, Rebeccah, and the wife of one of the elders had come into the room with pans of warm water. Rebeccah was at the foot of the bed Saul was lying on. A stone had evidently struck him on the big toe of his right foot. As Rebeccah softly bathed it with warm water, Saul moved the foot and a sharp pain shot up his right leg. The other woman was bathing the bruises on his head. Saul closed his eyes, enduring the pain. As Rebeccah was applying a poultice of healing herbs to his foot, Saul whispered, "My body is sown in dishonor, to be raised in power."

Ananias touched his fingers to Saul's eyes and said, "Again your body needs rest and restoration. The Holy Spirit desires to dwell in a healthy temple."

Saul lay still, feeling the warm healing herbs at Rebeccah's hand. And where his head had been aching, the pain had disappeared at Ananias's touch.

Saul opened his eyes and looked at Ananias. "Though I am nothing, Ananias," he said, "even in my nothingness shall I be the chief apostle of Jesus. His grace is sufficient for me. His strength is made perfect in my weakness."

Saul sat up on the side of the bed, removed the poultice from his foot, and stood up. The women were surprised that he was able to stand so soon, and they were aghast when he walked across the room without a limp and mounted the stairway that led to the open, spacious roof of the house of Ananias. He turned and said to his host as he climbed the stairs, "I shall take pleasure in infirmities for Christ's sake, for when I am weak, then I am strong."

Ananias turned, smiling to his wife. "Tell the other women to call the saints to the rooftop. This day shall be spent in prayer for the new mission that our zealous brother Saul of Tarsus has set for himself."

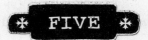

FIVE

THE WANDERING

Early in the morning toward the end of the week, Ananias searched the household for Saul and couldn't find him. His bed had not been slept in, and there was no indication that he had been in the room. Rebeccah was afraid when Ananias awakened her to tell her that Saul had disappeared. She put on her robe, washed her face and hands thoroughly, then, brushing her long black hair before the copper mirror, said, "I fear for Saul, Ananias. I had not mentioned it earlier for fear that you would think it was just women's idle conversation, but for the last two days I have heard bits of information here and there that there is a plot afoot to kill Saul."

Ananias put his arms around his wife, looking at her beautiful but troubled face in the mirror. He said gently, "Where does this talk come from, Rebeccah?"

She turned and faced her husband. "Indirectly from the Synagogue Moriah," she said, twisting her hair and arranging it on the back of her head.

"I cannot say for sure, but some of the women have reported that Judas, the chief rabbi, sent a messenger to Jerusalem to report to Jonathan ben Annas that Saul had abandoned his mission of destroying our congregation and that he had become one of us."

Ananias studied the information for a while, then said, "Saul would be happy for that bit of truth to be broadcast." He looked at his wife a moment, then turned and walked down the stairs and across the vestibule to the front door. Just as he reached the front door, he heard a noise behind the door to his left that led to the basement. A dim light was shining under the door.

He opened the door and walked quietly down the stairs. Saul sat on a stool, his head resting on his folded arms on the large horizontal loom where he had worked all night. Dawn was breaking through a small window near the ceiling, bringing more light into the room now than the nearly burned-out candle hanging from the lamp near Saul's head.

Ananias smiled down at the sleeping guest and gently shook him awake. "Saul," he said sympathetically, "wake up."

Saul arose with a start. When he saw Ananias, he smiled sheepishly and rubbed his tired, red eyes.

"You haven't slept in your bed," said Ananias.

"I couldn't sleep," he said.

Ananias studied him a moment, then asked, "What troubles you, Saul? May I help?"

Saul slowly turned and walked over to the front wall and looked up at the small window where the sunlight was just breaking through.

"The Lord Jesus spoke to my mind again last night, Ananias," said Saul.

"Did the Lord tell you that your very life is in danger?" asked Ananias.

Saul walked across the room and stood facing his friend. "I do not fear what men can do to my body. Yet I must survive now to go about the business for which the Lord calls me. Yes, Ananias," he said, "those who oppose me are quite prepared to kill me, and the Lord does not at this time require martyrdom of me, but service."

"What will you do, Saul?" asked Ananias. "The city gates are being watched, and you will be arrested."

"I know how you can leave the city safely," said Rebeccah, descending the stairs. Saul and Ananias turned toward her. "What about the window in the east wall of the city?" she suggested.

Ananias's face brightened. The library was next to the eastern wall. The only opening in the wall, barely large enough for a man to squeeze through, was a window on the third floor of the library, the place of ancient scrolls. In this room of the Jewish library were the large scrolls, writings by the prophets and seers of Israel, as well as writings by Solomon and Ezra and many works of commentary on the Prophets. There were timeless precious books on ethics, medicine, agriculture, and philosophy, all meticulously copied from earlier works. Some were on sheepskin, some on parchment, and some on papyrus made from reeds that grew along the Jordan and along the Nile in Egypt. The small window was opened and closed every morning and evening to allow the warm, dry east wind to circulate in the room, protecting the precious scrolls from mold and mildew.

Saul smiled. *The Lord provides a way,* he thought. He looked down at the candle, which was burning out.

"You can gain access to the room of the scrolls tonight," said Rebeccah. "You will need two or three men to come with a basket and a rope at least seventy cubits long."

Ananias thought a moment, then said, "The window is so small. How will we get a basket and Saul through it?"

"You will need the long basket," she said, "the kind used for carrying long stalks." She looked at Saul and smiled, thinking how small he would be wrapped up tightly in the long basket. "Just be sure, Ananias, that you have some steady hands ready to let him down the wall."

Ananias turned to Saul. "Meanwhile, you must get some sleep."

"I shall try," he said.

A frown crossed Rebeccah's brow. "Getting you out of Damascus should be fairly easy, Brother Saul," she said, "but I worry what happens then. If you go toward Jerusalem, you could be seen and arrested. If you go into Arabia and find a caravan route, you could be fallen upon by robbers."

Saul smiled. "I carry nothing to tempt robbers." He looked down at the candle as it sputtered out and then at the faces of Ananias and Rebeccah. "The love of God that is manifested in you is like that candle that burned gloriously for its entire life. The fire of his love in you burns brighter because you share it with me, and for this purpose have I been called, that I go and take his light of love and light his flame in other lives." He paused, then said, "Yes, I must go tonight! Unless the seed be scattered, there is no increase."

"At least I can prepare you a food pouch and a skin of water to take with you," said Rebeccah.

✳ ✳ ✳

Two pairs of hands pushed Saul through the hole in the upper eastern wall. He had helped Ananias and the two elders twist his shoulders through. Now his safety was temporarily in their hands. The upper half of his body was hanging head down, wrapped in the straw basket to the neck.

The rope was the problem. It was tied at his waist, and they were having trouble getting the basket and the rope all through the hole. Suddenly he was through and falling. In the darkness he couldn't see the ground below, but he knew it was a long way. Abruptly the rope took up the slack with a hard jerk; the loop at his waist slipped down to his hips, hanging him upside down. Slowly the men let him down, and spinning in circles, suspended from the hips, he strained to see the ground.

Down, steadily down he went, first with his arms hanging straight to cushion his contact with the ground. But when he made first contact, it wasn't with the ground but with a hedge-thorn bush. He wanted to shout out for his friends to stop but thought better of it. The eastern gate wasn't far away, and he mustn't be discovered.

He closed his eyes and steeled himself for what he knew was coming.

When his hands felt the thorns, he tried to protect his head, but it was next to impossible. The men inside the window felt the tension relax, and realizing Saul was down, they let the rope fall on out the window.

"He's down," whispered Ananias. He and the other men hurried down the stairs and stepped out the door and into the street.

Saul was indeed down—headfirst into a thornbush and tied up in a thin basket. Every moment was agony as he reached through the wiry thorn vines to untie the rope around his hips. As he twisted side to side to do so, the thorns scratched and stuck him in the hands, arms, face, even on top of his head.

Even with the rope untied he still felt imprisoned. He closed his eyes and lay still for a moment. The afterimage of the Man in White appeared on the backs of his eyelids, and he remembered the dream. The crown of thorns. The nails in the hands and feet.

With fearless determination, he started to stand up, but the strong vines and sharp thorns he had fallen through prevented it. His fingers felt the soft ground, and he started to pull himself out from underneath the thorns. He felt them cut and rip him all over, but he didn't stop. He kicked at the dirt, turning over on his back and twisting out from under the clawing vines.

His head, shoulders, and arms covered with bloody scratches, he sat against the wall looking out into the darkness. A dark red half-moon was rising, and the hills beyond began to take shape. Saul moved into the bushes and headed eastward. Up the tributaries of the River Abana lay the city of Haran. Perhaps he would go there. It lay directly under the rising moon, which, rising higher, did not lose its deep red color.

The kadim, *the hot east wind from the great desert, is coming,* thought Saul. From time to time it would come—no one knew when. The *kadim* blew furiously for three days and nights, bringing with it the dust of the desert that penetrated everything. Livestock and wild animals often died from choking on the flying dust. It came inside houses, under doorways; it got into the bread, the milk, and the clothes of everyone, rich or poor. Various superstitions abounded concerning the *kadim*. Children born during its passing would be criminal or demented. A woman's monthly cycle would be either delayed or prolonged. More people would be murdered or maimed during the *kadim* than at any other time.

People kept their faces covered when the terrible wind blew. There were tales of people losing their senses. Everyone dreaded the screaming, stinging wind that brought the maddening sand.

With the redness darkening as the moon rose, Saul was sure that it wouldn't be many hours before the *kadim* struck from the very direction he was headed.

With the wind rising, he stumbled among the bushes and rocks of the dry riverbed. He had lost count of the hours and had come upon no caravan routes. He only saw the moon occasionally now, and the sky breaking into dawn was dull and overcast.

Saul, weary and sore from the ordeal of his escape and stumbling all night against a constantly rising wind, stopped and sat upon a great tree trunk that had fallen into the riverbed. The day should have been breaking brighter by now, but the wind was bringing the dust. He surveyed his predicament.

He removed his cloak and tied the two arms of it to two limbs of the log. Then he took two sticks and, driving them into the sand on the downwind side, made himself a shelter. He lay down under the cloak against the log and covered his mouth and nostrils with his prayer shawl. From the small pouch Rebeccah had given him that hung from his belt, he removed some figs and cheese. After saying his prayers, he ate his meager breakfast and finished it with water from a small wineskin tied to his sash.

The wind and dust were increasing and the sky was darkening eerily as the exhausted Saul slept soundly, his prayer shawl covering his face. The wind whistled and howled, and the red dust became thicker, but Saul slept on, well protected by the log and his cloak. The dust whirled in ringlets about his head, and small piles of dust and sand encircled him, giving him even more protection from the raging *kadim*.

In the earsplitting shrill of the wind around midday, Saul started at the sound of a voice calling his name. "Saul," the Voice said softly. He opened his eyes, then closed them, and there again was the negative image of the Man in White. "Saul," the Voice said again.

"Yes, Master. Here I am," Saul whispered back in a dreamy half sleep. He was feeling a strange sensation, as if he were leaving his own body.

Suddenly he was above the storm, whirling into space, around and around like the little whirling streams of sand where he had lain.

"Look down, Saul," said the Voice.

"Yes, Master."

He saw the coastal city of Joppa and the blue Mediterranean tapping its shores.

"Observe," said the Voice, "the instruction of your fellow servant Simon whose name is Peter, the one I called Cephas."

"I see him, Master," whispered Saul, "on the rooftop."

The *kadim* had vanished, and the noonday sun shone down bright and clear upon Simon Peter in the vision that Saul beheld. He was in Simon Peter's presence, yet he was not. He was above him, yet he was beside him. He was out of the body, yet the auburn hair and beard and the broad shoulders of the fisherman seemed very tangible. Saul waited and observed, glorying in being allowed to witness Peter's experience.

"I am not worthy, Lord," Saul whispered.

"Be still and observe," said the Voice, "and know that the Holy One makes straight the way and certain the purpose for calling his saints to service."

Simon Peter's eyes were turned toward heaven as he received the vision. A great white sheet tied at the four corners, descending like a great vessel, approached the rooftop. Peter, and Saul, saw that tied in the sheet were all manner of four-footed beasts of the earth, domestic and wild, swimming and crawling things, and many different kinds of fowls.

Saul heard a voice directed to Peter say, "Arise, Peter, kill and eat."

Peter gasped in astonishment at seeing the great menagerie. "Oh no, Lord," he said. "I have never eaten anything that is common or unclean."

The Voice spoke to him a second time. "What God has cleansed, that you do not call common."

Peter covered his face for a moment, then looked up. The sheet was again descending from heaven. Again the Voice said, "Arise, Peter, kill and eat." And again Peter repeated his objection.

After the third time, the vision was gone. Peter fell prostrate on the roof and prayed, "O Lord, reveal the meaning of this thing to me."

Immediately Saul was again taken up and away from Joppa as the Voice said to him, "See how the Father cares for you, Saul. Your fellow workers are likewise prepared as you are with the knowledge that the Gentiles may receive the salvation of God through Jesus Christ. To them shall be given the gifts of the Holy Spirit also.

"This is the meaning of the living things which Simon Peter called 'common.' He henceforth knows that God is no respecter of persons and esteems no man over another; therefore, every nation that fears him and does his work of righteousness is accepted by him. Now the Word of God as given to the children of Israel is to be preached to all the world."

Saul suddenly opened his eyes. At first he was uncertain of where he was in the howling wind and sand, then he remembered and realized he had slept for a long time. But the dreamlike trip to Joppa was real, and he knew it. He had been blessed with another vision himself, observing Simon Peter's vision and hearing the meaning of it.

The sand was whirling in little eddies around Saul's body, and occasionally he had to take the prayer shawl off his nose and mouth and shake out the sand. He thought the sun must be high, though. Looking out under the edge of his cloak, he saw the sky was dark with the blowing sand.

All day and into the night, then into the next morning, the wind raged and the sand piled up around him. From time to time he would kick the tops of the piles down to allow the dust-filled air to circulate. He would hit the cloak above his head as it became weighted down with the sand. He was very thirsty.

Toward dawn he ate his second handful of fruit and cheese and drank his last bit of water from the skin. He knew he would have to suffer through the dust storm. He would quickly lose his sense of direction if he tried to move. He continued praying, "O Lord, when the coming storms of life rage about me, teach me to be still and wait upon you." He never thought to pray for personal deliverance from his plight. It never occurred to him that he was in any danger. It was just a matter of waiting until the scorching, blistering wind died, then he would be on his way.

"To where?" he asked prayerfully. The wind did not answer him.

After eating he again became sleepy. The constant sound of the wind had a lulling effect, and he closed his eyes.

Which direction will I go? he wondered. He was eager to be up and about the business for which he was called, but for some reason God had deemed that he wait here in this riverbed. He knew that the wonderful vision of Simon Peter's which he had shared was one reason for the delay in his journey. Still, hour upon hour the wind whistled and screamed, blistering everything it touched with the sand and dust it carried. The dust was like a great cloud, moving at a gale force, bringing not rain but dirt from foreign soil. *When will it end?* he wondered dreamily.

He remembered a scene from his youth. Jemimah was sitting beside him against a palm tree. The cares of the world and the business of the Temple were far from his mind. They had walked to the banks of the Jordan from the shop where her father sold cooked food. They were both very young, and they had laughed that morning. He threw stones into the blue-green water of the Jordan, skipping them across to the far bank.

"You did it, Saul!" she shouted. "It skipped three times."

What a pleasant person she is, thought Saul, admiring her snow-white teeth when she smiled. Her green eyes sparkled in the afternoon sun. He admired everything about her. Her long hair was braided into two long plaits that hung down each side of her face and whipped around her head when it turned. Her face was very animated.

"What are you looking at?" she asked.

He started to answer, "You," but quickly turned his face away from her and picked up another stone to throw at the water. "Nothing," he said, skipping the flat rock to the far side of the Jordan.

She continued looking at him. "You're a strange one, Saul."

He flushed. "What do you mean by that?" he mumbled.

"Nothing," she said, leaning back against the trunk of the palm tree. She picked up a fallen palm frond and swished it back and forth in the air. "It's just that you're so *serious* all the time. You need to laugh more. Just when I think you're going to enjoy yourself, your mind goes off into some other world."

"Not another world," Saul stammered. "This world. Jemimah! The reign of Israel! The steeling and tempering of my soul to be a true vessel of the Most High. There is nothing to laugh about! Roman standards are in the streets of Jerusalem. Many men are torn away from the worship of the true God—the one God! I know of nothing better to live for than to serve him through the study and practice of his Law! When the Romans are cast into the sea and a Jewish king sits again on the throne of Israel, then will I laugh."

"You're shouting at me, Saul," she said evenly.

He stood and looked at her, perplexed.

She arose to her feet and said resignedly, "We had better go. Take me back to Jericho."

"No, wait," he said, quick to apologize. "I'm sorry I shouted at you." He sat down on the grass and asked her to sit beside him, which she did reluctantly.

"The Romans!" she said finally. "And Israel!"

"I said I'm sorry," he said, putting his hand on her shoulder. Her eyes were captivating, and she returned his stare.

"I would like to look deep inside your soul, Saul, into the secret you, to see what you're really like."

He moved his face within inches of hers and said, "Look, then."

Before either of them realized it, their lips met and his arms were around her. At first she didn't resist, but as he held her tighter, kissed her more deeply, she felt herself being carried down. Suddenly she broke free and stood away from him. In embarrassment, she turned her back to him and said, "You shouldn't kiss me that way. We are not yet betrothed."

He was instantly on his feet. "Betrothed? We shall never be betrothed!" he shouted.

She turned and faced him. At first her eyes showed disappointment, but then her expression quickly changed to one of anger.

"Take me back to Jericho," she said, "to my father." And she struck out ahead of him.

✳ ✳ ✳

Saul startled at what he thought was a great noise. He listened. But it was the sound of silence that had awakened him. The wind had stopped, and everything was amazingly quiet and still.

Immensely troubled by the memory of that day with Jemimah, he lay still, looking at the patch of clear blue sky that showed under the edge of his cloak. No, he was not just troubled but very, very lonely. Now he was sure to dream of Jemimah again. He tried to erase the image of Jemimah from his mind, but in the naked light of day, with the sun streaming in upon him, his loneliness was as real as his thirst, which was severe. *I must,* he thought, *forget Jemimah. As I once believed that there was no room in my life for a wife and family, so it is even more so now. My home will be in the homes of the followers of Jesus. My family will be any congregation that worships the Lord. Whosoever does the will of the Father shall be my kinsmen. O Lord, deliver me from desires of the flesh and all such temptations; refine me for a surety of my purpose.*

He looked at his hands and arms covered with dried blood from the cuts and scratches of the hedge thorns. If he could have seen his own face, he would have been alarmed at the tortured, weary countenance. He felt his stomach and thought surely if he pressed hard enough he could feel his backbone.

He bent his legs to test their flexibility. *I must find water,* he thought, rising to his feet. He stood high upon the log and looked to the west. Far in the distance, shining like a jewel in the clearing sky, was the city of Damascus. He had come a long way. The city sat on a higher elevation, on the foothills rising toward the mountains of Lebanon. The long, high city wall looked like a golden band around the city.

To the south lay the endless stretches of arid desert land—the direction he would be traveling in. It was a wilderness where only the crafty survived. Unless traveling under the protection of a caravan, a man lived only by common sense and respect for the desert.

Saul surveyed the farther reaches of his vision. *There lies my mission,* he thought. Then he looked to the east, and down the riverbed just a few steps away was cool running water. "Praised be the Most High," Saul said aloud as he stepped down off the log and walked to the edge of the pool.

Before he drank and washed, he fell to his knees and gave thanks. Even in his severe thirst, in pouring his heart out for the seemingly miraculous discovery of water, he forgot himself and his needs and gave thanks for his blessings.

He raised his head and looked at the pool before him. The water came out of the ground, circled slowly in pools and eddies, ran a short way farther, and disappeared back into the ground. In prayerful meditation, he watched the ripples whirling, carrying off the dust from the stone, bringing more clear, pure water into the pool.

He closed his eyes, and the afterimage of the Man in White formed again behind his eyelids.

"Saul," it said.

"Yes, Lord."

"Drink, and learn this truth."

He lay down with his face in the pool and drank deeply.

"Whosoever drinks of this water shall thirst again. But whosoever drinks of the water that I shall give him shall never thirst. The water that I shall give him shall be a well springing into everlasting life."

"Yes, Lord," said Saul.

"Do you understand me?" asked the Voice kindly.

"Yes, Lord," he replied. "Whosoever believes in you, from within him shall flow rivers of the living water. You speak of the Holy Spirit."

"If any man thirsts, let him come to me and drink," said the Voice. "You shall pour out my living water to the whole world. Let him who is thirsty come. Whoever will, let him take of the water of life freely." The image disappeared, and the Voice was gone.

Saul bathed himself thoroughly, filling his skin with water, and stood up. He walked upon the rocks on the riverbank. He looked down upon the refreshing pool going in circles and remembered the dream he had had what seemed like a long, long time ago—the voices in the water that called out to him, the Jews and the countless numbers of the Gentile nations calling out his name in various languages.

He spread out his arms and smiled broadly. He raised his face to the sun and laughed. "The earth receives blessings from God," he said. "Make me worthy to be a vessel to pour out your living water."

Saul started out eastward. Everywhere the whirling, drifting sand covered all. Then on a rise ahead he saw a caravan and knew he was about to reach the great north-south trade route that traversed the western edge of the Arabian desert. Upon reaching it, he turned south.

This road was not a straight road of hard-surface stones like the ones the Romans built, but a wide path beaten by centuries of camels' and donkeys' feet, by noble and ignoble chariot wheels, and by the bare feet of slaves carrying royal cars whose occupants kept their costly curtains closed to keep out the fleas, the heat, and the smell of the animals. The bare feet of pilgrims traveled the road, as did the heavy wheeled carts and wagons laden with goods to be bartered in Philadelphia or Macherus, east of the mountains, east of the Dead Sea, or taken farther, across the vicious broiling Sinai to Memphis and Alexandria.

The road meandered as nearly as possible to the lay of the land, going around hostile terrain yet making as straight as possible the southern route from the Orient to its destinations. In addition to robbers who sometimes traveled in bands of a dozen or more, the outcroppings of rocks and canyons were feared as well because of lions. The farther south Saul traveled, the wilder and rougher the terrain became. He saw each day hundreds of fellow travelers and always stayed close to a well-protected caravan. At night he ate little and seldom slept. On the third night on the road, a terrible wind rose again, and Saul, lying in a ditch for protection, watched as litters overturned and animals broke their halters and disappeared in the desert.

An oriental man stood by his overturned litter and called for his slaves to aid him. His wife broke through the curtains under which she had fallen and clung to her husband's feet. As the slaves uprighted the litter, Saul leaped to his feet and ran to their aid. He drew from his belt the needles and hooks of his craft. The man huddled on the ground, protecting his wife from the fierce wind and dust.

In the darkness Saul heard the bleating of a goat, and reaching out into the darkness, he took the goat by the horns and twisted its neck until it fell upon the ground. From its shoulders and sides he pulled out strands of long black hair. Letting the animal go in the darkness, threading the hair in the needle, and reaching for the torn cloth of the royal litter, he urged the man to take his wife back inside. Then he worked as a blind man quietly mending the tear in the cloth until it was sewn together again. He felt along the sides of the litter and, upon finding another torn area, again threaded the goat hair and sewed and mended until the litter was whole again.

Finally the coughing and weeping of the woman inside ceased, and with his nostrils and eyes burning form the fury of the wind and sand, Saul lay upon the ground on the downwind side of the litter and slept.

Morning broke calm and clear, and Saul awoke to the sounds of stubborn animals being brought back to the caravan from where they had been lost and wandering aimlessly the night before.

He sat up, and to his surprise, well within sight was the lush green valley of the Jordan River and the city of Jericho beyond. The turmoil and madness of the night before was matched only by the loneliness and confusion of the morning. Inside the litter beside him and still asleep lay the man and his wife. Their slaves observed him curiously, but he paid them no attention.

The agony of this journey and the trauma of the weeks preceding it had left him weak, and as he looked across the short expanse of desert to the emerald-watered Jericho, he tried to pray. But the flesh cried out; the humanness in him cried out, "Jemimah! The beautiful woman Jemimah of Jericho." He could now be enjoying a comfortable home, food, rest . . . He confessed aloud, "I am lonely, Lord."

He felt bitter. Did not the coming of the Messiah mean that peace and joy were to be his? The conversion on the Damascus road already seemed a long time ago.

A very earthbound east wind had blown mercilessly until dawn, and now in the clarity and calm of the day, he could not turn his eyes from the west and the refuge he could find in Jericho.

A long black finger tapping him on the shoulder brought him out of his reveries. He looked up into the face of a dark-skinned giant. The man spoke to him and motioned toward the litter that still held the reclining figures of the king, if he was a king, from the East and his queen, or wife.

Saul arose to his feet, barely coming up to the waist of the servant who had brought his attention to bear upon the partially untied entrance flap to the litter.

Inside looking at him was the "king," reclining on his back, his head resting upon a cloth-covered board. Beside him, her face veiled in exquisite lace, lay the woman. Only her eyes moved in Saul's direction.

The servant prodded Saul closer to the opening in the curtain, saying, "My master will speak with you."

Saul unhesitatingly leaned toward the face of the man, keeping his eyes from the eyes of the woman.

The servant spoke in broken Aramaic, with a dialect strange even to Saul. "From beyond the two rivers, the Tigris and the Euphrates, we come. The master will now speak with you."

"Come closer," said the royal man. "Let me see your face."

Saul bent over and allowed himself to be studied.

"You are a Jew," said the king, a statement rather than a question.

"Yes," said Saul. He paused. The king opened the flap more, and Saul saw that the king and his wife, lying on their backs, had their hands resting upon another cloth-covered board. Then he saw a strange thing he had only heard of. The fingernails of the pair were longer than the fingers themselves. The man's fingernails were twice as long as his fingers, and they were curled and polished.

A sign of beauty? A sign of patience and endurance? Surely with such long, perfectly twisted, and unscratched fingernails, the royal couple never used their fingers for any labor or task that might in any way affect the growth and beauty of their fingernails. Was it a religious custom? Saul wondered. Or was it a symbol of their position, to be perpetually served in every way by their liege of servants? Or was it a thing only of vanity?

Their clothing was beautiful. The king wore a turban with many precious stones mounted in it. His mustache, like his fingernails, was long and twisted. He wore a red silk robe with a golden sash and golden sandals. His wife was very tiny but very beautiful. Her hair was black, as were her eyes. Her tiny sandals were red, trimmed in gold. Precious stones hung from her ears and around her neck. Inside the litter Saul smelled the musky, sweet odor of frankincense.

The world outside of Israel already mystified Saul, and his journey had just begun. How much more mystifying would he be to others, when he began proclaiming Jesus of Nazareth, the Messiah of God?

The king spoke, and as he did, he pointed toward the place in the litter where Saul had repaired it the night before.

"You have done such a marvelous job in repairing my litter that the stitches appear to be more of a decoration in the cloth than a repair."

"Thank you," said Saul humbly. He did not know what title to use in addressing the man. "Master" he would not use, and "King" he was not sure of.

The servant saw Saul's confusion and quickly informed him, "You stand in the presence of Batu-Han, king of the province Delbad. His one million subjects are loyal. You will kneel to him and offer your unworthy service. You will not look into the eyes of the wife of Batu-Han, king of Delbad, upon pain of death."

Saul stood up full length and looked up into the face of the king's servant. "I kneel before no man," said Saul. "I kneel only to the Most High, Lord of Israel. I have rendered a service to your king as I saw the need last night. However, he is not my king."

Saul next found himself sprawled upon the ground. The servant had slapped him with a stunning blow across the side of the head, and at the same time kneed him in the groin. At first Saul was stunned from the agony; then the pain returned. His breath was gone, and as he lay curled on the ground, trying to breathe again and overcome with pain, he heard the king shouting commands to the servant who had struck Saul. The servant bowed his head, turned, and stepped back.

Finally the pain subsided and Saul sat up, his head in his hands, rubbing away the numbness from the stunning blow he had received. Batu-Han, king of Delbad, was quietly observing him with a twinkle of a smile in his black eyes.

"What is your name?" Batu-Han asked Saul in atrocious Aramaic.

"I am Saul of Tarsus. A Jew of the tribe of Benjamin," Saul replied.

"From Jerusalem?" asked Batu-Han.

"Yes," said Saul.

"Where are you going?" asked the king.

"On a journey to prepare myself to serve the Most High through his Son, the promised Messiah," said Saul.

"Messiah?" asked Batu-Han.

"Yes," said Saul, "Jesus, the Deliverer."

Batu-Han smiled at Saul's testimony. He nodded as if he had heard this before. "Has this Messiah come?" asked Batu-Han.

"Yes," said Saul, "he has come."

"Are you delivered from your enemies?" asked Batu-Han.

"No," said Saul.

"Who are your enemies?" asked Batu-Han.

Saul found the questioning complicated and sought to simplify the matter. "I have no enemies," said Saul.

Batu-Han cocked his head at Saul, then shook it in confusion. "Then who are your friends?" he asked.

"Those who do the will of God," Saul said, pausing, "but more than that, my friends are the beloved followers of the Son of God and Anointed One of Israel."

Batu-Han paused and gave Saul a curious look. Then finally he said, "I have heard of your people and more than a little of your traditions and religion. God is one, is he not? Do you not proclaim this daily in your praise of him? Are you saying that your god has a son?" asked Batu-Han. "If he also is a god, then is not your god two?"

"God is one," said Saul, "yet he is now three—the Father, the Son, and the Holy Spirit. Still, he is one. You can come to know the omnipotence of him through his Son by the Holy Spirit."

Batu-Han laughed. "I have been to all the great cities of the world, and in all that world ruled by Rome your people are in the cities. You are many sects and synagogues."

"I know," said Saul.

Batu-Han smiled warmly, then said, "Saul of Tarsus, you are wrong in that you say you have no enemies. The whole world hates you."

Saul's mouth fell open. This remark left him speechless.

"In all the great and small cities of the world, your people are severely persecuted. They live in crowded districts of the worst sort. They are forced to live all together for many reasons. Your people are a clannish people who generally oppose civil authority and will tolerate no religion except their own."

"How do you know so much about the dispersed of Israel?" asked Saul.

"I have been everywhere in the world where men and women love gold, silk, and exotic spices. All men and women have this vanity in common, and my camels and carts supply these worldwide needs. In turn, I am a man of great wealth and influence."

Saul did not appear impressed.

Batu-Han had more to say. "You will have enemies everywhere you go. When you least expect rejection, watch for the stones to fly."

"I have a special calling," said Saul.

"Yes?" asked Batu-Han.

"The Son of God, in great glorification, descended from the right hand of God in heaven and appeared to me."

Batu-Han then looked at Saul as if he were seeing him for the first time. Then Saul thought it best to completely explain the Damascus road experience, answering unbelieving questions and explaining his mission to the Gentiles. Then he filled him in on what had preceded it.

Batu-Han understood his staunch Jewishness before the conversion. He had seen many Zealots. But the Damascus road experience and the appearance of a glorified Son of God singling Saul out for such a mission were incomprehensible.

His first words to Saul after Saul spoke were, "You're going the wrong way," and he laughed at Saul. "Your Gentile world lies at Antioch, Tarsus, Antioch of Pisidia, Ephesus, Troas, Thessalonica, Athens, Corinth, Rome . . ."

"I am going first to Sinai," said Saul, "to the rock from which I was hewn, so to speak. Then when he bids me, I shall go to those cities."

Saul bowed his head, and Batu-Han spoke warmly and personally. "You cannot do such a thing, Saul. All cities and all people have gods. You will bring yet another god into the lives of those who already have too many gods."

"There is only one God, the God of the Covenant. And through the Covenant with his people in Israel, his chosen people, a Savior, the Son of God, was sacrificed for all who will believe," said Saul.

Batu-Han relaxed and closed his eyes, then asked quietly, "Is your god a respecter of persons? Is one race lesser or greater in his eyes?"

"You do not understand," said Saul. "He is no respecter of persons. He doesn't esteem one race or one man above another. That is why I have been called as an apostle to the Gentiles. Under the new covenant, or the fulfilled covenant through Jesus the Savior, God does not want any man to suffer, but offers salvation to all through belief in him."

✳ ✳ ✳

The caravan moved slowly but steadily down the eastern side of Lake Asphaltitis. Hundreds of noisy animals could be seen, and people of many races and religions with many reasons for making the journey. Great carts of food and supplies followed the litter of Batu-Han. Tall bronzed slaves walked alongside each cart, prodding the beasts of burden. Day after day Saul walked with the caravan, earning his food and protection by mending tents, coverings, and clothing at every stop.

The road became a rocky gully as the entourage slowly climbed the plateau that was crowned in the distance by the fortress Macherus. For a day, then two days, then three, the tower steadily moved closer. The country was bleak and arid on the rises, and the heat was stifling. Down and across the valleys was like another world. The temperature dropped, and there was much vegetation.

Saul lay down under the stars at night to the sounds of night birds and the cries of wild animals. Jackals and dogs were always in the distance, warning of dangers in the strange darkness.

And stranger and stranger still the country did become. The canyons were deeper and the rocky mountains sharper and steeper. More vegetation grew out of the rocks, tangling vines, thornbushes. Crossing the eastern slopes of Machaerus, Saul began to see the beautiful and rare rue tree. The towering giants with the smooth, cool trunks were found only here, and because of its beauty, hardness, and rarity, the rue wood was much used in the fine chambers of the Temple.

The servants of Batu-Han spread their evening meal on an exquisite carpet, and a dozen or more men sat around this ready-made table. Oil fires heated the water, and soon the king and his lady were drinking a warm beverage. They moved into the tent, which was quickly set up by slaves, and reclined under the silk canopy, relaxing in the cool western breezes that came toward sundown from the direction of the great sea.

The many courses of the evening meal were served to Batu-Han and his queen by a seemingly endless line of servants. Saul did not take a place at the meal, but in deep thought he walked a few paces off from the entourage and gazed thoughtfully up at the fortress Machaerus.

The citadel was built by Herod the Great, his luxurious quarters being fifty cubits above the rock it stood on. A prison was carved out in this rock, and it was in this dungeon that John the Baptist was chained and finally beheaded by Herod, tetrarch of Galilee.

Before the death of Herod the Great, the tower had been raised another forty cubits. Fearing attacks by Egypt or Rome, the king built himself what he considered an impregnable refuge, notwithstanding the fact that to Rome there was no such thing as an unscalable wall. Like the Babylonians before him, the Romans, with their earthen or wooden ramps and great machines of war, mounted or destroyed every wall built to keep them out.

Gold reflected on the roof of the tower from the sun going down in the west. It shone like a jewel in the sky. *A man's monument to himself,* thought Saul, *will fall as surely as the Tower of Babel. And what cruelties the Baptist suffered in that dungeon.*

Saul's thoughts were interrupted by the braying of a donkey. Two men had the animal in harness and were trying to prod it to move. Behind the donkey was a great mound of dirt, and upon a closer look, Saul saw that it had come from an attempt to dig up a plant. Enough of the roots were cleared so that a rope could be looped around it and attached to the donkey's harness. The men continued to shout at the beast of burden and to strike him, but he refused to move.

Saul watched them curiously for a long time. The plant had just a few limbs and leaves rising just above the ground. The root of the plant, however, was long and deep and as big around as the man's leg.

"What is that plant?" Saul finally asked the men. They ignored him and continued to work with the animal.

"The barras root," said Batu-Han. He had heard the commotion and stood beside Saul, watching the men.

Then Saul remembered—the legendary, mysterious barras root. He had never seen one, since they, like the rue tree, grew only on the slopes of the mountains to the east of the Dead Sea, but he had heard many stories about it and the healing powers claimed by the people of this area. Proper application of the root was believed to cure all manner of disease. The plant was said to be dangerous, however, supposedly possessing powerful magical properties. The taproot of the plant was reputed to have a shocking power greater than the deadly eels in the Red Sea.

An Egyptian magician had appeared at the circus in Jerusalem just a few years ago, and it was claimed that he had turned night into day. Saul, seeking an answer to this supposed miracle, had discovered that he had stood on a large box that evidently contained many barras roots. From the box ran thin strips of tin to a large tin bowl set facing the audience. With great ceremony and flamboyance, calling down the powers that magicians call upon, he touched two strips of tin together, and the bowl exploded in a flash that for an instant lit the stadium. The tin bowl smoked, then melted.

The box was covered with great sheets of silk of various colors, and the magician was quite impressive as he stood upon the box and bowed repeatedly, twirling his magnificent cape. The audience stood and applauded. Even the Roman governor and his party were impressed by the miracle.

Such were the powers attributed to the root these men were now attempting to pull out of the ground. A sharpened stick finally accomplished this. The donkey lurched and the rope pulled the plant out of the hole with such force that it flew through the air and fell on the animal's back. When the roots struck the donkey, the animal bellowed, then leaped in agony. A great shock rippled through him, and he fell to the ground unconscious.

The men wailed at the apparent loss of their animal. The root lay across his back. Batu-Han stood beside Saul and studied the strange situation. Then a stranger thing happened. The sun was setting, and as it did, sparks of fire and streaks of lightning began shooting from the horizontal root in the direction of the setting sun. Batu-Han's eyes grew wide at this phenom-enon, and the men took a step back.

Saul seized the opportunity. "Do not worry," he said, stepping forward. As everyone watched, he knelt and whispered, "In the name of Jesus of Nazareth, that men might believe." With his right hand he grasped the leaves of the plant, and cradling the root in his left arm, he lifted it off the dead donkey.

The men gasped, and Batu-Han stared speechlessly. Saul lay the root on the ground, then closed his eyes and prayed again. Meeting Batu-Han's stare, he reached out and with one finger touched the donkey. Instantly, the animal opened his eyes and leaped to his feet, braying.

Saul met Batu-Han's stare. He stepped to face him but was distracted for a moment by the two men with the donkey. They had fallen to their knees, worshiping Saul. He raised them to their feet.

"I am a man as you are," he said. "The resurrection is by Jesus, the resur-rected Son of the Most High."

"By what power did you do this?" Batu-Han asked.

"As I said," Saul replied evenly, "by the power of Jesus of Nazareth, by faith in him and his Word."

"What word?" asked Batu-Han.

Saul turned away from the crowd and started walking slowly toward the tent. "He himself is the resurrected Word," said Saul. "By the power of his Spirit in me was the dead animal quickened."

Batu-Han stopped and looked at Saul. "Was this done for my benefit?"

"Yes," said Saul. "The salvation of God has been revealed to you."

❋ ❋ ❋

After leaving the caravan, Saul continued on the pilgrims' trail as it wound its way alongside gullies, around salt flats, and across barren, scorching wilder-ness. Saul traveled along on foot alone. When the sun rose high, the heat was unbearable, and he sought refuge in the shade of clumps and bushes, "the burning bush," a plant common to the Sinai Peninsula. It had red leaves and in a certain light appeared to be on fire. But the leaves afforded ample protection for Saul, as he spent his middays in the cool sand beneath the bushes. Even in the shade, it was too hot to sleep in midday, but to travel on foot across this desert with the sun bearing down overhead would be to invite death. He used his water sparingly and ate sparingly. Someone had once told him, "You need a slim horse for a long journey." Slim and wiry he was, and his skin was darkened from many days in the sun.

Here in the desert the strugglings and sufferings of his people were brought home to him. This was the wilderness where Moses and the children of Israel had lived for forty years after their release from Egyptian bondage. This was the land where Moses struck the rock and living water gushed forth. This was the land where the Law was handed down directly from God.

The Law. A stern law from a jealous God for a stiff-necked people. The Law had to come to Israel that humankind might live with a conscience and know their shortcomings without God. To know the Law and their inability to live up to its order made humans know their great need.

By the Law, men knew of their sinful nature. But now, as witnessed by the Law and the Prophets, and by Saul himself, the righteousness of God by the fulfillment of the Law is manifested through Jesus to all who believe. All are alike, Jew and Gentile. All have sinned and come short of the glory of God, but by his grace through the redemption that is in Jesus for all who believe, all can be justified by faith. Is the Law made void by faith? "No," Saul said aloud. "By faith, the Law is established."

SIX

REVELATION

At last, one morning immediately following his prayers, he found himself at the foot of the holy mountain—Sinai. With other pilgrims he began the long ascent to the top; three thousand steps cut in stone wound their way around sheer cliffs and up the sides of the rugged peaks on the way to the summit. The summit was hardly ever in view, the going was so hazardous. Occasionally the steps would end, and Saul, leaving behind less hardy climbers, clawed his way up the rock to the bottom of yet another flight of steps.

The original flight of stairs, "the Stairway to Heaven" as it was called, was ancient. No one knew just how many centuries ago the stairway had been cut into the sides of the series of peaks. It must have been many years, Saul thought, proceeding up another section of the stairway that was intact. Each step was bow-shaped, its center having been worn away by millions of bare feet and sandals of believers who had struggled to the top in order to be able to stand where Moses had stood when God talked to him.

The morning sun reflecting off the surrounding mountains gave the world a strange violet, pink, gold, and azure glow. *Unearthly looking,* Saul thought, *and how appropriate for the mountain of God.*

By midday, Saul was halfway to the top when he met two young men coming back down. Their faces, hands, and feet were bloody, and their clothing was torn. A hot wind blew off the desert; Saul stopped to rest and to let them pass. He took his prayer shawl from his sash and draped it across his shoulders. As he was kneeling, the boys passed and one of them said, laughing, "You should pray for deliverance from this miserable place."

Saul looked up into a dirty face half-covered with dried blood. The other boy stopped a couple of steps above Saul. They had either been in a terrible fight or fallen on the rocks somewhere along the way. Their skin was almost black, and they wore the headdress of the desert nomads.

"I do not wish to be delivered from this place," said Saul. "I am returning to the top of the rock from which I was hewn."

Suddenly he was kicked in the back and he felt his clothing being stripped away. He heard one of the boys say, "Another crazy Zealot from Jerusalem going to look for his God." More blows fell upon his back and head. He was nearly naked now, wearing only a loincloth. They had taken his belt, his pouch and skin, his robe and sandals. He struggled once, and another blow struck his head. Then all was darkness.

He was awakened by a bee buzzing in his face. The sun was burning down upon him, and he was in terrible pain. He realized just how badly he had been beaten when he tried to raise his hand to brush the bee off his face. His shoulders, arms, and back ached sharply from the beating the two boys had given him. He lay in a clump of bushes near the stairs where he had been thrown or kicked, but he couldn't understand the terrible buzzing sound in his head. His eyes cleared, and suddenly he realized that the sound was not just his imagination; the air around him was thick with honey bees. Amazingly enough, he had not been stung. Rising slowly and painfully, he looked around. Honeycomb hung in clusters from the rocks by his head; it was a working hive with thousands of bees.

He sat up and examined himself. Apparently there were no broken bones, but he was badly bruised. His attackers had abandoned him with a loincloth as his only worldly possession. He reached out and touched the honeycomb, gently brushing off the bees. He was not stung. He remembered that as a boy in Tarsus, he had gathered honey with his father and never had to wear a net or any kind of protection. He was one of those people whom bees didn't sting for some reason.

He puzzled over his condition. He had been brought down, beaten, and stripped of his garments, then immediately provided with food to sustain himself. He thought of Elijah, the prophet of old, and how the Lord had sent ravens to feed him as he lay dying near the brook Cherith. The honey was a rich golden color, and after offering thanks, he broke off a comb and slowly ate the golden nourishment. He chewed the wax, then spit it out and broke off another piece; he ate until he was satisfied.

He arose and walked out of the cloud of bees and found his way painfully back to the stairs. Upon reaching the spot once again where he had knelt to pray, he surveyed his position.

The desert of Sinai spread out endlessly before him. Out there, the first "Temple," the wilderness tabernacle had been raised up by Moses' brother, Aaron, the exact specifications of the portable building given by the mouth of the Lord himself. *A miracle,* thought Saul, *that in this desert were made the marvelous golden vessels, the laver, the candelabra, and the holy ark of the covenant.* Down from this mountain itself the cloud had come and covered the door of the tabernacle. Out of the cloud God had spoken to man.

Wasn't that the purpose of the centuries of pilgrimages by countless millions to the top of this mountain? That perhaps today might be the day that God would speak again to man? That possibly today's dark destiny might again be enlightened and directed by the divine Voice?

Why must I scale these heights? Saul asked himself. *I know many of the reasons. Maybe some are selfish and others charitable, but there is a darkness in my vision that I feel will be removed once I scale the mountain.*

He looked up at the dizzying heights. The stairway disappeared in the thin clouds at the top. *Perhaps I can reach the summit before nightfall,* he thought and slowly began climbing again.

He gave no thought to his body, that although the sun bore down upon him now, when darkness fell the air would be chilled. He did not consider that fact that he had no food and water, and he would be ending this day much farther away from any. He would not eat. He would not drink again until he prayed and fasted three days and nights at the summit.

As he struggled upward, he lost himself in meditation. He surrendered his mind to the Lord and to the momentous events that had transpired here. Here the Lord had proclaimed and confirmed his omnipotence. "You shall have no other gods before me," he had written in stone.

Saul stopped to rest. He gazed out across the desert northward toward Jerusalem. Suddenly he was very lonely again. What of his sister? He knew that by now she had heard the news of his experiences in Damascus, as had Baanah ben David. He would certainly face arrest in Jerusalem at this time. So he would have to wait, to work. There were the other cities of the Decapolis that he must go to as well as Damascus again before returning to Jerusalem. There was restitution to make to those he had harmed; his friends and family needed and deserved an explanation—but not yet.

He glanced toward the summit again. He felt drawn there; an eager feeling of anticipation filled him. "Like countless millions before me, I return to the rock of the Covenant, but this time I seek a deeper understanding of the new testament of God, a fuller understanding of the justification of the old with the new."

At the top of the three thousand steps, he walked under an ancient arch called "the Gateway to Heaven." The massive stone arch was five times higher than his head and had withstood centuries of desert wind and sand. It was built in the Greco-Roman style popular in its time and made with massive blocks of black basalt, but hammers and chisels in the hands of pilgrims had defaced the stones with names, dates, and names of cities. Resting under the arch, Saul recognized dates carved before the time of Alexander the Great.

Tracing with his finger along the letters of a name, he wondered if this was the kind of stone in which the finger of God carved the command-ments. *Probably not,* he thought. The holy words would most likely have been written in a harder, cleaner stone than this rough volcanic rock. Then again, maybe this was the kind. It was brittle, and Moses *had* broken the tablets the first time. *Yes,* thought Saul, *possibly this was the kind of stone God used—rough, dark, and pliable like the lives, deeds, and devotion of humankind.* Into this texture, the finger of the Most High had written steel-ing, refining words to live by.

Walking through the arch, Saul found himself in a broad, flat area, which according to tradition was the spot where God had come down to Moses. One side dropped off in a sheer cliff, and this side afforded a breathtaking view of the wilderness stretching out for many miles below. Above the flat area, giant bubblelike boulders of black volcanic rock gave the environment an unworldly appearance. Some of the boulders were hollow, and looking into a hole in one of them, Saul could see that there was room enough inside the boulder for a man to stand up. *So this will be my home for this pil-grimage.* "A shelter in the rock. Praised be the Most High," he said aloud. "He has provided."

While there was still daylight, he set to work gathering armloads of the coarse brown grass that grew in bunches among the rocks. He found sev-eral of the bushes called "the burning bush" and brought their leaves as well to make his bed in the hollow boulder he had chosen. He broke off a few leafy branches he would lean against the hole from the inside when he was ready to retire for the night. After his "house" and bed were prepared for the night, he walked near the edge of the cliff and, facing in the direction of Jerusalem, knelt and began his evening prayers.

He noticed again the soreness from his beating, but as he prayed he seemed to leave his pains behind and rise up to meet his Creator in his devo-tion. He prayed into the darkness.

Late into the evening he lay his bruised body down upon his bed of leaves and grass, and leaving the opening above him uncovered, he stared out at the few stars that showed through. But immediately the stars disappeared as his eyelids came down and the afterimage of the Man in White appeared before his eyes. He trembled slightly in anticipation, and a warm, comforting feeling flooded over him. Then he seemed to hear, not with his ears, but in his mind, singing. He could recognize no words, but the hundreds, thousands of voices were shouting and singing in praise and adoration. He lay enthralled with the beauty and glory of the sound. Then he heard the rushing of wind and the roaring and churning of water. It poured and boiled. It pounded with the awesome sound of the rolling sea. It made sounds like that of water cascading upon rocks. Then softly he heard the Voice, faint at first, then closer and warm, personal yet authoritative. The Voice came whispering at first, out of the multitude of celestial voices and water. He recognized the Voice, of course, as that of the Master.

"Saul," said the Voice gently. It called him again commandingly, "Saul."

He finally managed to answer. "Yes, Lord."

"My new covenant, my testament, is to be confirmed by the hands of you, my chosen disciple," said the Voice.

"I am unworthy, Lord," said Saul.

"You shall make yourself an empty vessel to pour me out," said the Voice. "Many are called, but few are chosen."

"Teach me, Master," said Saul.

"Beware of false teachers. Beware of polluters of my gospel. Beware of men-pleasers," said the Voice.

"Forgive my hesitation," said Saul. "I have returned to Sinai for a fuller understanding of my calling."

"Your mission is not at Sinai," said the Voice. "Revelation is through me."

Saul paused, then said quietly, "I suppose I am afraid. I would like to see beyond . . . beyond the veil."

"You will be shown the sphere of your mission and the scope of your work. My new testament is to be preached to the ends of the earth," said the Voice. "The tabernacle was built with its Holy of Holies that the Most High might dwell among men.

"Your body is to be the temple of the Most High. I am your High Priest under the new covenant. My Spirit in you brings you into oneness with the Father, for the Father and I are one. My people are dispersed over the earth. Through them you shall bear my covenant to the Gentiles. My servants in Jerusalem shall assemble for yet a little while only. God does not live in a temple made with hands, but in the hearts of men."

Saul lay quietly for a long while in peaceful communion with the presence. Though the revelations ended, as did the sound of the Voice, he felt a great inspiration. He seemed to be experiencing an inflowing of the channel of divine wisdom, for he began to clearly understand all that the Spirit was teaching him.

He slept soundly until the stars disappeared in the hole in the rock and the first light of early dawn turned the sky a dull gray. He climbed the stones above his rock-house and, finding a comfortable spot, sat and rested, facing toward Jerusalem and the Temple. From his perch he could see halfway across the Sinai wilderness, beyond which lay the Dead Sea, the mountains of Judea, and the Holy City.

He knew the Voice would come again. Suddenly he could feel the warm presence, and he closed his eyes. The afterimage was there immediately, the outline of the Man in White against the backs of his eyelids. All feeling left his body, and he felt detached, floating.

"Saul," said the Voice.

"Yes, Master," he said.

"Now I will show you the physical end of Temple worship in ritual and form, which the chosen fell into. You shall see the great extremities to which this nation is to be reduced. A remnant shall be saved, and the dispersed shall survive. The Father still loves his chosen, and through the chosen such as yourself shall my gospel be carried to the world. Thirty years you shall labor, and you shall carry my new testament to all men. Then it shall come to pass at about the same time that you finish your labors . . . Observe."

Saul listened expectantly, hardly breathing. He heard the sounds of battle first, then the afterimage slowly faded, and a picture terrible and sad appeared before his eyes; then as the scene enveloped him, he saw himself actually there, a part of it.

His dream body walked through the burning city of Jerusalem. It was totally destroyed, its magnificent walls torn down and lying in heaps in the valleys around the city. The Romans had fully accomplished the job. The dead filled the streets, and the few living were the very old and the very young.

The Temple itself was the most abominable place of all. Human and animal carcasses lay rotting in the holy courts. Roman soldiers staggered through the Temple courts, drunk from the confiscated wine. Vessels and utensils of gold and silver as well as holy brazen ornaments were stolen and carried off. The Temple treasury was broken into and its hoards taken away.

The sacred oil that had been kept by the priests was poured out on the ground. Priests lay dead on the altar in the Court of Israel, and the Temple veil was gone. The Holy of Holies was dark. No incense burned. The golden candlestick lay on the floor. A pack of dogs roamed the Court of Israel, tearing at animal and human carcasses.

Saul was greatly troubled and cried out, "No! My people! My people!" His whole body shook with the weeping.

The Comforter spoke to him then. "This is only the beginning of sorrows. See now the abomination of desolation."

Saul, in spirit, stood in the ruins of the Temple, in the Court of Israel near the spot where he had often made sacrifices. He watched as seven Jewish defectors were caught by the rebel leader Simon, and the few former priests who survived were summoned to the Temple altar. There the priests were forced to cut the throats of these seven men as they lay upon the altar.

Then the Romans came again with their great battering rams to destroy what was left of the Temple. But the rebel leaders, in order to deny Rome the final victory, set fire to the Temple. A great conflagration followed, and the holy Temple fell.

So, on the seventeenth day of the month of Tamuz, according to Daniel's prediction, the daily offerings and sacrifices ceased. But had the Temple not been afire, there still would have been no sacrifices. There were no priests alive to offer them. Those who did not die of starvation or commit suicide were killed by the Romans.

Saul was shown that the fiery holocaust raged for days. Just when it appeared that the fires would burn out, the winds changed and another section of the city burned. Sparks and flames shot high into the air. From any point in the length and breadth of the country, the smoke could be seen by day and the fires by night. Especially eerie were the nights when clouds covered the sky. Strange images reflected upon the clouds from the fires of Jerusalem.

In the horror of the knowledge that this was the end of their city, of their country, and of their very lives, thousands of people professed to having seen visions in the clouds of horses and chariots, of great battling, of machines of war, of marching armies, of people in chains moving en masse along roads guarded by soldiers.

Visions of scenes of crucifixion in the clouds were reported. These mirage-like tableaus, reflected and illuminated in the sky, were seen by Titus and his army, and after many, many days the news reached Rome that the gods smiled favorably upon Titus and the tenth legion.

Caesar Vespasian, upon hearing of his son Titus's triumph and the favorable omens shown by the gods in the clouds, declared that Titus (as well as he himself, since this favorable revelation had come during his reign) should be deified and that their status should stand in every city in the empire. Vespasian further suggested to Titus that the eagle standard of the tenth legion should be changed to a more appropriate emblem denoting Roman victory in Judea.

As the vision continued in stark reality, Saul watched. Titus walked among the ruins of the Temple. No rains had come for weeks, and fires still smoldered in the many subterranean chambers of the compound. He stopped at the altar, which was badly damaged and polluted with the bones and refuse of animals and men. He laughed aloud as he thought of the new design for the standard of the tenth legion.

Then in just a few days he marched over the Temple compound beneath the new standard carried by his soldiers. The image the banner bore symbolized total victory and ultimate abomination for any Jew who still lived to see it.

It was modeled after the emblem that signified the origin of Rome, the bronze statue of the fabled infants Romulus and Remus being suckled by a she-wolf which stood in the forum at Milepost Number One in the eternal city.

But Titus modified the images more than a little. Instead of a wolf, his legion's standard now showed a sow suckling two pigs. Through the ashes and rubbish the standard-bearers marched three times daily at what had been the hours of prayer.

At the place where the Most Holy Place had been, the soldiers stopped and waved their banner with its images of swine and shouted obscenities upon the God of the Jews. Then followed the drinking of wine and the pouring out upon the holy ground ablations to Jupiter and Mercury.

Certain pieces of the Temple furniture and vessels had survived the fires intact and were being made ready to be transported across land and sea for the triumphal march into Rome. The table of shewbread, the laver, and the massive seven-branched golden candlestick were salvaged. Molten in the fierce heat, however, was ton upon ton of gold—the golden cornices, the sacrificial vessels, gold borders in the fine chambers, the gilt that was laid upon most of the doors and along hallways, and even priests' garments made with golden thread. Most of the gold in the Temple treasury had melted, as well as the most massive layers of all—the golden strips, sheets, orbs, and moldings atop the Temple walls, parapets, and roofs.

Being porous and very heavy, the precious metal had flowed in shining streams from the fire. The soldiers had watched it day and night, running in tiny streams and rivulets, seeking cracks and crevices where it disappeared. Nightly, as new fires broke out, the bright molten metal ran down from new heights to sink and disappear into new depths.

Weary of battle and of Judea itself, Titus's army made ready to return to Rome. An occupation force commanded by centurions laid out a camp in the middle of the city's ruins.

In the midst of the Romans' preparing to depart, desert nomads began looting. A great number of them, working at night, managed to move one of the giant stones of the Court of Israel. Deep in the ground lining the sides of a foundation stone were great sheets of gold that had hardened as the fires had cooled.

The looters were caught and executed. The spoils of war were brought before Titus. Sheets of gold that required twelve men to carry them were brought to show him the treasure recovered from the moving of only one stone. Titus gave the order: "Move every stone. Don't leave one stone upon another." When Saul heard these words, he remembered Jesus' prophecy.

The entire tenth legion worked overtime collecting the spoils of war. The subterranean tunnels and chambers were stripped of their secret wealth. Great hoards of coins and precious bars of metal were discovered. Strips, fingers, balls, rods, nuggets, chunks, and sheets were brought forward as stone after great stone was moved and overturned. The soldiers were eager and anxious to return to Rome, and they worked furiously and thoroughly. The battering ram and the war machines were put into use.

From where Titus had originally surveyed the city atop the Mount of Olives, he now gazed upon a startlingly different scene. Ten teams of oxen pulling their wagonloads of spoils moved slowly behind a long line of marching men. Mount Moriah, the Temple mount, was bare and devoid of any evidence that it had ever been inhabited. There showed no indication that any walls had ever existed on that smooth, rounded hill where the strongest walls in the history of the world had only recently stood.

Not one stone was left upon another.

Saul had been sitting with his eyes closed, seeing all this. The scenes were disappearing now, and he began to be aware of the rock he was sitting on. A scripture was coming to his mind, and the words formed an audible sound in his ears. It was from the sections of the scroll of Chronicles that had been partly eaten away by a rat that night in his room just before he had begun his persecuting. "This house which I have sanctified in my name will I cast out . . ."

Then the Voice spoke to him directly. "Saul."

Slowly and weakly, he came out of his trance. "Yes, Master," he said.

"Arise," he commanded.

Saul walked to the edge of the cliff and looked out over the land. His vision was clear of the afterimage, but the presence was still there.

"What would you have me do?" asked Saul.

"Get down off this mountain," said the Voice, "and be about my Father's business."

Without a word of hesitation, Saul struck out, passing again under the Gateway to Heaven and beginning his descent.

"Go into all the world," said the Voice. "Preach the gospel and baptize them in the name of the Father, and of the Son, and of the Holy Spirit. And I am with you always."

SEVEN

THE FELLOWSHIP, AD 40

As Saul skirted the Mount of Olives and the city and the Temple came into view, his heart leaped within him. Jerusalem, the Holy City, Jerusalem that slays her prophets. Jerusalem, O Jerusalem!

His feet and legs ached, and he was very hot. He stopped beside the road at a spot where he had a good view of the city and sat down in the shade of a cedar tree. The tree, with its gnarled, scrawny branches, afforded little shade, but it would refresh him. He loosened the straps of his sandals and rubbed his feet. They were well calloused but ached sharply. He loosened his clothes and basked in the breeze that blew up from the Kidron. Memories flooded him, some sweet and some bitter.

Far off the end of the valley there was the mountain where he had, upon returning to the city that day, seen the terrible crucifixion and had watched his friend Michael die. There below in the Kidron itself was the spot where Stephen had fallen. No remorse filled him, and he wondered at his own feelings. There a brother in the Lord had died at his own hand, and he felt at peace about the matter.

The face of Stephen came back to his mind, and he understood fully the reasons God had for his martyrdom—a dying witness of the glories to come, a testimony of faith and devotion, an example of the ecstasy in the agony of suffering for the Lord. As the Lord himself gave his life for all, so did Stephen, and so did he especially give it for Saul. Stephen's classic testimony before the Sanhedrin would always be fresh in Saul's mind, and many times when called to the task he would use Stephen's style in his own testimony.

The magnificent Temple itself brought to mind many scenes in the life of his people. But the Temple heights with all the gold, bronze, and fine wood brought to mind a parable of the Lord: "bright and shiny outside, but full of corruption inside."

What a burden he had cast off—the Temple with its spiritual bondage. He felt a sense of freedom and elation he had never known before upon viewing the Temple. He would never speak of his vision of its destruction, but he was saddened in knowing what was to happen.

And it was not without a little grief and awe that he looked upon this city of his forefathers, and not without a little yearning that he thought of the alienation of those who had been his warmest associates. Surely they would receive his testimony now! When the Pharisees, even Gamiliel, saw the miraculous change in him, knowing what a persecutor he had been, surely they would believe him. Yet as strongly as he wanted them to believe him, deep in his being he knew that they would not.

Theophilus was now high priest, appointed by the Roman governor, Marcellus, who, to stay in favor with the emperor Caligula, placed a man in that position who would keep the peace by strict adherence to Rome's demands.

Saul knew that in the Temple he had lost all favor and that he was called a "turncoat." Under Theophilus his arrest and trial would certainly mean his execution. The few friends he might have remaining in the Sanhedrin would most certainly be outvoted in his case. Still, he must see the Temple, must walk those halls and chambers again.

As he strapped his sandals back on his feet, he thought of his sister, Sarah, and her family, the child Jacob and her husband. He smiled as he thought of Levi ben Lamech. *I might not win him over,* he thought, *but at least he will not be able to deny the change in me that the love of the Lord has made.*

The hand of the giant water-clock adjacent to the Temple pointed to the sixth hour. Feeling suddenly like a stranger, Saul walked past the tower and up through the southern porch, then crossed the Court of the Gentiles. He had come here every day of his life since as a child he had come from Tarsus, but in a way he felt he had never been here before. His feet hurried across the large open area toward the Court of Israel, where he would go to pray, when suddenly he stopped. He had the feeling he was being followed. He turned and looked behind him, and as he did, a man stopped some distance away. Saul stared for a moment, then continued. Just as he approached the steps to the Court of Israel, he stopped and turned, and there was the man again, but closer.

The follower did not stop this time but continued walking toward Saul. The man was barefoot and dressed in homespun. By his haircut, he was obviously a Greek.

"Saul of Tarsus," the man said. And his voice was familiar to Saul. More than familiar—the voice struck a sensitive nerve deep within his soul, for he recognized Barnabas the Cypriot, whom he had once confronted in the Synagogue of the Isles of the Sea.

Saul didn't speak at first; he just gazed into Barnabas's eyes. Then his eyes dropped to the hollow of Barnabas's neck, and he saw the ugly scar his own sword had made that night when he had disrupted the worship service.

Barnabas smiled. "I recognized your walk, Saul. No one but you walks with such, uh . . . determination."

"Barnabas . . ." Saul groped for words at first, then put his hands on the man's shoulders and looked deep into his smiling eyes. "It is strange that you are the first person I should see upon my return to Jerusalem."

"Yes," said Barnabas. "Come and let's sit in the shade of the colonnades and talk. I have heard many things of you since you left Jerusalem."

On the cool stone steps in the shade of Solomon's Porch they sat and looked out across the sprawling Temple compound. At first neither spoke—there was so much to say.

Barnabas started laughing, and Saul looked at him curiously. "You are a wanted man in this very Temple, yet here you sit unrecognized. But who would? I should think you look more like John the Baptist in your homespun robe and sandals than the fearsome Pharisee you were when you left here."

Saul smiled back. "Probably so."

Barnabas's face clouded. "As you may have heard, a new man sits in the high priest's seat. Theophilus ben Annas is quickly gaining favor with the governor, Marcellus."

"I understand," said Saul. "To stay in favor with Rome, a high priest must be more Roman than Jew."

"Yes, especially now," said Barnabas. "The madman Gaius Caligula is on the throne, and already the Roman standards are displayed publicly in Caesarea and other cities. Terrible times are coming upon this city. Everyone is choosing sides."

Saul paused and looked evenly at Barnabas. "This concerns me personally, does it not?"

"Yes," said Barnabas. "The Sanhedrin declared you a traitor soon after the news arrived of your conversion at Damascus. If you are recognized by the priests and elders here, you will be arrested."

"And my trial and execution would soon follow," said Saul. "I know the procedure well."

"You seem to have no fear," said Barnabas.

"My friend," said Saul, "those who walk in the Law are mindful of things of the flesh. The new law of the spirit of life in Jesus has set me free from the Law of sin and death in the flesh."

"You have been gone a long time," said Barnabas. "You must go with me to the house of Peter and meet your fellow workers in the Lord. And be prepared—most of them will fear you and will not believe that you are one of us."

"I long to show them I am," Saul laughed. "I will go to the house of Peter, but first I must visit my sister. I have peace to make with her husband."

They stood and embraced. "Come soon," said Barnabas. "I will try to pave the way for you."

Barnabas watched Saul walk toward the street. *A man born anew,* he thought. *No longer a hawk, but an eagle with a dove's heart.*

As Saul stood at Sarah's door, she didn't recognize him at first. Then she cried out and embraced him. "Saul, what has happened to you? You look like a beggar. It breaks my heart to see you this way."

"I am well, sister," he said as she led him in. "And I am not a beggar. I ply my trade as always and am very happy in my work. However, my tools, my loom and spindle, are in my room where I left them. I will need my tools to pay my keep."

"Where have you been?" she pleaded. "I have heard strange reports of you from Damascus. Is it true? You have abandoned your work and alienated all your friends here?"

"I have only just begun my work, Sarah," he said. "You, of all people, must understand me. I have come to know the fulfillment of the promises of the Covenant. I have become a teacher and a preacher of the new testament of our Messiah, who has come as promised. I am a man of peace, Sarah, and the peace is of my Lord."

Levi entered the room. He did not approach Saul to embrace him but only stared at him as if he were an intruder.

"You are a brave man for returning to this city. Not only the Temple authorities, but the Greeks, the Gentiles among whom you wreaked havoc, will try to kill you. Your life isn't worth a shekel."

"Levi," Sarah cried, "you are talking to my brother."

"He is no brother," said Levi. "You are a traitor!" he shouted at Saul.

Sarah clung to Saul and wept. "Please, Levi," she said.

"Where is my nephew, Jacob?" asked Saul.

"Fortunately, he is in school at the moment," said Levi. "And I'm sure you would be more welcome in the congregation of your friends."

Saul turned to Sarah. "I shall be at the house of Simon Peter, the one they call Cephas. Come there to see me," he said.

"I remember his trial and his scourging when he mocked the elders in the judgment hall. It is a matter of time for all of them in this city," said Levi.

"My dear brother-in-law," said Saul, smiling, "how is it that you are now concerned with the sect of the Nazarene?"

"Because you are one of them!" shouted Levi. "And don't call me brother," he said with hostility as he turned and walked out of the room.

Sarah again embraced Saul. "Be careful," she said. "I will come."

With a heavy heart he left for the house of Simon Peter. "I regret losing Levi, but I cannot cast my pearls before swine," he murmured.

❋ ❋ ❋

Simon Peter's oldest son was named Jesse, the youngest David. Jesse at twelve years old showed a wisdom beyond his years. He had the wiry, copper-colored hair of his father and the dark eyes. He was square-shouldered and strong. David favored his mother, Leah, with his straight black hair and slim features.

The Temple torches had been lit and the water-clock had sounded the twelfth hour. The family held hands around the table and recited the prayer. "Give us this day our daily bread . . ."

Barley bread it was, the round, heavy loaf of the common people. Peter broke the first piece and gave it to Leah. Then each one took a piece of bread and dipped it into the lentil stew. Jesse was the first to speak after the prayer.

"I had a strange dream last night, Father," he said.

"What did you dream?" Peter asked. Streaks of gray were beginning to show in Peter's beard, but his eyes were quick and youthful, his hands and face deeply tanned from traveling in the sun.

"I dreamed," said Jesse, putting his bread down and looking into his bowl thoughtfully, "that a man was praying in the Temple, and everyone wanted to kill him."

"Was I that man?" Peter asked, smiling.

"No," said Jesse. "He was a stranger. Yet I seemed to know him. I told him in the dream that he could come to our house."

Peter studied his son. "That was kind of you," he said, then continued eating.

"It was just a dream, I guess," Jesse said, passing it off. "Lots of people pray in the Temple."

"Yes," said Peter. "And many people have been killed there. Perhaps it isn't just a dream. Many have come to this house in the past as a place of refuge."

Leah got up from the table to close the damper on the brazier, and there was a knock at the front door. Peter started to rise, but Leah said, "I'll go."

The room where they dined served as kitchen, dining room, and sleeping room. Leah crossed the small courtyard and went through the foyer to answer the front door. In the courtyard were the stairs to the roof, where it was custom for families to spend their evenings after supper.

"Jesse," said Peter as they waited for the boys' mother to return, "and David, always remember to welcome guests who knock on your door. Though it may be dangerous to receive those who come after the doors are bolted, angels have been entertained unawares. And especially in this house, where . . ." Peter stopped, for Leah stood before them with her eyes wide and her face pale from fright.

Peter was immediately upon his feet. "What is it, Leah?" he asked. "Who is it?"

"I think it is Saul of Tarsus," she said. "The persecutor. He is at our door." She was trembling.

"Stay here, my sons," said Peter as he walked past Leah to the door. "Sit with the boys," he said to her. "I will see."

"So it is you, Saul," Peter said, studying the face of the Pharisee who stood at the door. "Is it true? Have you come in peace?"

"The peace of the Lord Jesus be upon all in this house," said Saul.

Suddenly Peter knew. "The chief persecutor, Saul of Tarsus, has come to know the Lord."

"Barnabas sent me," said Saul. "I come as a brother. May I come in?"

"Have you seen the Lord as is rumored?" asked Peter.

"Yes," said Saul. "I have come to share with you my joy in him."

"Leah, Jesse, David," Peter said, bringing Saul to the table, "make a place for our brother Saul. Sit at my right hand and dine with us."

"What fine boys you have, Peter," Saul said. When he looked into the questioning eyes of Leah, he said, "I realize that you felt fear upon seeing me, mistress, but please know that I come in the name of the Lord Jesus."

Peter nodded to Jesse and said, "I think my son expected you. He had a dream."

Saul studied the boy. "Many times the Lord has spoken to his people in dreams and visions," he said. "His hand is upon this household."

When they had finished, Peter said, "Bring a pan of cool water, Leah, that I might wash our guest's feet.

"This is a humble household, Saul. I have no couch for you to recline upon, but if you will turn your feet around where you sit, I will wash them."

Saul said, "You do me a great honor, Peter."

"No, my brother," said Peter. "I honor my Lord with an act of humility."

Leah brought the water and knelt beside Peter.

"I am not a man of great learning, Saul," said Peter, "and I was slow to understand much that the Lord said to me. It was on that last night with him and the other disciples that he knelt and washed all our feet. When he came to me, I tried to refuse him. He told me that if he did not wash my feet, then I would have no part with him in his kingdom. He even told me that I did not understand why he was doing it, but that I would later."

Peter paused and looked up at Saul. "It was a great lesson that he taught me. All must humble themselves as a little child to come into his kingdom, and how better to humble ourselves than to wash each other's feet.

"But the deeper lesson I have come to realize," said Peter, "is that he is the living water, and to be washed in him is to be spiritually cleansed. So it is he who washes you, Saul. I do it in remembrance of him."

Leah, kneeling beside him, dried Saul's feet with her hair. The boys gently brushed Saul's hair and beard, adding a few drops of olive oil to make it glisten. The warmth of the family feeling touched Saul deeply. How beautiful the boys were, laughing and taking turns with the brush. Leah was softly singing a psalm at his feet.

Peter kissed his family good night, and he and Saul mounted the stairs to the rooftop, for there was much to talk about.

The stars were out on the clear, warm night, and the giant torches on the Temple pinnacles cast an orange glow over the city. The two men sat facing each other, and Saul took a long time explaining his experience on the Damascus road. He described in as much detail as he could the glory of the Man in White. Saul paused, then said, "Peter, you first saw the Lord in flesh and blood. I saw him come in glory from the right hand of God."

"I saw him in glory also, Saul. I was with him on the holy mountain when the Voice from glory declared, 'This is my beloved Son, in whom I am well pleased,'" said Peter. "I also saw him after the resurrection."

"His glorified countenance," Saul said. "I was blinded by the pure glory of his countenance. I can still close my eyes and see his afterimage behind my eyelids."

"But we must remember that he was very human," said Peter. "He ate, slept, and laughed. He got tired, thirsty, and angry, and his feet hurt. He felt pain as you and I do. And there was one particular human thing that he had to do, Saul—bleed."

"The blood," said Saul. "I saw his blood in dreams."

"Yes," said Peter, "the blood of redemption. Our divine gift brought about through grace by the shedding of his blood."

"And in my case," said Saul, "the Lord, like a skilled physician, healed me when my fever was at its worst—my fever of zeal."

"Never has a man spoken as my Lord has spoken," said Peter. "He had the words of life.

"The Sabbath is coming, Saul, and our brother James will be here. With him we will read the words of the Master to the congregation."

"Read?" asked Saul.

"Yes," said Peter. "Once when he was teaching and healing at my house in Capernaum, a scribe came and told the Lord that he would follow him wherever he went. He had a bag of parchment and wrote down every word that the Lord said as long as he could keep up with us," Peter laughed. "The Lord told him that foxes have holes and birds have nests, but the Son of man has no place to lay his head. We went on to the lake then, and a storm came up. The scribe watched from shore as the Lord stretched out his hands and calmed the sea."

"And you have those sayings of the Lord that the scribe wrote?" asked Saul.

"Yes," said Peter. "Matthew Levi recopied his sayings, and James now keeps that copy. He will read from it on the Sabbath."

"He has revealed many things to me," said Saul, "but it will be good to hear his own words read."

"He often taught us in parables," Peter said, "because his message was so new and profound. Once when some Pharisees came testing him, asking him to give them a sign from heaven, he answered them by saying, 'When it is evening and the sky is red, you say it will be fair weather tomorrow, and in the morning if the sky is red, you say it would be foul weather.' Then he said, 'You hypocrites! You can discern the face of the sky, but you cannot discern the signs of the times.' They were puzzled by this, so he told them, 'You shall have no sign from me except the sign of the prophet Jonah.'"

"The three days in the belly of the fish," said Saul.

"Yes," said Peter. "Symbolic of his coming death and three days in the grave before his resurrection.

"He was extremely kind to the poor wherever he went. And if a person humbled himself before him, he made no distinction between Jew, Gentile, or Roman, male or female, bond or free.

"Once a Canaanite woman came to him, asking him to heal her daughter. We asked him to send her away, but he replied by saying, 'I am not sent just to the lost sheep of the house of Israel.' She fell at his feet, worshiping him. He tested her by saying, 'It is not meant to take the children's bread and cast it to the dogs.'"

"What did he mean by that?" asked Saul.

"He was the bread, and we were the children," said Peter. "Then she said, 'Lord, let the dogs eat just the crumbs that fall from the master's table.' The Lord answered, 'Great is your faith, woman.' And her daughter was healed . . . just a few crumbs of the bread of life from the Master's table."

They were silent for a moment, then Saul said, "I was privileged to witness your vision on the rooftop in Joppa."

Peter was amazed. "You saw the sheet and all the animals?"

"Yes," said Saul. "The Lord has made it clear to us that the door to his kingdom is open to all who will come in, Jew and Gentile. But there are problems we must discuss. We must not offend our own people, yet we must not let new converts feel that they must be bound by the traditions of the Law."

"The Lord was of the house of Israel as we are, Saul," said Peter. "The Lord did not make null and void the Law. He came to fulfill the promise of the Law and the Prophets. As a matter of fact, he told us that we must keep the commandments, for in keeping them is the love of God, and in keeping them is to be like him, for as the fulfillment of the Law, Jesus was the perfection of the Law."

Saul paused for a moment. He closed his eyes, and there, behind his eyelids, was the image of the Man in White.

"I know the way of salvation, Peter," said Saul. "It has all been revealed to me, and not by man, lest any man should boast, but by the Lord himself, through angels, through divine visitation of the Holy Spirit, and by his very voice itself."

Peter studied Saul for a moment, then smiled. "Then we were both taught by the Lord himself."

"Yes," said Saul, "we are blessed above all men."

"There were twelve of us," said Peter, "whom he publicly and personally called to minister with him. But he sent out many others and called many others such as yourself. And, Saul," said Peter, "no man should boast, even if he did receive direct revelation from the Lord himself."

Saul thought for a moment about what Peter was saying, then said, smiling, "I suppose that was a rather presumptuous statement I made, implying that I had a higher calling."

"We all have a high calling, Saul," said Peter.

"Will the other apostles be here to worship on the Sabbath?" asked Saul.

"Only James," said Peter, "and probably Barnabas. Many come here to worship who once went to the Synagogue of the Libertines or the Synagogue of the Isles of the Sea." Peter smiled. "But now, Saul, we have talked long enough. Let us pray, then we should retire."

Peter's household was very busy very early. First the boys were up with their talk and laughter. Then they were off to school, Leah following them to the door with a hairbrush in her hand, grooming as best she could the wild locks on Jesse's head.

"Uncle James is here, Father," he called out before closing the door.

Saul had said his morning prayers and was dressed to meet James. As he came in, Peter started to introduce them but stopped as they stared at each other.

Finally Saul said, "I have seen the Lord in glory, James. He has called me to be a witness of him to the Gentiles."

James looked around to Peter, who smiled at him, and said, "I am sure that if Cephas has received you as one of us, then it is so."

"I know my reputation as a persecutor, James, and I am prepared to face the congregation today. If I will be allowed to speak, I will convince them that I have seen the Lord."

"Very well," said James. "But I doubt that you will convince them all." He turned to Peter. "I must put these scrolls in the ark. It is a blustery, windy day. Perhaps the inner court would not be a good place to meet."

"We shall use the upper room," said Peter.

Suddenly there was a clamor outside, and Peter went to the door. There at the gate stood a donkey and a cart carrying a woman, her young son, and certain pieces of furniture.

"What brings you here?" asked Peter.

"I am Sarah, sister of Saul of Tarsus, and this is my son, Jacob."

Saul came out the front door, and upon seeing him, Sarah leaped from the cart.

"Saul," she said, crying, "I had to come. I feel that you need me as I need you, for now I have no one, only Jacob."

"Where is your husband?" asked Saul.

She hesitated to answer, first looking shamefully at Peter, then back to her brother. "He has gone to the temple priests and scribes to obtain a bill of divorcement."

"Divorcement!" cried Saul. "Why?"

"When I told him I was coming to find you, he went into a rage. He said I, too, would become a polluter of the Covenant by befriending this outlawed sect. But you are my brother, Saul. I didn't mean to desert my husband and my home."

"Perhaps when his temper subsides, he shall change his mind, Sarah," said Saul comfortingly.

Peter put his hand on her shoulder and looked at her kindly. "The women in my house are preparing food for the coming Sabbath. We have many people to feed. Perhaps you will join them, then stay for the worship service this evening." Then looking at Jacob, he said, "Your son can find a corner to sleep in with my own sons. Welcome to my home and to the congregation."

"Thank you," she said. "I hired a donkey and cart," said Sarah, "in order to bring you your tools, Saul. I have your loom, your shuttle, spindle, needles, and pliers, plus the cotton and flax that you left with Baanah ben David." She paused, looking at Saul. "He asked about you."

"I will go to see him as soon as possible," said Saul.

He set about bringing his equipment in and set it up in a corner of the courtyard. He began to make a curtain for the inner courtyard. His fingers flew at the task, and the long piece of material expanded. Jacob helped him while Sarah busied herself with the other women.

Later in the afternoon she came out to talk to him. "Saul," she said, "regardless of what Levi is doing, my home is still my home. You should go back there with me, for it is dangerous for you to stay here."

"Why is it, Sarah?" he asked.

"Through my husband," she said, "word will reach the Temple authorities that you are here. They will come for you."

"I do not fear men," he said. "I must commune with my fellow apostles."

"I am concerned for your safety," she said.

"My dear sister, you have always worried about me," he said. "Now is a time of joy in my life."

"There is none in mine," she said. "What must I do?" she pleaded. "He is serious about divorcement, and he is a lawyer. He will secure it."

"You must do nothing to fight him," said Saul. "You have not broken up your home just by coming here, but if it happened, so be it. The Lord Jesus said that his coming would not bring peace but a sword to divide families against each other, and that whosoever receives him shall receive the blessings of the Father."

"Saul," said Sarah, "there is much I do not understand. I only know that I love what I see in you, the kindness, the gentleness, the love, even your steadfastness with an attitude of joy against my husband's ravings."

"You shall learn of the Lord, Sarah," said Saul, "and you shall come into his peace."

Before sundown they started coming—Jews, Greeks, Cilicians, Galileans, Samaritans, men, women, and children.

He continued working with his back to the courtyard until nearly sundown. The congregation was assembling in the open court, for the wind had died and the evening was becoming cool.

"Shalom, Saul," said Barnabas, who suddenly appeared beside him. "That canvas you have woven will make a good backdrop for the altar."

"So it will," said Saul.

"The congregation has assembled. Peter and James would have you join us at the altar."

Saul looked around the courtyard and recognized none of the people there except Sarah and Jacob, who were sitting toward the back with Leah, Jesse, and David.

Peter, James, and Barnabas were sitting on high seats near the altar facing the congregation. As Saul was sitting down, he looked at Sarah and smiled. When he recognized the two men leaning against the wall behind her, however, his smile faded. There were the Hebronites Cononiah and Shemei.

Apparently they didn't recognize Saul, for they were looking around at all the people, and not once did their eyes rest on him. Shemei stood on his one good leg with the other resting at a curved angle. Cononiah's one good eye glared wide and darted from one face to another in the congregation.

Simon Peter stood up to address the people, and they immediately became attentive. "Welcome in the name of the Lord Jesus," he said. "Let us kneel and join hands and pray as he taught us to do. Our Father who is in heaven, hallowed be your name . . ."

Sarah and Jacob knelt with the others, but they did not recite the prayer. Sarah felt a stirring behind her, quietly and slowly turned her head, and saw that the two men leaning against the wall were whispering and looking in Saul's direction. When the prayer ended and Peter began speaking again, Sarah looked at the two men once more and saw that they were still looking at Saul.

"Our congregation continues to grow," said Peter. "There must be hundreds here today. I would like to welcome our visitors from out of the city. Would you please stand so we might recognize and welcome you?" Half of the crowd stood, and the visitors were welcomed. As the greetings ended, Peter sat down and Barnabas stepped forward.

"I am Barnabas of Cyprus," he said, taking the scroll of the prophet Isaiah.

"The prophet spoke thusly of our Lord," Barnabas said. He read, "Beyond Jordan in Galilee of the nations, the people who walked in darkness have seen a great light. They who dwell in the land of the shadow of death, upon them has the light shined . . ."

As he read, Cononiah and Shemei slowly and silently moved around the congregation until they were halfway to the altar. There they stopped and stared at Saul, who had not moved but ignored them as he listened attentively to Barnabas.

"For unto us a child is born, unto us a son is given. And the government shall be upon his shoulders, and his name shall be called Wonderful Counselor, Mighty God, Everlasting Father, Prince of Peace."

Barnabas rolled the scroll up and placed it in its cubicle, then said, "This Scripture is fulfilled in our time." Then he stopped, for he suddenly recognized the Hebronites. Their eyes were locked on Saul. Barnabas looked at Saul, who only smiled and nodded for him to continue.

"An angel appeared to the carpenter Joseph in Nazareth and said, 'Son of David, do not fear to take Mary for your wife, for the child she is bearing was conceived by the Holy Spirit. She shall bring forth a son, and you shall call his name Jesus, for he shall save his people from their sins,'" said Barnabas.

"This was a fulfillment of the prophet Micah, who said," continued Barnabas, as he unrolled another scroll and read from it, "'You, Bethlehem Ephratah, though you be little among the thousands of Judah, out of you shall he come forth who is to be ruler in Israel, whose goings forth have been from of old, from everlasting.'"

Barnabas sat down and whispered to Saul, "I see two of your old friends here."

"Yes," said Saul, smiling. "He who has an ear, let him hear," he quoted. "Perhaps they will receive the Word today."

James addressed the congregation and said, "I am James, brother of the Lord. From Deuteronomy I would like to read: 'The Lord your God shall raise up unto you a prophet from your midst, of your own brothers, like unto me. Unto him you will listen.' And the Lord said," James continued, "'I will raise them up a prophet from among their brothers, like me, and will put my word in his mouth, and he shall speak to them all that I command him.'"

He laid down the scroll of the Law and, opening a long leather canister, took out a scroll upon which were copied the sayings of Jesus. He rolled and unrolled the scroll until he found the passages that were pertinent to the message he wanted to deliver. "The prophet Isaiah said much that told of our Lord's coming. I was with the Lord in the synagogue in Nazareth upon the Sabbath when he stood up to read. This is the Scripture he read: 'The spirit of the Lord is upon me because he has anointed me to preach the gospel to the poor, he has sent me to heal the brokenhearted, to preach deliverance to the captives and recovering of sight to the blind, to set at liberty those who are bruised, to preach the acceptable year of the Lord.'"

"And then, my beloved friends," said James, "the Lord announced to the synagogue that he was the fulfillment of that Scriptures." James placed the scroll back in its place, and Peter stepped forward again.

"Let us welcome a brother who has come in peace," said Peter. "A man to whom the Lord has revealed his glory!" He paused. All eyes were on Saul, and there was some murmuring in the congregation.

"Saul of Tarsus!" Cononiah screamed and pointed to him.

Sarah was immediately on her feet, but so was half the congregation, some staring in stark fear. Many mothers hurried their children out as other men took up the shout. "My wife is dead because of him," said one man. "My son is dead at his hands," said another. Women began screaming and running out the front door into the street.

"Please," said Peter, trying to shout over the voices being raised against Saul, who still sat. "Let him speak."

"His actions have spoken for him," said a man as he hurried his family out. A few people, mostly men, stayed.

Peter said to those remaining, "God forgive us this day for judging our neighbor. Now I would like for you faithful to hear of his knowledge of the Lord from the lips of Saul of Tarsus himself."

"I will listen," said Sarah, standing and holding Jacob by the hand, "although I already believe. The change in his countenance is enough proof for me."

"I am a Jew," Saul began, "born in Tarsus, a city in Cilicia, yet brought up in this city at the feet of Gamaliel. I was taught according to the perfect manner of the Law of our fathers and was zealous toward God, as you are.

"I persecuted you, even to death." There was a murmur of agreement in the small crowd, but Saul continued, relating his mandate to go to other cities and arrest the followers of the Nazarene and the way he was blinded on the Damascus road. He told of his conversation with the glorified Christ and his commandment to take the gospel to the Gentiles. It was a strong, convincing oration, and one by one the people embraced him.

The service had ended, and Sarah knelt at the altar. All hands were gently laid on her, Peter's, James's, Saul's, Barnabas's, and Leah's, who knelt beside her.

"Receive unto your service, O Lord," said Peter, "Sarah, sister of Saul of Tarsus."

The boys Jesse and David brought the wine and flat cakes of unleavened bread. Peter broke off a piece of the bread and, giving it to Sarah, said, "In remembrance of the Master. This is his body which he sacrificed for us." And giving her the wine, he said, "This is his blood of the new testament, which is shed for the remission of sins."

She stood and they each embraced her, Saul last of all. He said, "Go in his love now and try to heal your broken home. I will see you in a day or so."

"I fear for your safety, Saul," she said.

"Don't worry," he said. "His hand is upon me."

Cononiah watched the administering of the bread and wine to Sarah through the cracked front door; then the Hebronites ran all the way to the house of the high priest. They rattled the latch at the outer gate several times before anyone answered. Finally a Temple guard came down the flower-banked path from the palace. He was angry.

"What do you want . . . on the Sabbath?"

"We must speak to the high priest," said Cononiah. "It is urgent."

"Nothing is urgent," said the guard. "Master Theophilus is having supper with his family. Now go away."

"But the persecutor turncoat is back in the city," said Shemei. "Saul of Tarsus."

"Go to the Temple tomorrow," said the guard. "You have already broken the Law by coming here," and he left them.

"What shall we do?" asked Shemei.

"We shall watch the house of the fisherman tonight," said Cononiah. "Then tomorrow we go to the Temple."

At Peter's house, the four men retired to the rooftop to talk.

"Theophilus will be a hard man to deal with, Saul," said Peter. "They will not accept your testimony. You will be imprisoned."

"There is still Roman law, Peter," said Saul, "and I am a Roman citizen."

"There are plots and subplots," said Peter. "They will take you when you least expect it."

"We must bring our congregation back together," said Barnabas. "When they hear your testimony, you will be accepted here at least."

"Perhaps I should leave the city," said Saul. "There was peace until I came."

"The problem with the Temple," said James, "is that we have separated into a group on our own and allow the Gentiles to freely become a part of it, even the women. What we are doing we have been told to do by the Lord himself—all may freely come by faith in him."

"We must stand firm," said Saul. "We cannot freely receive Gentiles into his kingdom if we first bind them with our laws and our traditions."

"Do we not, being Jews, have the advantage?" asked James.

"Wasn't that a question we asked the Lord himself?" asked Peter.

"Yes," said James. "We asked who would be the greatest in the kingdom of heaven."

"What did he say?" asked Saul.

"He said," said James, "that except we humble ourselves as little children, we cannot enter."

"He also said, 'The first shall be last and the last shall be first,'" said Peter. "So no one shall be greater. All are equal in him."

"Listen, my brothers," said James, "God has chosen the poor of this world who are rich in faith and full of love for him as heirs to his kingdom."

"We have the advantage only in that the oracles of God were committed to us," said Saul. "But under the Law, justification is impossible, while now the righteousness of God is manifested through faith in him who is the fulfillment and perfection of the Law. The righteousness of God is received in faith by all who believe."

Into the night they talked, and the next night the same. A larger debate was held over circumcision.

"God shall justify the circumcised by faith and the uncircumcised by faith," said Saul. "By faith the Law is established."

"What of those already circumcised who come to the Lord?" asked James. "Do you think it means nothing?"

"Neither circumcision nor uncircumcision is the most important thing. Rather, it is faith, working through love."

"My brothers," said Peter, "he requires nothing but to come to him just as we are. We must not confuse the gospel of Christ. It is the gift of God. He said to the burdened, 'Come unto me and I will give you rest.' He bears our sorrows. He lifts our yoke of bondage."

"He lifted our yoke of bondage from under the Law," said Saul. "No man can be justified by the deeds of the Law. By the deeds of the Law comes the knowledge of sin."

"And he bore our sins," said Barnabas. "That is how he lifted the yoke."

"Even David in his time spoke of the blessedness of the man to whom God imputes righteousness without works," said Peter.

"Faith without works is dead," said James, his voice rising steadily.

"Abraham had faith, and it was accounted to him for righteousness," said Saul.

"Yes!" said James, pointing his finger directly into Saul's face. "But his faith was manifested through works! He offered his own son upon the altar. What greater work could a man do?" James paused and took a deep breath, then said, "By Abraham's works his faith was made perfect."

"Yes," said Saul. "But to win certain converts we must ask them to come on faith alone, then teach them the duties of following the Master. Works will follow."

"I do not agree with you," said James. "If a brother or sister is cold and hungry and you say to them, 'Go your way and be full and warm,' yet they continue to be hungry and cold, what good have you done?"

"On the Damascus road when he revealed himself to me," said Saul, "from that moment on I knew that I was reconciled with God through faith."

"So you say you have faith," said James. "And I say I have works." He stared at Saul challengingly. "Show me your faith without your works, and I will show you my faith by my works."

"All right, brother," said Saul. "Your point is made and accepted. My point is that converts must know that in coming to our Lord they are justified by faith in him, that the righteousness of the Law is attained by total faith in him."

Peter spoke up. "Our congregation is in the holy capital Israel. We shall have to honor certain traditions and rituals; else we shall all be put out of the city."

"Which ones?" Saul asked.

"Traditional national feast days and holy days," said Peter.

"Yes," said Saul.

"And on the question of circumcision . . ." Peter began.

"Circumcision is of the Jews who keep the Law," said Saul.

"The Gentiles who come to the Lord through faith," said Barnabas, "need not be circumcised."

"We will have many problems," said Peter. "The Temple authorities are watching us for the least malefaction against the Law."

"Is God the God of the Jews only?" asked Saul. "Is he not also the God of the Gentiles? Yes. He is God of all, and he shall justify the circumcised by faith and the uncircumcised by faith."

"Circumcision *is* the seal of faith for the Jew, Saul," said James.

"James, God's promise to Abraham that he should be the heir of the world was not to Abraham and his seed through the Law, but through the righteousness of faith," said Saul. "Therefore, being justified by faith we have peace with God through our Lord, Jesus."

"We are concerned, my brothers," said Peter, "as to how we come into his glory and become partakers of the divine nature and how to so lead others. By faith comes virtue, by virtue knowledge, by knowledge temperance, by temperance patience, by patience godliness. And from godliness comes brotherly kindness and love. We must strive, therefore, with all diligence to bring others into his kingdom freely with no yoke and no price."

"The question of circumcision has not been settled," said James. They all looked at each other for a moment.

"We must pray for wisdom," said Saul.

"The answers are in the Holy Scriptures," said James.

"Then we must pray that we agree upon the proper interpretation," said Saul. "Circumcision is nothing to me," said Saul, "and uncircumcision is nothing. Let the circumcised stay so, and the uncircumcised stay so. I will place no burdens on Gentiles who turn to God through Jesus."

"You may lose converts for that reason alone," said James.

"James," said Saul, "if my eating meat offended anyone, I would never eat meat again. In Jesus Christ all things are lawful to me when necessary to win some to him."

"What about the flesh of swine?" James asked testily. "Is that lawful for you?"

"James," Saul said, "all things are not expedient, though lawful. And some things, though lawful, do not edify him and could even be a stumbling block. No, of course not. I would not eat the flesh of swine."

Peter spoke up. "God showed me on the rooftop in Joppa that all men are the same. He accepts any man who will come to his righteousness."

"As Saul just said," said Barnabas, "we should place no burdens upon the Gentiles who turn to God through Christ."

The men paused and were silent for a while, each of them knowing in his heart that the issue was far from being resolved to everyone's satisfaction.

"We must pray for wisdom," said Peter. "In every circumstance we must seek the Lord's guidance. He called the scribes and Pharisees 'hypocrites.' In the Temple itself he admonished them for binding men with heavy burdens that were impossible to bear."

They remained silent for a time, each of them meditating on the Lord's words and their meaning.

Then Peter said, "Men, we must bring our congregation back together."

"Yes, we must," said James. "Our congregation must know also that reconciliation with God doesn't necessarily mean that there automatically follows reconciliation with your fellow man." James looked directly at Saul when he spoke.

"Yes," said Saul. "I know that very well from personal experience—and in the case of my brother-in-law, Levi." He paused. "On the other hand, to become a follower of Jesus, you bear a cross. Men everywhere will hate us and want to kill us for claiming him Lord."

"The Master once said, 'You shall know the truth, and the truth shall make you free,'" said Peter.

"We need to be free from worry and care as to what the world can do to us, for we have not told cunningly devised fables concerning the power and glory of our Lord Jesus. We are eyewitnesses to his majesty."

✳ ✳ ✳

The next day Sarah came back and handed Saul a parchment. "This was nailed to my doorpost when I came home from here last night." There were tears in her eyes. Saul took the paper and put his arms around his sister, knowing what it was.

They sat down on a bench in the inner courtyard of Peter's house. "What reason does he give for a bill of divorcement?" he asked gently.

"Abandonment of devotion to him and the traditions of our faith," she said. "He told me that I had forsaken the true religion of our fathers and had become as a pagan Gentile to him." She held back more tears.

"Well," he said, looking at her evenly, "you have just come to know a new Master. Love is the way into his kingdom, but he said that in building his kingdom he comes as a sword, and a man's enemies shall be those of his own household."

Sarah stared at him. "He is more fearful than the God of Abraham who burned Sodom and Gomorrah. I don't understand, Saul. Barnabas called him the Prince of Peace. Why does this terrible pain come to me just as I accept him?"

"The trying of your faith works patience, Sarah, and with your faith through patience, you gain wisdom," he said as he put his arms around her shoulders.

"Endure, Sarah, endure, and the Prince of Peace will comfort you."

She looked straight in his face and said, "Saul, your words are nice." Then she paused. "Give me a little time. You have no idea how hard it is for a woman to be given a bill of divorcement. The reason for such is almost always adultery." She trembled. "And I can't face my friends. Jacob never said a word all morning before he left for school. He knows that something too terrible to talk about has happened. And he had been so happy to see my joy here on the Sabbath."

Saul thought for a minute, then said, "You often talked about going back home to Tarsus, Sarah. Have you thought of that?"

"I have been here ten years, Saul. Memories grow dim. I rarely hear from our friends and relatives there," she said. "Still, I have no one here now except you and Jacob, and you won't be staying."

"Perhaps I will," said Saul. "I must make the people believe."

"You will be killed, Saul," she said. "The high priest, Theophilus, stoops to please Marcellus. And speaking of peace, you are a threat to the peace."

"I have a gospel of love to preach, Sarah," he said.

"Yes, but you said yourself it pits husband against wife, and as you know, it pits Jews against Jews, and that Marcellus will not condone. Things were different when Jonathan ben Annas sat in the high chair. He practically ignored the fact that Rome ruled. Caesar Caligula is insane, and he hates us.

Theophilus will not allow men like yourself to speak to the people on Solomon's Porch with Marcellus's soldiers looking down upon you."

They sat quietly for a while, then Saul said, "Put your trust in the Lord, Sarah." He paused. "I must go into the Temple again soon," he said.

"Why?" she asked.

"To pray, Sarah."

"I must go get Jacob now," she said, rising. "And, Saul, I would like something."

"What would you like?" he asked, smiling.

"I want to be baptized in his name," she said. "Somehow I feel the need to be. I have made one step; now I must go all the way with him."

✿ ✿ ✿

For the third day in a row, Cononiah and Shemei knocked on the outer door of the high priest's chamber at the Temple.

"You cannot see Father Theophilus now," said the guard who opened the door and faced them.

Cononiah spoke out quickly, "The turncoat persecutor, Saul of Tarsus, is in the city and congregating with the Nazarenes."

"The high priest can't be bothered with the Nazarenes again," the guard said.

Cononiah put his foot in the door. "The high priest wants Saul of Tarsus arrested," he growled, "and we know where he is."

"Where is he?" asked the guard.

"We must speak with Father Theophilus," said Cononiah.

"Just a moment," he said, closing the door.

Theophilus did not look up from his papers when the two men entered, and it was a few moments before he said anything.

"What is this I hear about Saul of Tarsus?" asked the high priest.

"He is in the city," said Shemei.

"At the house of the Galilean Simon Peter," said Cononiah.

"How long has he been there?" asked Theophilus.

"A few days, Master. They profaned the Sabbath with their rituals honoring the Nazarene," said Cononiah.

"In what way?" asked Theophilus.

The two men looked at each other, each hoping the other would speak. Finally Cononiah said, "They drink the Nazarene's blood at their service!"

Theophilus didn't react.

Shemei said, "This is forbidden by Law!" He paused, then said, "They also eat his flesh. They pass around little pieces of it and they all have a bite."

Finally the high priest said, "I am tired of these horrible tales of the Nazarene's worship services. If they are true, their so-called Lord would have to have been as tall as Mt. Hermon and had a bloodstream as big as the River Jordan."

"We have seen it, Master Theophilus," said Shemei.

"Out with you! Begone!" said Theophilus.

As the door opened and the Hebronites went out, the high priest called in the guard.

"Saul of Tarsus is at the house of the Galilean preacher Peter," he said. "Get a cohort of soldiers from Antonia and arrest him. Have him imprisoned at the fortress."

✠ ✠ ✠

They were near the spot on the Jordan where John the Baptist had baptized Jesus. The river was wide and shallow here. The stream of the Jordan was responsible for a lush green belt through the bare wilderness.

The oasis of Jericho was within sight, but Saul stood with his back to that city, and his memories of the girl Jemimah were as if she had been in another life. He wondered about her, though, and if she had married. *Does she have children? Is she happy?* He dropped his eyes, and the memories pained him, not just memories of her and the time they had spent together, but memories of his own loneliness from the time he had rejected her until that day on the Damascus road when his whole life was suddenly changed.

The words of Barnabas brought him out of his reverie. "Insomuch as you have professed your faith in the Lord Jesus, I baptize you, my sister Sarah, in the name of the Father, and of the Son, and of the Holy Spirit."

The waters of the Jordan swept over her, and she came up crying tears of joy. Leah and Barnabas led her out of the water, and Leah covered her shivering shoulders with a blanket. The four of them had come to this spot as Sarah had requested. As she dried her hair, she said, "I want to be more like Jesus, and more like those who know him."

Saul embraced his sister. "Welcome into his kingdom," he said.

"Saul," she said, shivering in her wet clothes, "how can I find peace in my family situation?"

"You must try to reconcile with Levi," he said. "Love him more. Try, Sarah, and pray."

"Let's change your wet clothes," said Leah, taking her aside.

Saul turned his back to her, saying, "Thank you, God, for bringing her into your service." Now he was facing Jericho. It was as if a war began inside him. "Jemimah." He mouthed her name as he looked at the city. "Jemimah." He closed his eyes upon the city.

On the way back to Peter's house as they were going around the southern colonnades of the Temple, Saul stopped. "Go ahead without me," he said. "I must go once more into the Temple to pray."

"Be careful, Saul," said Sarah.

She watched him go up the steps with that great stride of his, his homespun cloak flaring out behind him.

"Come, Sarah," said Leah. "The children will be hungry."

Barnabas watched Saul until he disappeared between the columns, headed for the Court of Israel, then he turned and followed the women to the house of Simon Peter. When they were in sight of the house, they stopped. Something was wrong. Roman soldiers stood at the door in the street. One of the Temple guards seemed to be in a heated discussion with Cononiah and Shemei. Barnabas and the two women were blocked by the soldiers as they approached the gate.

"Where is Saul of Tarsus?" the guard demanded of Barnabas.

He didn't answer and was knocked to his knees. The terrified women forced their way into the house and joined the children, who were just as terrified. "Are you all right?" Leah asked.

"Yes," said Jesse. "They want Saul."

Sarah held Jacob in her arms. "They will go away, my son. They won't hurt us."

The soldiers prodded Barnabas along the street, and when he hesitated, they put chains on his arms and pulled him roughly up the incline to the Temple area, past the Judgment Hall and into the Hall of Flagellation, where they chained him to a post.

The elders and chief priests questioned him about Saul and about his activities at the house of Peter. He spoke not a word, and the lashes began falling on his bare back. He fainted before the thirty-ninth one fell. They unchained him and took him out of the Court of Israel and cruelly pushed him down the steps, where he came to rest, bleeding and broken, in the Court of Women.

In the Court of Israel, Saul knelt praying. "Guidance, O Lord, please, guidance," he said. "Like David of old, I am encompassed about with my enemies.

"You have called me; you have bought me. You have given me friends in your work. You have brought my sister to my side for your service. You have blessed me by bringing me Barnabas. Now do I present my body as a living sacrifice. In my midst are those who would kill me. Do I offer my neck to the executioner? Do I offer my body to be stoned? What would you do with me, Lord?

"For me to live at all is to preach your gospel, to tell of your salvation. If I must die, I shall die in you; if I am to live, I must live in you. For me to live is to be your minister, your apostle.

"I do not seek to please men, for I understand now that to please all men I would not be a proper servant. Speak to the minds of us all. Strengthen Cephas and James in wisdom as you strengthen me.

"I am crucified with you, Lord; nevertheless, I live, yet not I but you in me, and the life I now live in the flesh, I live by faith in you.

"May I stand fast in the liberty by which you have made me free. Let me walk in your Spirit and not in the flesh.

"My flesh is crucified to your glory. Let me know the fruits of the Spirit, the fruits of love, joy, peace, long-suffering, gentleness, goodness, faith, meekness, and temperance.

"Send me where you will, Lord. Enlighten me that I may teach men the fellowship of the mystery which from the beginning of the world has been hidden. May I impart to your church your manifold wisdom.

"May I bear the just fruits of righteousness which are by Jesus Christ unto your glory."

He suddenly stopped praying, for he felt the presence. Saul was kneeling with his eyes closed when the afterimage of the Man in White appeared on the backs of his eyelids. He heard the rushing of the eternal water and over the waters came the voices calling his name in all foreign languages. Then the divine Voice whispered to him, and the implication of the Lord's pronouncing his name in this manner chilled and thrilled him.

"Paul," the Voice said. "Paul."

He tried to answer but couldn't speak.

"Paul, Paul," the Voice called again.

Then the image began to glow, and glory radiated from the face in the vision. The beautiful eternal Voice called him by his Gentile name again.

"Paul."

"Yes, Lord," he whispered.

"Go out of Jerusalem quickly," the Voice said. "They will not receive your testimony concerning me."

"Lord," said Paul, "they know that I imprisoned and beat in the synagogues those who believed in you, and when the blood of the martyr

Stephen was shed, I stood by and consented to his death. I held the clothes of those who killed him."

Not responding this time to his old confession, the Lord said, "Go. I send you far away to the Gentiles."

He arose immediately and strode back toward the Court of Women. He shivered as he remembered the vision he had had of the destruction of the Temple. *My Lord has many temples he is waiting to enter,* he thought, *the temples of human hearts.*

He shivered again as he came down the steps and into the Court of Women. There sat Barnabas against the bottom step. He had pulled himself up to a sitting position and was trying to get to his feet. Countless people passed him by, not wanting to be involved in helping a malefactor. Paul stopped even before he recognized him. Barnabas was covered with blood.

"There were soldiers at Peter's house," said Barnabas. "They were looking for you."

Paul helped him to his feet. "So they scourged you instead." Looking at Barnabas's wrists, he added, "And chained you."

"Yes," said Barnabas.

"Are they still at Peter's house?" asked Paul.

"Probably not," said Barnabas, his arm around Paul's shoulder as they walked slowly.

Paul was silent for a moment, then he said, "They have gone too far. We are Roman citizens, and it is unlawful to bind and scourge a citizen of Rome."

"It has happened, and it shall happen to you," said Barnabas.

The courtyard at Peter's house was crowded when they returned. As Paul and Barnabas walked in, Peter was leading them in prayer. When he raised his head and saw Barnabas, he said, "Our prayers are answered. He is alive."

Paul stood beside Peter, James, and Barnabas and looked out over the faces. Many were there who had fled upon recognizing him before.

"I summoned these people back, for now they confirm that you are no longer the persecutor but a true disciple," said Peter to Paul.

Paul took his cloak from around Barnabas's shoulders to show the results of the scourging. "Bear witness, brothers and sisters. Such are the afflictions that come from serving the Lord." He paused, then said, "But know that the present sufferings are nothing compared to the glory that is to come to us for faithfulness to his calling."

Sarah and Leah came forward to take Barnabas inside.

"Sarah," Paul said, "I must leave you now."

"Where are you going?" she asked. "Where can you safely go?"

He walked with them away from the congregation and into a room where Leah began bathing Barnabas's back and shoulders. He looked up at Paul from his chair.

"I have decided to go back to Tarsus," he said. "I have had a vision from God. I must go to the Gentiles."

"What you see that has been done to me is just a foretaste of the persecution that you will receive," said Barnabas.

"I know that very well, Barnabas. It is part of my calling."

"You are going home without me," said Sarah resignedly.

"I must leave now," said Paul. "I am going to Caesarea, where I will find sailing passage to Tarsus."

"I have no one here," said Sarah mournfully, "except my son."

"You have brothers and sisters in Christ," said Paul. "If your husband will not rescind the bill of divorcement, I would like for you to make arrangements to take Jacob out of school and join me soon in Tarsus. Of the people I know there, I know of none in the service of our Master. You would be a great help to me in establishing a church there."

His excitement was evident, and Barnabas smiled. "So you have finally resolved to answer the call of the Gentiles."

"Yes, my brother," he said, and with an arm around Sarah, he led Barnabas back out into the courtyard.

"Levi will never let me take Jacob," said Sarah.

"Still, you must come," said Paul. "Pray about it. God will bring it about that Jacob join us. He has been a witness to much testimony of the Master.

He has become an open channel for the love of Christ. He will go with you to Tarsus, Sarah. I know it. He shall be with us in the Lord's service."

A few people, mainly the elders of the church, were still there, a dozen or more men talking with Peter and James. Peter embraced Barnabas, who smiled and said, "I am privileged to suffer for my Master."

Peter called Paul aside and said, "I have just been told that the relatives of the Greek woman who died under your persecution plan to kill you."

"I had a vision in the Temple, Peter," he said. "I know about the plots to kill me. I am going to the Roman governor, Marcellus, to demand a military escort to Caesarea. One Roman citizen, Barnabas, has already been illegally scourged and chained. My Lord commands me to leave. I shall make sure nothing stops me from obeying him."

"I will go with you," said Peter.

"No," said Paul, "You need not be seen in that place. I shall go alone."

Paul turned to Sarah. "Find peace in this decision, Sarah. It is God's plan."

"I don't know what will happen to me," she said.

"I will expect you in Tarsus soon, Sarah," he said.

Peter said, "Would you speak to the elders, to all of us before you go?"

Paul turned to the group of men and said, "Brothers, it was with joy that I gained your fellowship. I now must leave you to follow the Master's bidding.

"I have testified to the Jews and Greeks repentance toward God and faith in the Lord Jesus Christ. Now I go, bound in the Holy Spirit, knowing that persecution and afflictions await me. But into the cities I go. I shall become all things to all men that I might win some to Christ, and the afflictions that I shall suffer do not concern me, neither do I count my own life dear, so that I might finish my course.

"I am not fleeing Jerusalem in fear of the men who would kill me. I go at his command to take the testimony of his gospel to the Gentiles. Concerning those who feared me in this congregation, I am pure of the blood of all men, having been justified by my surrender to the Master's love."

He paused, then looking into all their faces said, "I leave you with a reminder of our Lord's commandment, that you love your neighbor as yourself."

He turned to Barnabas and laid one hand on his shoulder and the other on his head. "Join me, Peter," he said, "to pray to the Lord to heal Barnabas's wounds."

They bowed their heads with their hands upon Barnabas as Paul said, "Lord, Creator of worlds, you who raise the dead to life, renew the flesh of our wounded brother."

They stood quietly for a moment. The image of the Man in White was behind Paul's closed eyes, and when he opened his eyes to look at Barnabas, he saw that the scar on his neck was gone. There was no sign of it.

"The cuts from the lash are gone, Barnabas," said Peter. "He who raises the dead can easily heal broken flesh; we need only have faith in him."

Paul embraced Peter. "Surely we shall meet again."

"Yes," said Peter. "In God's own time."

"Good-bye, Barnabas," said Paul. "I have found in you a kindred spirit. We shall minister together someday."

He turned to James. "The love of Christ will settle all confusion and differences of opinion, my brother," he said, embracing him.

"Look into the perfect law of liberty," said James, "and continue in it, doing his work, and you will be blessed."

He turned to Sarah last. "Stay here for the time being. Pray for God's will in your life. If it be his will, I will soon see you in Tarsus." They embraced tearfully, and he was gone.

✠ ✠ ✠

He stood outside the door of Marcellus, the Roman governor. A guard blocked the door as he approached.

"I demand protection," said Paul. "I will not go into this place, but you can tell him to supply me with a military escort to Caesarea."

The guard turned on his heel and went inside.

Paul could see down a long hallway of marble flooring. The interior was very rich and ornate. A large bust of Caesar Caligula and one of Tiberius sat on tall pedestals, both images well lighted by polished tin reflectors behind oil lamps on the floor.

Someday, he thought, *I will enter buildings like this to witness to kings and rulers and will more than likely be scorned and abused in such places. But not tonight. Not for this business. Besides, I am not worthy to enter this hall and stand where the Master stood before Pilate.*

Soon Marcellus appeared at the door with the guard, and looking Paul up and down, he sneered. Marcellus wore a crown of laurel leaves on his head. He was robust and fully dressed in his Roman military armor, with a flowing blue silk cloak with a golden fringe.

"So you are the fearful turncoat persecutor," Marcellus laughed. "I must say, you do not appear very fearsome," he said as he fingered the sleeve of Paul's homespun robe and eyed his dusty sandals.

"I am a Roman citizen," said Paul. "I come from Tarsus of Cilicia, to which I would return now."

"Then go," said Marcellus, starting to turn away.

"I demand a soldier escort to Caesarea due to the plots against my life."

"You demand?" Marcellus asked incredulously.

Paul stared at him evenly. "My brother Barnabas the Cypriot was chained and flogged in your prison; this is a violation of Roman law inasmuch as he is a citizen of Rome. Various groups in this city are plotting to kill me; should they do so, it would be yet another violation of your law, for they plan to kill me on religious grounds, and we are guaranteed freedom of worship since the days of Pompey." Paul lowered his voice and stared unwaveringly into the eyes of Marcellus. "If you do not provide me with safe escort out of this city, I shall see that these injustices and legal infractions reach the ear of Caesar himself."

"Are you threatening me?" Marcellus asked loudly.

"Yes," said Paul firmly.

Marcellus turned his back to Paul for a moment and told the centurion beside him, "Organize a detail of six soldiers to go to Caesarea. Get this man out of the city immediately." The centurion saluted and was gone.

"Thank you," said Paul.

"Just go," said Marcellus, "and don't come back." He turned and went inside.

"No time soon," said Paul, waiting for his escort.

As he passed the Temple with his guards, he wasn't aware if anyone recognized him or not. He could barely see the Temple for his tears. He was thinking that the Lord himself wept that night in Gethsemane and grieved in his soul, knowing of the coming destruction. *My people must be made to understand that God does not live in a temple made with hands,* he thought.

Yet at a certain point along his journey and knowing that soon he would no longer be able to see the Temple, he stopped a moment and looked back. He whispered the Shema. "Hear, O Israel: The Lord our God, the Lord is One."

As he turned his back to the city and continued on with the soldiers, he said aloud to the soldiers in Latin, "And he gave his only Son, that whosoever believes on him shall not die but shall have eternal life."

The soldiers looked at him questioningly but didn't say anything.

They will have much to say and many questions, thought Paul, smiling, *for I have much to tell these, my first Gentile audience, on my first journey.*

THIS STORY
HAS NO
END

EPILOGUE, AD 70

They had escaped for just a while, this remnant of the last surviving citizens of Jerusalem. The Romans had found them in caves, in burned-out buildings, and in the rocks and cliffs of the wilderness around the city.

Thousands had been enslaved, mostly the young and strong, male and female; they would be sold in Rome or given as gifts to certain select citizens of the city. Those slaves, part of the spoils of Judea, would be marched in chains on foot into the Eternal City, where they would suffer public humiliation. Before them in Titus's triumphal procession would be other spoils of the war—the ark of the covenant, the golden candlestick, and other treasures and sacred objects from the destroyed Temple.

But those who had been caught later and brought back to the scene of total desolation prayed for death, if indeed they prayed at all, for they moved leadenly under the lash of the soldiers. They were forced to pick up the bodies of their fellow Jews, men, women, and children, and toss them onto carts.

The oxen pulled their frightful burden westward to the Valley of Gehenna, where their remains were dumped into a burning pit. Other slaves poured out buckets of pitch to keep the fire constantly burning. The oxcarts and slaves, under the lash of the soldiers, returned time and time again to the city until the last of the bodies were found and burned.

Then from Lake Asphaltitis, the dead salt sea, came a long line of sons of Israel shouldering heavy bags of salt into the city that was no more. The salt was poured onto the ground until it covered the whole of the Temple area. Day after day the bags of salt were brought until a layer of white covered the whole city area.

Then as a final act to make the conqueror's point, oxen and plows were brought in and the salt was plowed into the ground throughout the city. Never would plant life grow here as it had before. And the blood of the citizens of the city was plowed under, not to be seen again, for it had covered the ground.

Over most of the Roman Empire, the sect calling themselves Christians was flourishing. The apostles had established churches from Jerusalem to Rome to Spain. In Asia they grew, and in Cilicia and Macedonia.

Order had been established in the churches. Bishops and elders were appointed or elected in each city, and the fight for the protection and propagation of the gospel of Jesus Christ was tirelessly waged. In Africa and India the apostle established churches, appointing elders and deacons to see that the gospel was spread.

But a few years before the war in Judea, a great persecution arose against the Christians in Rome. The great fire that burned Rome under Nero was blamed on the Christians, and many died cruel deaths in the arena. Some were forced to face wild beasts unarmed; some were sewn up in animal skins and set upon by dogs; some were dragged around the arena behind a team of horses.

Of the twelve disciples who had walked with Jesus as his friends, companions, and servants—not counting Judas Iscariot, who was already dead—eleven died by violence; one was flayed alive, one was pulled apart by wild horses, and one was crucified on a St. Andrew's cross. James was killed by the sword under Herod Agrippa's orders.

Only one lived long and died at an old age—John, the beloved, who wrote Revelation while in exile on an island in the Aegean Sea. He was finally allowed to return to his church at Ephesus, where he continued to care for Mary, the holy mother.

Two of the chief apostles of the Nazarenes were executed. Simon Peter, who refused Roman citizenship, maintaining that he was a citizen of the Land of the Lord, was, according to Rome's way of executing foreigners, crucified. At the last minute he begged his executioners to crucify him upside down, because he deemed himself unworthy to die upright as his Lord had done.

The other apostle was a freeborn citizen of the empire, although he was a prominent Pharisee in Jerusalem. This man, the most outspoken proponent of the gospel of the Nazarene, later established Christian churches all over the known world. Under his direction and pastorate, the church at Tarsus, his birthplace, grew in numbers and power.

His journeys, during a time when transportation was primitive, are well documented and more than impressive. Wherever he felt the call to go, he went, often by direct command through visions of the Lord and of angels sent from God. Throughout the lands of Cilicia, Asia, Cappadocia, Pontus, all the provinces that are now Turkey, he traveled, establishing churches among the believers and suffering the most severe persecutions. He was stoned at Iconium and barely escaped with his life. In Derbe, he was stoned again, thrown into the city dump, and left for dead.

With Barnabas, he was run out of the city of Antioch. But he returned to Antioch in Syria and, with Barnabas and another helper named Silas, brought great numbers into the congregation.

In a vision at Troas, a man of Macedonia called him to come there, and he answered that call to go into the continent of Europe. Perhaps the gospel would not have reached us on this continent through our European ancestors had he not answered that call.

He established a church at Philippi, where he and Silas were stripped naked, beaten with rods, and imprisoned. In Philippi, he and Silas preached in the synagogue and established a church in that city. At Athens, his message was generally rejected after he preached, but a few believed, and from those few a great church grew.

In Corinth, he challenged the ruler of the synagogue, for in a vision Jesus had told him, "Don't be afraid to speak, for I am with you." He stayed there a year and a half. His church flourished. At Ephesus, he performed miracles. Invalids and the diseased were healed just by touching his clothing. In that city he gained so many followers that people stopped buying idols of Diana, the goddess of love. The silversmiths rioted, but he had gained followers and left Ephesus.

In Jerusalem after one journey, he was dragged out of the Temple and beaten. He was imprisoned for two years at Caesarea, charged with sedition. He was shipwrecked and bitten by a deadly poisonous snake, but he survived. He was imprisoned again and taken to Rome, where he continued to gain converts even among Caesar's own household.

He always left his churches solidly established and appointed elders at every place to keep order and preach the gospel of Christ. He never took pay for his service as an evangelist and pastor, but continued to ply his trade as a tentmaker wherever he stayed to pay his keep.

But now, he had finished the fight, run the race, and kept the faith. The apostle was taken outside the city walls to be beheaded. With a Stephen-like expression on his face, he closed his eyes and turned his neck to the executioner.

The dark outline of the Man in White suddenly appeared behind his eyelids, and just as he was dying, the image became as white, as dazzling, as glorified as the one that struck him on that day on the Damascus road. This time, however, the vision did not stop, and a truly brilliant light streamed from a countenance whose piercing eyes of love beckoned the apostle Paul.

I've been to Damascus
And I didn't go by air
I walked upon the paved Roman Way
I stood at the very spot
Where a brilliant light once shone
And I saw a fleeting flicker there that day
But it needn't be Damascus
And it needn't be on a road
And it needn't be a lofty mountain height
It could be in a closet
And it could be at the door
That, if opened, glows the glorious, blinding light

AFTERWORD:
THE THORN REMOVED?

My father felt a kinship with the apostle Paul. In many ways, they were of the same ilk. Paul was a poet, traveler, and visionary. My father, who traveled most of his life, maintained his purpose and Christian standards as best he could. My father read Paul's words as the poetry they were, and found inspiration in them throughout his life. He felt he knew Paul personally. To my dad, Paul was a mentor, friend, and companion. This book you hold was one of my father's greatest visions.

When I was very young, I slammed my finger in the car door. The nail was torn off, and it took a long time to heal. I feared that my finger would never be the same, that I would never be able to use it as before.

When I told my father my fears, he smiled and said: "Son, I am sure your finger will be fine in no time, but if it doesn't heal right, use it as a thorn in your flesh."

"But Dad, there's no thorn in there," I said, confusedly.

"God can turn our hurts and weaknesses to our own advantage," he said, "and ultimately, to His."

I looked at my missing nail and black fingertip and had no idea what he meant.

My finger healed and was as good as new in weeks, but I never forgot what he said.

When I first read *Man in White,* I understood what he meant. The thorn forces us to rise above the hurt. Somehow, the pain makes the focus more important, the goal more meaningful.

We do not know exactly what Paul's thorn was . . . epilepsy possibly, or a hearing defect . . . or even a speech impediment.

I know some of my father's: the loss of his brother at an early age, his struggles with his own demons . . . Later in life, his neurological disorder and his diabetes. These thorns may have slowed my father down, but not only did he stay strong in faith, he actually gained momentum through these struggles. I believe Paul did the same.

"Some thorns are never removed, during the time we live and breathe. I believe Paul's were not ever removed, and as my father, he accepted them as his personal burden, something to rise above, something to sharpen his courage, to define purpose, and to help him remember to stay grateful for his blessings."

I am grateful my dad's words are still there to bless us, and that his music continues to touch the world. And now that his thorns have been removed, I feel certain their purpose is clear.

Through a glass darkly,
John Carter Cash
May, 2006
Hendersonville, TN

ONLY
JOHNNY
CASH
COULD
MAKE
A FILM
THIS
SPECIAL

DVD AVAILABLE NOW!

The Man Called CASH

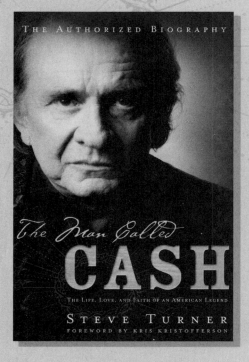

ifferent from other books written about him, The Man Called CASH brings Cash's faith and love for God into the foreground and tells the story of a man redeemed, without watering-down or sugar-coating. The Man Called CASH has been a huge success with his fans and will continue to draw in many new fans with this inspiring story of faith and redemption.

W PUBLISHING GROUP
A Division of Thomas Nelson Publishers
Since 1798
www.wpublishinggroup.com

JOHNNY CASH
REMEMBERED
Gospel Music Listening and Viewing

ALBUMS RECORDED	RECORD COMPANY	YEAR
Hymns by Johnny Cash	Columbia/Sony	1959
Hymns from the Heart	Columbia/Sony	1962
The Holy Land	CBS/Sony	1969
Timeless Inspiration	Reader's Digest	1986
Precious Memories	CBS/Sony	1975
Believe in Him	Word	1986
Just As I Am	CBS/Sony Records	1999
My Mother's Hymn Book	American Recordings	2004

CROSSINGS®
THE BOOK CLUB FOR TODAY'S CHRISTIAN FAMILY

A Letter to Our Readers

Dear Reader:

In order that we might better contribute to your reading enjoyment, we would appreciate your taking a few minutes to respond to the following questions. When completed, please return to the following:

Andrea Doering, Editor-in-Chief
Crossings Book Club
401 Franklin Avenue, Garden City, NY 11530

You can post your review online! Go to www.crossings.com and rate this book.

Title _____ Author _____

1   Did you enjoy reading this book?

❑ Very much. I would like to see more books by this author!

❑ I really liked_____

❑ Moderately. I would have enjoyed it more if_____

2   What influenced your decision to purchase this book? Check all that apply.

❑ Cover
❑ Title
❑ Publicity
❑ Catalog description
❑ Friends
❑ Enjoyed other books by this author
❑ Other _____

3   Please check your age range:

❑ Under 18   ❑ 18-24
❑ 25-34   ❑ 35-45
❑ 46-55   ❑ Over 55

4   How many hours per week do you read? _____

5   How would you rate this book, on a scale from 1 (poor) to 5 (superior)?
_____

Name_____

Occupation_____

Address_____

City_____ State_____ Zip_____